D1756153

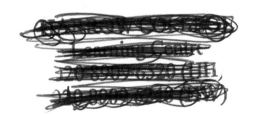

HARROW
COLLEGE

170275

CIVIL RESISTANCE IN THE ARAB SPRING

Civil Resistance in the Arab Spring

Triumphs and Disasters

Edited by
ADAM ROBERTS
MICHAEL J. WILLIS
RORY McCARTHY
TIMOTHY GARTON ASH

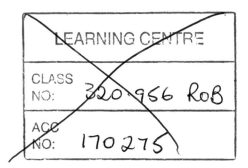

OXFORD
UNIVERSITY PRESS

OXFORD
UNIVERSITY PRESS

Great Clarendon Street, Oxford, OX2 6DP,
United Kingdom

Oxford University Press is a department of the University of Oxford.
It furthers the University's objective of excellence in research, scholarship,
and education by publishing worldwide. Oxford is a registered trade mark of
Oxford University Press in the UK and in certain other countries

Published in the United States of America by Oxford University Press
198 Madison Avenue, New York, NY 10016, United States of America

British Library Cataloguing in Publication Data

Data available

Library of Congress Control Number: 2015940147

ISBN 978–0–19–874902–8

Printed and bound by
CPI Group (UK) Ltd, Croydon, CR0 4YY

Preface

The Editors

This book provides an account and analysis of the role of civil resistance in the dramatic series of events that began at the end of 2010, leading to the fall of governments from Tunisia to Yemen. It covers not only the early months and years, when civil resistance predominated and was the hallmark of the Arab Spring, but also the prolonged crises that ensued in many countries—for example, the military intervention in Bahrain, the wars in Libya and Syria leading to huge refugee flows both to countries in the region and beyond, and the reversion to authoritarian rule in Egypt. It explores why it was Tunisia, the country where the Arab Spring began, that experienced the most political change for the lowest cost in bloodshed. Tunisia is the only country where a popular uprising was followed by a relatively liberal, democratic constitutional order—albeit one that faces many challenges and threats, both internal and external.

Why did so much go wrong in so many countries? Did the problem lie more with the methods, leadership, and aims of the popular movements, or in the conditions of the societies that they were attempting to change? Our authors provide expert, detailed accounts of developments in each country. They place them in their historical, social, and political contexts, and relate them to the wider story of civil resistance. They take note of specific characteristics both of the postcolonial history of the Arab world and of political Islam in the early twenty-first century. They look at domestic forces and at external ones, including the highly controversial policies and actions of the United States and Europe. They emphasize the vital part played by ordinary men and women, and look at the complex interplay of social media, television, and the physical organization and courage of protesters on the streets. They show the wide variety of forms that civil resistance can take—including protests on the streets but also political action in a constitutional framework, strikes, and flight as refugees. They describe the widely differing ways in which those in power responded to popular protests: how, for example, Arab monarchies in Jordan and Morocco undertook to introduce reforms to avert revolution, while President Bashar al-Assad in Syria abandoned tentative reform in favour of violent repression. They also ask why the Arab Spring failed to spark a Palestinian one. Above all, they show how civil resistance aiming at regime change is not enough: building the institutions and trust necessary for a stable, pluralist constitutional order is a more difficult but also crucial task.

A word about the terms used in the title of the present work may be useful. First, 'civil resistance'. This present work is a companion to the first book produced under the auspices of the Oxford University research project on Civil Resistance and Power Politics. That book, entitled *Civil Resistance and Power Politics: The Experience of Non-Violent Action from Gandhi to the Present*, edited by Adam Roberts and Timothy Garton Ash, was published by Oxford University Press in 2009. 'Civil resistance' is defined in it as a type of political action that relies on the use of non-violent methods. It is largely synonymous with certain other terms, including 'non-violent action', 'non-violent resistance', and 'people power'. It involves a range of widespread and sustained activities that challenge a particular power, force, policy, or regime—hence the term 'resistance'. A fuller version of this definition, including a brief outline of the mechanisms of change involved, and an indication of the variety of reasons for the avoidance of violence, can be found in the introduction to *Civil Resistance and Power Politics*. From its initiation, the Oxford research project has been predicated on the recognition that the relationships between civil resistance and other forms of power and struggle are highly complex: the Arab Spring confirms this.

And why 'Arab Spring'? As discussed by Adam Roberts in the concluding chapter of this book, many other terms have been advanced, including Arab Awakening and Arab Uprisings. We opt for 'Arab Spring' because it is succinct, widely understood, and captures some of the special features of these events—not least the fact that spring was in so many countries followed by fall.

Our first volume looked at nineteen major cases of the use of civil resistance across nearly a century, from Gandhi in India to the 'moment of the monks' in Burma in 2007. Like this one, it asked systematic, comparative questions about the relationships between historical agency and structure, ends and means, analysis and advocacy, external and internal forces, and, not least, failure and success. Many of those nineteen cases could by then be said to have ended in success. That cannot, at this writing, be claimed for most of the countries covered here. But we can learn from failure as well as from success. Moreover, as some of those earlier cases show, one decade's failure can ultimately contribute to another decade's success, especially if people are ready to learn from the history that they have experienced and helped to shape.

The chapters in the book, and the electronic addresses (URLs) mentioned in the footnotes, were finalized and checked in March–May 2015.

A.R., M.J.W., R.M., T.G.A.

Oxford
May 2015

Acknowledgements

This is the second and final book containing the findings of the Oxford University research project on 'Civil Resistance and Power Politics: Domestic and International Dimensions', established in 2006. In addition to the many funding bodies that supported generously the first phase of the project's work, we owe special thanks to the funders who have supported our work on this volume: the International Center on Nonviolent Conflict in Washington, DC, and in particular its founding chair, Peter Ackerman; and the late Professor Nina Byers of the University of California Los Angeles, who made a generous donation to this project in 2014, and died while this book was in preparation.

As regards the shape and content of the book, we owe thanks to the numerous friends and colleagues—in Oxford and elsewhere—who provided us with information, advice, and helpful feedback on draft chapters. It would be problematic to name them all individually, and we cannot name the anonymous reviewers of our proposal to Oxford University Press, who were notably constructive. We thank you all.

We also owe a special debt of gratitude to our Oxford colleagues and fellow members of the project's Organizing Committee, Judith Brown, Peter Carey, Rana Mitter, Alex Pravda, and Jan Zielonka, who have all contributed notably to our work on this subject.

At Oxford University Press we thank particularly Dominic Byatt, Commissioning Editor for Politics and International Relations; and his colleagues Sarah Parker, Olivia Wells, and Franziska Bröckl. In addition, we owe special thanks to Rohan Bolton for her highly skilled work in preparing the index.

The University of Oxford has, as ever, provided excellent resources for research. The Social Sciences Library, and the Library at the Middle East Centre at St Antony's College, offered rich resources and friendly assistance. At the Department of Politics and International Relations, which has managed administrative aspects of the project, we particularly thank Kalypso Nicolaidis, Director of the Centre for International Studies, Andrew Hurrell, Montague Burton Professor of International Relations, and Neil MacFarlane, Lester B. Pearson Professor of International Relations, for their consistent support for this work; and, from the administrative staff who kept the project on the rails, especially Kate Candy, Lana Fisher, Genevieve Garrido, Matthew Kennedy, Julie Page, and Rasangi Prematilaka.

Contents

List of Illustrations

TABLE

List of Contributors

Jacob Amis was previously a freelance researcher on Jordanian politics. He holds an M.Phil. in Modern Middle Eastern Studies from St Antony's College, Oxford University, for which he won the 2012 Walter Zander Prize. Between 2011 and 2013 he regularly conducted fieldwork in Jordan, and spent many hours in the crowds of the Jordanian *hirak*. He now works for the Foreign Office.

M. Cherif Bassiouni is Emeritus Professor of Law at DePaul University in Chicago. Born in Cairo, he studied Law at Cairo University and then at three US universities. Among other appointments, in 2011 he served as Chair of the Bahrain Independent Commission of Inquiry; and in 2011–12 as Chair and member of the UN International Commission of Inquiry on Libya. He is the author of numerous books and articles on international legal issues and practice, including *Crimes against Humanity: Historical Evolution and Contemporary Application* (Cambridge University Press, 2011) and *International Extradition: US Law and Practice* (6th edn, Oxford University Press, 2014).

Elham Fakhro is a doctoral candidate in Socio-Legal Studies at St Antony's College, Oxford University. She previously acted as a researcher with organizations including Georgetown University, the International Institute for Strategic Studies, and the Bahrain Independent Commission of Inquiry, and as a Lecturer at the University of Bahrain. She holds a Master of Laws from Harvard Law School and Bachelor of Laws from the University of London.

Timothy Garton Ash is Professor of European Studies at Oxford University, Isaiah Berlin Professorial Fellow at St Antony's College, Oxford, and a Senior Fellow at the Hoover Institution, Stanford University. As a journalist and 'historian of the present', he witnessed a number of episodes of civil resistance. His books include *The Polish Revolution: Solidarity* (3rd edn, Yale University Press, 2002); *The Magic Lantern: The Revolutions of '89 Witnessed in Warsaw, Budapest, Berlin and Prague* (3rd edn, Vintage, 1999); and (joint editor) *Civil Resistance and Power Politics: The Experience of Non-Violent Action from Gandhi to the Present* (Oxford University Press, 2009).

Raymond Hinnebusch is Professor of International Relations and Middle East Studies at St Andrews University and Director of the Centre for Syrian Studies. He has written a number of major books on contemporary Syria including *Authoritarian Power in Baʿathist Syria: Army, Party and Peasant* (Westview,

1990), *Syria: Revolution from Above* (Routledge, 2001), and (co-edited with Tina Zintl) *Syria from Reform to Revolt: Political Economy and International Relations* (Syracuse University Press, New York, 2015). His works on the Middle East region include *The International Politics of the Middle East* (2nd edn, Manchester University Press, 2015).

Omar Imady is a Senior Fellow and the Deputy Director of the Centre for Syrian Studies at the University of St Andrews. He is the author of various studies, books, and UN reports on Syria and the Middle East. He is also a published poet and novelist and his novel *The Gospel of Damascus* (MSI Press, Hollister, CA, 2005) has been translated into several languages.

George Joffé teaches a postgraduate course on the international relations of the Middle East and North Africa in the Department of Politics and International Studies at the University of Cambridge, where he also supervises M.Phil. and Ph.D. dissertations. He was previously Deputy Director of the Royal Institute of International Affairs (Chatham House) in London.

Helen Lackner first visited the People's Democratic Republic of Yemen (South Yemen) in 1973, and lived there in 1977–82. Since then she has lived and worked in all parts of Yemen. She has worked as a consultant in social aspects of rural development, mostly in Yemen, but also in thirty other countries. She is author of *PDR Yemen: Outpost of Socialist Development in Arabia* (Ithaca Press, 1985), and editor of *Why Yemen Matters* (Saqi Books, 2014). She writes on Yemen on openDemocracy. She is currently working on governance and water management in Yemen in the past century. She is particularly interested in social movements, especially their role in development.

Rory McCarthy is completing a D.Phil. in Oriental Studies at St Antony's College, Oxford, where he is researching Islamism in contemporary Tunisia. He was formerly a foreign correspondent of the *Guardian* and was posted in Islamabad, Baghdad, Beirut, and Jerusalem. He is the author of *Nobody Told Us We Are Defeated: Stories from the New Iraq* (Chatto & Windus, 2006).

Driss Maghraoui is Associate Professor of History and International Relations at Al Akhawayn University, Morocco. He co-edited a special issue of *Mediterranean Politics* (2009) on 'Reform in the Arab World: The Experience of Morocco'. He is editor of *Revisiting the Colonial Past in Morocco* (Routledge, 2013). Recent publications include 'Searching for Normalization: The Party of Justice and Development in Morocco', in Quinn Mecham and Julie Chernov Hwang (eds), *Islamist Parties and Political Normalization in the Muslim World* (University of Pennsylvania Press, 2014), and 'The Moroccan "Effort de Guerre" in World War II', in Judith Byfield et al. (eds), *Africa and World War II* (Cambridge University Press, 2015).

Chibli Mallat is Presidential Professor of Middle Eastern Law and Politics at Utah University, and Jean Monnet Chair of European Law at Saint Joseph University in Lebanon. His first tenured position was at the School of Oriental and African Studies, London. In 2005–6 he was a leader of the Cedar Revolution in Lebanon, and ran for president. In 2009 he established Right to Nonviolence, an NGO based in the Middle East. He has written or edited over thirty-five books in English, French, and Arabic. They include the award-winning *Renewal of Islamic Law* (Cambridge, 1993) and *Philosophy of Nonviolence* (Oxford University Press, New York, 2015).

Edward Mortimer is a Distinguished Fellow of All Souls College, Oxford. He was a foreign correspondent and specialist on the London *Times*, focusing on southern Europe and the Middle East, 1967–85; the main foreign affairs commentator of the *Financial Times*, 1987–98; chief speechwriter and director of communications to UN Secretary-General Kofi Annan, 1998–2006; and Chief Program Officer of the Salzburg Global Seminar, 2007–11. His books include *Faith and Power: The Politics of Islam* (Faber, 1982) and *Roosevelt's Children* (Hamish Hamilton, 1987). He also co-edited *People, Nation & State: The Meaning of Ethnicity & Nationalism* (I. B. Tauris, 1999).

Wendy Pearlman is the Crown Junior Chair in Middle East Studies and Assistant Professor of Political Science at Northwestern University. She graduated magna cum laude with a B.A. in history from Brown University and earned her Ph.D. in Government at Harvard University. She is author of *Occupied Voices: Stories of Everyday Life from the Second Intifada* (Nation Books, 2003); *Violence, Nonviolence, and the Palestinian National Movement* (Cambridge University Press, 2011); and numerous articles in academic journals. She has studied or conducted research in Spain, Morocco, Egypt, Lebanon, Israel, and the West Bank and Gaza Strip.

Adam Roberts is Senior Research Fellow in International Relations at Oxford University, and Emeritus Fellow of Balliol College, Oxford. He was President of the British Academy, 2009–13. His books include: as editor, *The Strategy of Civilian Defence: Non-Violent Resistance to Aggression* (Faber, 1967); and (joint editor), *Civil Resistance and Power Politics: The Experience of Non-Violent Action from Gandhi to the Present* (Oxford University Press, 2009). He has written extensively on military occupations in the Middle East, and co-authored *Academic Freedom under Israeli Military Occupation* (International Commission of Jurists, 1984).

Michael J. Willis is H.M. King Mohammed VI Fellow in Moroccan and Mediterranean Studies at St Antony's College, Oxford. His research interests focus on the politics, modern history, and international relations of the Maghreb. Before taking up his position in Oxford in 2004, he taught politics for seven years at Al Akhawayn University in Ifrane in Morocco. His books include *Politics and Power in the Maghreb: Algeria, Tunisia and Morocco from Independence to the Arab Spring* (Hurst and New York University Press, 2012). He conducted research in Tunisia both before and after the revolution of 2011 with a particular focus on opposition to the Ben Ali regime.

Tina Zintl is Project Coordinator for the Comparative Middle East Politics and Society Programme at the University of Tübingen in Germany. From 2009 until 2013 she was Research Assistant at the Centre for Syrian Studies at the University of St Andrews. She was awarded a doctorate in International Relations by St Andrews University in 2013. She is joint editor (with Raymond Hinnebusch) of *Syria from Reform to Revolt: Political Economy and International Relations* (Syracuse University Press, New York, 2015).

1

The Background to Civil Resistance in the Middle East

Chibli Mallat and Edward Mortimer

The Arab Spring that began in Tunisia in December 2010 was widely viewed, in much public and political discourse, as a striking phenomenon using methods of action that were new—at least in the countries concerned. This view is wrong. It had deep roots in the countries of North Africa and the broader Middle East.

In this chapter we look critically at the 'myth of Arab exceptionalism'—the idea that deep cultural factors made the Arab world predisposed to accept dictatorial rule. We show that non-violent forms of resistance have long been used in political action and in political debate. We then look at social changes—especially those relating to demography, unemployment, and the new media—that created strong pressures for change. We examine throughout the chapter dilemmas proper to the massive earthquake unfolding in the Middle East since 2011, including its specific religious and sectarian dimensions.

THE MYTH OF ARAB EXCEPTIONALISM

The fact that dictatorships in the Middle East were long lived in the period 1950–2010 compared to some other regions of the world can be explained by various historical and geopolitical contingencies, not by any deep cultural predisposition of Arabs or Muslims to accept despotism. Any such theory is simply a late version of orientalism, comparable to similar reifications of Catholicism, Orthodoxy, and 'Asian (or Confucian) values' in earlier periods. In a seminal book published in 1978 by the late Edward Said, orientalism as an academic discipline was criticized as an expression of colonial power.[1] While

---

[1] Edward Said, *Orientalism* (London: Routledge and Kegan Paul, 1978).

the criticism may have been excessive, it does underscore the dangers of apparent academic impartiality and 'science', of which the latest version is that Arabs/Muslims are intrinsically/culturally incapable of, or adverse to, democracy and human rights.[2] The number of journalists, lawyers, professors, human-rights activists, and political leaders who have been imprisoned, assaulted, or killed is probably larger in the modern Middle East than in any other part of the world in recent decades. Opposition to Middle Eastern dictatorships was constant, but wilfully ignored by the rest of the planet. Hence the false narrative of 'surprise' in 2011.

The model of dictatorship that dominated the region for more than half a century arose from the military coups, which the Middle East shared with several countries of the postcolonial world: in Latin America, Africa, and large important South-East Asian countries such as Myanmar and Indonesia. Already in the 1920s the military takeover in Iran by Reza Khan (who made himself Shah and took the family name Pahlavi) and the growing authoritarianism of Mustafa Kemal (Atatürk) in Turkey had foreshadowed later putsches in the Middle East. Both purported to carry a modernizing agenda as well as a social revolution. The theme of order, social redress, and reform would endure as the justification of the 'strong man' seizing and retaining power.

In countries under foreign rule, colonial governments devalued the rule of law they otherwise proclaimed (and in varying degrees established) by denying proper self-government to the local populations. They systematically undermined mass parties that demanded full independence (such as the Wafd in Egypt), jailed their leaders, and yielded little or no ground to the deafening call for self-determination. During two decades of struggle in the interwar period, moderate nationalist leaders and movements that shunned violence were

---

[2] On Islam (or previously 'the Arab mind', as in the title of a notorious book by Raphael Patai published in 1973) being incompatible with democracy, it may be sufficient here to point out the exceptional nature of the question itself, which recurs time and again in the media and has seeped into 'silver bullet' scholarship about Islam. 'Is Christianity or Hinduism compatible with democracy?' would mostly be frowned upon as a leading and overbearing question.

Academia is responsible for its own version of the wrong question, when it (*a*) presents Islamic law as the exclusive or dominant normative reference in Arab–Muslim societies, a norm that is 'frozen' in time and therefore 'incompatible with democracy', or (*b*), more subtly but equally wrongly, when it purports to provide in a single essay the key to Muslim/Arab societies progressing, regressing, or stagnating through the lens of Islamic law. Examples in recent scholarship of Islamic law as the fulcrum of Muslim/Arab societies include Timur Kuran, *The Long Divergence: How Islamic Law Held Back the Middle East* (Princeton: Princeton University Press, 2011), suggesting that all economic progress was undermined by Islamic law principles on commercial partnerships and property, Noah Feldman, *The Fall and Rise of the Islamic State* (Princeton: Princeton University Press, 2008), suggesting that Islamic law and its legal scholars were a good countervailing balance to power that was lost in the modern world, and Wael Hallaq, *The Impossible State: Islam, Politics, and Modernity's Moral Predicament* (New York: Columbia University Press, 2013), considering classical Islamic governance and the modern state at deep odds for producing two different types of subjectivities/human beings.

weakened and discredited. The sense of failure in jettisoning Western dominance made societies more fragile, and soon more willing to embrace 'strong men' who seized the helm through military coups. And so, to the profound frustration caused by a cynical colonial divide-and-rule policy was added the sense of a regional destiny shaped only by war and violence.

Within a complex set of debilitating factors, some local and regional, others international, several stand out as particularly Middle Eastern. One is economic: the region was plagued by oil, which acted as an explicit focus of national security in industrialized countries from the First World War onwards.[3] In a meeting aboard the USS *Quincy* on 14 February 1945, while the Second World War was still raging, the president of the United States confirmed his country's commitment to support the rule of the Saudi royal family so long as oil was sold with the help of American companies at an affordable price, and the lines of supply to the West secured. Even the massacres committed by mostly Saudi nationals in the heart of Manhattan and Washington in September 2001 would not shake the USA's commitment to absolute Saudi rule. The alternative thought by some of the Iraq War architects, that a pro-American Iraq would enable the USA to dispense with the support of the Saudi regime, floundered; and the initial unease across the USA at the fact that fifteen out of the nineteen young men who carried out the massacres on 9/11 were Saudi nationals has all but dissipated. Democracy and human rights continue to be sacrificed on the altar of oil.

What the Saudi rulers did with oil revenues for domestic repression and the support of extreme movements worldwide was never seriously called into question. Structurally, oil transformed the whole region into a system of direct or indirect rentier states with no healthy connection between citizen and government. Governments in Algeria, Libya, Iran, and Saudi Arabia belong to the first category of direct rentier states. No taxation is required. No representation is granted. In other countries with less or no oil, such as Jordan, Morocco, or Egypt, baksheesh governments live off a halting tax system and the subsidies of the oil countries. In the early 2000s a series of Arab Human Development Reports, prepared by Arab intellectuals under the aegis of the UN Development Programme, highlighted important deficits in Arab countries as compared with other parts of the world: a deficit of knowledge (more books were being translated in Spain alone than in the whole Arab world); a deficit of women's education and empowerment; and a deficit of freedom, democracy, and human rights.

---

[3] This is elegantly described through the career of the young Winston Churchill by David Fromkin, *A Peace to End All Peace* (New York: Avon Books, 1990). On the shaping of the Middle East by oil, see also Daniel Yergin, *The Prize: The Epic Quest for Oil, Money and Power* (New York: Simon and Schuster, 1991).

A second Middle Eastern factor is the continuous, massive violence of a hundred-year-long civil and regional war over Palestine, starting with Zionism's colonial project in the late nineteenth century. In the heart of the Arab–Muslim world, the shock occasioned by the establishment of Israel in four-fifths of Palestine west of the Jordan in 1948, and the expulsion/flight of 90 per cent of that area's non-Jewish population, undermined any remaining trust in regimes created by or aligned with the West. Syria started its own series of coups immediately after its government's conspicuously helpless performance in the war of 1948, and Egypt followed suit in 1952, with General Neguib's Free Officers easily removing the monarchy, then quarrelling with each other until the 'strong man' emerged in the person of Gamal Abdel Nasser—a 1954 coup within the 1952 coup. This would be replicated in similar terms in countries such as Iraq, with Ahmad Hasan al-Bakr's coup in 1968 and Saddam Hussein's takeover in 1979, and Syria, with Salah Jadid's coup in 1966 followed by Hafiz al-Assad's one-man leadership from 1970 to his death in 2000.

The form of the military junta takeover was invariably a 'Declaration Number One' ('balagh raqm wahed'), which decreed the death of the *ancien régime* and empowered a group of obscure army officers to exercise all powers taken over from the previous autocrat.[4] Constitutionally, the Revolutionary Command Council was put in charge. In law, subsequent constitutions that followed the Nasser model were tailored accordingly: self-designated enlightened groups, each propelling a leader in its midst to be president-for-life, would dominate Somalia, Sudan, Libya, Tunisia, Mauritania, Algeria, Yemen, Iraq, Syria, and the Palestine Liberation Organization (PLO) for the better part of the second half of the twentieth century (see Figure 1.1).[5]

Where emirs and monarchs survived the attempted coups in their countries, they aligned themselves on the model of the sole and absolute ruler with a similar fog of constitutionalism. The king/emir/sultan was invariably established constitutionally as the absolute wielder of executive and legislative powers, and the judiciary formally marginalized and made insignificant.

There is also the evident weight of religion in politics, Islam in particular, because of the wide majority of Muslims among the population of the Middle East. Religion creates a vector of identity that often stands in conflict with citizenship within a given nation state to the detriment of followers of other religions and non-observant or atheist compatriots. It also opens the door to medieval practices that are flaunted as 'authentic' by zealot groups, rendering

---

[4] Note the ominously similar *balaghs* issued by Egypt's Supreme Council of the Armed Forces (SCAF) after the first declaration on 10 February 2011, the day before Mubarak was forced to resign. The most expansive such declaration was issued on 18 June 2011 'constitutionally' to empower the junta: 'English Text of SCAF Amended Egypt Constitutional Declaration', *Ahram Online*, 18 June 2012 http://english.ahram.org.eg/News/45350.aspx.

[5] See Roger Owen, *The Rise and Fall of Arab Presidents for Life* (Cambridge, MA: Harvard University Press, 2012).

Figure 1.1. Self-confident rulers on the eve of the Arab Spring. On 10 October 2010, two months before the protests began, there was laughter and joking as the Afro-Arab summit met in Sirte, Libya. In the front row from left are Tunisian President Zine El Abidine Ben Ali, Yemeni President Ali Abdullah Saleh, Libyan leader Colonel Muammar Gaddafi, and Egyptian President Hosni Mubarak. Within 16 months all four were overthrown following popular protests.

©AP Photo/Amr Nabil

mainstream those Muslim apostates who need to be brought into the fold of 'authenticity' by force.

More subtle is the sectarian, as opposed to the religious, factor. In both Iraq and Syria, long dominated by opposing branches of a secular Arab nationalist Ba'ath party characterized by the ruthlessness with which its leaders cracked down on even the slightest hint of opposition, a key explanation is offered by the fact that the respective dictators were drawn from religious minorities— Sunni in Iraq and 'Alawi (a local version of Shi'ism) in Syria. They had every reason to fear the outcome of majority rule, and made sure that that fear was widely shared by their co-religionists as well as by other minorities.

In the Middle East, sect trumps religion, and the main divide is Sunni/Shi'i. This is part of the sectarian 'overdetermination' of the region, where the three monotheistic religions command an overt political expression in Judaism (Israel), Christianity (Lebanon, for part of the population), and Islam (in all the other countries of the region). Because of sheer numbers, the Muslim factor has played an important role in both government and dissent through the Middle East revolutions. As in all religions, such expression is protean. In government, the rulers in Saudi Arabia or Iran portray Islam as a central definer of their respective states despite their evident differences. In dissent, the revolutionary tide of 2011 has included non-violent expressions by the dominant Tunisian, Egyptian, or Jordanian Islamic parties. Some of the dissident Islamic movements espouse democracy as their 'natural' choice of government. But there are also openly violent movements, of which ISIS (the Islamic State in Iraq and Syria, or more recently SIC, the State of the Islamic Caliphate, a name it uses to distinguish itself from al-Qaeda and other extremist groups) is the latest expression. The menu is therefore vast and unruly. Practice is the ultimate test for the propensity of a self-styled Islamist movement in its relation to the use of violence for advancing its political interests, in government or in opposition.

Similar sectarian dynamics prevailed in Bahrain, Lebanon, and the eastern province of Saudi Arabia, where Sunni elites feared lest a combination of demography and democracy should bring about Shi'i dominance. And on the regional level the same Sunni elites feared the influence of Shi'i Iran, especially after the revolution of 1979, and even more so after the 2003 invasion moved Iraq into the Shi'i camp. Since 2011 these sectarian tensions have fed into, but have also been exacerbated by, the Syrian revolution turned civil war.

Long before that, however, people were resisting oppression across the region, as in other parts of the world. A serious study has yet to be written on the multi-formatted shape of civil resistance, which ranged from everyday gestures of impatience by individual citizens subjected to the brutal activities of the regime's apparatus of repression to more collective action through civil society: pressure groups, labour unions, bar associations, women and the disenfranchised, clerical circles, and political parties. Action ranged from civil resistance from within the system, including honest civil servants and the judiciary, to separatist movements eventually taking up arms against central power. There is no such work covering the whole Middle East,[6] but the late Hanna Batatu (d. 2000) brought all the social movements in twentieth-century Iraq together in a model book.[7] Kanan Makiya, writing under the pseudonym Samir al-Khalil, provides an impressive account of the brutality of the Ba'ath regime under Saddam Hussein in *The Republic of Fear*, but fails to take into account the amount of resistance that Batatu illustrated.[8] In the midst of domestic and regional violence of sometimes epic proportions, as in the Iran–Iraq War of 1980–8, the logic of non-violent resistance was always there, battling for its place against the

---

[6] However, see Charles Tripp's remarkable book on the 2011 revolution in its wider historical context, including in the struggle of women and in artistic expressions of dissent: *The Power and the People: Paths of Resistance in the Middle East* (Cambridge: Cambridge University Press, 2013).

[7] Hanna Batatu, *The Old Social Classes and the Revolutionary Movements of Iraq* (London: Saqi Books, 2004; original Princeton, 1978).

[8] Kanan Makiya, *Republic of Fear: The Politics of Modern Iraq* (Berkeley and Los Angeles: University of California Press, 1998; original by 'Samir al-Khalil', 1989).

logic of force. Already in the 1950s, with the hope of a third way inspired by the Bandung Conference, the figure of Gandhi towered high in the Middle East.[9] As elsewhere, it was undermined by civil and regional wars. Cicero's 'inter arma silent leges' (often rendered simplistically as 'In war laws are silent') had its enhanced equivalent in the Arab adage 'la ya'lu sawtun fawqa sawt al-ma'raka' ('No voice rises above the sound of battle') and in the Nasser regime's pedestrian motto: 'What is taken by force can only be taken back by force.'

Amid the sounds of battle, there always was a different logic at play. In the case of Nasser, the symbol of civil society resistance appears in the picture of the most respected jurist of Egypt, and of the Arab world, 'Abd al-Razzaq al-Sanhuri (d. 1971). On 29 March 1954, he was mobbed, beaten, and bludgeoned by Nasser's thugs in his courtroom.[10] From 1954 onwards, the judiciary would time and again rise against the three military rulers in Egypt, from Nasser's 'socialist' dictatorship through Sadat's idiosyncratic *infitah* ('opening'— to the market, to the West, and to reactionary, oil-funded Islam) to Mubarak's ever-increasing corruption and nepotism.[11] Other countries had their similar hero-judges, none though more successful than the embattled Chief Justice Iftikhar Chaudhry of Pakistan and the lawyers who supported him, who eventually achieved the removal of military dictator Pervez Musharraf in 2008.[12]

---

[9] See Elias Khoury's novel *Rahlat ghandi al-saghir* ('The Journey of Little Gandhi') (Beirut: Dar al-Adab, 1989). Gandhi and Nehru have long been icons of Middle Eastern societies, in Gandhi's case seeping, as in Khoury's novel, into the first names given to children. Nehru's books were translated into Arabic and widely read. The Lebanese leader Kamal Jumblatt, who was assassinated in 1977, most likely on the orders of Syrian dictator Hafiz al-Assad, was a prominent advocate of Gandhi's lifestyle and non-violence, which he put into effect in his leadership of what may be considered as a proto-non-violent revolution in 1951 against the extended presidency of first Lebanese president Bishara al-Khouri (it was called 'al-thawra al-bayda', the white revolution, as opposed to blood-shedding 'red' revolutions current then). On Jumblatt's contradictions and appeal, see Chibli Mallat, 'Fi sirr iqbal bidayat al-qarn 'ala kamal junblat: al-tariq al-thaleth wa dinamiyyat al-la'unf' ('On the Allure of Kamal Jumblatt for the Century: The Third Way and the Dynamism of Non-Violence'), *An-Nahar*, Beirut, 14 April 2001.

[10] Photo of beaten-up Sanhuri at his office in Majlis al-Dawla on 29 March 1954, courtesy of Tarek al-Bishri http://weekly.ahram.org.eg/2005/747/_bo3.htm. Tarek el-Bishri is a leading Egyptian jurist who was tasked with removing the authoritarian, anti-democratic clauses of the Egyptian Constitution in the early days after Mubarak's resignation, a task that he accomplished with remarkable effectiveness. (For this effort, accompanied and mirrored by a team of researchers at Harvard Law School, see Chibli Mallat, 'Revising Egypt's Constitution: A Contribution to the Constitutional Amendment Debate', *Harvard International Law Journal*, 22 February 2011, pp. 182–203 http://www.harvardilj.org/2011/02/online_52_mallat/.) Unfortunately, this purposeful amendment to the Constitution, which was confirmed by referendum, was undermined by SCAF's constitutional declaration mentioned at n. 4. Bishri, a 'moderate Islamist', is described as 'a staunch supporter of non-violent resistance to Mubarak's regime' (Jean-Pierre Filiu, *The Arab Revolution* (New York: Oxford University Press, 2011), 27).

[11] Tamir Moustafa, *The Struggle for Constitutional Power: Law, Politics, and Economic Development in Egypt* (Cambridge: Cambridge University Press, 2009).

[12] Daud Munir, 'Struggling for the Rule of Law: The Pakistani Lawyers' Movement', *Middle East Report*, 251 (2009), 37–43; 'The Pakistani Lawyers' Movement and the Popular Currency of

Judges and lawyers were not alone. Non-violence took many other forms, but was crowded out by the violence of the government, combined with that of covertly state-sponsored groups, or mobs, which governments tolerated, encouraged, and sometimes even conjured into existence for ulterior reasons: Islamists and others against communism in the early days, various groups against Islamism since the late 1970s. These were both threats that Western governments were ready to believe in, and against which they were generally happy to condone the use of violent repression, sometimes by silence, sometimes with explicit support. Since the 1980s, most remarkable was the violence by the rulers against Islamic factions. In Syria, Hafiz al-Assad had the centre of the city of Hama levelled to the ground in 1982. In Algeria, the military engaged in a long battle against Islamic groups after the Islamic Salvation Front (FIS) had won a lead in the first round of parliamentary elections in December 1991 and the army had then cancelled the electoral process. In Saudi Arabia, the violence of the Saud family against the Islamic opposition, especially in the first decade of the twenty-first century, was relentless. Extreme regime violence fed on extreme religious factions waging armed insurrection against the state, with the massive majority of non-violent civil resistance caught in between.[13]

This made the non-violent route even more difficult: the source of violence against people was not solely the apparatus of repression of the state. It also came from groups, mostly sectarian, capturing the political high ground through violence. Nor were those groups exclusively Muslim: unimpeded Jewish extremism in Israel has driven the colonization of the West Bank since 1967, and undermined the two-state solution, long the most reachable formula of peace between Israel and the Arabs; while the Christian militias of Lebanon were the first in 1975 to practise wide-ranging ethnic cleansing of Muslims living in their midst.[14] Still, a strong non-violent thread was there throughout, even when stifled by the battle between a violent government and activist violent factions, or military adventures against neighbours. This history of silent resistance and pain tends to be less well written than the one that

---

Judicial Power', *Harvard Law Review*, 123 (2010), 1705–26; Ran Hirschl, *Constitutional Theocracy* (Cambridge, MA: Harvard University Press, 2009), 99.

[13] For an account of the extent of non-violent Saudi dissent, see Human Rights Watch, *Challenging the Red Lines: Stories of Rights Activists in Saudi Arabia* (New York: HRW, December 2013) (detailing the contributions of eleven non-violent dissenters). The most scholarly accounts of violent and non-violent dissent can be found in the works of Madawi al-Rasheed, including *A Most Masculine State: Gender, Politics, and Religion in Saudi Arabia* (Cambridge and New York: Cambridge University 2013), which she augments by activism partly expressed in her tweets at @MadawiDr.

[14] The best book on the early period of Christian fascism in the Lebanese wars remains Jonathan Randal, *The Tragedy of Lebanon: Christian Warlords, Israeli Adventurers and American Bunglers* (London: Chatto & Windus, 1984). Wide-ranging ethnic cleansing of Christians followed at various points, especially by the Druze in the Shuf mountains in September 1983.

derives from the fracas of arms. In one of Bertolt Brecht's poems, a worker, reading in history that 'Philip of Spain wept when his fleet went under', asks: 'Did no one else weep?'[15] The question is even more pertinent for those who have suffered the violence of their rulers, and resisted without shedding their torturers' blood, in what is expressively described as 'unviolent' activity.[16]

All this long history of civil (and violent) resistance, and the corresponding entrenchment of regimes across the Middle East into ever more brutal and uncompromising rule, makes the 'surprise' expressed, as the revolutions started to break out across the Middle East in late December 2010 and January 2011, itself somewhat surprising.

A BRIEF HISTORY OF MIDDLE EASTERN NON-VIOLENCE

In so far as a regional context is useful, events in countries such as Egypt, Libya, Syria, Tunisia, and Yemen are better understood as part of a broader Middle East including Iran, Israel, and Turkey than as exclusively Arab phenomena. This region had witnessed many developments regarding the idea and practice of non-violence.[17]

There was a long stream of imperfect precedents. Although it may be questioned whether the overwhelming majority of demonstrators was *self-consciously* non-violent, Erica Chenoweth and Maria J. Stephan remind us that the Islamic revolution in Iran in 1978–9 shunned armed resistance.[18] Mary King makes the same point about the First Palestinian Intifada in Gaza and the West Bank, which began in December 1987.[19] At the beginning of the Arab

---

[15] *'Phillip von Spanien weinte, als seine Flotte Untergegangen war. Weinte sonst niemand?'* from Bertolt Brecht, *Fragen eines lesenden Arbeiters* ('Questions of a Reading Worker') (1935).

[16] Timothy Garton Ash (quoting Kenneth Boulding), 'A Century of Civil Resistance: Some Lessons and Questions', in Adam Roberts and Timothy Garton Ash (eds), *Civil Resistance and Power Politics: The Experience of Non-Violent Action from Gandhi to the Present* (Oxford: Oxford University Press, 2009), 371.

[17] 'Non-violence' can refer both to a general principle, and to a mode of action—and the two can be very different. Here the focus is mainly on the second. For a more comprehensive view of non-violence, see Chibli Mallat, *Philosophy of Nonviolence: Revolution, Constitutionalism, and Justice beyond the Middle East* (New York: Oxford University Press, 2015).

[18] Erica Chenoweth and Maria J. Stephan, *Why Civil Resistance Works: The Strategic Logic of Nonviolent Conflict* (New York: Columbia University Press, 2009). But see the criticism in Mallat, *Philosophy of Nonviolence*, 53.

[19] Mary Elizabeth King, *A Quiet Revolution: The First Palestinian Intifada* (New York: Nation Books, 2007). In fact, this was not strictly a non-violent movement—the use of stones, which echoes David and the killing of Goliath, is still violent—but the main 'fighters' on the Palestinian side were young people throwing stones at heavily armed Israeli troops and police. In purely military terms the Israelis had overwhelmingly superior force, but politically the first intifada was much more successful than the second, which began in September 2000, and in which the

Spring, Sadiq Jalal al-Azm noted the 2000–1 precedent—the Damascus Spring—foreshadowing the term that was so quickly and widely adopted for the revolution.[20] The Damascus Spring started with a relaxation by the new president, who literally inherited power from his father and had the constitution changed overnight just for this purpose.[21] Whether this relaxation was a ploy or reflected a genuine intention to open up, he changed his mind soon after people tried to take him at his word and test the limits of the new tolerance. Repression was back, but there was continued civil resistance, and Syrians spoke up more openly, especially after the Cedar Revolution in Lebanon in 2005 had forced Syrian troops out of the country, after almost four decades of continued military dominance (1976–2005).

It was during the Cedar Revolution in Lebanon that the concept of revolutionary non-violence was massively demonstrated on the streets of Beirut. When former Prime Minister Rafiq Hariri was murdered in a car bomb explosion that took the lives of another twenty-one innocent victims in downtown Beirut, the street reaction against the Lebanese–Syrian security order spiralled quickly, culminating in the largest demonstration in Lebanese history on 14 March 2005. The revolution was remarkable for its rejection of violence from the very first day. The response of Syria and its supporters, in contrast, was extremely violent: more than 100 people, including many leaders of the revolution, were assassinated or injured in the following two years, and the revolution was finally derailed when Hezbollah launched a violent attack against Israel in July 2006 (see Figure 1.2).

The impact of the Cedar Revolution was tangible. Street power was asserted, and yielded results, in the shape of the formal withdrawal of Syria's troops. A Special Tribunal for Lebanon, intended to find and try Hariri's killers, was established by the UN against strong opposition from the Assad government and its allies. However, these achievements were incomplete. The revolution failed to get its leaders into effective positions of power.[22] Moreover, the

---

unarmed demonstrations of the first few days were quickly overtaken by suicide bombings and other violent attacks on Israel's civilian population. Mubarak Awad has led the non-violent movement in Palestine, but was repeatedly stifled by the authoritarianism of the Fatah and Hamas leadership, and by the Israeli government. See, e.g., Mubarak Awad, 'Nonviolent Resistance: A Strategy for the Occupied Territories', *Journal of Palestine Studies*, 13/4 (Summer 1984), 22–36. See also Wendy Pearlman, Chapter 10, this volume.

[20] Sadiq Jalal al-Azm said in July 2011 in Berlin that the Damascus Spring of 2001 was a dress rehearsal for the Arab Spring of 2011. See, e.g., Carsten Wieland, 'A Decade of Lost Chances: Past and Present Dynamics of Bashar al-Asad's Syria', *Ortadoğu Etütleri*, 4/2 (January 2013), 9–29. This was also variously expressed by al-Azm in Arabic interviews and articles from the early days of the Middle East revolution.

[21] The Syrian constitution mentioned at Article 83 that the president must be at least 40 years old. It was amended to 34, the age of the young Assad. See Article 83, Constitution of Syria http://www.law.yale.edu/rcw/rcw/jurisdictions/asw/syrianarabrep/syria_constitution.htm.

[22] One of those leaders, Saad Hariri (son of Rafiq), eventually became prime minister for a time, but there is no real power in Lebanon without control of the presidency. The revolution failed because (*a*) Hariri's murderers have still not been brought to justice, although the Special

Figure 1.2. Civil resistance had a long history in the region before the Arab Spring. On 21 February 2005 thousands of Lebanese gathered in central Beirut to protest the assassination a week earlier of former prime minister Rafiq Hariri, who was killed in a car bomb in front of the St George Hotel, which stands in the background. The crowds chanted 'Syria out' and Damascus withdrew its troops two months later, ending a 29-year occupation.

© *Ramzi Haidar/AFP/Getty Images*

Special Tribunal has been a signal disappointment for those who believe in justice. Still, two important characteristics of the Cedar Revolution would endure and spread in the region: the potential of the people to use non-violent action to bring about a change in a deeply oppressive situation, and the call for judicial retribution.[23]

A similar movement took to the streets in Tehran in July 2009. There, too, the electoral manipulations of the incumbent president, supported by the ruling dictator in Iran, 'Supreme Leader' Ali Khamenei, led to a series of spontaneous non-violent street demonstrations. Repression was immense: dozens were killed and hundreds arrested, and the two opposition contenders for the presidency,

Tribunal for Lebanon has charged five Hezbollah operatives and is conducting their trial in absentia; (*b*) Hezbollah continues to act as a Syrian/Iranian surrogate, with support from the Shi'a community, so that Lebanon can still not be considered a truly independent country, while the Hariri camp held diminishing autonomy vis-à-vis the Saudi rulers; (*c*) the pro-Syrian president Émile Lahoud served out his full (illegally extended) term, from 1998 to 2007, and the Lebanese political system remains fundamentally unchanged.

[23] See, generally, Chibli Mallat, *March 2221: Lebanon's Cedar Revolution: An Essay on Non-Violence and Justice* (Beirut: LiR, 2007).

Mir-Hossein Mousavi and Mehdi Karroubi, themselves old pillars of the Islamic regime, have remained under house arrest since. Iran is a central factor in the Middle East non-violent revolution and remains one of its greatest hopes.

Meanwhile, in Bahrain, the mainly Shiʻa opposition had long established itself as a strong non-violent movement seeking to hold the king to his many promises of power sharing. In 2010, the movement grew significantly across the full political spectrum of Bahraini political forces. Thus, when more populous and less wealthy Arab countries erupted, Bahrain quickly joined in with its Pearl Revolution in February 2011. Caught off balance, the regime at first sought to preserve itself through compromise, and its reformist wing, led by the Crown Prince, was about to start formal discussion with the opposition on 'constitutional options', under the aegis of the US State Department.[24] On 14 March 2011 it abruptly changed tack and resorted to a vicious crackdown, evidently encouraged, if not imposed by, neighbouring Saudi Arabia, which sent in a large force, including contingents from other Gulf states.[25]

Since the 1980s, protests in the street took several forms, including localized and widespread strikes by workers. In Egypt, a precedent was established with the strikes of al-Mahalla al-Kubra on 6 April 2008, the best-known workers' strike of many examples in Egypt and elsewhere.[26] It led to the April 6 Youth Movement, one of the most active non-violent groups in Egypt. In the Arab world generally, in the aftermath of 11 September 2001 and the removal of Saddam Hussein by the US-led Iraqi invasion in 2003, a considerable fault line between the people and their governments was exposed. Hundreds of meetings of reformists and activists underlined the yearning for reform, but the grip of dictators was such that any reform short of removing the president/king/ayatollah looked insignificant. The dictators' grip on power remained steadfast, raising the difficult question of where civil resistance should set the bar of its demands, and how flexible it should remain, even when it turns into massive non-violent street protests.

Before Tunisia's revolution in 2010–11, civil resistance was not all expressed in the street. Nor were all street protests directed at the removal of the regime.

---

[24] See Caryle Murphy, 'Bahrain Becomes Flashpoint in Relations between US and Saudi Arabia', *Global Post*, 13 April 2011; Chibli Mallat and Jason Gelbort, 'Constitutional Options for Bahrain', *Virginia Journal of International Law*, 12 April 2011, pp. 1–16 http://www.vjil.org/articles/constitutional-options-for-bahrain.

[25] Martin Chulov, 'Saudi Arabian Troops Enter Bahrain as Regime Asks for Help to Quell Uprising', *Guardian*, 14 March 2011. See further details in Elham Fakhro, Chapter 4, this volume.

[26] For an early history of the Egyptian revolution, see Robert Solé, *Le Pharaon renversé: 18 jours qui ont changé l'Egypte* (Paris: Les Arènes, 2011). In North Africa, Michael Willis has documented dissent in various forms, including violent action, notably among Islamists. See his *Politics and Power in the Maghreb: Algeria, Tunisia and Morocco from Independence to the Arab Spring* (London: Hurst, 2012). See also M. Cherif Bassiouni, Chapter 3, this volume, and Mallat, *Philosophy of Nonviolence*, index entries for revolution (Nile); Kefaya; and other early non-violent Egyptian resisters of Mubarak.

But the governments actively anticipated any form of expressed dissent, and cracked down severely. Typically, prominent figures commanding national, sometimes worldwide, respect and a strong domestic following would be targeted by the government. The name that stands out in Syria is Riad al-Turk, probably the closest equivalent in the Middle East to Nelson Mandela. Turk was jailed by Assad the elder for two decades. When he was released by Assad the younger, he was rocklike in his refusal to compromise. As a leading figure in the Damascus Spring of 2000–1, he soon found himself in prison again, with several others. In total, he spent some twenty-four years in the Assads' jails. His article, 'The Time of Silence is Gone', published two days before the revolution broke out in Damascus (quickly followed by Dar'a) in March 2011, is testimony to his stature.[27] Aged over 80, Riad Turk has been living underground in Syria since, actively participating in civil resistance.

There are many such stories in the region, of leaders jailed for their opinion and courage. In Egypt, Saad Eddin Ibrahim and Ayman Nour are the two prime examples of resistance to Mubarak's autocracy. In 2000, Ibrahim wrote a mocking column about the passage of Syria's rule from father to son, coining the word 'monarblic' (*jumlukiyya*, from *mamlaka*, monarchy, and *jumhuriyya*, republic). He was jailed that night by Mubarak, who at the time was grooming his own son Gamal for the succession, and saw where Ibrahim's criticism was leading. Ibrahim spent three years in jail before being cleared by Egypt's highest court in 2003, and then from 2007 had to live in exile to avoid being imprisoned again (in 2008 he was given a two-year sentence *in absentia* for 'defaming Egypt'). Meanwhile in 2005, fearing that Lebanon's Cedar Revolution might spread to Egypt, Mubarak changed Article 76 of the Constitution to allow for a more competitive presidential contest. Ayman Nour, former MP and outspoken activist, took up the challenge. He was hounded by Mubarak, his party destroyed, and he too was jailed for three years.

Two major figures in the struggle against Muammar Gaddafi stand out. In 1978, Lebanese Shi'a leader Musa al-Sadr, invited officially to Libya, was 'disappeared' by Gaddafi. Apart from one brief acknowledgement by Gaddafi in 2002, no hard news about him has yet surfaced in Libya.[28] The abduction

---

[27] Riad Turk, 'Laqad walla zaman al-sukut: lan tabqa suria mamlakat al-samt' ('The Time of Silence is Gone: Syria will No Longer Remain the Mute Kingdom'), published on the Syrian *al-Ra'i* website http://www.arraee.com/portal, 12 March 2011, but no longer available there.

[28] On 31 August 2002, two years after a case had been lodged against Gaddafi by the family of Musa al-Sadr before the Lebanese courts, Gaddafi admitted in halting Libyan vernacular how great the imam was, what a loss his disappearance was, and what a pity it was that he 'disappeared here in Libya...we don't know how'. See, e.g., Amnesty International, *Amnesty International Report 2003: Libya* (London: AI, 28 May 2003) http://www.refworld.org/docid/3edb47da4.html, which notes: 'In his annual speech on 1 September Colonel Mu'ammar al-Gaddafi gave an official acknowledgement that Imam Musa al-Sadr, a prominent Iranian-born Shi'a cleric living in Lebanon, "disappeared in Libya" during a visit in 1978.' (In fact Gaddafi mentioned the disappearance on Libyan television a day earlier.) This went against a quarter of a

and disappearance triggered a continuous, massive protest in Lebanon. In 2000, the families of Sadr and the two companions who were with him on the visit sued Gaddafi in a Lebanese court. An indictment followed, and Gaddafi found himself under a persistent judicial sword of Damocles, making it impossible for him to visit Lebanon and a number of other Middle Eastern countries for fear of arrest.[29]

Another less judicially successful case was that of Mansur Kekhia, a distinguished former foreign minister of Libya who was abducted in Cairo in December 1993. His remains were identified in 2012 after the regime had fallen, but question marks persisted, including over the outrageous fine and dismissal of a case his wife had brought before an Egyptian court. Even more than Assad, who had been feted at the 14 July celebrations of the French president in 2008, Gaddafi was shamelessly courted by presidents and prime ministers in the last years of his reign: the British prime minister, the president of France, the latter's former wife on a separate trip, the chancellor of Germany, and sundry senior US officials visited Gaddafi's Tripoli in search of oil contracts or other concessions. Most egregious in Europe was the case of former Italian prime minister Silvio Berlusconi, under whom a new investigation was started to whitewash Gaddafi over the disappearance of Sadr. While it did not change the reality of Gaddafi's own acknowledgement, it shows how the judiciary, in at least some Western countries, can be manipulated by the executive on such important international human-rights cases.

It also illustrates, on a more positive note, how the families of victims carry heroic battles, and are increasingly vindicated. Ariel Sharon was defeated before the Supreme Court of Belgium by the victims of the massacres at Sabra and Shatila, before the law was changed retroactively to stop the proceedings. Saddam Hussein was tried and hanged (admittedly in a flawed and inhumane manner). Some of the alleged killers of Rafiq Hariri are under indictment before the UN Special Tribunal for Lebanon. Gaddafi was brutally murdered, unfortunately depriving his victims of his crucial testimony, while, as of May 2015, his son and chief security man were both in jail awaiting trial. Ben Ali in Tunisia has been tried *in absentia* and hides in Saudi Arabia. There is continuing pressure for Syria's Assad and Yemen's Saleh to be pursued for crimes against humanity. And Mubarak sat in the same orange jail where both Ibrahim and Nour had been incarcerated.[30] Justice operates in fits and starts.

century of systematic denial by the Libyan government that the imam and his companions had disappeared in Libya upon their visit, and an elaborate ploy to suggest that they disappeared in Rome.

[29] Notably he was obliged to miss the Arab Summit in Beirut in March 2002.

[30] Tora Prison, located south of Cairo. See Mallat, 'Al-zanzana al-burtuqaliyya tantazir mubarak' ('The Orange Cell Awaits Mubarak'), *al-Hayat*, London, 8 August 2011 (relating that the same cell where Ayman Nour was jailed had been painted in his party's orange colour to receive Mubarak; his two sons were reportedly held in the cell where Saad Eddin Ibrahim had

The last episodes in Gaddafi and Saddam's lives are not glorious moments in the history of non-violent resistance, but at least many of their opponents and victims could be heard calling loudly for their lives to be spared. In all these instances, the silver lining of accountability appears in the midst of setbacks and disappointments. Mubarak and his sons were released from jail a year after Sisi had taken over the presidency; Libya's collapse into chaos and Gaddafi's death made it much harder to find out what happened to Sadr and the hundreds of Libyan and non-Libyan killed and 'disappeared'; and the UN Special Tribunal for Lebanon has yet to see the accused behind bars, let alone those on whose orders they probably acted. Massacres in Syria and repression in Bahrain and the Gulf proceed without any form of domestic or international accountability. Even in Tunisia, the protection provided by the Saudi Government to Ben Ali and his family have prevented their proper trial in Tunis or elsewhere. These are just a few examples of the ongoing battle between crime and punishment.

Despite the setbacks, many histories of civil resistance are available across the Middle East for those who wish to avoid being 'surprised' again as they were in 2011. For every Saad Eddin Ibrahim or Riad Turk, there are hundreds whose names are unknown. Many of the leaders of civil resistance are women, repressed both by the government and by the Islamist extremes. Such is the case of Razan Zaituneh, who was an iconic resistant to Assad's rule in Duma, near Damascus, and 'disappeared' in December 2013 together with three of her close companions, under the watch of Zahran Allush, a local Islamist thug.

Even in a country such as Saudi Arabia, where resistance is generally associated with brutal, extreme, groups, the forest is missed for the trees. Particularly significant is the number of women who have been jailed, denied their passports, and harassed. The repression can take the basest of forms: attacks on husbands and fathers (who are supposed to keep their wives and daughters in line); confiscation of property; and threats, even abroad. All are common. Their stories occasionally surface thanks to groups such as Amnesty International and Human Rights Watch, or when protest takes an apparently newsworthy form, such as women driving in downtown Riyadh, or a particularly egregious decapitation, but none of this affects the standing of the Saudis with Western (and other) governments.

A warning has come since 2011, however. In the following two years there were more demonstrations than in the whole history of Saudi Arabia, since King Abdulaziz Ibn Saud occupied the cosmopolitan Hijaz in 1924 and subjected it to an increasingly puritan version of Islamic rule. On 9 March

---

lived months of solitary confinement). The transfer of Mubarak to house arrest in August 2013 did not prevent him from being brought to court a month later, but the relaxation of his detention conditions was a clear sign of the extent of the counter-revolution orchestrated by the army.

2013 the co-founders of the Saudi Civil and Political Rights Association (ACPRA), Mohammad bin Fahad al-Qahtani and Abu Bilal Abdullah al-Hamid, were sentenced to long prison terms. Women's challenge to the driving ban has become a recurrent staple of their leadership in resisting social oppression by males. On 9 January 2015, blogger Raif Badawi, who had earlier been sentenced to 10 years in jail and 1,000 lashes, turned into a world symbol of resistance when 50 lashes were publicly administered as a first instalment. The battle for non-violence is joined in Saudi society, but the persistence of impunity for an egregious style of governance effectively sends the message that there is no room for reform from within the margin allowed by the regime, pushing future opposition groups to adopt more radical objectives and methods. Considering the precedent of the early 2000s, however, and the Syrian turn of events, the Saudi people may well conclude that non-violent action is the far better route for change.

DEMOGRAPHY, UNEMPLOYMENT, NEW MEDIA

Saudi Arabia, the Middle Eastern country with by far the largest oil revenues (92 per cent of its $330 billion national income in 2012, according to official figures), is a useful example of the difficulty of subduing one's population for ever, even in highly liquid oil-rentier countries. There are not enough positions in government to satisfy all members of the ruling family, which is generally put at some 6,000 individuals;[31] and the financial demands of the Al Saud on the budget are increasingly heavy. More important, there has been a rapid and unplanned increase in the Saudi population, from around 9 million in 1980 to 27 million in 2010.[32] This has resulted in high unemployment.[33] With higher numbers come also higher demands for food, shelter,

---

[31] Opposition groups say closer to 20,000.

[32] Some have seen this population increase as in itself a form of civil resistance, though more probably it reflects the limited access of Saudi women—especially among Saudi tribes—to education and employment. Meanwhile, there has also been an enormous increase in the number of expatriate workers in Saudi Arabia.

[33] In 2006 the Saudi Minister of Labour announced that there were 120,000 unemployed on the basis that 120,000 people had applied for work at job centres. Sceptics observed that, since there is no unemployment benefit in Saudi Arabia and job centres rarely find people jobs, this figure was probably an underestimate. It was later revised to 440,000 unemployed, or about 9% of the workforce. Three million women were also described by the government as 'housewives' not seeking work, even though many are unmarried and some as young as 15. Interior Ministry documents obtained by opposition groups based in London suggest the real figure is much higher. According to the government's own figures in 2004, the total number of people in the workforce was 9,929,358, of whom 2,237,529 were students, 435,511 were retirees, 850,000 worked in the public sector, 750,000 worked in the private sector, and 266,910 were disabled or otherwise ineligible to work, leaving 5,389,408 men and women in the workforce unaccounted

and—most important—education. Educated youth, even if the education leaves much to be desired, carry expectations, not least that of finding a job that corresponds to their years of work at school and university. There are few jobs available, since rentier states dependent on oil revenue produce little of anything except oil and oil derivatives, and most of the work that needs doing is done by expatriates—a much more biddable and exploitable workforce than Saudi citizens would be. How many Saudis can be put to work in an oil industry dominated in its middle management by foreign experts, in the oilfields kept going by imported labour from South Asia, and in domestic service where workers come from the Philippines?

Middle Eastern governments are also kleptocratic nepotisms, with theft and corruption starting at the top: what correspondence was there between Saleh's or Mubarak's official salaries as presidents and their actual wealth? Nepotism is inherent in monarchies, and has successfully been cloned in self-styled republics, whether they are 'socialist' or 'Islamic'. The gulf between educated expectations and backward-looking government grows.

It gets worse for governments. The more people are educated, the more attuned they are to other models—popular music (rap in Yemen and Harlem, shake in Tunis and Cairo) is one small sign of resistance, in this case using Western symbolism—and the more they are technology savvy, the more they are likely to be critical of their governments. The revolutions in the Middle East are not merely Twitter or Facebook revolutions. Technological tools are just that: tools. For revolutionary change, it is the street that matters. But the street will be moved by information, and the technology of the 2010s is one where the citizen–journalist–witness is a click away from reporting an event, expressing his disagreement, and connecting with soulmates. As a rule of thumb, educated citizens are ahead of their governments in grasping new technology and its potential. In 1978, Khomeini's sermons and fatwas were brought into Iran through cassette tapes. The BBC World Service, carried by shortwave radio, was accepted as a source of accurate news long before satellite TV channels proliferated in the region. In 2011, national dissent was carried by the Internet, with the latest applications being Twitter and Facebook, and by satellite television. Text-messaging is second nature to adolescents the world over. In a report commissioned

for, presumed unemployed. However, according to leaked confidential government census documents, the total number of Saudi males in 2004 was approximately 16.5 million, of whom almost 10 million were adults (aged over 15). The total number of men in the workforce in 2004 was 5,012,223, of whom 124,030 were students, 418,076 were retirees, approximately 700,000 were employed in the public sector, 600,000 worked in the private sector, and 168,446 were disabled or otherwise 'not fit for work'. This suggests that in 2004, out of a total male workforce of just over 5 million, approximately 60% were unemployed. (Note kindly contributed by Hugh Miles, March 2013.)

by the BBC, Edward Mortimer summarized the development of 'user-generated content':

> For several years before the Arab Spring, the role of the 'citizen journalist' had
> been widely debated among media professionals and scholars. It had become
> clear that, at a time when fewer and fewer 'traditional' news organizations could
> afford to maintain extensive networks of professional journalists and cameramen
> around the world, technology had placed in the hands of 'ordinary' people the
> capacity to film and record events as they were happening, and transmit them
> around the world in a matter of minutes, or even seconds. The iconic example of
> this was the photograph of the dying student, shot (in both senses) during the
> demonstrations that followed the 2009 election in Iran, which is said to have been
> on President Obama's desk within 15 minutes. Yet nothing had quite prepared us
> for the sheer volume of footage of street protests, and of violence used to repress
> them, combined with the inaccessibility of much of the action for independent
> professional media, which has characterized the Arab Spring.
>
> Indeed one might say that, combined with the existence of satellite TV
> channels able and willing to transmit these images, it has *made* the Arab Spring.[34]
> Without those endlessly repeated jumpy images of crowds marching, crowds
> chanting, people running, falling, bleeding, and smoke rising from buildings, how
> many Arabs would have known that there was an Arab Spring, and felt embold-
> ened to take part in it? If that question is unanswerable, another admits of only
> one answer: can we, the outside world, imagine the Arab Spring without those
> images? Surely not. UGC [user-generated content] has not simply made the story
> more vivid, more exciting, more telegenic. It has *been* the story, or at very least
> has transformed its nature.[35]

Governments panic when the mass of critical views multiplies across
the population. They learn quickly how to crack down, enlisting the help
of unconscionable foreign high-tech companies, and pooling together their
repressive resources. The Gulf is typical, as too is the symbiosis of repression
between the Syrian and Iranian governments, with some governments looking
as far as China (and vice versa) to respond to the technological threat. There
are also unintended consequences: when Mubarak shut down the Internet and
the mobile phone networks in the early days of the then relatively limited

---

[34] Among many testimonies to the importance of satellite TV, here is that of Ian Pannell,
whom the BBC deployed in practically every arena of protest and struggle in the Middle East
during 2011: 'Most important [in spreading the protests from one country to another], rather
than social media, was Al Jazeera Arabic—people were glued to the screen watching events that
took place elsewhere' (telephone interview, 12 April 2012). Al Jazeera Arabic (in contrast with
the moderate tone carefully honed for its far less impactful English channel) was also peddling its
own, biased, and often vociferous Islamist world view, which rendered immense disservice to the
unity that characterized the initial moment of the Middle East non-violent revolutions.

[35] Edward Mortimer, 'Independent Assessment for the BBC Trust', in *A BBC Trust Report on
the Impartiality and Accuracy of the BBC's Coverage of the Events Known as the 'Arab Spring'*
(London: BBC, June 2012), 68 http://www.bbc.co.uk/bbctrust/news/press_releases/2012/arab_
spring.html.

demonstrations, worried parents went down in massive numbers into the streets to look for their children, swelling the numbers of demonstrators.[36] But some regimes—notably the Syrian—have been catching up, learning for instance how to infiltrate and manipulate the email accounts, blogs, and tweets of some of their opponents. In Sudan, the government was quicker on the uptake, and succeeded in nipping an incipient Arab Spring protest movement in the bud. As one news report put it: 'Pro-government agents infiltrated anti-government sites, spreading disinformation and looking to triangulate the identities of the chief organizers. They'd barrage Facebook pages with porn-ography, then report the pages to Facebook for violating the rules.'[37] It is notable that, of five 'state enemies of the internet' identified by Reporters Without Borders in its 2013 report, three—Bahrain, Iran, and Syria—are in the Middle East.[38]

There is much to say about the mass media technological factor in the 2011 revolution. Some is evident; some requires better research and more solid figures. What is certain is that cheap new media and educated (and un-employed) youth have at their fingertips an extraordinary, versatile, immediate, and always creative tool that can be used to support non-violent action.

A DEEPER CULTURAL HISTORY OF NON-VIOLENCE

There is also a deeper culture and longer history of non-violence in the Middle East. To be Braudelian is easy: all three great monotheistic (Abrahamic) religions were born in the heart of the region, and, whatever their subsequent terrible slips into conquest and cruelty, their message of peace remained throughout three millennia or so unperturbed in its core. All three have a strong message of non-violence. It has been an irony well underlined by the great philosophers Baruch Spinoza (d. 1677) and Abul 'Ala al-Ma'arri (d. 1058) that each religion is so perceived by its adherents, but not usually by those of the other two.[39] Yet Islam is by definition 'entering into peace',

---

[36] On the main Internet and mobile phone shutdown on the night of Thursday, 27–Friday, 28 January 2011, see Christopher Rhoads and Geoffrey A. Fowler, 'Egypt Shuts down Internet, Cellphone', *Wall Street Journal*, 29 January 2011 http://www.wsj.com/articles/SB1000 1424052748703956604576110453371369740. The shut-down lasted until about 2 February.

[37] Alan Boswell, 'How Sudan Used the Internet to Crush Protest Movement', McClatchyDC, Washington, 6 April 2011 http://www.mcclatchydc.com/2011/04/06/111637/sudans-government-crushed-protests.html.

[38] Reporters Without Borders, *Enemies of the Internet: 2013 Report (Special Edition: Surveillance)* (Paris: Reporters Without Borders, 12 March 2013) http://surveillance.rsf.org/en.

[39] Spinoza's excommunication in 1656, at the age of 24, remains shrouded in uncertainty as to the exact particulars, but there is little doubt that his critique of the biblical canon and the refusal

Jesus wilfully died on the cross, forbidding his followers to resist by violence, and *salam/shalom* is the greeting accolade of all Middle Easterners, rooted—like the word *Islam*—in the Semitic stem/*s/l/m*/, which means peace.

Such broad brushes may not be particularly helpful, and the sad truth is that violence has dominated regardless, including mob violence among the grass-root supporters of all three religions. Yet there is a language of protest that is largely *non-violent* and can also be documented more specifically than the initial, recurrent propensity of religions to associate with peace: its tangible expression is the recurrent use of 'silmiyya, silmiyya' ('peaceful, peaceful') in the demonstrations, and the increased adoption since 2011 of *la'unf* ('non-violence') by several authors and commentators on the Arab Spring.

Non-violence as a language of protest is certainly as old as some of the major crises in recorded Islamic history. Yes, there was 'terrorism', practised by the 'assassins' (followers of the Sheikh of the Mountain) in the eleventh and twelfth centuries. But all the leading thinkers of Islam rejected assassination as a mode of political action. Here one must operate in dualities, rehabilitating *fitna* (sedition/strife) and *bid'a* (innovation/heresy) as positive concepts that find their way into popular language—first names Badi', Badi'a, Faten, are common. There is a more intellectual aspect to this debate, including in the criss-cross legacy of, on the one hand, Ibn Hanbal (d. 855), who is claimed as an intellectual ancestor by today's 'fundamentalists', but is also the symbol of civil resistance to the absolute power wielded by Caliph al-Ma'mun (d. 833), and, on the other hand, his Mu'tazilite opponents—cited by Islamic rationalists and modernizers today, but allies of absolute power in their time. The evolving legacy of Imam Hussein for his Shi'a followers—from armed rebellion through martyrdom to separation of religious and political authority, with quiet acceptance of 'usurping' Sunni rule in the political sphere, and then back

to recant was behind it. The excommunication decree mentions 'the abominable heresies which he practised and taught'. See, e.g., Asa Kasher and Shlomo Biderman, 'Why was Baruch de Spinoza Excommunicated?', in David S. Katz and Jonathan I. Israel (eds), *Sceptics, Millenarians and Jews* (Leiden: E. J. Brill, 1990), 98–141. Spinoza's *Theological-Political Treatise* (1670) is relentless in its treatment of both Jewish and Christian religions as superstitions, and in it his argument moves from the harsh textual criticism of canonical texts to the advocacy of freedom as the 'objective of the republic' in the final chapter. Abul 'Ala al-Ma'arri, the blind poet–philosopher who ended his life in seclusion in his native Ma'arra in northern Syria, is most famous in the Arab world for the following verses: 'fil-ladhiqiyyati dajjatun (or fitnatun) | ma bayna ahmada wal-masih; hadha bi-naqusin yaduqqu, wa dhaka bi-mi'dhanatin yasih; kullun yumajjidu dinahu/ya layta ruhi ma al-shahih?' ('In Lattakieh is a rumour (also comes as fitna, revolt) as between (the supporters) of Muhammad and those of Jesus. The one rings his church's bells, the other shouts from his minaret; each glorifies his religion, o my soul, which one is right?') In February 2013 Ma'arri's small monument in his native village was desecrated, in what was probably an act of Islamic extremists, another sign of the ill-fated descent of the initially non-violent Syrian revolution into iconoclasm and intolerance.

again with Khomeini, who prided himself on being a Husseini not a Hasani,[40] to the assertion that the right-thinking Islamic jurist has a duty to exercise power—is another example of a tradition crossing back and forth between violent and non-violent resistance.

Violence and non-violence live uneasily together in the history of the region. Reading them with the correct lens revives treasures of subtlety, including refusals to resort to violence, which tend to be all too easily forgotten. While this is a vast intellectual research and education programme, it has started with a treatise on the non-violent society in Islam.[41] In this treatise, Hasan Bahr al-Ulum, a leading Shi'a cleric in Najaf (who died at age 50 in 2014), echoed a significant moment of non-violent resistance featured by historic leader of the Egyptian Muslim Brotherhood Hasan Isma'il al-Hudaybi (d. 1973),[42] who was also followed on this path by the successor 'guide' of the movement, Umar Tilmisani (d. 1986).[43]

NON-VIOLENCE: THE RULE AND THE EXCEPTION

While this history is being slowly reconstructed, the people on the street are way ahead. Non-violent resistance was a massive reality of the 2011 revolutions. Carried out with the motto 'silmiyya, silmiyya', it captured the imagination of the world in the early months of 2011.[44] The fidelity of Middle East revolutions to non-violence is remarkable. Even the Cicero rule of thumb about the sound of battle smothering all law was belied, if only one pays attention to the sheer numbers of people and countries involved in non-violent dissent and civil resistance. It took four months in Syria for the massively non-violent movement to be overtaken by arm-carrying rebels, first among the fracturing army, then by the influx of extremist Islamist

---

[40] Hasan, the elder son of Imam Ali, is considered to have chosen the 'non-violent' route for his opposition to the Umayyads, whereas his younger brother Hussein took up arms against them.

[41] Hasan Bahr al-Ulum, *Mujtama' alla'unf: dirasa fi waqe' al-umma al-islamiyya* ('The Non-Violent Society: A Study in the State of the Muslim Nation') (Kuwait: Marafie Foundation, 2004).

[42] Bahr al-Ulum, *Mujtama' alla'unf*, 98.

[43] The non-violent advocacy of Hudaybi and Tilmisani may be described by sceptics as opportunistic, and the Muslim Brotherhood in power adopted a worrying policy that mirrored those of Mubarak and of SCAF. Still, that strand of non-violence is worth noting (and building upon), against another tendency in the movement inspired by Sayyid Qutb (executed by Nasser in 1966), which was explicitly violent. A more puzzling question is whether non-violence can be merely a tactic, advocated only when the chances of winning through an alternative violent method are perceived to be remote.

[44] Including that of President Barack Obama, who said in a speech at the State Department on 19 May 2011: 'And through the moral force of nonviolence, the people of the region have achieved more change in six months than terrorists have accomplished in decades.'

combatants. Since the revolution in Syria started arming itself in the summer of 2011, it lost its soul to the increasing brutality of the insurgents and the government, turning the country into a wasteland and the Syrian crisis into a tragedy of biblical proportions.

The *dérive* in Libya and Syria should not distract us from the extraordinary persistence of non-violent methods on the revolutionary side in Lebanon since 2006, Saudi Arabia, Bahrain, and—most counter-intuitively—Yemen, let alone the revolutions of Egypt and Tunisia. In countries where the dictator has fallen through non-violence, a strong attachment to non-violent methods continues to be flaunted repeatedly even by the Islamic movements and leaders. The killing of a leading opponent to an-Nahda in Tunisia in early 2013 triggered the most significant crisis for the government since the fall of Ben Ali. In 2014, after the Huthi movement took over Sana'a by force, massive non-violent demonstrations followed, heralded and supported by numerous tweets and press declarations by Tawakul Karman, the iconic 2011 Nobel prize winner.

Of course, violence remains a temptation across the region as groups vie for power in the smouldering aftermath of dictatorship. For one, the repressive apparatus of the former government is at best numbed, at worst waiting for revenge. The shadow of the military—which had created Nasser, Sadat, and Mubarak—was so heavy in 2011–12 that Egypt's revolution was continuously haunted by the spectre of another coup. The first elected president of Egypt, Mohamed Morsi, and his Muslim Brotherhood are no saints either, and the veneer of non-violence does not strike observers as being particularly deep in their case. In June 2013, a massive street mobilization against Morsi was used by the army to reassert its power violently. Still, the philosophy of non-violence remains the distinguishing (as well as most alluring) characteristic of the region-wide phenomenon. The more it loses ground, the less attractive the revolution appears to its own protagonists as well as to those watching it in the wider world. Nowhere is this more important than in Libya and Syria, where the absence (Libya) or loss (Syria) of the non-violence impetus is increasingly identified by leading protagonists as the central cause for the respective failures of the Libyan and Syrian revolutions: in Libya with the chaos brought to the post-dictatorship period by revolutionary militias, in Syria with the militarization of the revolution in the summer of 2011 opening the door to ISIS and similarly brutal movements.

One difficult problem for civil resistance basing its ethos on absolute non-violence comes after the revolution. There is a complex link between non-violent revolution, the coercive nature of any state, even democratic ones, and judicial accountability for fallen dictators.

This set of complex factors interacting can be summarized as follows. The revolution can be non-violent, absolutely so. In Lebanon in 2005–6, in Egypt during the eighteen days that led to Mubarak's ousting, in Tunisia, in Yemen, it is hard to find a single recorded instance of violence deliberately targeting an agent or representative of the government. If any, police officers killed during each revolution can be counted on one hand.

Once the revolution has succeeded, however, the first question for the transition is the revival of the monopoly of violence in the hands of a new government. Here there is no choice: a government is obliged to use a degree of coercion (implying at least the threat of violence) to implement its most basic functions, not least the punishment of the common criminal. Even more significantly, one of the most important demands of the non-violent revolution is the trial of the former dictator and his aides. This cannot be done without the violence inherent in judicial power, but the trial cannot take place before the dictator's fall.

The non-violent spirit of a revolution cannot endure beyond its success other than through democratic mechanisms, which include an important dose of violence, best illustrated in the penal system. The criminal system is bound to be revived, and the call: 'The people want to try the president' ('al-sha'b yurid muhakamat al-ra'is') is of the essence for the non-violent revolution itself. In the case of dictators rightly tried as authors of massive crimes, usually crimes against humanity in the systematic repression against civil resisters, the state monopoly of violence is back for their trial. Maybe the removal of the death penalty can act as an effective reconciliation between the rule of law and the continuing spirit of a non-violent revolution.

CONCLUSION

To sum up, the Arab Spring derives from long traditions of civil resistance in the Middle East—a region that contributes more to, and derives more from, the global trends in human development than is often understood. More immediately, it sprang from recent events in the region—notably the Damascus Spring that began in 2000, the Cedar Revolution of 2005 in Lebanon, and the Green Movement of 2009 in Iran—as well as those that preceded the dramatic events of early 2011 in each of the Arab countries where they occurred. In Tunisia, Egypt, Yemen, Bahrain, and for many months also in Syria, the typical pattern of these events was an escalating non-violent mass protest movement, in which many thousands of unarmed protesters faced violent and brutal reactions from the forces of the regimes in power—the official security forces as well as paramilitaries and agents provocateurs—with extraordinary courage, and without themselves resorting to violence.

The regimes of Zine El Abidine Ben Ali and Hosni Mubarak were brought down not by force of arms but by masses of largely unarmed protesters against whom, after a short trial of strength, the security forces were unwilling to use the level of violence that would have been needed to crush them. They simply collapsed. For the non-violent movement, the turning point in the revolution is the moment when the dictator can no longer rely on his apparatus of repression to shoot into the unarmed crowds. Since his typical reaction is to give such orders when it is clear that the tide against him is rising by the day, one of the hardest tasks for revolutionaries is to gauge the precise moment when the dictator's apparatus of repression is about to collapse. There is no hard and fast rule, and the history of the Middle East revolution is young, to coin a phrase. But hard questions are upon us: is it not better for the non-violent revolution to cut its losses and 'go home' or seek a painful compromise that keeps the dictator in power, than to confront a regime that is not likely to collapse? Is it possible to continue a more low-level resistance, as in Bahrain after 2011, rather than escalating and ending with tens, if not hundreds of thousands, killed, as in Syria?

The early successes of the Arab Spring in Egypt, Tunisia, and Yemen were more or less textbook cases of how civil resistance is supposed to work. Some of the activists involved had benefited from training and advice provided by the International Center on Nonviolent Conflict, which had been carefully honing and encouraging such tactics for a couple of decades. This was discovered by the international media in the days after Mubarak's fall, and gave rise to a number of conspiracy theories, according to which the whole Arab Spring was engineered by American agents to serve Western interests, as well as to some understandable resentment on the part of activists not directly connected with the groups in question, who felt that those groups were unjustifiably claiming much too large a share of the credit for what had happened.

Indeed, their role should not be exaggerated. It would be a classic orientalist mistake to imagine that Arabs, Muslims, or Middle Easterners were not capable of working out a strategy of non-violent resistance for themselves. The essence of such a strategy is not, as they say, rocket science. Its starting point is the simple proposition that a weapon is of no use except in the hands of a person willing to use it. There are, of course, psychopaths who enjoy killing other people for its own sake, and it is also possible to train people to fire on unarmed crowds, and to use torture. But spontaneous psychopaths are the exception rather than the rule, and an important element in the training, generally, is inculcation of the idea that one has simple choices—between killing and being killed, between torturing and being tortured. The task of the non-violent activist is to counteract this training by somehow convincing the person with the weapon that these are *not* the only choices. Thus, the less threatening the protestor appears to the individual member of the security forces, the more threatening he becomes to the dictator who relies on those forces to suppress the protest.

For most non-psychopaths, killing and torturing people have disadvantages—one becomes odious to society and potentially to oneself. Without a strong counter-incentive to continue, the chances that security forces will desist, and/or seek to change the government that orders them to behave in this way, are quite high. In Syria, the brutality of the regime eventually bore fruit. In the summer of 2011, when significant groups began to desert from the army and other security forces, they saw it as their duty to protect unarmed people against their oppressors, and began to organize armed counter-attacks. This played into the hands of the regime, which had all along maintained that it was defending the country against 'terrorism', and in time also provided cover for jihadist groups to enter the struggle, so that by early 2012 there were indisputably two sides involved in a desperate and violent, if unequal, sectarian conflict. Many would argue that the brutality of the regime's response to civil resistance left its opponents no choice but to take up arms. But, by doing so, and by allowing themselves to be drawn into sectarian brutalities of their own, they forfeited much support both at home and abroad, and supplied the regime with a rationale for clinging to power. To continue purely non-violent resistance in the circumstances of late summer 2011 would have required extraordinary courage and discipline, but might well have been more effective in undermining support for the regime, including within its security apparatus. What would make such persistence of non-violence possible requires more careful thought, but, within the Middle East, Bahrain has offered since the massive crackdown of March 2011 a remarkable example of an obdurate non-violent resistance persisting for several years.

What makes non-violent resistance difficult is that it requires great courage, strong discipline, and a capacity for cool and rational strategic thought—all of these in at least as high a degree as does armed resistance. Yet in many societies there is a quite false popular perception that it shows weakness, and that armed resistance is the more manly, and also the more effective, response to oppression. People are often ready to accept that armed struggle is a long-term strategy, and to go on supporting it at great personal cost, even when there are no visible positive results. But non-violence they are ready to abandon, unless it has almost immediate and overwhelming success. In the case of the Egyptian and Tunisian revolts, it did. This is certainly testimony to the courage, discipline, and skill of the revolutionaries, but also to the weakness of the regimes. In one respect it is unfortunate: it created expectations of rapid success in other countries whose regimes were not quite so weak, or where circumstances were in other respects less favourable. The success of these revolts was certainly a great triumph for non-violent action. But by making it look too easy it may also have been a setback for the use of similar tactics elsewhere.

Nor is the flight or arrest of the dictator the end of the non-violent revolution. How does a non-violent revolution carry its central message into the post-dictatorship period, as it drafts a new social contract in the form of a constitution, and accounts for the long years of criminal behaviour by the fallen dictator and his aides? And are these two necessary moments, constitutionalism and accountability, not part and parcel of the same philosophy of non-violence that triggered the world's enthusiasm in the early 2011 months of the Arab Spring? How can the development of a non-violent, democratic way of carrying out politics, and of judicial and other forms of accountability for the leaders of the *ancien régime*, continue and reinforce revolutionary non-violence?

One area where one might have expected these tactics to be applied was the Palestinian–Israeli conflict, where the Israelis enjoyed overwhelming military superiority but would probably have found it hard to sustain a ruthlessly brutal reaction against a determinedly non-violent protest movement. For a moment, in May and June 2011, such a movement appeared to be materializing. Thousands of unarmed Palestinians marched on the Israeli border in Lebanon and on the ceasefire line in the Golan Heights. Israeli troops responded by opening fire, and tens of protesters were killed. These marches were problematic, because obviously engineered by Assad and Hizbullah to deflect the growing revolution in Syria. But similar protests were held in the West Bank and the Gaza Strip. However, the movement was not sustained. This may have been yet another example of the famous aphorism, attributed to Abba Eban, that 'the Palestinians never miss an opportunity to miss an opportunity'. It was absolutely to be expected that Israel would respond very harshly at first, but it is hard to imagine that Israel could have continued firing on unarmed Palestinians in large numbers, week after week, month after month. Neither international nor domestic Israeli opinion would have tolerated it, and the soldiers themselves would soon have refused to carry out orders.

Why did the Palestinians not pursue this strategy? Apparently it was discussed among the elite in Jerusalem and the West Bank, but the political leaders there were greatly afraid of following it through. They correctly anticipated that Israel would react at first with considerable brutality, and they feared that under this pressure it would not be possible for the movement to remain non-violent. Palestinians would again resort to armed attacks on a significant scale, the cycle of violence would resume, and any hope of a negotiated solution would be moved even further off. The leaders of Fatah, which was in government in the West Bank—and perhaps also, to a lesser extent, those of Hamas, in power in Gaza—were well aware that their own authority, as well as the Israeli occupation, was a likely target of any mass protest movement. In this confused situation a general disillusionment with politics prevailed, and the relative improvement of the economic and security situation in the West Bank also took the edge off political anger, at least among some of the educated youth who might otherwise have taken the lead.

Reasonable as these explanations may be, they all seem defeatist and depressing. Indeed, they speak eloquently to the frame of mind of the Palestinian leadership, which had been worn down by too many failures and frustrations over the years. In fact that was already true of the exiled PLO leadership in 1988. At that time their hand had been forced by a new, more enterprising leadership that sprang up inside the occupied territories— much as, in 2011, the cautious leaders of Egypt's Muslim Brotherhood were bounced into joining the protests in Tahrir Square by their movement's more enterprising youth wing. But, in the demoralized and divided Palestine of 2011 and after, no such new leadership appeared. The activities of Ziad Abu Ein, a Palestinian minister who had espoused non-violence in a creative campaign focusing on planting olive trees against the Israeli policy of settlement and orchard destruction, indicated that the strategy of non-violence had some prospect of gaining ground, but his death in December 2014 from a heart attack after a confrontation between demonstrators and Israeli forces was a setback for this cause. A strategy of non-violence is unlikely to make headway without a strategic shift of Palestinians inside and outside Israel–Palestine, and it cannot succeed if it does not make serious inroads among Jewish Israelis.[45]

Such are the dilemmas faced by all movements of civil resistance against regimes of systematic brutality. The political context and culture of the Middle East have subjected such movements to a particularly harsh test. Even in countries such as Egypt and Tunisia where the revolutions at first achieved spectacular success, the new leaders have found it very difficult to turn this success into the foundation of a long-term constitutional order, given the very low level of trust between different factions and the fact that the best organized groups (notably those that emerged from the Muslim Brotherhood) were not really committed to democracy as an end rather than a means.[46]

Here, again, practice is decisive. For some 'young' movements such as al-Qaeda and ISIS in Syria and Iraq, violence is part and parcel of their

---

[45] Abu Ein was reportedly struck by Israeli soldiers and succumbed to a heart attack. Lawyer Gabi Lasky, a Tel Aviv City Council member for the Meretz party, had this comment: 'Instead of ending the injustice they try and curb and prevent non-violent protests. In doing so, the security forces use violence against anyone who attempts to realize their most legitimate right—to protest. That's what happened here. And this time, like in previous incidents, it ended with death.... The Israeli occupation has found many ways to use force against Palestinian violent struggle. But it doesn't have an answer to non-violent struggle, aside from sending its leaders to prison.' (Yael Marom, 'Palestinian Non-Violent Activists: Army Violence Won't Stop our Resistance', +972 *Magazine*, Israel, 10 December 2014 http://972mag.com/ziad-abu-ein-wanted-2015-to-be-the-year-of-non-violent-struggle/99918/).

[46] As of May 2015, the outcome was very different in the two countries. In Egypt, the coup of July 2013 had spawned a full-blooded counter-revolution, while in Tunisia (perhaps awed by the Egyptian example), An-Nahda had shown willingness to compromise, allowing the election of a secularist-led government in the winter of 2014–15 and thus preserving the original non-violent spirit of the 2011 revolutions.

ideology and action. This is not necessarily the case of the Muslim Brother-hood, which in its long history has manifested contradictory stances towards the use of violence, or the Tunisian An-Nahda, which has clung much more firmly to non-violent practices, both in government and in opposition. In all cases, however, the non-violent movement's response can only be inscribed in human-rights-honed processes. There is nothing essentially 'Islamic' or 'Arab' compelling violence as a mode of political actions. The 'Islamic' reference always falls short of explaining why the massive majority of Muslims despise them as well as suffer most from their rule. There will never be a dearth of political movements or individuals who seek to hijack non-violent revolutions. This is true for the military replicas of Mubarak in Egypt, the Muslim Brotherhood under Sisi, Saleh, or the Huthi rebels in Sana'a, or the self-anointed 'caliph' al-Baghdadi commanding atrocities from his hiding place in the Syrian–Iraqi desert. Political Islam must make existential decisions between violence and non-violence, in government and in opposition. If it is to survive the risk of associating the religion it claims as guide with the naked, intolerable use of force characteristic of sheer barbarity, then its tradition of humanism needs to be reclaimed and genuinely applied. The alternative is death and misery. Non-violence divides the future of the planet between those who espouse it as mode of political expression, and those who glorify violence as part and parcel of their world view.

It is important to recognize that the Middle East, including its Arab component, is a region of enormous diversity, culturally as well as in socio-economic terms. While Islam and the Arab heritage may be unifying elements facilitating the transmission of ideas, the political context and culture still vary greatly from one country to another. It would, therefore, be a great mistake to imagine that events in one will necessarily follow the same pattern as those in others—a mistake unhappily made by many Syrians in the spring and summer of 2011, but also by some Western powers, which rushed to call for Assad's departure without having any strategy to help bring that about.

One of the lessons may be that oppositions engaging in non-violent action should be more strategic in choosing their objectives as well as their methods. Rather than calling for the downfall of the regime—as most Arab Spring movements have done—it may sometimes be wiser to make more limited demands, such as respect for freedom of expression and of peaceful assembly, which may be harder for the regime to refuse but which, if granted, may also crucially limit its own freedom of manœuvre. Alternatively, the strategy may well need to be conceived as a set of actions moving back and forth in a staggered manner with a view to dislodging the dictator qua individual, by making it harder for the regime as a whole to launch an all-out repression that decimates the revolution or forces it into violence. Non-violence requires a creativity to which the revolutionaries of the Arab world have already contributed significantly. It requires also a philosophical reflection that is commensurate with the historical earthquakes seen in intensive moments— both successes and failures—from the eastern European revolutions in 1989 to China and the Middle East.[47]

[47] The authors wish to extend particular thanks to Hugh Miles and Mara Revkin, and to Trudi Hodges and several colleagues at Right to Nonviolence, for their help with this chapter.

2

Revolt for Dignity

Tunisia's Revolution and Civil Resistance

Michael J. Willis

Tunisia has been surprisingly neglected in accounts of the popular uprisings that shook the Arab world from early 2011, despite the critical role it played. It was here that the whole dramatic chain of events began. Sustained and widening protests culminated in tens of thousands of Tunisians thronging the main avenue of the capital, eventually toppling the twenty-three-year rule of President Zine El Abidine Ben Ali on 14 January. It immediately became the model to follow. The crowds that similarly flowed onto the streets of Cairo, Benghazi, Sana'a, and Manama in the weeks that followed explicitly acknowledged this example, not least through the adoption of the slogan chanted by the crowds in Tunisia: 'ash-sha'ab yurid isqat al-nizam' ('The people want the fall of the regime'). Tunisia also became notable for achieving the most amount of political change for the lowest cost in terms of bloodshed. For, while neighbouring Libya arguably became the first Arab state to break definitively with its previous regime with the fall of the last Gaddafi strongholds in October 2011, Tunisia's break, through the election just one week later of a new Constituent Assembly dominated by long-time and inveterate opponents of Ben Ali's regime, was at once less bloody and more profound. Whereas tens of thousands had died in the battle to oust the Gaddafi regime, those killed in securing the departure of Ben Ali and his system, while equally individually mourned, numbered less than 300. Tunisia's subsequent path to the approval and introduction of a new fully democratic constitution in January 2014 was certainly rocky and not without bloodshed, most notably with the assassinations of two leading politicians, but such incidents were rare, especially when compared to the transitions occurring elsewhere in the region. Indeed, as the death tolls mounted in Yemen, Bahrain, Egypt, and especially Syria, the achievements of the Tunisian revolution became even more remarkable. Tunisia thus appears to represent the most complete and accomplished example of civil resistance emerging from the Arab Spring.

A TRADITION OF PEACE?

Exactly why Tunisia emerged as the most successful example of civil resistance is worth exploring. An explanation that is commonly heard is that the country has an ingrained tradition and preference for peaceful change and an abhorrence of violence. Some academics dismiss this as 'culturism' based on the impressions of tourists to the country, which 'confuse the professional obsequiousness of the lift boy with a quasi-natural favouring of conciliation over conflict'.[1] Yet it is an argument that is commonly advanced by Tunisians themselves. Mokhtar Yahyaoui, a dissident judge who stood up to Ben Ali and who was dismissed and persecuted for his stand, states that he never feared that opposition to the Ben Ali regime would turn violent, arguing: 'Even under colonial rule, Tunisians were never violent.'[2] Ahmed Nejib Chebbi, the leader of the largest opposition party to Ben Ali, asserts: 'We are a peaceful people...we are softer than others.'[3] The evidence for this argument is inevitably mixed. Historically, the country experienced periods of violence and peace much like any other. It was certainly true that the French were able to establish colonial control over the country in the final quarter of the nineteenth century far more easily and with less bloodshed than accompanied the establishment of their rule in neighbouring Morocco and particularly Algeria. Yet this had much to do with the country's small size and population when compared to its neighbours. Moreover, resistance to French colonial rule did turn violent by the early 1950s, particularly in the countryside, and was comparatively short lived owing to Paris's decision to grant independence to the country relatively swiftly to allow it to concentrate on maintaining its presence in Algeria.

Violent resistance to the state did not end with the departure of the French in 1956. A bitter internecine conflict within the victorious nationalist movement, the Neo-Destour, killed as many people as the conflict with the French over independence. The victorious faction led by the new President Habib Bourguiba ruthlessly suppressed his rival, Salah Ben Youssef, and his supporters, and survived two coup plots before relative political calm was established in the country. Violence returned to the country's streets again in the late 1970s with clashes emanating from a general strike organized in January 1978, killing possibly hundreds of people. Two years later, a group of insurgents in the Gafsa region attempted an uprising backed by Libya and Algeria. In 1984 there was widespread rioting across large areas of Tunisia in protest at austerity measures, which resulted in more than 1,000 casualties and nearly 100 deaths,

---

[1] Entretien de Béatrice Hibou avec Sadri Khiari, 'La Révolution tunisienne ne vient de nulle part', *Politique africaine*, 121 (March 2011), 25.

[2] Author's interview with Mokhtar Yahyaoui, Tunis, 19 September 2011.

[3] Author's interview with Nejib Chebbi, leader of the Progressive Democratic Party (PDP), 2001–6, Tunis, 26 September 2012.

overwhelmingly at the hands of the police.[4] Indeed, the Tunisian state was itself responsible for significant levels of violence, especially during the 1990s, imprisoning and torturing hundreds of opponents of the regime, more than thirty of whom perished in official custody.[5] Although such incidents of violence were smaller in scale and less bloody than in many other states, they still make it difficult to argue convincingly that Tunisians are fundamentally pacific.

A more considered analysis of the revolution of January 2011 itself is, therefore, needed. One of the difficulties in analysing the revolution is both the absence of an identifiable leadership and the remarkably heterogeneous nature of the movement that forced Ben Ali's departure. These features, which were notably shared by the protest movements that emerged in other Arab states in the wake of the Tunisian uprising, precluded easy identification of the causes of the revolution but at the same time spoke of both the complex but also the comprehensive nature of the protest movements. Indeed, support for the revolution came from a very wide cross section of Tunisian society, each element with its own motivations for seeking the overthrow of the regime and its own methods. An examination of each of these constituent elements is, therefore, important for an understanding of the broader picture.

REVOLT IN THE RURAL INTERIOR

The uprising that ultimately brought down Ben Ali began in the provincial interior of the country. The story of Mohammed Bouazizi, the young vegetable-seller who set himself on fire outside the local governorate office in protest at his mistreatment by the local authorities on 17 December 2010, is now well known.[6] Yet the popular narrative of how the actions of this one

---

[4] Mustapha Kraïem, *État et société dans la Tunisie Bourguibienne* (Tunis: MIP, 2011), 446–9.

[5] Sdiri Wafa, 'Liste nominative des personnes mortes à cause de la torture dans les prisons tunisiennes depuis 1987', *Tunisie numerique*, 16 October 2011 www.tunisienumerique.com/liste-nominative-des-personnes-mortes-a-cause-de-la-torture-dans-les-prisons-tunisiennes-depuis-1987/81081.

[6] The precise details of the initial event remain slightly disputed. Bouazizi was punished for selling fruit and vegetables either in an unauthorized place or without a licence. A policewoman confiscated some of his vegetables and his weighing scales and may also have slapped him across the face, although a court case against her was later dropped. Bouazizi went to protest at the municipal building and then the governor's office, but was turned away. He then set fire to himself, apparently with paint thinner, outside the governor's office. See Kareem Fahim, 'Slap to a Man's Pride Set off Tumult in Tunisia', *New York Times*, 21 January 2011 www.nytimes.com/2011/01/22/world/africa/22sidi.html, and Elizabeth Day, 'The Slap that Sparked a Revolution', *Observer*, London, 15 May 2011 www.theguardian.com/world/2011/may/15/arab-spring-tunisia-the-slap.

individual suddenly and spontaneously ignited the whole of Tunisia, and ultimately the wider Arab world, in revolt obscures a more profound appreciation of the deep-rooted origins of the Tunisian uprising. The small town in which Bouazizi lived, Sidi Bouzid, is part of the southern interior of Tunisia, which not only has a long history of resistance to governments in Tunis but, more importantly, had been the locus of undoubtedly the most serious, organized, and sustained social unrest during the Ben Ali regime just two years before Mohammed Bouazizi set light to himself.

The Gafsa governorate just to the south-west of Sidi Bouzid had been a prominent centre of resistance during the rule of the French. It also provided significant support to Salah Ben Youssef, the defeated contender for the leadership of both the Neo-Destour Party and the country after independence. Significant investment in the region, notably its profitable phosphate mines, made for a more tranquil period in the 1960s and 1970s, but the decline in the international price of phosphates together with government austerity measures revived unrest in the 1980s. It was the region that the Libyans and Algerians chose for their attempt to overthrow the Tunisian regime in 1980, and was home to major points of unrest during the general strike of 1978 and the riots of 1984.[7] Progressive neglect of the region during the rule of Ben Ali, who channelled resources and especially jobs disproportionately to the capital and the coastal towns and cities, stoked resentment, which was exacerbated by two further factors. Official rhetoric about Tunisia's 'economic miracle' failed to chime with local experiences, and the marked growth of clientelism and nepotism, particularly during the latter part of Ben Ali's presidency, led to widespread local feeling of being excluded and cheated out of the fruits of Tunisia's supposed economic success.[8]

Resentment at the perceived nepotistic way in which jobs were allocated by the local office of the national phosphate company led in January 2008 to a series of protests in the town of Redeyef, in the Gafsa governorate, which spread out to the surrounding towns in the weeks that followed. The fact that the authorities took a full six months to quell these protests was an indication not just of their size and level of support but also of their degree of organization. The local and unofficial association of unemployed graduates, together with similarly unofficial local independent trade unionists, came rapidly to the fore to coordinate the protests and managed to launch a national support

---

[7] Amin Allal and Karine Bennafla, 'Les Mouvements protestaires de Gafsa (Tunisie) et Sidi Ifni (Maroc) de 2005 à 2009: Des mobilisations en faveur du reengagement d l'état ou contre l'ordre politique?', in Sarah Ben Néfissa and Blandine Destremau (eds), *Protestations sociales, révolutions civiles: Transformations du politique dans la Méditerranée arabe* (Paris: Armand Colin, 2011), 31, 39.

[8] Béatrice Hibou, 'Tunisie: Économie politique et morale d'un movement social', *Politique africaine*, 121 (March 2011), 9–10.

committee before the authorities were able successfully to isolate the region from outside scrutiny.[9]

The precedent, lessons, and organization produced by the Gafsa protests of 2008 provide an important explanatory backdrop to the unrest that was to erupt in the adjacent governorate of Sidi Bouzid, which shared many of the same problems, at the end of 2010. Indeed, in the period in between many smaller protests had continued. Thus the events in Sidi Bouzid were not so much the spark that lit a revolution, but rather the latest expression of gathering social unrest in the region.[10] In July 2010 local police used batons and tear gas brutally to break up protests about the abusive practices of an agricultural bank by farmers and agricultural workers in front of governor's offices in Sidi Bouzid.[11]

Six months later, on 17 December 2010, it was in front of the same governor's office at Sidi Bouzid that Bouazizi stood and poured paint thinner over himself, and it was also where a crowd, consisting mainly of local traders and youths, gathered on the night of Bouazizi's self-immolation. There they organized a sit-in in protest at his treatment. The following day more people joined the sit-in and protests, and the day after that a Coordination Committee was formed and protests spread to neighbouring towns, following a very similar pattern to that of Redeyef and Gafsa two years earlier. The local police responded by trying to break up the protests and began to arrest people, which prompted retaliatory violence from some of the protestors, who burned down a police station in the neighbouring town of Menzel Bouzaïane. The confrontations reached a new and ultimately pivotal level with the shooting dead of the first protestor by the security forces in Menzel Bouzaïane on 27 December, just over a week after Bouazizi's initial protest.[12] From this point, the size and spread of the protests increased dramatically, stoked by the death of Bouazizi in hospital on 4 January: 5,000 people attended his burial the following day.[13] Yet, even after the unrest had reached the cities, the small towns of the interior continued to bear the brunt of the regime's attempt to repress the gathering uprising: some fifty protestors were killed in the town of Kasserine in the days leading up to the departure of Ben Ali (see Figure 2.1).[14]

---

[9] Allal and Bennafla, 'Les Mouvements protestaires', 29–30.
[10] Entretien de Hibou avec Khiari, 'La Révolution tunisienne', 33. Bouazizi was also neither the first nor the last young Tunisian to set light to himself. See Slah Westlati, *Démocratie ou guerre civile? Chronologie de la révolution tunisienne* (Tunis: Nirvana, 2011), 41–6.
[11] *Dégage: La Révolution tunisienne. Livre-témoignages* (Tunis: Éditions du Patrimonie, 2011), 20.
[12] *Dégage: La Révolution tunisienne*, 20, 23.
[13] Mohamed Bouamoud, *Bouâzizi, ou l'étincelle qui a destitué Ben Ali* (Tunis: Almaha Editions, 2011), 58.
[14] *Dégage: La Révolution tunisienne*, 32.

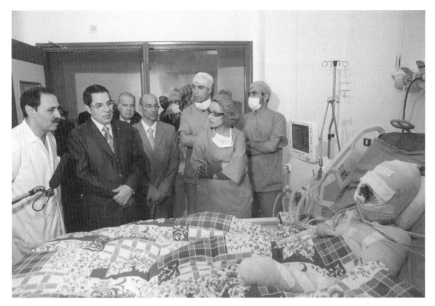

Figure 2.1. An unlikely starting point. Tunisian President Zine El Abidine Ben Ali visits Mohammed Bouazizi in hospital on 28 December 2010. The young vegetable seller from Sidi Bouzid set himself alight in a desperate protest at his apparent mistreatment by the local authorities and unleashed a region-wide wave of protest. Bouazizi died from his wounds on 4 January 2011; Ben Ali fled the country 10 days later.

© *AFP Photo/Tunisia*

CENTRALITY OF TRADES UNIONS: THE UGTT

Local independent trade unionists had played a role in organizing the Gafsa protests and they came to play a similar and expanding role in the opening days of the 2010 protests. Several attended the second day of the sit-in in Sidi Bouzid. Very significantly, members of the official national trades union, the UGTT (Union générale tunisienne du travail), began to join the protests. The UGTT had a stature and historic role in Tunisia that was greater than any other trades union in any other Arab state. It had played a crucial role in the liberation struggle against the French, taking on the leadership of the struggle when the politicians of the nationalist party were imprisoned and in exile. After independence it enjoyed a level of prestige and independence that was a source of ongoing concern to the regime, which made repeated attempts to co-opt and neutralize the union. It became a significant pole of opposition to President Bourguiba in the 1970s and was the driving force behind the highly politicized general strike of 1978. After coming to power, Ben Ali appeared to be more adept than his predecessor at co-opting the union through patronage, intimidation, and the effects of economic reforms that reduced its bargaining power. This succeeded in bringing the national leadership of the union to heel but was not able to control the local and regional sections of the organization, which engaged in increasing conflict with the leadership in Tunis. Dissidents succeeded in entrenching themselves in certain important sections of the union, such as the postal workers and the teachers, and it was these groups that began to organize and mobilize their members, as the protests spread from the provinces to the towns and cities of the coast, including the capital, by late December and early January.[15] Dissidents progressively took control of the local and regional branches of the union, and very rapidly large sections of the ordinary membership of the UGTT, which numbered half a million, appeared to be in open revolt against the union's leadership.[16] The national leadership of the union finally succumbed to huge pressure on 11 January and authorized a general strike the next day in Tunisia's second largest city, Sfax, and then in Tunis two days later. The huge success of the Sfax strike rang for many observers the death knell of the Ben Ali regime: on the day of the planned strike in the capital the president fled.[17]

THE REVOLUTION COMES TO TOWN: WORKING AND MIDDLE-CLASS RESPONSES

Before the internal struggle within the UGTT had been definitively resolved, unrest had spread by the second week of January to the capital and other main cities, and the first calls for the departure of President Ben Ali were heard at protests. Beginning in working-class districts of the cities, the unrest was led by youths in a rather more anarchic and arguably violent fashion than the more coordinated protests of the interior and by the trades unions.[18] Police were attacked, especially at night in these districts by youths who sought to drive them out and claim or 'take' the neighbourhood or *quartier*. Stones and even domestic gas bottles were thrown from windows and roofs at members of the security forces who tried to enter the *quartier*. Clashes with the police, like those of the interior, had a precedent but of a rather different sort. Many of the young men leading the violence against the police in the working-class districts of Tunis were supporters of the main Tunis football club, EST (Espérance Sportive de Tunis), who had experience of fighting the police in

---

[15] Entretien de Hibou avec Khiari, 'La Révolution tunisienne', 33.

[16] Pierre Puchot, *Tunisie: Une révolution arabe* (Paris: Gallade Éditions, 2011), 165.

[17] Olivier Piot, *La Révolution tunisienne: Dix jours qui ébranlèrent le monde arabe* (Paris: Les Petits Matins, 2011), 89, 100–1. According to some accounts, the mass demonstration in Sfax on 12 January attracted as many as 50,000—nearly one in five of the city's population. Puchot, *Tunisie: Une révolution arabe*, 164.

[18] Tunisian youth played a particularly prominent role in the revolution, not least because of its relative demographic strength—40% of the Tunisian population being under the age of 25. Piot, *La Révolution tunisienne*, 90.

Tunisia's football stadia, which had witnessed increasing levels of violence in the years up to 2011. Many hard-core supporters, or *ultras*, had been excluded from matches three years earlier and thus brought with them not only experience of combating the police and their tactics but also considerable grudges to be avenged.[19] This was evident in the widespread graffiti in working-class districts of Tunis and elsewhere proclaiming 'A.C.A.B. Winners'. 'All Coppers are Bastards' drew on similar slogans used by European football supporters and originally from anti-police slogans used by delinquent youth in Britain, and symbolized the importance of this dimension to many of the urban working-class young in Tunisia's revolution.

Evidence of the engagement of significant parts of Tunisia's middle and professional classes in the revolution became most apparent in the demonstrations in the final week of the protests before the departure of Ben Ali. Well-heeled individuals, often holding placards and banners in foreign languages, had a large presence in the crowds on the central Avenue Bourguiba in particular. Yet they were not opportunistic or late converts to the uprising. The lawyers' syndicates became some of the earliest activists in the protests in urban areas. There were demonstrations by lawyers in most cities, including Tunis, on 28 December, and three days later they came together in a national demonstration.[20] Moreover, lawyers had been stalwarts of most of the organized opposition to the Ben Ali regime over previous decades in human-rights organizations and political parties. Unhappiness with the regime's arbitrary and prejudiced use of the law and legal system against its critics and in favour of its supporters had long enraged the legal profession. Mokhtar Yahyaoui had sent a letter to the president in 2001 detailing his dismay and stating that it was 'intolerable to continue' as a senior judge.[21]

Other sections of Tunisia's sizeable middle class, one of the largest in the Arab world, also deeply resented the political constraints, repression, and mounting venality of the regime. Educated Tunisians felt humiliated by the enforced sycophantic banality of the state media that detailed and lavished praise on the daily activities of the president while depriving them of the most basic accurate information about their country. Teachers and academics chafed at official controls on what could be taught and discussed in classrooms and businessmen quietly seethed at the way senior members of Ben Ali's family blithely muscled in on successful enterprises and were able to direct the selective application of regulations and taxes. Many middle-class Tunisians travelled regularly to Europe and were thus aware of the contrasts. Those

---

[19] Amin Allal, '"Avant on tenait le mur, maintenant on tient le quartier!" Germes d'un passage au politique de jeunes homes de quartiers populaires lors du moment révolutionnaire à Tunis', *Politique africaine*, 121 (March 2011), 56–7. Author's interview with Mehdi Mabrouk, Professor of Sociology, University of Tunis, Tunis, 22 April 2011.

[20] *Dégage: La Révolution tunisienne*, 24, 27.

[21] Author's interview with Mokhtar Yahyaoui, Tunis, 19 September 2011. For details of his charges, see *Le Monde*, 17 July 2001.

middle-class Tunisians brave enough to confront the regime before the revolution chose peaceful and notably scrupulously legal and constitutional means to do so. Mokhtar Yahyaoui wrote a letter; others joined parties and non-government organizations. A small group of young, middle-class Tunisians systematically explored the officially sanctioned ways of expressing dissent in the country by formally applying to hold demonstrations and attempting to register to run as independent candidates in elections. Through this they sought to expose the insincerity and absurdities of the system and indeed revealed the absence even of a bureaucratic mechanism to process such legally sanctioned requests. They also hoped to open a new front of opposition against the regime, believing that the existing, more organized forms of opposition had largely failed. As Yassine Ayari, one of the main organizers of these initiatives, argued: 'We saw that the political parties had achieved nothing in twenty years, so perhaps we have to change our methods.'[22]

THE ABSENCE OF THE POLITICAL PARTIES

The absence of the country's political parties from the protests of December 2010–January 2011 was a notable feature of the Tunisian revolution. Ben Ali had substantially liberalized the political party landscape following his assumption of the presidency in 1987, legalizing a number of new political parties, ostensibly to compete with the ruling RCD (Rassemblement constitutionnel démocratique) party. The space and freedom given to these parties was, however, drastically limited in the years that followed; most were bribed or intimidated into not simply passive submission but frequently active support for the president and his regime. Those that resisted were either banned or were sufficiently harassed and hemmed in to prevent them making any meaningful stand against the regime.[23] This largely explains their modest contribution to the uprising of 2010–11. The leadership of the Progressive Democratic Party (PDP), the largest and best-organized opposition party, called a press conference and called for an end to the arrest of protestors and the opening of negotiations a week into the strike on 24 December, but with little effect. Local offices of the PDP and the formerly communist Ettajdid Party did become gathering places for protesting crowds in the days that followed, but the small size of the parties and their weak presence beyond the capital meant that they were not able to provide the mobilizational structures that the UGTT was rapidly able to supply.[24] It was also true that

---

[22] Author's interview with Yassine Ayari, leading opposition activist, Tunis, 21 September 2011.
[23] See Michael J. Willis, *Politics and Power in the Maghreb: Algeria, Tunisia and Morocco from Independence to the Arab Spring* (London: Hurst & Co, London, 2012), 131–5.
[24] *Dégage: La Révolution tunisienne*, 23–4.

the parties were as surprised as the regime by the spread of the initial protests. Nearly all had come to discount the possibility of a popular mobilization and had instead invested in a war of attrition against the regime, publicizing its iniquities to the outside world in the hope of reform that would allow them a greater role.

Hope of a popular uprising against the regime had been nurtured among some political parties but notably among those that were banned or exiled. The small proscribed workers' communist party, the POCT (Parti des ouvriers communistes de Tunisie), endorsed the idea out of ideological necessity, as did the exiled human-rights campaigner Moncef Marzouki, who had formed his Congress for the Republic Party in Paris in 2001.[25] More significantly, the inevitability of a popular revolution was also advocated by what was undeniably Tunisia's largest banned opposition party: the Islamist An-Nahda party. Created in 1981 as the MTI (Mouvement de la tendance islamique), An-Nahda had emerged as the most substantial and best-organized opposition force to the Tunisian regime in the last years of Habib Bourguiba's presidency. It was Bourguiba's determination to crush the movement definitively and the likely turmoil that this would cause that led to his removal by Ben Ali, his prime minister, in November 1987. Ben Ali had initially adopted a conciliatory approach to the MTI. Once he was in power, he freed the movement's leadership from prison, meeting them and allowing its members to contest elections as independent candidates. Relations, however, rapidly soured between the presidential palace and the Islamist party. The regime embarked on a brutal repression of the party, imprisoning thousands of its members and, by the end of 1991, removing any institutional manifestation it had.

In spite of the success of the repression, An-Nahda was able to retain a significant organizational presence in exile in Europe through a number of its leaders who had fled Tunisia before being arrested. Chief among these was the president of the movement, Rachid Ghannouchi, who successfully gained political asylum in London. From Britain he confidently predicted the fall of the Ben Ali regime to a popular intifada, telling the author in April 1995: 'If Ben Ali continues in this way . . . there will be a revolution. People will react slowly, but Ben Ali has possibly 5–6 years, not more.'[26] This popular intifada eventually arrived more than a decade and a half later. Yet, despite predicting it, An-Nahda appeared as institutionally absent as the other opposition parties from the gathering protests that eventually unseated Ben Ali. Much of this was due to the success of the regime's repression of the party, the continued suppression of which was the overwhelming focus of the regime's efforts to protect itself during the entire Ben Ali period. Some observers have even speculated that it was this narrow focus by the regime's intelligence and

[25] Entretien de Hibou avec Khiari, 'La Révolution tunisienne', 25.
[26] Author's interview with Rachid Ghannouchi, London, 18 April 1995.

security services that left it blind to the storm brewing in the interior of the country far away from the traditional urban strongholds of the Islamists.[27] The rapidity with which An-Nahda came to throw off the repression of the Ben Ali years and reassert itself as the largest single political force in Tunisia, notably through winning 40 per cent of the seats in the first post-revolution election to the National Constituent Assembly on 23 October 2011, spoke of the resilience and mobilizational capacity of the movement. It was also potentially indicative of the strength and success of the movement's strategy during this difficult period.

From its bases in exile, An-Nahda had publicized the human-rights abuses, lack of democracy, and other failings of the regime in Tunis through pamphlets and interviews with the press and academics. The few contacts it retained within Tunisia itself it used to attempt to ameliorate the conditions of the thousands of members of the movement imprisoned by the regime. What it notably did not do was organize any more muscular resistance to the regime's rule within Tunisia's borders through the adoption of more violent or even armed methods. This may well have been due to an inability to do so given the effectiveness of the Tunisian police state coupled with a reluctance to upset relations with the European governments that had granted its leaders exile.

THE FAILURE OF THE ALGERIAN EXAMPLE

The absence of violent or armed resistance organized by An-Nahda was explained by the movement itself as a function of the party's commitment to exclusively peaceful methods to achieve its aims. The Ben Ali regime poured scorn on these claims, pointing to a string of violent acts attributed to the movement before its official repression, which it claimed had been provoked by the violence practised by An-Nahda. The evidence put forward by the Tunisian regime to support this assertion was somewhat sketchy. Even the regime's courts had failed to link the party to a series of bomb attacks in 1987, which were laid at the feet of a smaller largely unconnected group. Other alleged incidents were of much smaller scale and of uncertain authorship and occurred when the senior leaders of the movement were in jail.[28] The Tunisian government's supply of stories to the British media allegedly linking Ghannouchi to radical views and terrorism failed to achieve their intended aim and resulted in an unbroken series of successful libel actions by Ghannouchi against major British newspapers.[29]

---

[27] Béchir Chorou, Professor at University of Carthage-Tunis, to author, Tunis, 19 April 2011.
[28] For a fuller discussion of these incidents, see Willis, *Politics and Power*, 174–7.
[29] Azzam S. Tamimi, *Rachid Ghannouchi: A Democrat within Islamism* (Oxford: Oxford University Press, 2001), 203–4.

An-Nahda's endorsement of non-violent methods in the period after the movement's repression may have made tactical sense in terms of securing and maintaining Ghannouchi and his colleagues' application for asylum in Britain and other European states, but it contrasted markedly with the stance and behaviour of the Islamist movement in neighbouring Algeria. Like An-Nahda, the main Islamist movement in Algeria, the FIS (Front islamique du salut), had suffered a brutal repression by the Algerian authorities following a period of strength and growth in the late 1980s and early 1990s. Yet, in contrast to An-Nahda, FIS members and leaders did not simply succumb to the repression inside the country and advocate non-violence from exile. Within Algeria, party activists formed armed groups to oppose the repression and dissolution of the FIS. Leaders of the party who had fled into exile justified and supported the use of force and violence against the regime. A concerted and widespread campaign of violent armed resistance thus began and sought initially to force the regime to re-legalize the FIS and restore electoral victories it had won. Soon, as elements within the movement radicalized, it increasingly sought the overthrow of the Algerian regime itself.

The leadership of An-Nahda was not unaware of the comparisons with Algeria and found itself under increasing pressure from a number of directions to abandon or at least relax its formal endorsement of non-violent methods, particularly as the violence directed at its members by the Tunisian state worsened. Consciousness of the prevalence of torture against its members in Tunisia's prisons, and especially of the incidence of rape, was particularly difficult for the rest of the party to bear. The party's leadership in exile met several times in 1991–2 in Germany and the Netherlands to discuss how it should respond to the growing violence against the party in Tunisia. Critics of the movement's pacific stance cited the Prophet Muhammad's endorsement of Muslims' right to respond if attacked and highlighted the contrast with Algeria. As one leading An-Nahda figure in exile recalls: 'People were saying "Look at the brave reaction of the Algerians, but you do nothing."'[30] Proponents of non-violence within the party responded with a mixture of strategic and moral arguments. Moving away from the existing stance would, they argued, lead to the party abandoning the moral high ground in its battle with the Ben Ali regime and would undermine the party's long stated claim to being committed to non-violent methods and the establishment of a democratic government in Tunisia. Moreover, they maintained, the Tunisian regime was well aware of this and was using torture and rape against An-Nahda members in prison to provoke the party outside into violence. Turning to violence would also probably unleash a cycle of violence that the party would

---

[30] Author's interview with Seyyed Ferjani, member of the Majlis Shura (Guidance Council) of the An-Nahda Party, Tunis, 20 September 2011.

not be able to control.[31] For Rachid Ghannouchi, the party's leader, it was important that, in seeking to resist an evil, a greater evil was not created: an important principle in Islamic jurisprudence.[32]

The issue was not fully resolved until a party congress in 1995, when the party definitively rejected any resort to violent methods and stated that any member who disagreed would have to leave the movement.[33] This victory of the advocates of non-violent methods had been significantly helped by the escalation of violence in Algeria during the period 1993–5, which had become increasingly brutal and indiscriminate on all sides. This allowed Ghannouchi subsequently to argue that 'the party had refused to let itself be dragged into the cycle of violence and reaction to the violence of the regime, as had happened in Algeria, permanently reaffirming, both in terms of ideas and practice, its pacific and democratic nature.'[34]

SOCIAL MEDIA: THANK YOU FACEBOOK?

One aspect of the Tunisian revolution that attracted significant attention was the role played by newer forms of communication technologies. Their apparent importance in the uprising was highlighted by banners held aloft by protestors in the mass demonstrations in central Tunis in the final days before the departure of Ben Ali that proclaimed slogans such as 'Thank you Facebook' in reference to the social networking website. This led many foreign commentators to dub the fall of Ben Ali the 'Facebook revolution' or the 'Twitter revolt'.[35] The reality of the role played by social media and newer communications technologies such as Twitter, YouTube, and the Internet more generally was inevitably more complex.

Tunisia on the eve of the revolution had one of the higher Internet usage rates in the Arab world, a reflection largely of its relatively large urban and middle-class population. The rapid expansion in this usage in the 2000s had

---

[31] Author's interview with Seyyed Ferjani, Tunis, 20 September 2011. The connection between torture and violence was acknowledged by senior members of the party who had been imprisoned by the regime. Ziad Doulatli, a senior figure in the party who had spent fourteen years in prison, stated: 'Our movement never used violence despite torture.' Author's interview with Ziad Doulatli, Tunis, 21 April 2011.

[32] Tamimi, *Rachid Ghannouchi*, 165.

[33] Author's interview with Seyyed Ferjani, Tunis, 20 September 2011.

[34] 'Entretien avec Rachid Ghannouchi', in Olfa Lamloum and Bernard Ravenel (eds), *La Tunisie de Ben Ali: La Société contre le régime* (Paris: L'Harmattan, 2002), 262.

[35] The Tunisian revolution was also widely dubbed the 'Jasmine Revolution' after the national flower of the country and in evocation of the other popular 'colour' revolutions elsewhere, such as the 'orange' revolution in Ukraine in 2004. However, this term was rarely used by Tunisians themselves, who associated the flower with the ousted dictator Ben Ali, who had used it in his own propaganda. See Olivier Malaponti, 'Révolution de jasmin?', *Mediapart*, 15 January 2011 http://blogs.mediapart.fr/blog/olivier-malaponti/150111/revolution-de-jasmin-0.

alerted the Tunisian regime to the potential threat that it posed to the hitherto tight grip it had been able to exercise over what information about events inside the country Tunisians were able to access, but it was not until the events in Gafsa province in 2008 that any concerted attempt was made to restrict rather than monitor this access. Attempts by activists in the region during the unrest to upload news and images onto the Internet led the authorities in August 2008 to block access to the most commonly used site for these uploads: Facebook.[36] It proved to be a wholly counterproductive move, as it led to the site's 300,000 users in Tunisia not only discovering and personally resenting regime censorship but also finding ways to bypass it through use of proxies as they consulted friends and other Internet sites to overcome the interruption to what had become for very many a major aspect of their social lives.[37] As one cyber activist who was to become very active in the revolution observes: 'Up until this point, most of the 300,000 were more interested in football, girls et cetera... In 2011 these 300,000 made a difference in the revolution.'[38]

The public outcry that the blocking of Facebook created alerted the regime to the mistake it had made: within a month the site was unblocked, reportedly on the personal initiative of the president himself.[39] The damage, however, had been done, and there rapidly developed what one Tunisian newspaper described as a 'cyber war' between the regime and campaigners against censorship, with the latter organizing small demonstrations, flash mobs, and protest blogs from 2009.[40] These culminated in 2010 with an online petition against continued attempts at Internet censorship by the regime that attracted 10,000 signatures. When, at the end of November that same year, the Wikileaks website began publishing large numbers of leaked US government cables, activists set to work translating and disseminating those relating to Tunisia on Facebook and even created a dedicated website entitled 'Tunileaks'.[41] The cables not only provided detailed confirmation of the venality and corruption of the Ben Ali entourage but, more importantly, revealed the extent of American unhappiness with the regime. This revelation surprised activists, most of whom had long seen the USA as a staunch supporter of Ben Ali, and

---

[36] Laryssa Chomiak and John P. Entelis, 'The Making of North Africa's Intifadas', *Middle East Report*, 259 (Summer 2011).

[37] The head of Tunisia's Internet Agency, the ITA, Moez Chakchouk, revealed after the revolution that private foreign companies had used Tunisia as a testing ground for censorship software given the Ben Ali regime's commitment to surveillance and censorship of its citizens. 'Tunisian Internet Agency Defends Net Neutrality', *FreeSpeechDebate*, 12 April. 2012 freespeechdebate.com/en/media/tunisian-internet-agency-defends-net-neutrality.

[38] Author's interview with Yassine Ayari, 21 September 2011.

[39] *Réalités*, Tunis, 21 April. 2011.

[40] *Réalités*, 21 April 2011; interview with Slim Amamou, leading cyber activist, in *Dégage: La Révolution tunisienne*, 193–4.

[41] *Réalités*, 21 April 2011 https://tunileaks.appspot.com.

who were now encouraged by this evidence suggesting that Washington might not come to the regime's aid.[42]

When the protests began in Sidi Bouzid on 17 December, demonstrators rapidly made use of the Internet: the first images of the clashes with police were online within forty-eight hours. By the end of the week the footage captured on digital cameras and mobile phones began to feature on the slightly older medium of satellite television through foreign channels such as France 24 and Al Jazeera.[43] This dramatically expanded awareness of the events in Sidi Bouzid province given the many more Tunisians who had access to satellite television than the Internet. The images from the interior were picked up by the campaigners against Internet censorship, who, despite coming from largely urban, educated, and elite backgrounds, realized their power and significance and began to use their technological expertise to disseminate and publicize the protests and the regime's attempt to crush them. Some, such as Yassine Ayari, found themselves abroad at the time of the outbreak of unrest but contributed to the processing and dissemination of news, pictures, and footage coming out of Tunisia, arranging to work in shifts with fellow activists to ensure an unbroken flow of coverage. 'During the revolution I tried to turn my Facebook page into a press agency,' he recalls.[44] In addition to Facebook, dedicated websites and Twitter hashtags, often relating to events in specific towns, were established further to speed the spread of information. As the uprising gathered pace, news of protests and demonstrations were instantly communicated to thousands of people, thus aiding mobilization of large numbers of Tunisians for further protests. Belatedly aware of the role being played by the Internet activists, the authorities arrested some of the most prominent in Tunisia on 6 January, but by then the revolt was in full swing.

The role played by the Internet, social media, and mobile technology, such as camera phones, in spreading information and mobilizing the public would seem to support the notion of a 'Facebook' or 'Internet' revolution. However, while these media contributed hugely to spreading information and awareness and facilitating the mobilization and coordination of large numbers of people, they did not explain nor embody the revolution. Most Tunisians were painfully aware that they had lived in a police state before the advent of Facebook, and the iniquities and venalities of Ben Ali and his family had no need to trend on Twitter to become common knowledge. The revolution itself could not occur online but only offline. Yassine Ayari comments: 'I am annoyed by the idea of an "Internet Revolution"—it is an insult to those people who went onto the streets and were shot down. I saw no bullets being used on Facebook.'[45]

---

[42] 'iRevolution: Online Warriors of the Arab Spring', CNN, 19 June 2011 http://transcripts.cnn.com/TRANSCRIPTS/1106/19/cp.01.html.

[43] *Dégage: La Révolution tunisienne*, 20, 23.

[44] Author's interview with Yassine Ayari, 21 September 2011.

[45] Author's interview with Yassine Ayari, 21 September 2011.

AN ORGANIC REVOLUTION?

One of the striking features of the uprisings in Arab states, certainly in the early weeks of 2011, was their seemingly organic quality, emerging from within the local societies and contexts with no apparent input from outside besides the example of their neighbours. The first anniversary of the uprisings began to see the appearance of books and articles critiquing this view of the organic character of the uprisings and pointing to the activities of foreign, mainly Western governments, in the run-up to the revolts. Most focused on the periods spent in Europe and North America by activists, and links established by Western governments with opposition figures and the pressure they put on regimes at crucial junctures.[46] It is difficult to the point of impossible, however, to make a plausible case for the Tunisian uprising being the product of some prefabricated plan by foreign governments. The alignment of domestic factors already set out demonstrates the complex, deeply domestic, and hugely popular origins of the revolt that it would have been unfeasible to have stage-managed. Moreover, the record of Western states' interaction with Tunisia in the years before the revolution provided only the scantiest of evidence of their interest in provoking a popular revolution in the country. Tunisia had largely been off the radar of most Western governments in the early decades of its independence from France, with only the former colonial power devoting much time to mutual relations. Tunisia's small size, and the low-profile, domestically oriented, and pro-Western stance of Habib Bourguiba's regime, meant that most major powers paid it little attention. Any concerns about the progressive turn towards authoritarianism by the Ben Ali regime from the early 1990s were largely offset by worries about the spread of the violence from neighbouring Algeria. Criticism of the poor human-rights record and lack of democracy in the country began to surface with the decline of the violence in Algeria at the end of the decade but disappeared overnight following the attacks on the USA of 11 September 2001. These allowed Ben Ali, along with other regimes in the region, to present themselves as staunch allies of the West in the fight against global terrorism, which became the guiding concern in Western governments' policy in the region from this point. Moreover, Ben Ali's savage repression of Tunisia's Islamists, which had succeeded in removing any organized manifestation of Islamism, rapidly came to be seen in many Western policy-making circles as a model to be followed rather than a flaw to be criticized. In a trend that became dominant elsewhere, concerns about democracy and especially human rights

---

[46] See, e.g., Tariq Ramadan, *The Arab Awakening: Islam and the New Middle East* (London: Allen Lane, 2012), 23–5.

came to be seen as unaffordable luxuries in the face of the supposedly global threat of al-Qaeda and its allies.[47]

There was thus no international appetite on the eve of the Tunisian uprising for an overthrow of the Ben Ali regime. It is possible that contact between foreign governments and figures inside the Tunisian regime in the final days before Ben Ali's departure may have influenced and especially hastened his exit, but this is a long way from the suggestion that the whole revolt was planned from abroad. The enormous crowds on Avenue Bourguiba on 14 January planned to head to the presidential palace in Carthage to force Ben Ali to leave and were forestalled only by the news that the president had already fled the country. The swift pace of events in the previous days had left most foreign governments struggling to keep pace, making the execution of any coherent plan impossible. Even the country with the largest presence and best contacts inside the state, France, revealed how unaware it was of the turn of events when its foreign minister offered 'know-how' to help maintain public order just three days before Ben Ali fell (see Figure 2.2).[48]

Figure 2.2. The height of the Tunisian uprising. Lawyers wave the national flag as they demonstrate in a crowd of thousands on 14 January 2011 in front of the interior ministry on Avenue Habib Bourguiba in Tunis, the feared symbol of this police state. Within hours the regime had collapsed and Ben Ali had fled.

© *Fethi Belaid/AFP/Getty Images*

---

[47] As one leading Tunisian journalist commented, 11 September was 'a huge gift' for the Ben Ali regime. Author's interview with Salah Eddine Jourshi, Tunis, 15 April 2009.
[48] *Le Monde*, 11 January 2011.

THE COLLAPSE OF THE REGIME: THE FAILURE OF POWER POLITICS?

One of the factors that had elicited speculation about foreign intervention in the Tunisian revolution was the surprisingly rapid capitulation of the regime. This raises questions as to the tactics used by the regime to defend itself against the popular uprising. The size, robustness, and pervasiveness of the Tunisian state security apparatus had been impressive even by the high standards of the Arab world, and its effectiveness in controlling dissent was attributed to Ben Ali's career experience in the security sector before moving into politics.[49] An estimated 100,000 people were employed by the regime in the direct business of controlling the population in addition to the two million members of the ruling RCD party—one in five of the total population—whom the regime used to monitor their fellow citizens.[50] Quite why this security apparatus failed to deal with the revolt can be attributed to a number of specific factors and some general ones. As has been shown, the regime made specific mistakes in dealing with the constituent elements of the revolt: focusing its attention on the urban areas and the Islamists rather than the rural interior; thinking that the shooting of demonstrators would intimidate rather than inflame protestors; and provoking and then being technically unable to respond to opposition on the Internet. At a more general level, the regime arguably displayed the essential brittleness of very repressive regimes: notably an inability, born of inexperience, to adopt the sort of multifaceted response of concession, co-option, and communication that might have saved it, instead of relying on simple physical repression that had appeared to have served it well over the decades. Once this repression was seen to fail, not least in its provocation of further popular unrest, the regime was at a loss for an alternative strategy.

Much has also been made of the failure of the Tunisian military to come to the aid of the regime in its final week, its intervention being seen as being crucial in potentially crushing the revolt. Unlike its counterparts in the most of the rest of the Arab world, the army in Tunisia had long been kept relatively small and separate from politics and the regime. This was a function of Habib Bourguiba's deep suspicions of the putschist impulses of armies in most other Arab states and his consequent preference for the European model of the small, apolitical professional military. Ben Ali retained these suspicions especially after purging Islamist infiltration of the military in the late 1980s and early 1990s and preferred to rely on the police and the security forces to maintain domestic order and to act as a check on the army. Alienated by these purges and this suspicion, the Tunisian army was thus disinclined to rush to

---

[49] Ben Ali had started his career in the military but had served as Director of National Security and Interior Minister before becoming president.

[50] Puchot, *Tunisie: Une révolution arabe*, 168.

save Ben Ali and his interior security forces, preferring to keep to its trad-itional apolitical ethos.[51] Still emerging evidence about the events of early January paints a complex and confusing picture about reactions within the Tunisian regime in the run-up to 14 January. It appears that the senior leadership of the Tunisian army was initially as confused as most other actors as to how to respond but sought to ensure that their troops kept their distance from the internal security forces that were carrying out the bulk of the repression.[52] Many Tunisians were aware of these tensions: people in several towns in the interior of the country publicly appealed to the army to protect them from the police during the revolt.[53]

Some caution should be exercised in equating the Tunisian regime too fully with the person of Ben Ali and thus assuming that the former fell with the departure of the latter. It certainly appears that other senior elements in the Tunisian regime sought to save their own positions by sacrificing Ben Ali and his family, much as the Egyptian military appeared to do with Hosni Mubarak just a few weeks later. Attempts to retain most of the ministers of the Ben Ali government after his flight, with the simple addition of a few figures from the opposition, were defeated by further sustained popular protests, which forced the departure of Ben Ali's long-serving prime minister, Mohammed Ghan-nouchi, on 28 February and the appointment of an interim government of figures less directly associated with the old regime. The triumph of parties led by veteran opponents of the Ben Ali regime in the election to the National Constituent Assembly eight months later in October 2011 and their conse-quent formation of a coalition government seemed to signal the definitive departure of the wider Ben Ali regime. Pockets of resistance remained, how-ever, in certain ministries and began to reassert themselves through the reorganized internal security apparatus and police and even through new political parties, notably Nidaa Tounes (the Call of Tunisia), which was formed in 2012. Although portraying itself as a front against the allegedly Islamist orientation of the new government, Nidaa Tounes rapidly came to be seen as a rallying point for loyalists of the old regime. Taking advantage of the networks of the old ruling party and benefiting from popular disillusionment

---

[51] Willis, *Politics and Power*, ch. 3.

[52] Noureddine Jebnoun, 'In the Shadow of Power: Civil–Military Relations and the Tunisian Popular Uprising', *Journal of North African Studies*, 19/3 (2014), 296–316.

[53] Puchot, *Tunisie: Une révolution arabe*, 156, 157. One leading cyber activist has even claimed that he drew on family connections in the military to disseminate the very influential story that the military had refused the regime's requests to fire on protestors, intentionally overstating the army's inaction both to encourage the protestors and to win at least the passive support of the army through making heroes of its members. Author's interview with Yassine Ayari, 21 September 2011. Ayari's father was a senior military commander. When he learned that his father had not yet received orders from the regime to move against the protests, Ayari deliberately refashioned this fact as the army's refusal to act.

with the new government's failure to address the country's ongoing social and economic problems, Nidaa Tounes emerged as the leading party in legislative and presidential elections held in the closing months of 2014. The resultant return to senior positions in government by former members of the Ben Ali regime elicited some concerns that the pre-2011 regime might be reconstituting itself four years on from the fall of the former dictator.

THE QUEST FOR DIGNITY

In assessing the Tunisian revolution one is struck by the heterogeneity of the different sections of Tunisian society that came together to remove the established regime. Itinerant vegetable sellers, lawyers, agricultural workers, trades unionists, computer technicians, football supporters, academics, and the urban unemployed came together to oust Ben Ali and his system. Analysts and commentators have struggled to find an overarching motive for these disparate groups: explicitly political factors seemingly absent from the early protests in Sidi Bouzid and in the working-class districts of the cities but economic deprivation similarly irrelevant to the well-heeled lawyers and middle-class cyber activists who took up the revolution with equal gusto.[54] There was one common theme that did, however, come remarkably consistently to the fore when those who participated in the revolution spoke about their reasons for doing so: the quest for dignity, or *karama* in Arabic.[55] Michaël Ayari, a political scientist, noted the increasing use of the word in diverse opposition literature and discourses throughout the 2000s, which he believed to be essentially uncoordinated but symptomatic of an emerging broad consensus within Tunisian society about the need for dignity in the face of humiliation suffered at the hands of the regime.[56] The unemployed of the small towns of the Gafsa and Sidi Bouzid governorates felt humiliated by their exclusion from Tunisian's economic 'miracle' and by the nepotism in job hiring by local employers; lawyers and judges, such as Mokhtar Yahyaoui, felt humiliated by increasingly blatant political interference in legal cases; football supporters felt humiliated by the beatings meted out to them by the police in

---

[54] Explicitly political slogans and those targeting Ben Ali did not appear at protests until towards the end of December. Larbi Chouikha and Éric Gobe, 'La Force de la désobéissance: Retour sur la chute du régime de Ben Ali', in Néfissa and Destremau, *Protestations sociales, révolutions civiles*, 221.

[55] One of the main popular slogans of the revolution was 'shughl, hurriyya, karama wataniya' ('work, freedom, national dignity').

[56] Michaël Béchir Ayari, 'Des maux de la misère aux mots de la "dignité": La Révolution tunisienne de janvier 2011', in Néfissa and Destremau, *Protestations sociales, révolutions civiles*, 209–18.

the football stadiums and their exclusion from matches; young Internet-users felt humiliated by the shutting-down of websites and interference in their use of social media; businessmen felt humiliated by having to cede partnerships in their enterprises to venal relatives of the president and his wife; the senior leadership of the army felt humiliation through the purges and surveillance to which they were subjected; teachers and journalists felt shamed by the severe limitations on what they could read, write, and teach imposed by a thuggish and undereducated president (popularly known as 'Mr Bac minus 3'[57]) and his gold-digging hairdresser wife. Thus, when Mohammed Bouazizi stood outside the governorate office in Sidi Bouzid on 17 December and set himself on fire, he was protesting at his sense of humiliation at the hands of the local police and officials rather than his poverty and it was this humiliation that resonated with so many other people in Tunisia.[58]

The importance of notions of dignity and humiliation in understanding the root causes of the Tunisian revolution is also instructive in comprehending the methods used by protestors in opposing and ultimately unseating the dictatorship of Ben Ali, particularly the relatively low levels of violence employed. Notions of dignity and humiliation indicate a sense of a proper or correct way or code of doing things that has not been observed and has indeed been flouted. One is struck by the remarkable attention to proper procedure, structure, and organization that featured in much of the opposition to the Ben Ali regime both before and during the revolution. Cyber activists put together a petition against Internet censorship; trades unionists organized sit-ins and strikes and put together national coordination committees; An-Nahda held conferences and formally endorsed principles that Rachid Ghannouchi felt were in accordance with Islamic jurisprudence; Mokhtar Yahyaoui wrote a letter to point out abuses of the legal system; Yassine Ayari and his friends sought official approval for their demonstrations and their candidacy in elections; even Mohammed Bouazizi tried to lodge formal complaints with the local authorities before setting himself on fire. Although not all groups resorted to such means to express their unhappiness with the regime, surprising numbers did. This attachment to procedure, process, and forms of legality has echoes in Tunisian history in which one could argue it finds its origins. Tunisians are proud to tell people that Tunisia was the first Arab country to adopt (albeit briefly) a written constitution, in 1861. The nationalist parties that led the struggle for independence from France were named *Destour* (Constitution in Arabic) and *Neo-Destour*, reflecting a demand for a legal

---

[57] Standing for 'Baccalaureate Minus 3', this was a popular, humorous, and derogatory epithet for Ben Ali referring to his alleged lack of education and playing on the more usual 'Bac Plus' formula used to indicate a person's years of education subsequent to finishing the baccalaureate examinations.

[58] Entretien de Hibou avec Khiari, 'La Révolution tunisienne', 30.

framework for colonial rule, a reference that Ben Ali felt compelled to retain when he established his own ruling party—the Rally for *Constitutional* Democracy. Even the succession from Bourguiba to Ben Ali was managed with scrupulous attention to constitutional provisions.[59] Although counterexamples to this tendency are not difficult to find, its presence is noticeable and not found to the same degree in most other Arab states.

The emphasis on procedure, process, and forms of legality was continued in the aftermath of the revolution with the setting-up of interim governments, councils to oversee the process of transition, the election of a national constituent assembly, and ultimately the approval and introduction of a new, permanent constitution for the post-revolutionary era. It was reaffirmed by the peaceful transfer of power that occurred following the defeat of the An-Nahda Party by its arch-rival Nidaa Tounes in the elections of 2014, Rached Ghannouchi telephoning the leader of Nidaa Tounes, Beji Caid Essebsi, formally to concede defeat and congratulate him on his party's victory. The subsequent inclusion of representatives from An-Nahda in the government formed in the wake of the elections spoke not just of the necessity to command majority support in the new legislature but also of a recognition of the benefits of inclusion and compromise and bolstered confidence that Tunisia's new democratic institutions would be able to resist a resurrection of the old pre-revolutionary dictatorship. Despite the noise and controversy that, even in Tunisia, often accompanied this process, it was achieved remarkably smoothly and with minimal violence and bloodshed. Much attention was drawn to the assassination of two leftist politicians in 2013 and the attack by Islamist extremists on the Bardo Museum in Tunis in March 2015, but the public horror and outrage that greeted these and the handful of other killings that occurred in the period only served to distinguish Tunisia yet further from the violent carnage occurring elsewhere in the region, notably in Libya, Syria, and increasingly Egypt.[60] Moreover, major parties and actors consistently resolved regular apparent impasses in the transition process by sitting down and negotiating a way through, most notably in the compromises that were struck to pave the way to the final approval of the country's new constitution by a near unanimous vote in the National Constituent Assembly on 26 January 2014, which was regarded as a day of national triumph: the victory of due process and compromise over violence and division.[61] Nearly all the major

---

[59] The increasingly senile Bourguiba was declared medically unfit to rule by a panel of doctors and was replaced by his prime minister (Ben Ali).

[60] The assassinations of Chokri Belaid in February 2013 and Mohamed Brahmi the following July led to large-scale protests across the country, the largest since those of January 2011.

[61] Of the 216 members of the National Constituent Assembly, 200 voted for the final draft. 'Tunisia Assembly Passes New Constitution', *BBC News*, 27 January 2014 www.bbc.co.uk/news/world-africa-25908340. For the text of the new constitution, see http://test.jasmine-foundation.org/en/?p=791.

politicians and political parties played their part in these achievements, but the contribution of An-Nahda was particularly striking. Although An-Nahda had advocated the introduction of democracy to Tunisia during its long period in exile under Ben Ali, the movement was regarded with huge suspicion by many of the other parties who feared that it would seek to impose an Islamist theocracy on Tunisia when it emerged as the clear victor in the 2011 elections. The party sought to alleviate such concerns by forming a coalition government with two non-Islamist parties and by consistently arguing for the maintenance of inclusive and broad-based multiparty administrations. Its attachment to peaceful and legal procedures seemed to be borne out by its withdrawal from government in January 2014 in favour of an interim technocratic government, the significant compromises it made on the final draft of the new constitution of 2014, and its fully and formally conceding defeat to Nidaa Tounes in the legislative elections of October 2014.[62] The party's senior figures argued not only that such an approach contributed to the stability of Tunisia but also that the entrenching of the rule of law and democratic institutions would be the best protection for the party against returning to the imprisonment and torture its members had suffered under Ben Ali.[63] Such a stance stood in marked contrast to that taken by the Muslim Brotherhood in Egypt, whose refusal to compromise and work with other parties was heavily criticized in private by senior figures in An-Nahda.[64]

It is this element of Tunisian national culture, attachment to values of procedure, process, and forms of legality, rather than a simple aversion to violence, that arguably marks out Tunisia and explains the success of forms of civil resistance in this opening encounter of the Arab Spring. As some Tunisians like to joke: 'We are the only country that had a revolution on the Friday and went back to work on the Monday!'

---

[62] It was widely acknowledged that the text had been approved largely through the acquiescence of the An-Nahda party on key issues. See Monica Marks, 'Convince, Coerce, or Compromise? Ennahda's Approach to Tunisia's Constitution', Brookings Doha Center Publications, 10 February 2014 www.brookings.edu/research/papers/2014/02/10-ennahda-tunisia-constitution-marks.

[63] See, e.g., Isabelle Mandraud, 'Rached Ghannouchi: "Ennahda a quitté le pouvoir par choix éthique"', *Le Monde*, 14 January 2014 www.lemonde.fr/tunisie/article/2014/01/14/rached-ghannouchi-nous-avons-quitte-le-pouvoir-par-choix-ethique_4347544_1466522.html.

[64] Author's conversations with senior figures in An-Nahda, 2012–13.

3

Egypt's Unfinished Revolution

M. Cherif Bassiouni

In 2011 a popular revolution in Egypt, born out of a campaign of civil resistance, heralded the fall of the autocratic regime of President Hosni Mubarak. After eighteen days of mass protests by pro-democracy supporters, starting on 25 January and articulating calls for freedom, justice, and human dignity, the military establishment convinced Mubarak to resign. However, subsequent attempts to follow up this apparent success of the popular movement failed as the Muslim Brotherhood and the military establishment supplanted the pro-democracy revolution. In the following years, Egypt experienced in rapid succession a series of political and constitutional changes. In 2012, presidential and legislative elections were held, resulting in the success of the Muslim Brotherhood; then a new constitution was drafted, which was approved by popular referendum in December. On 3 July 2013, after barely a year of turbulent and ineffective Muslim Brotherhood rule, there was a military takeover preceded by an unprecedented popular demonstration by Egyptians seeking the Muslim Brotherhood's ouster from power. A new government was established by the military. It outlawed the Muslim Brotherhood and engaged in violent suppression of a wide range of political movements and activities. This was followed in short order by the adoption of a revised constitution in early 2014, and the election as president of a recently promoted senior army general, Abdel Fattah el-Sisi. The country remained in a deep economic crisis with no apparent government solution. This chapter explores key aspects of Egypt's troubled and still unfinished revolution, the reasons why the popular movement succeeded initially, and why the revolution was followed by such turbulence and ultimately by military rule. It also considers briefly whether the civil resistance movement of 2011 has left an enduring legacy in Egypt.

ORIGINS OF THE REVOLUTION

The Egyptian revolution has long been a work in progress, and has long been centred on resistance to foreign control.[1] In 1798 it took the form of opposition to the Napoleonic occupation. In 1882 it was against a British invasion. In 1919 a major uprising against the occupying British led to Egypt's formal independence in 1922. In 1956, during the Suez crisis, Egypt resisted an attack by Great Britain, France, and Israel; and, by December of that year, Egypt was free from foreign occupation until 1967, when Israel occupied the Sinai, only leaving it in 1979–82. In July 1952 a military coup removed the monarchy, resulting in the establishment of a republic in 1953. Egypt has been independent since its 1923 Constitution, but it had British forces in the country until 1954, when, by treaty, Britain evacuated all of its forces. As of 1954 a dictatorial military regime was established that has lasted for more than sixty years, with only the one-year interlude of Mohamed Morsi's presidency and the ill-fated rule of the Muslim Brotherhood. The May 2014 presidential election saw Field Marshal el-Sisi become president for the next four years (renewable for one more term under the 2014 Constitution). In the meantime, democracy will have to wait, as it has since at least 1952. However, Egyptian aspirations for democracy, freedom, dignity, and justice go on, as does the struggle for the attainment of these rights.

By the end of 2010 the economic situation in Egypt had deteriorated significantly and the abuses of the Mubarak regime had become so blatant as to be no longer tolerable. The November and December 2010 parliamentary elections were openly rigged. Corruption was rampant. Mubarak and his oligarchs were widely perceived to be treating the country as a private farm and the people as their indentured servants. The army was no longer the visible face of these abuses, as it had been in the past: it had receded into the background under Field Marshal Hussein Tantawi's leadership since 1991. Instead it was the interior ministry under Habib el-Adly that became the most visible instrument of political repression and the protector of the corrupt oligarchy.[2] Pro-democracy and labour union opposition had been mounting since 2005.[3] The worsening economic situation affected millions as the

---

[1] See Eugene Fisher and M. Cherif Bassiouni, *Storm over the Arab World: A People in Revolution* (Chicago: Follett, [1972]), 61 ff.

[2] Habib el-Adly was convicted in June 2012 for having participated in the killing of protesters during the 2011 uprising, and was sentenced to life in prison along with Hosni Mubarak: 'Mubarak Sentenced to Jail for Life over Protest Deaths', *BBC News*, 2 June 2012 http://www.bbc.co.uk/news/world-middle-east-18306126.

[3] A useful account of the wave of worker protests in the last decade of Mubarak's rule is Joel Beinin and Hossam el-Hamalawy, 'Strikes in Egypt Spread from Center of Gravity', in David McMurray and Amanda Ufheil-Somers (eds), *The Arab Revolts: Dispatches on Militant Democracy in the Middle East* (Bloomington, IN: Indiana University Press, 2013), 83–91. This account, first published in 2007, is also available at http://www.merip.org/mero/mero050907.

population rose to more than 85 million in 2009 with 50 per cent under the age of 30, of whom 60 per cent were unemployed. An estimated twenty million Egyptians lived at, or below, the poverty line. The winds of discontent were blowing, but the interior ministry's State Security Investigating Police remained focused on the perceived threat from the Muslim Brotherhood while disregarding the rest of the people, for whom they showed only disdain. They never imagined what would happen on 25 January 2011, and they were taken totally by surprise. Over the years, a sort of vendetta had developed between State Security and the Muslim Brotherhood, the world's oldest and most influential Islamist movement, founded in 1928.

Under presidents Gamal Abdel Nasser (1954–70) and Anwar Sadat (1970–81), the state's ruling oligarchy had consisted mostly of military and former military personnel, their relatives, friends, loyal politicians, and senior bureaucrats. Under Mubarak (1981–2011), it expanded to encompass a growing class of businessmen (and some women) who dominated the economy and public life through corrupt practices. The political establishment institutionalized and legalized such abuses of authority and public corruption by promulgating laws and administrative procedures that facilitated these practices. The greatest profits were made from the sale of publicly owned industries and property, and by giving highly lucrative concessions for business and other investment projects, including the sale of public lands at nominal prices. By 2011 it was unofficially estimated that 200 families owned 90 per cent of Egypt's private-sector wealth. On the other hand, the Mubarak regime had eased up on repressing freedom of expression so long as it did not threaten the existing order, but it firmly controlled the political process and the security apparatus.

Just as there is a long history of Egyptians opposing foreign occupation by force, there is also a long history of non-violent movements promoting democracy and freedom, though these too have occasionally turned violent. It started in 1919 against British occupation, and then continued against King Farouk's corrupt regime (1936–52). In 1954, the first year of Nasser's sixteen-year rule, there was only one peaceful pro-democracy demonstration: starting from the University of Cairo's Law School, it crossed University Bridge over the Nile at Giza, and was stopped by overwhelming police force. From then until Nasser's death in 1970 no demonstrations were allowed. Under Sadat's rule the Judges' Club and the Lawyers' Syndicate undertook a few peaceful protests. During the later phase of the Mubarak period, there were demonstrations by such emerging pro-democracy groups as *Kefaya* (the Arabic for 'enough'), a loose-knit coalition that was brought together in 2003 because of shared opposition to Mubarak's plans to transfer power to his son Gamal.[4]

---

[4] Sherif Mansour, 'Enough is not Enough: Achievements and Shortcomings of Kefaya, the Egyptian Movement for Change', in Maria J. Stephan (ed.), *Civilian Jihad: Nonviolent Struggle, Democratization, and Governance in the Middle East* (New York: Palgrave Macmillan, 2009),

Kefaya revived street politics. Growing out of demonstrations of solidarity for Palestinians during the Second Intifada and then opposition to the US invasion of Iraq, it soon focused on a cross-ideological effort involving leftists, nationalists, and Islamists to demand reforms from the Mubarak regime.[5] It staged street demonstrations without asking for official permission, and, though this often resulted in arrests, it offered a new, bold challenge to both the regime and the often-stilted actions of opposition political parties. Another new pro-democracy group was the April 6 Youth Movement, which emerged in 2008 in the form of youth activists acting in support of striking textile workers at the industrial town of el-Mahalla and soon grew into a large movement. It held public demonstrations but most importantly sparked a vibrant online debate, particularly on Facebook, about freedom of expression and government corruption.[6] Its leaders were frequently arrested but went on to play a key role in the early protests in 2011.

Against this background, it is widely agreed that the immediate causes of the Egyptian revolution of 2011 included: general dissatisfaction with Mubarak's rule, growing economic problems, abuses by the police, and public corruption.[7] Awareness of the events in Tunisia that led to the fall of President Zine El Abidine Ben Ali on 14 January 2011 contributed to the timing of the revolution.[8]

THE EIGHTEEN DAYS OF DEMONSTRATIONS

The 2011 revolution began with an online invitation to all Egyptians to join a 'Day of Rage' to be held on 25 January, National Police Day. Concerns about

---

205–18. See also, in the same volume, the chapter by Shaazka Beyerle and Arwa Hassan on 'Popular Resistance against Corruption in Turkey and Egypt'.

[5] See Manar Shorbagy, 'The Egyptian Movement for Change—Kefaya: Redefining Politics in Egypt', *Public Culture*, 19/1 (2007), 175–96.

[6] Samantha Shapiro, 'Revolution, Facebook-Style', *New York Times*, 22 January 2009 www.nytimes.com/2009/01/25/magazine/25bloggers-t.html.

[7] See Adel Iskandar, *Egypt in Flux: Essays on an Unfinished Revolution* (Cairo: American University in Cairo Press, 2013); Aly El-Samman, *Egypt: From One Revolution to Another: Memoir of a Committed Citizen under Nasser, Sadat and Mubarak* (London: Gilgamesh, 2012); Ashraf Khalil, *Liberation Square: Inside the Egyptian Revolution and the Rebirth of a Nation* (New York: St Martin's Press, 2012); Robert Solé, *Le Pharaon renversé: Dix-huit jours qui ont changé l'Egypte* (Paris: Les Arènes, 2011); Stephen R. Grand, *Understanding Tahrir Square: What Transitions Elsewhere Can Teach Us about the Prospects for Arab Democracy* (Washington: Brookings Institution Press, 2014).

[8] See Esam Al-Amin, *The Arab Awakening Unveiled: Understanding Transformations and Revolutions in the Middle East* (Washington: American Educational Trust, 2013); Marc Lynch, *The Arab Uprising: The Unfinished Revolutions of the New Middle East* (New York: Public Affairs, 2012); M. Cherif Bassiouni, 'The "Arab Revolution" and Transitions in the Wake of the "Arab Spring"', *UCLA Journal of International Law & Foreign Affairs*, 17 (Spring 2013), 133.

police violence had been increasing, and were reflected in the work of such pro-democracy groups as the April 6 Movement. Thousands are believed to have been tortured and many killed during Mubarak's thirty-year reign, with total impunity for the perpetrators.[9] The invitation to take part in the 'Day of Rage' came from the online Facebook page 'We are all Khaled Said', named after a young Alexandrian who had been beaten to death by police in June 2010.[10] Wael Ghonim, at the time a Google marketing executive, was joint author of this web page, which was one of several calling for public protests and demonstrations.[11]

The call was successful, and the first demonstration took place at Tahrir ('Liberation') Square in Cairo. As many as 200,000 people (many claimed that the number reached 400,000) filled the square, while others participated in similar peaceful protests throughout the country. Their numbers increased in subsequent days. The movement used the methods of civil resistance for a variety of reasons that were not explicitly enumerated, but can be inferred from its actions and statements: a revulsion against political violence; an awareness of the success of some 'people power' movements, most recently in Tunisia; a belief that only by eschewing the use of violence could large numbers be mobilized; a desire to match moderate and constitutional ends with moderate means; and perhaps, too, an awareness that by using such means they had a better chance of exposing the brutality of the police, and also of avoiding the army's hostility, perhaps even of engaging its support.

For three weeks, millions throughout the country would join demonstrations after Friday prayers. In ten to fifteen cities people took to the streets on a daily basis. The major cities that participated in the uprising included Cairo, Alexandria, Suez, Port Said, Beni Sweif, Mansoura, and el-Mahalla. During those weeks it was an extraordinary sight to see the people in unison make basic demands for democracy, jobs, freedom, dignity, justice, and a decent life. For the most part they were not violent: for a few days at Tahrir Square, the protests were reminiscent of the Indian non-violent independence movement led by Gandhi, the US civil-rights movement led by Martin Luther King, and the anti-apartheid struggle in South Africa led by Nelson Mandela. However,

---

[9] See, e.g., Amnesty International Report on Egypt for 2010 http://www.amnestyusa.org/research/reports/annual-report-egypt-2010?page=4. Egypt is a state party to the 1984 UN Convention against Torture, and torture is a crime in Egypt's Criminal Code.

[10] Jennifer Preston, 'Movement Began with Outrage and a Facebook Page that Gave it an Outlet', *New York Times*, 5 February 2011 http://www.nytimes.com/2011/02/06/world/middleeast/06face.html?pagewanted=all.

[11] For more details, see M. Cherif Bassiouni, *Egypt Update* (Background Paper), issued 7 February 2011, and *Egypt Update*, nos 1–4, issued 10–24 February 2011. All these are from my multi-part series of analyses of the situation in 2011–14 http://mcherifbassiouni.com/egypt-updates/. See also Wael Ghonim, *Revolution 2.0: The Power of the People is Greater than the People in Power: A Memoir* (Boston: Houghton Mifflin Harcourt, 2012).

the demonstrations and protests in Egypt had no unified leadership and no political programme for the country's transformation.

For a peaceful popular revolution, it was magnificently naive—an extraordinary, patriotic, and nationalistic movement involving many segments of society. Thousands of people spent the night at Tahrir, often in defiance of strict curfew orders. Thousands more came and left every day, bringing food and drinks to those who stayed there. There were speeches from religious and lay people, as well as actors and comedians. People played musical instruments and sang popular songs, while new songs were made about the ongoing event. Rich and poor mingled, women and men, Christians and Muslims, clergy and lay people, and many foreigners living in or visiting Egypt. Afterwards, thousands of individual accounts of the event surfaced in movies, documentaries, short stories, books, articles, and memoirs. Those who lived that extraordinary experience will never forget it, or the ideas of democracy, freedom, justice, and human dignity that the movement represented.

Even during those eighteen days of non-violent demonstrations in January and February 2011 considerable force was used against the pro-democracy activists by the regime; and, even when not used, its threat was there. The demonstrators also sometimes used force in response. Force took four distinct forms.

- The police and security forces were a constant challenge to the demonstrators, arresting and detaining many of them, and then in many cases subjecting them to mistreatment and torture. Foreign journalists covering the demonstrations were also targeted. Tear gas was used extensively in attempts to stop demonstrators advancing, or to break up demonstrations completely.[12]

- Although the demonstrations for the most part remained non-violent, there was a series of incidents from 25 January onwards in which crowds used some forms of violence.[13] Within a few days, such incidents included burning down the ruling party's headquarters, setting fire to police stations and police cars, and attacking the interior ministry.

- On several occasions, from 28 January onwards, army units were deployed on the streets, including in and around Tahrir Square. The presence of tanks was particularly striking. It is an interesting question whether they were sent there to be used or not, as they were inappropriate for crowd control in a confined space. While some demonstrators were initially concerned about the army presence, many saw the army as potentially a

---

[12] See, e.g., Robert Tait, '28 Hours in the Dark Heart of Egypt's Torture Machine', *Guardian*, London, 10 February 2011, 4, 5 http://www.theguardian.com/world/2011/feb/09/egypt-torture-machine-mubarak-security.

[13] Kareem Fahim and Mona El-Naggar, 'Violent Clashes Mark Protests against Mubarak's Rule', *New York Times*, 25 January 2011 http://www.nytimes.com/2011/01/26/world/middleeast/26egypt.html?pagewanted=all (published in print edition 26 January 2011).

Figure 3.1. Tanks were deployed during the protests in central Cairo, but at that time the army was seen as an ally of the demonstrators against the Mubarak regime. On 6 February 2011 protesters were photographed resting inside the tracks of a tank near Tahrir Square as protests grew in strength.

© *AP Photo/Ben Curtis*

protection against the police, or even a means of ousting Mubarak.[14] On 31 January the army pledged not to use violence against the peaceful protests. A common slogan of the demonstrators—perhaps reflecting hope rather than certainty—was: 'The army and people are one.' (See Figure 3.1.)

- Demonstrators also used force to protect themselves, particularly on 2 February, when pro-regime thugs, many riding on horses and camels, attacked them in Tahrir Square. In response, some in the crowd used a degree of force, including throwing stones at their attackers and arresting a number of them. By these means they succeeded in defending the square.[15]

The human cost of the January–February 2011 phase of the revolution was significant: an estimated 800 demonstrators were killed and more than 1,200 injured.[16] As the regime resorted to violence and the police and security forces

[14] David D. Kirkpatrick, 'Mubarak Orders Crackdown, with Revolt Sweeping Egypt', *New York Times*, 28 January 2011 http://www.nytimes.com/2011/01/29/world/middleeast/29unrest.html?pagewanted=all (published in print edition 29 January 2011).

[15] Amr El Beleidy, a travel writer, in 'This will Get Ugly', a collection of tweets sent on 2 February 2011, published in the *Guardian*, London, 15 April 2011, section G2, 14, 15.

[16] Verifiable numbers are unavailable. According to Human Rights Watch in New York, the Egyptian Ministry of Health indicated that 846 persons died during the protests in January and February, most on 28 and 29 January 2011: Human Rights Watch, *World Report 2012: Events of 2001* (New York: HRW, 2012), 546 http://www.hrw.org/node/79288.

to repression, so the regime's position rapidly weakened, both domestically and internationally. Popular support for the demonstrators increased, thanks to their restraint and civility, and international opinion moved perceptibly against the regime. Previously, the USA and Europe had tended to support Mubarak because of their concern with stability and the value they placed on Egypt's continued implementation of the 1979 Egypt–Israel Peace Treaty. But now that began to change.

US policy was particularly significant because of the long-standing US security relationship with Egypt. From the early days of the revolution there were close military-to-military contacts in which the Pentagon, like the State Department, inclined to support existing institutions of power, especially the military, while urging the military to act with restraint.[17] Throughout the crisis the US government struggled to come up with a clear policy. By the end of January the administration, while not at that stage calling explicitly for the replacement of its long-time ally Mubarak, emphasized that the repression had to end and that reform was urgently needed. In her memoirs, US Secretary of State Hillary Clinton wrote of the initial US response:

> Like many other young people around the world, some of President Obama's aides in the White House were swept up in the drama and idealism of the moment as they watched the pictures from Tahrir Square on television. They identified with the democratic yearnings and technological savvy of the young Egyptian protesters. Indeed Americans of all ages and political stripe were moved by the sight of people so long repressed finally demanding their universal human rights, and repulsed by the excessive force the authorities used in response. I shared that feeling. It was a thrilling moment. But along with Vice President Biden, Secretary of Defense Bob Gates, and National Security Advisor Tom Donilon, I was concerned that we not be seen as pushing a longtime partner out the door, leaving Egypt, Israel, Jordan, and the region to an uncertain, dangerous future.[18]

Of the situation in Cairo in early February, Clinton wrote:

> Things in Cairo got worse. Regime supporters came out in force and clashed violently with protesters. Men wielding clubs and other weapons swept through Tahrir Square on camels and horses, cracking heads. I called Vice President Suleiman to make it clear that such violent repression was absolutely unacceptable. The Egyptian leadership did not repeat this tactic in the following days.[19]

On 2 February, the day of the violent assault in Tahrir Square, President Obama supplemented the policy of opposing the violent repression by indicating that Mubarak should stand down: he stated that the transition in Egypt 'must be

---

[17] Josh Rogin, 'Gates and Mullen in Close Contact with Egyptian Military', *Foreign Policy*, Washington, 11 February 2011 http://foreignpolicy.com/2011/02/11/gates-and-mullen-in-close-contact-with-egyptian-military/.
[18] Hillary Rodham Clinton, *Hard Choices* (New York: Simon & Schuster, 2014), 339–40.
[19] Clinton, *Hard Choices*, 344.

Figure 3.2. Tahrir Square, symbol of the Arab Spring. Thousands of Egyptian demonstrators fill the square for their biggest protest in central Cairo on 11 February 2011. Later that day Mubarak was removed as president.

© *Patrick Baz/AFP/Getty Images*

meaningful, it must be peaceful and it must begin now'.[20] These, and similar pleas from Europe, may have contributed significantly to the avoidance of massive violence against the demonstrators in Tahrir Square, and perhaps also to the rapid outcome. Three weeks after it had begun, the protest movement achieved an apparent political victory when Mubarak resigned. However, that was not the end of the story, merely the beginning (see Figure 3.2).

POST-MUBARAK: THE SCAF AND THE BROTHERHOOD

On 11 February 2011, Mubarak resigned and the Supreme Council of the Armed Forces (SCAF) took over.[21] The SCAF consisted of fifteen top military

---

[20] Obama, press conference, Washington, 2 February 2011, reported on CNN http://edition.cnn.com/2011/POLITICS/02/01/us.egypt.obama/. On the background, see Chris McGreal, 'Obama Told Mubarak to Hold Free Elections and Step Down' (report from Washington), *Guardian*, London, 2 February 2011, 6.

[21] David D. Kirkpatrick, 'Egypt Erupts in Jubilation as Mubarak Steps Down', *New York Times*, 11 February 2011 http://www.nytimes.com/2011/02/12/world/middleeast/12egypt.html?pagewanted=all.

commanders and was assisted by a few select major generals who were not members of the SCAF, but who were called upon to play a role in the ongoing events. The SCAF was headed by Tantawi, who had served as defence minister since May 1991. He was to lead the country until a civilian government could be put in place. The SCAF announced the suspension of the 1971 Constitution, the dissolution of both houses of parliament, and the holding of new elections. It was too soon for the pro-democracy forces to rejoice at Mubarak's resignation, and indeed many of them initially refused the army's appeals to leave Tahrir Square. The SCAF acted as Egypt's sole ruler, and its aim was for the armed forces' leadership to remain in control for years, not least to retain its far-reaching political powers, social influence, and economic privileges. This they ultimately achieved by ousting Mohamed Morsi as president on 3 July 2013 and the election of Sisi to that post in May 2014. In the process, the glorious and naive pro-democracy revolution had been hijacked three times: first, in 2011, by the military; then by the Muslim Brotherhood; and finally, in July 2013, when the movement was once again hijacked by the military establishment, which was back in control.

However, the months after 11 February 2011 witnessed the continuation of considerable activism. There were labour strikes, whose bread-and-butter demands were often interpreted by the regime as threats to national security.[22] The pro-democracy movement, far from being passive, continued to exert pressure—either through additional demonstrations in Tahrir Square and elsewhere or through meetings of the youth leadership with members of the SCAF. It was partly through such pressure that Lieutenant General (Ret.) Ahmad Shafiq—the former Chief of Staff of the Air Force whom Mubarak had appointed prime minister on 31 January in response to the ongoing demonstrations—resigned from the premiership on 3 March 2011. Following a number of army and police assaults on demonstrators, some chants even demanded Tantawi's removal.[23] The SCAF was responsive to some of the demands of 'the street' or rather of the few leaders who were given the opportunity of meeting them. But the influence of the pro-democracy forces in this crucial period was limited. There were several reasons for this: the leaders of the Tahrir Square movement had relatively little power compared to the SCAF; they lacked a clear leadership structure; and, although continued demonstrations could remind SCAF of the risks that would arise if they went against the revolution's demands, the public was beginning to tire of such demonstrations. Time was not on their side.

---

[22] Hesham Sallam, 'Striking back at Egyptian Workers', in McMurray and Ufheil-Somers (eds), *The Arab Revolts*, 91–9 http://www.merip.org/mer/mer259/striking-back-egyptian-workers.

[23] Peter Beaumont, 'Raid on Cairo Protesters Raises Fear Army Has Hijacked Revolution', *Observer*, London, 10 April 2011 http://www.theguardian.com/world/2011/apr/09/egyptian-soldiers-tahrir-square-protesters.

In the weeks and months after 11 February 2011, perhaps the greatest failure of the movement that had brought down Mubarak was that it had few proposals for how Egypt should be governed. Despite the involvement of many talented individuals, the movement as a whole was simply not equipped for an effective part in discussions on that subject. As an interesting analysis published in late 2013 put it:

> The youth not only lost their direction after the revolution; they also lacked the focus necessary to achieve any of their strategic goals. This lack of interest . . . led to the death of the process of change and prevented the development of any alternative political system.
>
> . . . the youth's lack of interest stemmed from not wanting to participate in the decision-making process, which was dominated by old parties and the long-standing elite. The youth did not succeed in establishing new parties that would continue with the goals of the revolution.[24]

The leadership of the pro-democracy movement proved not to be up to the task. The movement floundered and was co-opted by the Muslim Brotherhood.

Concerned at being marginalized after the SCAF's takeover on 11 February 2011, the pro-democracy movement planned a comeback: some activists called for a 'second Friday of anger' on 27 May 2011. The leaders of the pro-democracy movement had numerous concerns, including about the overall performance of the SCAF; its reported intention to pardon Mubarak; and the incidents since 11 February in which the military police, the army, and the police 'have used disproportionate force, mass arrest, torture as well as live ammunition against protestors'.[25] In support of these demands, new demonstrations and protests took place. News reports put the number of demonstrators in Tahrir at between 50,000 and 250,000 people. Approximately 200,000 demonstrators took to the streets in Alexandria as well as a reported 10,000 in Suez. Smaller demonstrations were reported to have taken place in fifteen other governorates across Egypt. All this was evidence of the inevitable rising tension between the pro-democracy forces and the SCAF, but the smaller numbers participating also showed how the revolutionary zeal of a few months earlier had waned.

From February 2011 onwards, the pro-democracy revolution was gradually marginalized by the Muslim Brotherhood, which had not originally participated in the uprising. The Muslim Brotherhood had waited to see what the

---

[24] Abdul-Fatah Madi, an Egyptian researcher and academic, 'Where are the Youth of the Egyptian Revolution?', Al Jazeera net, 19/23 November 2013 https://www.middleeastmonitor.com/articles/africa/8467-where-are-the-youth-of-the-egyptian-revolution-.

[25] Article by Egyptian activist Wael Khalil, 'Why we are Holding Egypt's Second "Friday of Rage"', *Guardian*, London, 27 May 2011 http://www.theguardian.com/commentisfree/2011/may/27/egypt-second-friday-of-rage.

military establishment would do. When it became clear that this institution would not defend Mubarak and some of the cronies who rode on his coat-tails (other cronies, however, remained close to the military), the Muslim Brotherhood joined the revolution.[26] Then, in effect, it took centre stage. By the end of 2011 the pro-democracy revolution had been squeezed at both ends, by the SCAF and the Muslim Brotherhood.

The Muslim Brotherhood posed an increasingly serious challenge both to the creation of a fully democratic system and to the military establishment. In April 2011 it founded the Freedom and Justice Party (FJP), and in the parliamentary elections to the People's Assembly, held from November 2011 to January 2012, the FJP teamed up with several other pro-Islamist parties (such as the Salafists, who later in 2013–14 changed their alliance and supported the Sisi regime), winning a decisive majority of seats. Then, in May 2012 the Brotherhood's Morsi won election to the presidency. During the election campaign, it was rumoured and widely predicted that Morsi's opponent, Lieutenant-General (Ret.) Ahmad Shafiq—Mubarak's last appointed prime minister—was likely to win.[27] The final tally of the vote gave Morsi 13.2 million votes—about 882,000 votes more than Shafiq. The SCAF may have calculated that, had Shafiq won, the Muslim Brotherhood would have protested with force, the military would have had to intervene, and this would have produced a large number of casualties. The SCAF appears to have considered that it was best to let the Muslim Brotherhood win and then fall on its face. In both parliamentary and presidential elections, many of Egypt's electorate had stayed at home: thus it took only slightly more than 25 per cent of registered voters to put in place a Muslim Brotherhood presidency and legislature. The legislature proceeded to draft a new constitution, which was approved by referendum in December 2012 (with a modest 33 per cent turnout). This 2012 Constitution was seen by many as paving the way for a theocratic system of government.[28]

Having allowed Morsi to win the 2012 presidential election, the SCAF tested the Muslim Brotherhood's skills at the helm of the nation, with the relative certainty that it would be only a matter of time before it would fail to address the needs of the nation and become unpopular. That would pave the way for the military to be called back to power, as eventually happened. During the twelve months of Morsi's presidency, the military establishment made things

---

[26] It appears that, as from 28 January 2011, members of the Muslim Brotherhood encouraged worshippers to join the demonstrations across the country. Eric Trager, 'The Unbreakable Muslim Brotherhood: Grim Prospects for a Liberal Egypt', *Foreign Affairs*, 90/5 (September–October 2011), 120.

[27] My prediction to this effect was in Bassiouni, *Egypt Update*, no. 16, issued 8 June 2012, para. 25.

[28] See Articles 2, 4, 219 of the 2012 Egyptian Constitution. Between them, these added some detail to the brief mention of sharia in Article 2 of the previous (1971) constitution.

difficult for Morsi and the Muslim Brotherhood, which mishandled the many economic, social, and political crises that they faced. This was inevitable for an organization that had experienced eighty years of repression, and whose leadership was more adept at survival underground than government. As a former secret organization, the Muslim Brotherhood was ill equipped to run a country. Also significant is the secret history of how the Muslim Brotherhood and the SCAF dealt with one another during the year that President Morsi was in power. There is no doubt that there was an effort by the SCAF to work out a modus vivendi. But the Muslim Brotherhood missed many cues and acted without finesse in what was a delicate situation. In large part this was due to the fact that policies and their implementation were divided between the Guidance Office of the Muslim Brotherhood and the Presidency. Contradict-ory positions and decisions frequently emerged. The Guidance Office and some of the top leaders prevailed over Morsi. The SCAF could not possibly rely on such uncertainty to reach an accommodation that might have given the Muslim Brotherhood a better chance at government.

After Mubarak's fall in February 2011, democracy lost out to the apparent compromise between the military establishment and the Muslim Brother-hood. It took only six months for the military to realize that what they had thought was a possible modus vivendi with the Muslim Brotherhood could not work, since the latter now appeared in their eyes to be irrevocably committed to the establishment of a theocracy in which Egypt would, in time, be subsumed in a larger Islamic nation. It is possible that Tantawi and the SCAF anticipated most of the outcomes that subsequently occurred in 2011–12. They probably acted on the basis of the following assumptions:

- After 25 January 2011, popular revolutionary fervour was high and increasing. The military could not risk going against it without killing thousands of people. If they did, they would lose all legitimacy and any hope of governing the country. Thus, Mubarak had to be ousted and some apparent regime change was necessary. This conclusion was rein-forced by the awareness of existing corruption and of Mubarak's plans to have his son Gamal inherit the presidency. In addition, Mubarak's ap-pointment of Egypt's intelligence chief Omar Suleiman to the long-vacant post of vice president, announced on 29 January 2011, was particularly unacceptable to Tantawi, because of long-running rivalry between the intelligence services and the military.

- In the 2012 presidential elections, running a pro-military establishment candidate for the presidency to oppose the Muslim Brotherhood was worth trying, as a mechanism to assess the popularity of the Muslim Brotherhood, and the extent of the pro-democracy movement's hostility. If the Muslim Brotherhood and the pro-democracy forces did not oppose Ahmad Shafiq too strongly, the military establishment would back him, otherwise it would back off. In the end, the SCAF pulled the rug from underneath him. If the military had openly put their weight behind Shafiq in 2012, as they were to do for Sisi in 2014, Shafiq would have won. But a Shafiq victory, backed by the military, would have meant civil war between the Muslim Brotherhood and the pro-democracy forces on one side and the military on the other. This would have meant thousands of deaths and injuries, and it would have discredited the military. So they sacrificed Shafiq on the altar of democracy, and gained legitimacy and popularity to come back, as they did when the opportunity arose.

THE 2013 COUP AND ITS AFTERMATH

By 2013 most Egyptians had grown to dislike the Morsi government and the Muslim Brotherhood. More importantly, they had become concerned that Egypt would be turned into a theocratic state. Most Egyptian Muslims (88 per cent of the population) reject that form of government, as do the Christian 12 per cent of the population. Only an estimated 25 per cent favour it. The opportunity given to the Muslim Brotherhood to veer off to a democratic and somewhat secular form of government failed. The dangers in sight were far too significant to be overlooked. The military establishment saw this as an opportunity to return to power. However, they needed popular support. On 30 June an estimated thirteen million people took to the streets to demand that Morsi step down, and an electronic petition with an estimated twenty million names was circulated. Although the military establishment helped orchestrate the 30 June popular movement, the mass popular antipathy towards Morsi was genuine. The movement organizing the demonstrations and petition was called *Tamarod* (Arabic for 'revolt'). It gave Morsi an ultimatum to resign the presidency or face a campaign of 'complete civil disobedience'; and it urged 'state institutions including the army, the police and the judiciary to clearly side with the popular will represented by the crowds'.[29]

What followed was a very transparent scenario probably planned by military intelligence and implemented with military precision by Sisi, who, at the time, was Morsi's defence minister and head of the SCAF. On 3 July 2013 the military arrested Morsi and took power.[30] Technically the army's assumption of power on 3 July was a military *coup d'état*, but it claimed popular

---

[29] 'Profile: Egypt's Tamarod Protest Movement', *BBC News*, 1 July 2013, http://www.bbc.co.uk/news/world-middle-east-23131953.

[30] David D. Kirkpatrick, 'Egypt Army Ousts Morsi, Suspends Charter', *New York Times*, 3 July 2013, A1, A12; Evan Hill, 'Background: SCAF's Last-Minute Power Grab', Al Jazeera http://www.aljazeera.com/indepth/spotlight/egypt/2012/06/201261812449990250.html (18 June 2012).

revolutionary legitimacy—there being no constitutional means of removing the elected president from office before the end of his presidential term. Even the military establishment's strong push for Sisi to become the next president had popular support and hence some legitimacy. The population yearned for stability and supported the military, believing that the military would bring stability and address the nation's economic woes. Thus they did not oppose curtailing freedom of the media and other forms of freedom of expression. Repression of the peaceful pro-democracy movement was accepted by the strongly polarized majority, as was repression of the Muslim Brotherhood.

In a public referendum held on 14–15 January 2014 a new constitution was approved by a large majority of those voting.[31] Voter turnout was relatively low, and concerns about this will be mentioned later. On 26 March Sisi, like Nasser in 1956 before him, declared he was running for president and promptly won elections on 26–7 May 2014. The features of the new regime appeared similar to those of the Mubarak era, with two possible exceptions: first, the open and formal entry of the military establishment into public reconstruction—for example, in housing and infrastructure;[32] and, second, a claim to reduce corruption as practised by the oligarchy.

After the coup of 3 July 2013 the interior ministry, as under Habib el-Adly's leadership from 1997–2011, reverted to its pattern of abusive tactics against any and all demonstrations. The regime's thinking after the coup appears to have been that excesses by the police were accepted so long as they did not lead to more problems for the military; and, if there was trouble, then the police could be blamed and the military could even be seen once again as the nation's saviour. In time the targets of repression included not only the Muslim Brotherhood but also the pro-democracy movements. As the military establishment had accurately predicted, popular sentiment was on the regime's side. The repression of the Muslim Brotherhood and pro-democracy adherents was tactically led by the interior minister, Police General Mohamed Ibrahim, and strategically led by the head of General Intelligence, Major-General (Ret.) Mohamed Farid el-Tohamy, a previous head of Military Intelligence and Sisi's mentor, who had the rank of minister, but was retired by Sisi in December 2014.[33]

---

[31] Constitution of the Arab Republic of Egypt 2014 as amended on 15 January 2014 (hereinafter 2014 Constitution), unofficial translation available from http://www.sis.gov.eg/En/Templates/Articles/tmpArticles.aspx?CatID=2603#.VKfRdcZikqc.

[32] Major housing and infrastructure mega-projects will be given to the Army's Corps of Engineers. See Bassiouni, *Egypt Update*, no. 30, issued 31 May 2014, para. 23.

[33] David Ignatius, 'The Future of Egypt's Intelligence Service', *Washington Post*, 11 November 2013 http://www.washingtonpost.com/blogs/post-partisan/wp/2013/11/11/the-future-of-egypts-intelligence-service/; and David D. Kirkpatrick, 'Egypt's President Replaces Influential Intelligence Chief', *New York Times*, 21 December 2014 http://www.nytimes.com/2014/12/22/world/middleeast/egypts-president-replaces-intelligence-chief.html.

In the months after the coup, demonstrations by Muslim Brotherhood supporters campaigning against the military government took the form of a series of prolonged mass sit-ins in public squares. Their chosen method was an echo of the Tahrir Square demonstrations in 2011. The outcome was grim. The most extreme case of repression was the killing of more than 800 demonstrators in Raba'a Square in Cairo on 14 August 2013, ending a six-week mass sit-in of tens of thousands. The authorities claimed that some of the demonstrators had been carrying guns, but the number of such cases appears to have been low.[34]

Meanwhile, pro-democracy activists, many of whom had approved of the removal of Morsi from office, became critical of the country's military rulers. Their concerns included a law passed on 24 November 2013, which prohibited the kind of activities that had prevailed during the 2011 revolution: it effectively curtailed freedom of expression and assembly in Egypt, and also violated the International Covenant on Civil and Political Rights, which Egypt had ratified.[35]

On 25 January 2014 pro-democracy and other activists organized massive popular protests in Tahrir Square and elsewhere to commemorate the third anniversary of the 25 January 2011 revolution. Unfortunately, the situation they faced was similar to what it had been for most of the time since 1952. An estimated 49 persons were killed, 247 injured, and more than 1,000 arrested. The security forces made no distinction between demonstrators or whether they were peaceful or not.[36]

On the previous day, Friday 24 January, four bombs at four different sites in Cairo had left six people dead, and eight civilian protesters were killed in battles with the police. The first, and deadliest, of the attacks was a car bomb outside a security headquarters. Although many initially blamed the Muslim Brotherhood for the attacks, the bombings followed the model set by the Sinai-based Islamist terrorist group Ansar Bait al-Maqdis.[37] This group had issued an audio message the night before promising there would be attacks on police and army targets. The Muslim Brotherhood denied any part in the attacks and issued a statement condemning them as 'cowardly' and called for swift investigations. Within two hours of the first bombing, a crowd had gathered

---

[34] Human Rights Watch, *All According to Plan: The Rab'a Massacre and Mass Killings of Protesters in Egypt* (New York: HRW, 2014), 5–10, 94–7 http://www.hrw.org/reports/2014/08/12/all-according-plan-0.

[35] International Covenant on Civil and Political Rights, UNGA Res. 2200A (XXI) of 16 December 1966, *UN Treaty Series*, vol. 999, p. 171.

[36] Ali Omar, 'At Least 49 Killed, 247 Wounded in 25 January Anniversary', *Daily News Egypt*, 26 January 2014. This can be accessed via Twitter https://twitter.com/dailynewsegypt/status/427425107422625792.

[37] A reported al-Qaeda affiliated group of violent Islamists who had been fighting in the Sinai against Egypt's Second Army. They support Hamas in Gaza, and their fighters are reported to be from various parts of the world.

to cheer Sisi, shouting: 'The people want the execution of the Brothers', thus imitating and twisting the call of three years before, 'The people want the fall of the regime.'[38] By linking Ansar Bait al-Maqdis and the Muslim Brotherhood, the regime's propaganda machine heightened animosity against, if not hatred of, the Brotherhood. This made further repression more palatable.

The interior ministry announced that this was the beginning of the expected 'terrorist' campaign of the next day. Thus the regime had in advance labelled 25 January 2014 a day of 'terrorist' activities. The protests and demonstrations that day were mostly peaceful, but the security forces did not give these protestors and demonstrators the opportunity to exercise their constitutional and internationally protected rights of peaceful assembly and freedom of expression.[39]

The security forces and the Prosecutor-General's office frequently acted abusively, as they had under the Mubarak regime. The security and military forces arrested an estimated 20,000–24,000 people in the three years from February 2011; prosecutors subsequently validated their arrests. Thousands were charged and tried in ordinary and military courts: no one knows the exact number. Many of the charges were questionable. By December 2014 several hundred had been sentenced to more than ten years imprisonment, and more than 1,800 had been sentenced to death. However, their cases were automatically appealed to the Court of Cassation and their sentences were likely to be reversed.

On 21 June 2014 the leader of the Muslim Brotherhood, Mohamed Badie, and 182 supporters were sentenced to death on charges related to violence in the southern town of Minya. Morsi and the Muslim Brotherhood leadership of fifteen were put on trial for what appeared to be mostly absurd charges of escaping from prison in 2011, espionage, and similar accusations. Some charges, such as incitement to violence, were arguably valid, though the defence could certainly argue that use of force against a military coup was justified, as was resistance against the removal of a lawfully elected head of state. To say the least, the conduct of such trials left much to be desired. On 21 April 2015 Morsi, although he was acquitted of murder charges, was sentenced to twenty years in jail for involvement in arrests and torture of demonstrators during his rule. The following month he was sentenced to death in the prison escape trial. He faces several other trials, each with a separate sentence if he is found guilty.

---

[38] David D. Kirkpatrick, 'Prolonged Fight Feared in Egypt after Bombings', *New York Times*, 24 January 2014 http://www.nytimes.com/2014/01/25/world/middleeast/fatal-bomb-attacks-in-egypt.html. See also 'Cairo Rocked by Deadly Bomb Attacks', Al Jazeera, 24 January 2014 http://www.aljazeera.com/news/middleeast/2014/01/cairo-rocked-deadly-bomb-attacks-2014124103138914258.html.

[39] These rights were repressed as people were killed, injured, and at least 1,000 persons were arrested on that day. Since 3 July 2014, opposition leaders claim that an estimated 23,000 political activists have been arrested by the regime.

How many people were killed in the period following the military takeover of 3 July 2013? The government did not release figures on the number of people dead, injured, or arrested. Amnesty International was one of several bodies that published reports on the scale of the repression.[40] Amnesty also gave evidence to the UN Human Rights Council that, between 3 July 2013 and mid-February 2014, '1,400 people have been killed in political violence, most after security forces forcibly dispersed protests by Mohamed Morsi's supporters'.[41] I have estimated that, in the period from July 2013 to May 2014, more than 2,500 people were killed and 17,000 injured.[42] The government also did not provide information on those arrested, how many had been kept in detention, how many were released, or how many were prosecuted (whether in civil or military courts). Further, the government did not release, either by incident or cumulatively, information on the number of security officers killed or injured in confrontations.

In 2013–14 several new laws were enacted by Interim President Adly Mansour and by President Sisi that criminalized, with harsh sentences, a variety of conduct believed to be a threat to national security, attacks on the public, or demonstrations without a permit. These new laws also gave the military courts jurisdiction over civilians. This was also the case with the early anti-terrorism law. The 2014 Constitution recognized military courts as equivalent to ordinary civilian courts, even though in the military justice system there were only two levels and no civilian oversight court, not even the Court of Cassation, Egypt's highest law court. The military courts also had jurisdiction in north Sinai after Sisi had declared it to be subject to a new State of Emergency Law.

The regime's repression of both the Muslim Brotherhood and the pro-democracy movement continued even after the regime's victory in the January 2014 referendum on the new constitution, and after Sisi's election to the presidency in May 2014. By then it had had its full effect—there were far fewer protests and demonstrations. But that did not mean the end of periodic violence, including on Egypt's borders with the Gaza Strip and Libya, as mentioned below.

Repression and its practices were not new, nor were its protagonists and the means they employed. For most Egyptians the Mubarak regime—like its predecessors, the Sadat and Nasser regimes—represented corruption, brutality, and a general lack of respect for human rights. For most of that time military leaders ran the country, with the General Intelligence Directorate (GID) the dominant body. They engaged in arbitrary arrests and detention as

---

[40] Amnesty International, 'Egypt Three Years on, Wide-Scale Repression Continues Unabated', 23 January 2014 http://www.amnesty.org/en/news/egypt-three-years-wide-scale-repression-continues-unabated-2014-01-23.

[41] Amnesty International, *Egypt: The Human Rights Situation in Egypt: Amnesty International's written Statement to the 25th Session of the UN Human Rights Council (3 to 28 March 2014)*, 14 February 2014, 1.

[42] Bassiouni, *Egypt Update*, no. 30, para. 45.

well as torture and disappearances. Their work was supplemented by the police's State Security Investigations Service (*Mabahith Amn al-Dawla*) now referred to as National Security. After 2005, under Minister of Interior Habib el-Adly, this department took over most of the political repression work. Generally speaking, Adly and his senior leadership showed a total lack of concern for the law and for the people. They used all the repressive powers of the police and the Prosecutor's Office (which they influenced significantly) to engage in massive arbitrary arrests, torture, and other human-rights abuses against the Muslim Brotherhood and anyone else who dared oppose the government and the oligarchs. Adly and his subordinates were truly the servants of a corrupt oligarchy, and, in exchange, they came to acquire a new political, social, and economic status in the country. They were reputed to have received the largest bonuses and benefits of any security force or public employee in the country, and were unaccountable for any violations including torture and killings under torture.

Repression after the army takeover of 3 July 2013 targeted many pro-democracy activists. For example, on 22 December 2013, Ahmed Maher, a leader of the April 6 Movement, along with two other high-profile activists, Mohamed Adel and Ahmed Douma, were sentenced to three years in prison and a fine of 50,000 Egyptian pounds (roughly $7,180), for organizing a demonstration before the People's Assembly to protest the law passed in November 2013 infringing freedom of assembly. During that demonstration, seventy-nine other pro-democracy activists were arrested, including ten women. On 5 January 2014 a court imposed a one-year suspended sentence on Mona Seif, a popular activist known for her campaigns against torture, police brutality, and the use of military courts in civilian matters. She and eleven other activists, including Alaa Abdul-Fatah, were convicted of participating in an illegal demonstration. In January 2014 prosecutors charged seven activists for putting up posters urging people to vote 'no' in the constitutional referendum.[43]

Independent journalists have also been targets. On 23 June 2014 three Al Jazeera journalists were sentenced to prison terms of seven years (and one had an additional sentence of three more years) on charges that were widely condemned as completely baseless.[44] An additional fifty-three journalists were arrested and intimidated and many were imprisoned.[45]

---

[43] Human Rights Watch, 'Egypt: Activists Arrested for "No" Campaign', HRW, New York, 13 January 2014 http://www.hrw.org/news/2014/01/13/egypt-activists-arrested-no-campaign.

[44] 'Egypt Court Sentences Al Jazeera Staff: Network Says Jail Terms for Peter Greste, Mohamed Fahmy and Baher Mohamed defy "logic, sense, and semblance of justice"', Al Jazeera http://www.aljazeera.com/humanrights/2014/06/egypt-court-sentences-al-jazeera-staff-2014623135112242945.html (23 June 2014). In January 2015 the Court of Cassation announced a retrial for the three. In February Greste was deported and flown to freedom in Cyprus and then home to Australia; and then Fahmy and Mohamed were released on bail. At retrial in August their sentences were reduced to three years, and in September Fahmy and Mohamed were pardoned and freed.

[45] Bassiouni, *Egypt Update*, no. 30, para. 50.

The security forces and the Prosecutor's Office also targeted labour unions. For example, in July and August 2013 workers who had taken part in a strike against the Suez Steel Company over dismissals and the failure to pay salaries and other employee benefits were arrested and had their homes searched. The arrests were used as a bargaining chip to pressure the workers to end their strike. On 18 December 2013 the headquarters of the Egyptian Center for Economic and Social Rights, an NGO that focused on socio-economic issues, particularly labour rights, was raided by fifty armed men in civilian attire, later identified as police. Six members of its staff were detained, and a number of items and documents were seized.

Syrian refugees were unexpected casualties of the security forces' repressive practices. On the assumption that they were Morsi supporters, they experienced a backlash after his ousting in July 2013. The UN High Commissioner for Refugees (UNHCR) estimated that by September 2014 there were 139,000 Syrian refugees registered with it in Egypt.[46] Several media figures appealed to viewers to attack Palestinians and Syrians, describing them as pro-Morsi and as wanting to destabilize the country. Authorities began to treat Syrians as a security risk, and Syrians attempting to flee the civil war in their country were denied visas to enter Egypt. Many Syrian refugees already living in Egypt, but who did not have visas, were arrested. UNHCR reported that some 476 Syrians had been deported or denied entrance to Egypt during July 2013.[47] In addition to Syrians and Palestinians, sub-Saharan African refugees, mostly from Eritrea, were regularly kidnapped, tortured for ransom, and killed by traffickers, according to a report by Human Rights Watch.[48]

The extensive record of repression after 2013 encompassed the legal and judicial system. Prison conditions were, by international standards, subhuman. There was torture and physical abuse, including repeated sexual abuse in women's prisons by supervising male police officers. In January 2015 Human Rights Watch reported: 'Scores of Egyptians died in government custody in 2014, many of them packed into police stations in life-threatening conditions.' It cited one official report that 'at least 90 detainees held in police facilities in just the governorates of Cairo and Giza died in custody in the first ten and a half months of 2014'.[49] Official sources put the number of those who

---

[46] UNHCR, 'Update on UNHCR's Operations in the Middle East and North Africa', 17 September 2014, 2 http://www.unhcr.org/541aa1dd9.pdf.

[47] 'Egypt: UNHCR Concerned over Detention of Syrian Refugees amid Anti-Syrian Sentiment', Briefing Notes, 26 July 2013 http://www.unhcr.org/cgi-bin/texis/vtx/search?page=search&docid=51f242c59&query=476%20Syrians.

[48] Human Rights Watch, 'Egypt/Sudan: Traffickers who Torture: Egypt Should Use Sinai Security Operations to Suppress Trafficking', 11 February 2014 http://www.hrw.org/news/2014/02/11/egyptsudan-traffickers-who-torture.

[49] Human Rights Watch, 'Egypt: Rash of Deaths in Custody—Holding Police Accountable Key to Saving Lives', HRW press statement of 21 January 2015 http://www.hrw.org/news/2015/01/21/egypt-rash-deaths-custody.

died in detention and prison facilities in 2014 at more than 200, many because of unattended illnesses and diseases, and the terrible physical conditions of these locations. These deaths are disproportionately attributed to the police and prison personnel and not to those in the government who control the resources for these facilities and related medical and social services.

There was no accountability, and the judiciary exercised no meaningful control. Many judges and prosecutors became politicized and part of the oppressive apparatus. A number of judges and prosecutors acted in ways that violated due process, and an inordinately high number of people were prosecuted, convicted, and given heavy sentences, including the death penalty, with little or no evidence of culpability. In the end the policies and practices of repression succeeded. Demonstrations and protests became fewer and smaller.[50] The much-wanted stability had been achieved, and in part public safety. But the desired stability has not brought about economic development. Society also remains sharply divided and strongly polarized. Other forms of terror-violence are emerging from groups affiliated with ISIS.

Notwithstanding all of the above and certainly not with the intention of minimizing the levels of harm that have occurred, it is nonetheless important to have a balanced sense of proportion with respect to the context and consequences of the events that have occurred since 2011. During that period there were hundreds of demonstrations and protests in over fifteen cities, cumulatively involving millions of persons. They were faced with an overworked and overstretched police force (estimated at 450,000). The negative human consequences of an estimated 4,000 dead and 12,000 injured could statistically have been much larger. Also the comparative number of police officers killed (an estimated 600 and several thousand injured) is a high ratio in comparison to the civilian casualties—by comparison to the number of police officers killed and injured in similar demonstrations and protests in various countries of the world.

THE RELENTLESSNESS OF THE 'DEEP STATE'

Events between the 2011 revolution and Sisi's election in 2014 resembled those during the Nasser era of 1952–70: the promulgation of a series of

---

[50] On 25 January 2015, the fourth anniversary of the 2011 uprising, there were demonstrations in several places by disparate groups of demonstrators. At least thirteen protestors and one policeman were killed: Patrick Kingsley, '14 Killed during Pro-Democracy Rallies in Egypt', *Guardian*, London, 26 January 2015, 16 http://www.theguardian.com/world/2015/jan/25/11-killed-during-pro-democracy-protests-egypt-2011-uprising-anniversary.

constitutional proclamations and declarations by a military body;[51] the elaboration of constitutional texts by different appointed bodies; the conduct of public referenda to give the appearance of legitimacy; and, in the end, Egypt's 'deep state' reasserting itself.

The term 'deep state' reflects the reality of power as it existed in Egypt. There were several centres of power and influence that played different roles at different times, exercising their power and influence over policy and practice. Sometimes it was for the benefit of the nation, and sometimes it was for the benefit of their caste or group. The 'military establishment' refers to an informal structure headed by the defence minister who was also the chairman of the SCAF. From the 1952 revolution onwards, the minister was appointed by the president. However, the new 2014 Constitution formally gave the SCAF this role. It also stated that the minister of defence, who had to be an officer in the armed forces, could not be removed by the president, or any other authority in Egypt, for the next eight years.[52]

Since the military establishment also included industrial enterprises, some of which were purely military while others were in the civilian economic sector, the armed forces controlled a parallel economic structure that constituted between 20 and 40 per cent of the overall Egyptian economy. Although it was under the direct authority of the defence minister, rather than the SCAF, it was beyond any civilian oversight and paid no taxes on its profits, which were secretly distributed by the minister at his or the SCAF's direction.[53]

Two other agencies could be said to have fallen within the scope of the military establishment: the General Intelligence Directorate (GID) and the Administrative Control Authority (ACA). Both were directly under the president. Their respective heads were former military personnel (they had to resign their military position before assuming that function) who held the rank of minister, and since the 1952 revolution they had always been former heads of military intelligence. The GID comprised 90 per cent former military officers and only 10 per cent former police officers and civilians. The ACA was composed entirely of former military officers. The security forces—which are to be distinguished from other elements of the interior ministry that deal with public safety and other police functions—were another centre of power. They were controlled by the interior minister and answerable to him and to the president, though at different times the security forces were more or less under the control or influence of the GID. Thus, to some extent, this independent source of power of the 'deep state' was at times, as was the case after 2013, under the control of the military establishment.

---

[51] In 1952–6 the ruling military body was the Revolutionary Command Council, and in 2011–14 it was the Supreme Council of the Armed Forces (SCAF).

[52] 2014 Constitution, Articles 201, 234.

[53] Bassiouni, *Egypt Update*, no. 19, issued 1 July 2012, 10–13.

The 'deep state' encompassed two other groups. First, there were politically influential personalities, whether in office or not, and that included senior media personalities. The second group comprised business moguls who were more likely to exercise influence than direct power, except in economic and financial matters. It was the combination of these centres of power and influence that constituted the deep state. At different times, and with respect to different issues, the alliances between these groups varied, as did the power relations between them. After 2013 the military establishment was the preponderant force that dominated all others.

Any democratic society must necessarily be concerned about the existence of bodies such as these. The power and influence of such bodies—including their capacity to use their power and influence outside their specific institutional functions—was undemocratic, specifically given that they were not subject to legal and administrative control like any other public body. The question for Egypt was whether or not the 'deep state' had, since 25 January 2011, served the interests of the broader population. Strategically, the military establishment saved the country from a civil war in January–February 2011 by forcing the resignation of Mubarak. In 2012 it allowed what were probably the first free and fair elections in Egypt since 1952, which led to the election of Morsi. It then allowed the elected president and the Muslim Brotherhood-dominated legislature to run the country—even if only for one year. And, when Morsi's and the Muslim Brotherhood's failures became obvious, the tactical objectives of public opinion and the military establishment coincided. However, as indicated below, there were differences in long-term strategic goals between public opinion and the military establishment.

POLITICAL PERSPECTIVES

If, by the end of 2011, it was not obvious that the revolution had come to an end, this was surely clear by the end of 2013. The 30 June 2013 popular movement was against the Muslim Brotherhood but it was not pro-democracy. Most Egyptians genuinely wanted stability, even at the price of sacrificing democracy. Polarization was prevalent. It was a zero-sum game: neither side saw the other's position, let alone its merits, and each side was engaged in labelling the other as the enemy. Part of this process was to label as terrorist or terrorist sympathizer anyone who supported the Muslim Brotherhood, or was pro-democracy, or even who opposed the police's use of force. No principled opposition was acceptable. Polarization had reached such a level that public hospitals were reported to have refused treatment to injured demonstrators.[54] Deaths, injuries, and arrests continued with every new event: any critics, including foreign and domestic journalists, were likely to face arrest.

The candidacy and election of Sisi were a foregone conclusion.[55] According to official statistics, in the presidential election of May 2014 he received 23.8 million votes (96.9 per cent of all votes cast), while in the January constitutional referendum 19.9 million votes (98.1 per cent of all votes cast) had said 'yes' to the revised constitution.[56] Parliamentary elections scheduled for March and April 2015 were expected to produce a legislative body dominated by pro-regime figures. That the regime worked hard to ensure the election of Sisi did not detract from the fact that there was strong popular support for him and strong popular dislike for the Muslim Brotherhood. But that was only a transitional stage. Addressing the nation's economic and social problems would be the test.

Since January 2011 Egyptians had demonstrated how politically conscious they were and how much they were committed to Egypt as a nation and desirous of achieving democracy and a socially just system. In June–July 2013 they made it clear that they rejected the Muslim Brotherhood system of government: they rose up and then welcomed a military-backed regime in the hope that it would provide for a future transition to democracy. The numbers involved were impressive. According to some estimates, up to thirty million Egyptians participated by either going to the streets, through the social media, or signing the anti-Morsi petition. Perhaps twenty million is a more likely figure. Considering that Egypt had an estimated eighty-five million population, the fact that there were so many politically active people was quite telling.

However, equally telling were the divisions in society, and the weakness of the opposition so far as the articulation of practical policies was concerned. As one observer of these events wrote in June 2013:

> In conversations with opposition politicians over the past six months, I have been struck by two things: their vehement hatred of the Brotherhood, and their

---

[54] Amnesty International statement, 'Egypt: Detained Morsi Supporters Denied their Rights', 12 September 2013 http://www.amnestyusa.org/news/news-item/egypt-detained-morsi-supporters-denied-their-rights.

[55] 'Egypt's Sisi "to Run for President"', Al Jazeera http://www.aljazeera.com/news/middleeast/2014/02/egypt-army-chief-confirms-presidential-bid-201425225057233402.html (6 February 2014). This report cited Kuwaiti newspaper *Al-Seyassah* of 6 February 2014.

[56] Official figures from the website of *Al-Ahram*, Cairo, 18 January 2014 http://english.ahram.org.eg/NewsContent/1/64/91874/Egypt/Politics-/UPDATE—approves-postJune–constitution.aspx. For indications of certain concerns about the January 2014 constitutional referendum, see 'Egypt Constitution Approved by 98.1 percent', Al Jazeera http://www.aljazeera.com/news/middleeast/2014/01/egypt-constitution-approved-981-percent-201411816326470532.html (last updated 24 January 2014); and David D. Kirkpatrick, 'Overwhelming Vote for Egypt's Constitution Raises Concern', *New York Times*, 18 January 2014 http://www.nytimes.com/2014/01/19/world/middleeast/vote-validates-egypts-constitution-and-military-takeover.html.

inability to articulate solutions to the country's problems. People speak in vague terms about social justice and democratic values.... A recent survey by Zogby Research Services showed that seventy-four per cent of eligible voters lack confidence in the Brotherhood, and seventy-five to seventy-eight per cent lack confidence in the leading opposition parties.[57]

In the aftermath of the campaign of June 2013 there were many deep divisions in Egyptian society. First there was a generational gap, between a younger age group many of whom sought change, and an older generation that was more inclined to settle for stability and the status quo. Young voters were 'conspicuously absent' from the January 2014 constitutional referendum.[58] Secondly, there were important divisions between those who were sceptical about religious involvement in politics, and the two main political–religious movements, the Muslim Brotherhood and the Salafists.

Since 3 July 2013 the Muslim Brotherhood has pursued a multi-track strategy of peaceful protests, occasional violent confrontations with the security forces, and outright violence. The first two prongs of the strategy were designed to provoke a repressive reaction by the security forces and thus to obtain public sympathy at home and abroad. The third prong was more complex: it involved direct violence carried out by groups that the Muslim Brotherhood claimed to be separate. The Muslim Brotherhood has used this strategy throughout its history, and particularly in the 1970s and the 1990s.

The Muslim Brotherhood was marginalized and driven underground, much as it had been throughout its history. In December 2013, following a bombing at Mansoura, it was proclaimed a terrorist organization. It stated that it had no involvement in the bombing, responsibility for which had been claimed by Ansar Bait al-Maqdis. The Muslim Brotherhood's political party, the Freedom and Justice Party, was popularly discredited before it was declared illegal by the 2014 Constitution, through Article 74, which banned religious political parties. In April 2014 the Muslim Brotherhood's Secretary General, Mahmoud Hussein, issued an emphatic statement that the Brotherhood's 'activity and struggle against corruption and despotism is based on absolute peacefulness and the rejection of violence in all its forms and putting up with the harm, detentions, killing, torture and oppression [the group] suffers'. It stressed that 'anyone who engages in violence is at odds with the group'.[59] My prediction is that its members will continue their resistance and some will continue to fight.

---

[57] Leslie T. Chang, 'Egypt's Petition Rebellion', *New Yorker*, 27 June 2013 http://www.newyorker.com/news/news-desk/egypts-petition-rebellion.

[58] David D. Kirkpatrick and Mayy El Sheikh, 'A Chasm Grows between Young and Old in Egypt', *New York Times*, 17 February 2014, A1 http://www.nytimes.com/2014/02/17/world/middleeast/a-chasm-grows-between-young-and-old-in-egypt.html?_r=0.

[59] 'Brotherhood Releases Lengthy Statement Condemning Violence', *Al-Ahram*, Cairo, 8 April 2014 http://english.ahram.org.eg/NewsContent/1/64/98626/Egypt/Politics-/Brotherhood-releases-lengthy-statement-condemning-.aspx.

They have strong support in Egypt, in several Arab countries, and throughout the world. But they too in time will change and maybe recognize the value of some democracy and less theocracy. Ideologies such as theirs are necessarily subject to generational changes, particularly in the current era of globalization.

The only official remaining Islamist movement was the Salafists. In Egypt, as in other countries, the Salafists looked back to the earliest Muslims to provide a model of Islamic practice. Their main political party, which was set up in 2011 after the overthrow of Mubarak, was al-Nour, with its head-quarters in Alexandria. Presumably al-Nour ought to have been declared illegal in accordance with the 2014 Constitution, but, because of its support for the regime and its backing by Saudi Arabia, the party's status was in limbo. Egyptian Salafists publicly urged a 'yes' vote in the January 2014 constitutional referendum, and they managed to stay out of the confrontation between the Muslim Brotherhood and the regime, but future confrontation seemed likely. It was not clear exactly how many members they had, but they were able to obtain at least one million votes in the 2011 legislative elections.[60] Saudi Arabia, which funded them, had always guided the Egyptian Salafists. They were supportive of the Mubarak regime and were seldom subject to any repressive measures by the state security apparatus under Mubarak, or for that matter under the Sisi regime. Many in the military were believed to share their values. The regime hoped that the Salafists would help to improve what it saw as deteriorating social values in Egypt. But they were likely to surprise the regime as their Islamist goals began to surface. I am convinced that rank-and-file Salafists will press for some form of theocracy whenever they have the opportunity to do so. Already they were critical of the 2014 Constitution, which removed the provision in Article 4 of the 2012 Constitution that could have been seen as giving the *ulema* the right to decide on whether a given law complied with sharia.[61]

GEOPOLITICAL FACTORS

Geopolitical factors have long had a profound effect on developments in Egypt. They encompassed the foreign policies of the USA, Russia, Israel, Saudi Arabia, and the other Gulf states, European states—and also the region-wide conflict between Shi'a and Sunni Muslims. While most states involved in the region had a strong interest in ensuring Egypt's stability, they

---

[60] 'Many Stripes: Can Egypt's Salafists Take on the Islamist Mantle?', *The Economist*, London, 30 November 2013 http://www.economist.com/news/middle-east-and-africa/21590916-can-egypts-salafists-take-islamist-mantle-many-stripes.
[61] The *ulema* consists of those with special training in Muslim religion and law.

had different approaches regarding how to achieve it. The fluctuating US positions in 2013–14 were especially problematic.

The USA had for decades had a complex but largely supportive relationship with Egypt's governments. When the 3 July 2013 coup took place, the Egyptian military establishment anticipated likely White House reactions on the basis of the information they had from their counterparts in the US military and intelligence communities, the latter being historically anti-Muslim Brotherhood. What they and their US counterparts had not expected were the reactions of the US National Security Council and those close to President Obama whose commitment to democracy and human rights trumped geopolitical considerations. The result, the partial suspension of US military and economic aid, in turn led to the decline of US popularity in Egypt. Neither the Egyptian military establishment, nor for that matter probably the US military and intelligence communities, had anticipated the effect of the shift in US strategic interests in the Arab world at around this period, characterized by a US reluctance to get deeply involved. The shift coincided with Susan Rice taking up the post of US National Security Adviser on 1 July 2013. Such a shift was inevitable after the disastrous US policies in Iraq and Afghanistan; in addition, the worsening civil war in Syria added to US doubts about involvement in the Middle East. The partial thawing of US–Iran relations was another sign of a new US approach in the region. On the Syria civil war and the internal conflict in Iraq, the USA unexpectedly took a pro-Shi'a position. In Iraq it provided Apache fighter helicopters to assist the Shi'a-dominated forces of Iraqi prime minister, Nouri al-Maliki, against the Sunnis in Iraq's Anbar province.[62]

US influence seemed likely to remain limited. Egyptians had a consensus of antipathy for the USA and for Israel. The strong anti-American popular current was due to what was seen as the ambiguous and opportunistic US position towards Egyptian regimes from Mubarak to Morsi to Sisi. In 2014 this was aggravated by the disappointing US position on Syria, and by US support of Israel, not the least over its devastating military attack on Gaza (8 July to 26 August).

In 2014 the USA drew back from some of the positions it had taken in 2013. Following the Iraqi parliamentary election of 30 April 2014, the USA put pressure on Baghdad to agree on a less narrowly sectarian government: this finally happened in August, making it possible for the USA to take military action against the forces of Islamic State in Iraq and the Levant (also variously known as ISIL, Islamic State, or its Arabic acronym DAESH) without being necessarily perceived as part of a more general pro-Shi'a and anti-Sunni front.

---

[62] On 29 October 2013, on an official state visit to the USA, Iraqi President Maliki asked President Obama for military assistance to fight the Sunni rebellion against his Shi'a pro-Iranian government, using the argument that al-Qaeda-linked forces were behind it.

Then on 13 December 2014 the US Congress passed a bill establishing a procedure for the US government to resume full military aid to Egypt on the grounds of 'national security', even in the absence of credible progress towards democracy. This bill brought the USA closer to the Egyptian regime, not to the people.

Before these changes in 2014, the US line in response to the July 2013 coup had created an opening for Russia's re-entry into Egypt for the first time since Sadat had asked Soviet military advisers to leave Egypt in 1972. Russia saw an opportunity, offering to become a supplier of air equipment and air defence systems to Egypt, to be paid for by Saudi Arabia and the United Arab Emirates.[63] As of late 2014, a potential $3.5 billion deal was in the making.[64] If this deal went through, the geopolitical situation in the region could change significantly. Russia could even pull its fleet from the Syrian Mediterranean ports to put it in Egyptian ports. This was what occurred in the mid-1950s, with the Russians retaining a dominant position in Egypt until 1972. This may explain why, as already noted, the US Congress resolved in late 2014 to waive the statutory certification requirement by the Department of State that Egypt is in conformity with its international human-rights obligations. The USA was also concerned about the growth of ISIS and saw Egypt as a potential active participant against that violent extremist group.

The European Union and its members, in response to the events in Egypt after 2011, pursued a policy distinct from that of the USA. Together they formed Egypt's largest trading partner. They were perceived as carrying less historical baggage, and throughout the long crisis they could talk to a notably wide variety of Egyptian actors, but their repeated attempts to promote compromise and dialogue failed. They were reluctant to call what happened in July 2013 a coup. Despite proclaiming the importance of inclusiveness and progress towards democracy, European states had two particular reasons to favour stability and security in Egypt. First, there was concern that a different Egyptian government might get into a crisis or war with Israel, forcing European states to take difficult and potentially divisive decisions. Second, there was the worry that, if Egypt itself became the scene of internal conflict, there might be a new flood of refugees, many of whom would head across the Mediterranean to Europe. In any case, threatened or actual reductions of European aid for Egypt had limited effect: Saudi contributions were

---

[63] Ariel Ben Solomon, 'Russia and Egypt Complete $2 Billion Arms Deal Funded by Gulf States', *Jerusalem Post*, 9 February 2014 http://www.jpost.com/Middle-East/Report-Russia-and-Egypt-complete-2-billion-arms-deal-funded-by-Gulf-states-340847.

[64] On 17 September 2014 the head of the Russian Federal Service for Military–Technical Cooperation announced that Russia and Egypt had reached a preliminary deal for Cairo to buy arms worth $3.5 billion from Moscow, Reuters report from Moscow http://uk.reuters.com/article/2014/09/17/uk-russia-egypt-arms-idUKKBN0HC1A320140917.

significantly larger.[65] The EU and its member states were likely to continue supporting Egypt economically and politically.

Saudi Arabia and the Gulf States reacted negatively to the US line adopted in the wake of the coup in Cairo. Already involved in the anti-Islamist effort, which involved propping up Sisi, they increased their support for Egypt. This allowed Egypt not only to receive substantial economic assistance, but also to start reassessing its strategic relations with the USA and its reliance on the USA as its sole military supplier. On 9 December 2014 the Gulf Cooperation Council, which included Saudi Arabia, the Arab Emirates, and Bahrain, announced at its summit meeting in Doha the establishment of a joint military and police cooperation, and also stated that it unanimously supported Sisi and the political road map in Egypt.[66] This announcement indicated a softening of the position of Qatar, the small Gulf state that had been a prominent critic of Sisi's rule in Egypt. The home of Al Jazeera, Qatar had earlier supported the Muslim Brotherhood in Egypt, publicly disagreed with the Sisi regime's treatment of the media, and particularly opposed Egypt's imposition of prison sentences from seven to ten years on three Al Jazeera journalists for simply exercising their reporting rights. Now, following much pressure from its GCC colleagues, it seemed to be relenting; and on 20 December 2014 a Saudi-brokered reconciliation between Qatar and Egypt was formalized.

Another factor that was probably not prominent in the Egyptian military's strategic assessment in 2011, but that subsequently increased in importance, was the persistence of the ongoing struggle in the Sinai between the Second Egyptian army and the group Ansar Bait al-Maqdis. Notwithstanding the fact that Israel allowed an increase in Egyptian troops and military equipment to be deployed in the peninsula, the Egyptian forces faced a tough struggle against their guerrilla opponents. In 2014, on the third anniversary of 25 January 2011, four soldiers were killed and eleven injured. On 26 January 2014 militants shot down an Egyptian military helicopter. On 16 February at least two tourists and an Egyptian driver were killed in a bomb explosion targeting a tourist bus, the first such attack on tourists in more than three years.[67] On 24 October a suspected jihadist car bomb killed at least twenty-six Egyptian soldiers at a checkpoint in North Sinai. Immediately after this attack,

[65] Steven Erlanger, 'European Union Sets Emergency Session on Suspending Aid to Egypt', *New York Times*, 19 August 2013 http://www.nytimes.com/2013/08/20/world/middleeast/european-union-sets-emergency-session-on-suspending-aid-to-egypt.html?pagewanted=all&_r=0.

[66] 'GCC States to Create Regional Police, Navy', *Al Arabiya News* (a Dubai-based and Saudi-owned TV news channel), 9–10 December 2014 http://english.alarabiya.net/en/News/middle-east/2014/12/09/Regional-stability-on-table-as-GCC-summit-kicks-off-.html.

[67] Kareem Fahim and Mayy El Sheikh, 'Bombing of Tourist Bus Kills at Least Three in Sinai', *New York Times*, 16 February 2014 http://www.nytimes.com/2014/02/17/world/middleeast/bus-bombing-kills-tourists-in-sinai-egypt.html. Such events had been anticipated in Bassiouni, *Egypt Update*, nos 24, 25, 26, issued between 31 December 2013 and 12 January 2014.

the Sisi government ordered massive evacuations from the town of Rafah, which borders the Gaza Strip, in the attempt to create a buffer zone to stop the further influx of militants and weapons across the border. While understandable from a military–strategic point of view, these forcible evacuations were likely to increase polarization and radicalization, especially among North Sinai Bedouin. Ansar Bait al-Maqdis, in a statement on 2 November, indicated that the group had sworn allegiance to ISIS, thus further internationalizing the threat Egypt faced in the Sinai.[68]

At the same time, the instability in neighbouring Libya showed that Egypt faced serious trouble on another front. On 19 July 2014 twenty-one Egyptian border guards were killed close to the Libyan border by a group of Islamists believed to have been smuggling weapons into Egypt. In December 2014 twenty-one Egyptians working in Libya were kidnapped, and an Egyptian doctor, his wife, and daughter were killed. In February 2015 a video was released showing the brutal beheading of twenty-one Coptic Egyptian hostages, apparently those kidnapped months earlier. The Egyptian military launched immediate air strikes on targets in Libya in response, the first time it had openly acknowledged intervening in the Libyan conflict. Militant groups proclaiming their affiliation to ISIS appeared responsible for these attacks. In a perverse sense, both the Sinai and Libyan events may have benefited the Egyptian military establishment, which was seen as the nation's defender.

In 2014 the rise of ISIS, and its exercise of control in large parts of Syria and Iraq, reinforced the sense that Egypt faced a geopolitical threat both beyond and inside its borders. In September 2014 Egypt joined the international coalition against ISIS, but did not contribute to military operations in Syria and Iraq because of the military establishment's reluctance to commit troops outside Egypt. This was due to the negative experiences of the Nasser regime.

Geopolitically, Egypt will be seen as a necessary balance to Iran's new influence in the region, especially in the light of a possible conjunction of interest between the USA and Iran. Neither the USA nor Iran realized the deep-seated animosity that the Arab Sunni had for the Shiʿa and especially for Iran. Any conjunction of interest between the USA and Iran could have the unintended effect of unifying the Arab world that may henceforth become the Arab/Muslim/Salafist world. Iran, however, is an old imperial power that knows how to play its cards more wisely than the USA does. It will attempt to find ways to avoid confrontation with the Sunni Muslim Arab world, but respite does not mean stable and enduring coexistence.

The geopolitical factors briefly outlined here will continue to influence events in Egypt, and will provide a basis for external support of the Sisi regime.

---

[68] Shadi Bushra, 'Egypt's Ansar Bayt al-Maqdis Swears Allegiance to ISIS: Statement', Reuters report from Cairo, 4 November 2014 http://english.alarabiya.net/en/News/middle-east/2014/11/04/Egypt-s-Ansar-Bayt-al-Maqdis-swears-allegiance-to-ISIS.html.

While some of the regional support for Sisi was mainly at the political level, some was more substantial. Saudi Arabia will continue to help Egypt financially, as will the US militarily and strategically, particularly if Russia is competing with the US for influence in Egypt and the larger Arab world.

HISTORICAL REFLECTIONS

In Egypt's long history, the demonstration of power—not least by military means—has been an enduring theme. Pharaohs still keep coming, though few of the modern ones have left much, if anything, behind them except a record of abuse and harm. Even though some of them tried, none of these modern pharaohs stood as tall as Rameses II, whose glory still illuminates Egypt's history. Gamal Abdel Nasser was the closest aspirant. He died in 1970 of a heart attack in the aftermath of the infamous 1967 defeat that saw the Sinai lost to Israel. The defeat occurred at the place where in 1274 BC Rameses II defeated the Hittites at the Battle of Kadesh.

Anwar Sadat, who succeeded Nasser, took on the mantle of Rameses II by winning a partial victory in the October 1973 surprise attack across the Suez Canal into the Sinai on Yom Kippur. But the Egyptian foothold was soon overtaken by an Israeli counter-attack that crossed the Suez Canal in the opposite direction, cutting off the Egyptian Third Army from the Second Army. The former found itself encircled from the West and the East. A political settlement orchestrated by Henry Kissinger, then US Secretary of State, saved the situation before the Third Army had to surrender. Nevertheless Egypt has since then celebrated the success of the October War on an annual basis. As years went by, the event reinforced the public belief in Egypt's military supremacy over Israel. However, Sadat himself was assassinated in 1981 at the annual commemoration parade, by a small group of soldiers participating in the parade who were Islamists opposed to his 1979 peace agreement with Israel.

In time, the commemorative parades of 23 October increased in significance. Sisi, then defence minister and chairman of the SCAF, oversaw the parade of October 2013. This fortieth anniversary year was indeed the grandest of all. It included the presence of Nasser's daughter and Sadat's widow. What greater symbolism could there have been to link together the past and the present? But as the parade ended and the crowds faded away, there was nothing left on the ground but emptiness, harshly echoing the silent statues and tombs that dot Egypt's Nile banks.

Unlike Nasser and Sadat, Mubarak did not die in power, but fell from it in disgrace. His mediocrity and support of a corrupt oligarchy drained Egypt not only of its economic strength but also of its social vitality and political life. The successor to that dynasty, Sisi, was believed by many to be a shy and modest person. His honesty and integrity were well recognized. His effort to rebuild confidence within the Coptic community was well received. His emphasis on Egyptianhood was an important contrast to the Islamists' positions. He would surely rule as president with the same decisiveness and strong hand that he had displayed since 30 June 2013, and, for that matter, since 25 January 2011, when he was head of Military Intelligence. His picture hung in homes and public places along with some resurrected pictures of Nasser that had disappeared during the Sadat and Mubarak eras. The symbolism was uncanny. Both Nasser and Sisi appealed to the dignity of Egyptians, something so dear to those who have no more than a dream of regaining dignity, clinging to the illusion that by some miracle another military dictatorship will restore it. Alas, this was not likely to be the case, as Egypt had already started its slow descent into the quicksand of exponential demographic growth and economic decline. The Sisi regime continued a policy of unrelenting repression, as seen in the violent response to student demonstrations in October 2014.[69] Harsh sentences and unfounded convictions remained in place, and both judges and prosecutors were still politicized. An effective media campaign continued to present Sisi as the new, entitled pharaoh.

What it would take to pull the nation out of this situation was hard to foresee. There was nothing to indicate that those in power had made an assessment of the situation and what was needed to stop the decline. Without a plan, it was difficult to see how things could change. But then, as the late Sadat once told me at his home in Mit Abu al-Kum in 1974, 'Egypt has survived for 7,000 years, and will live for a long time to come.' The implication was that Egypt will go on surviving because of its people's resilience. Egyptians are indeed resourceful, imaginative, and adaptable. Whether these traits would be sufficient to overcome the present and future challenges was the question no one could yet answer. But hope springs eternal, and Egyptians are by temperament hopeful and optimistic. One example of this was the response when the Museum of Islamic Art and the National Archives was damaged by one of the car bombs detonated in Cairo on 24 January 2014. The bomb, meant to target the police building across the street, severely damaged these depositories of history. Irreplaceable artefacts from Islam's Golden Age as well as invaluable papyrus scrolls were lost. In the face of this great loss, however, Egyptians displayed their customary resolve. Volunteers rushed to the blast site, financial aid was promptly sought, and restoration of the facilities began without delay.[70]

---

[69] David D. Kirkpatrick, 'Crackdown on Student Protesters in Egypt', *New York Times*, 13 October 2014 http://www.nytimes.com/2014/10/14/world/middleeast/egypt-cracks-down-on-new-student-protests-arresting-scores.html.

[70] Sarah Gauch, 'Triage for Treasures after a Bomb Blast', *New York Times*, 31 January 2014 http://mobile.nytimes.com/2014/02/01/arts/design/sorting-through-the-rubble-of-museum-of-islamic-art-in-cairo.html?from=arts.music.

CONCLUSION

What has to be described as a glorious revolutionary effort was marginalized within just three years. Few who participated in the movement or witnessed it would ever forget the sense of freedom and empowerment as they succeeded in bringing down Mubarak in a matter of weeks. Maybe there was a parallel here. After the 1919 revolution it took time for Egypt to become an independent state and to be freed from British colonial occupation. That revolutionary spirit was rekindled on 25 January 2011. Of course the movement was not all equally revolutionary: some in the January 25 Movement wanted to change the regime, whereas others wanted only reforms. Even though the movement did not succeed in bringing about democracy, freedom, and the rule of law, it was neither in vain nor was it finished.

Are there any lessons that any future democracy movement in Egypt, and Egyptian society more generally, might learn from the failure to achieve the changes for which the civil resistance movement struggled? Ten such lessons emerge.

(1) While a mass movement may naturally have to focus on a central demand on which all can agree—and that may sometimes involve calling for the departure of a particular ruler—such a demand is problematic if there is no shared vision of a future constitutional framework. Such a shared vision was lacking. There was no clarity about the post-Mubarak political system nor any realistic assessment of the likely emergence of an elected dictatorship under Muslim Brotherhood rule. The demand for Morsi's departure, a mere twelve months after his election, was problematic in so far as it involved rejecting the decision of the voters a year earlier, and was thus extra-constitutional and resulted in a return to army rule.

(2) To focus on certain limited and intermediate goals—such as an end to torture, the right to demonstrate, the freedom of the media—might provide the possibility of attainable objectives that themselves could point the way to further legal and constitutional developments.

(3) A movement must have a leadership cadre. As was evident in some of the east European revolutions of 1989, such leadership structures can play a particularly important and constructive role in transitions towards democracy. They can help to set the terms of national debate, and also to negotiate a 'pacted transition'—a formal agreement to a changed constitutional system. Such pacted transitions are in principle more likely than unpacted ones to be peaceful. In Egypt, the pro-democracy movement had neither leadership nor a policy of the kind that would have been appropriate to guide it through the negotiations and compromises necessary in such a transitional period.

(4) Because of the 2013 law curtailing freedom of assembly, new forms of action different from the demonstrations in Tahrir Square and other similar locations that were at the heart of the events of January–February 2011 need to be developed. Civil resistance can assume a wide range of forms, many of which may be legal and constitutional in character.

(5) For at least sixty years, political and social development in Egypt has been hampered by what might be called a repression–radicalization dynamic, whereby state repression hastens the emergence of new cadres of youth who oppose the state and are willing to take up arms against it. To get beyond this dynamic requires fundamental changes in how the state is organized and responds to popular demands for political and social change. That is, of course, what democracy is supposed to achieve.

(6) Above all, both civil resistance and the process of constitutional democratic change require a degree of mutual understanding, tolerance, and respect on the part of the different political, social, and religious groups in society. This was in short supply. Perhaps the most serious problem was the lack of mutual respect between the two main political actors: the military establishment referred to the Muslim Brotherhood as terrorists; and, for its part, the Brotherhood accused the military of having seized power in an illegal *coup d'état*. That level of distrust, which has sadly been made worse by the events of 2011–14, would need to be tackled if Egypt was to have a chance of responding to the demand for a transformed political order that was so memorably exemplified in Tahrir Square in 2011.

(7) Egyptian society is in dire need of modern reconstitution. Sixty years of oppression and exploitation have shredded any social contract that may have once existed. No country can be reconstituted after crisis without a cohesive society. And that cannot be built on polarization; only national reconciliation will do.

(8) Egypt's new identity, if it can acquire it, will shape its new path towards economic, social, and political development. Without it, Egypt's short window of opportunity will soon close. Its population of 85 million will reach 100 million in a decade. Already every economic and social indicator is under severe stress.

(9) The inability to stabilize the country's ongoing economic crisis, let alone to relaunch the economy to meet the needs of the next ten years, may well usher Egypt into the category of a failing or failed state.

(10) Economic failure in this time period, with the posited demographic increase, is likely to produce a resurgence not of pro-democracy

forces, but of Islamist ones that may or may not be linked to the Muslim Brotherhood. The latter are certainly biding their time for a political comeback. If and when that occurs, violence is likely to be among its means of securing power and remaining in power.

If Egypt's peaceful transformation towards economic, social, and political development does not take place, then violent revolution remains a risk—unless the country falls into the category of a failed state, lacking the energy to produce even a violent revolution.

Revolutions are often characterized by chaos and violence. Public and private abuses take place: much harm and many wrongs occur in the name of a revolution. Truth and justice are distorted, and human beings suffer the consequences. History teaches us that it takes many convulsions after a revolution for a nation in turmoil to settle down along a path that aspires to democracy, freedom, justice, and human dignity. The pace depends on how fast a system of rule of law can be established to sustain institutions of government that have the capacity to achieve these goals. Egypt is no different, as it now goes through a transitional post-revolutionary phase. The 2011 'revolution', like many others in history, started with idealistic people of all walks of life motivated by the principles of democracy, freedom, justice, and human dignity. They, like their many other predecessors throughout history, sought political, social, and economic justice after decades of tyranny, repression, and exploitation. The demand for change will continue in Egypt, and may be strengthened by the five-million-strong expatriate population, who produce a major source of income for the country, and are aware of conditions elsewhere. The question that many Egyptians ask is whether the changes brought about by the presidential elections of May 2014 and the legislative elections scheduled for 2015 are likely to be steps in the direction of democratic change, or whether they will prove to have been merely cosmetic. No one can predict the future, but many careful observers can evaluate the past to project the likely shape of the future. Among history's many lessons is that a people's social culture and historic response to crises are far more telling than any other tangible factor. Victories are more often snapped from the jaws of defeat by determined and courageous people rather than by the empty oratory of pompous leaders.[71]

---

[71] Parts of this chapter draw on M. Cherif Bassiouni, *Egypt Update*, a series of analyses of the ongoing situation issued between 7 February 2011 (Background Paper) and 13 August 2014 (Final Message) http://mcherifbassiouni.com/egypt-updates/.

4

Revolution and Counter-Revolution in Bahrain

Elham Fakhro

Inspired by popular revolutions in Egypt and Tunisia, online activists declared 14 February 2011 a 'day of rage' and called for protests to take place across Bahrain, an island state with a population of 1.2 million off the eastern coast of Saudi Arabia. Crowds gathered in villages across the country calling for greater popular representation, constitutional reform, and an end to corruption. Security forces confronted protesters and shot dead a young demonstrator. Thousands attended his funeral the following day, which culminated in a sit-in at a central junction, the Pearl Roundabout. Security forces killed a second protester that day, prompting a larger turnout at the roundabout the next day. This series of events marked the beginning of a month-long uprising in which Bahrain's political parties, labour unions, and anonymous online activists joined the mass mobilization of tens of thousands of people calling for political reforms. Caught off guard, loyalist groups reacted to events by mobilizing similar numbers in a series of parallel counter-demonstrations.

Faced with growing protests, Bahrain's Crown Prince invited representatives from Bahrain's opposition political societies to engage in a national dialogue. The political societies, empowered by a rise in populist activism and simultaneously wary of losing this support to radical fringe groups, responded to the invitation by demanding reforms and preconditions to dialogue, including the resignation of the government. As the negotiation process stalled, pro- and anti-government vigilante groups began to exercise a growing presence across the country. State-run media began branding anti-government protesters, as foreign agents engaged in a conspiracy to impose an Iranian-style theocracy in the country. The government announced a state of national safety (akin to a national emergency, except that constitutional provisions remained in force), on 14 March 2011, inviting Gulf Cooperation Council (GCC) Peninsula Shield Force troops to enter the country to 'assist the Bahraini armed services in the defence of the Kingdom of Bahrain against foreign threats and in securing vital locations in the country'.[1] The first units from the Saudi Arabian Royal Guard entered Bahrain that evening, bringing a symbolic end to the mass uprising and ending prospects for an immediate negotiated solution between the Crown Prince and opposition groups.[2]

As of early 2015, Bahrain's political scene remains in flux. A long-awaited national dialogue between pro-government and opposition groups began in February 2013 and was officially suspended by the government nearly one year later. The suspension followed the withdrawal of opposition groups from the dialogue in September 2013, in protest against the arrest of an opposition leader that same month. The detention of Ali Salman, the head of the largest opposition society, in December 2014 on charges of 'inciting hatred and spreading false news' dampened hopes for the revival of any dialogue process.[3] Other opposition political leaders and human-rights activists remain imprisoned, and there is little evidence of accountability for officials implicated in the torture and deaths of detainees, one of the key recommendations made by an independent commission of inquiry established by King Hamad and tasked to investigate events surrounding the uprising. Political power has shifted towards radicalized elements on both ends of the political spectrum, including towards an increasingly violent street movement that calls for the downfall of the regime. The appointment of Bahrain's Crown Prince as deputy prime minister in March 2013 indicated a renewed consolidation of the power of centrist actors within the government, but the future direction of the country remains far from certain.

This chapter will first outline the events of early 2011, which attracted much attention internationally. Then there are summaries of the background to these events; the security crackdown especially after 14–15 March; the role of social media; the continuation of protests; and the fate of proposals for dialogue and reform. Finally, some questions are raised. Can the movement be considered a failure? To the extent that this was so, were the setbacks due to the divided nature of Bahraini society, to the movement making demands that were an uncomfortable mix of reformist and revolutionary, to the particular methods used by supporters of the movement, or to power-political considerations, including those relating to two particularly influential powers in this case, Saudi Arabia and the United States?

---

[1] Bahrain Independent Commission of Inquiry (BICI), *Report of the Bahrain Independent Commission of Inquiry* (Manama: BICI, final revision dated 10 December 2011), 385 www.bici.org.bh.

[2] The total number of troops deployed by the GCC-JSF in Bahrain was approximately 5,000. This included land and naval combat units, command and control units, and support personnel of various specializations. BICI, *Report*, 386.

[3] 'Bahrain Main Opposition Leader on Trial for Plotting Coup', *Guardian*, London, 28 January 2015 http://www.theguardian.com/world/2015/jan/28/bahrain-main-opposition-leader-trial-plotting-coup.

EVENTS OF LATE FEBRUARY AND
EARLY MARCH 2011

Following the funeral of teenager Ali Mushaima on the afternoon of 15 February, thousands of mourners poured into the Pearl Roundabout. By the evening, the number of mourners-turned-protesters reached several thousand, with dozens erecting tents and camping in the area overnight. Mimicking the occupation of Tahrir Square in Cairo, the roundabout functioned as an open platform for protesters to express their grievances, which ranged from demands for constitutional reform and greater economic opportunity to calls for the downfall of the regime.

A coalition of seven Islamist and leftist opposition political societies, including the largest Shi'a Islamist society al-Wefaq, immediately announced its support for the demonstrations. The sit-in continued for two days, with tens of thousands visiting the roundabout. Political societies and professional associations, such as the Bahrain Lawyers' Society, also set up tents in the area serving tea and coffee and inviting bystanders to attend political lectures.

Security forces raided the roundabout at 3 a.m. on 17 February, clearing the area of all tents and killing three civilians. Military armoured vehicles closed off the area to demonstrators. Later that morning, crowds flocked to Salmaniya Medical Complex, the country's main hospital, where approximately 2,500 people joined medical staff in protesting against the attack, amid unverified rumours that the hospital's administration had prevented ambulances from recovering injured people at the roundabout.

That same day, parliamentarians from the country's largest opposition bloc, al-Wefaq, announced their collective resignation from parliament in protest at the killings. In view of the attack on the roundabout, the February 14th Youth, an anonymous online group, which had called for the initial protests, escalated its demands from the creation of a constitutional monarchy to the downfall of the regime.[4] The General Federation of Bahrain Trade Unions (GFBTU) issued a call for a general strike on 20 February in protest against 'the extremely brutal attack by the army and police against the demonstrators peacefully gathered at the Pearl Roundabout'. The GFBTU was, at the time, the sole umbrella organization for all of Bahrain's officially sanctioned unions, representing more than 70 unions and 33,000 workers from the public and private sectors.

Faced with an escalating political crisis, Crown Prince Salman bin Hamad Al-Khalifa appeared on national television calling for calm and inviting the opposition to enter into a national dialogue. As a gesture of goodwill, he

---

[4] 'February 14 Youths Media', 17 February 2011 https://ar-ar.facebook.com/14FebruaryYouthsMedia.

promised the withdrawal of troops from the roundabout and reopened the area to protesters. He also announced that his father, King Hamad, had authorized him to head a national dialogue, and invited opposition parties to participate.

On 20 February the GFBTU went ahead with its planned strike, which gained the support of numerous professional associations, including the Gulf Air, Bapco (Bahrain Petroleum Company), and Alba (Aluminium Bahrain) trade unions.[5] Other professional organizations also adopted their own strike calls. The Bahrain Teachers' Society, for example, issued a statement calling on teachers to strike in front of their schools to demand accountability for the deaths of five protesters, some of whom were students. On 20 February, according to official records, an estimated 80 per cent of the total workforce stayed away from work. The mass absence came as a result of both the support of tens of thousands of workers for the call to strike, and the closure of key roads and highways by protesters, which prevented others from accessing their workplaces. The GFBTU announced the suspension of its strike one day later. The Teachers' Society continued its strike for an additional three days, until 24 February. By the end of the strike, the Ministry of Education had begun to hire new teachers to replace striking teachers, and a number of them were subsequently hired as permanent replacements.

The following day, on 21 February, Sunni cleric Abdul Latif al-Mahmoud headed a counter-demonstration under the banner of 'national unity and reform' outside al-Fateh mosque, in the centre of the capital Manama.[6] After leading a prayer, al-Mahmoud announced the establishment of the 'National Unity Gathering', which he described as an independent platform for people from all political and sectarian backgrounds. Al-Mahmoud adopted a conciliatory tone, affirming the legitimacy of the existing regime and the unity of all Bahrainis from both Shi'a and Sunni sects. He also called on the government to implement many of the same demands made by the political opposition, including the removal of all forms of ethnic and sectarian discrimination and an end to the misappropriation of wealth. Official estimates placed the number of attendees at 300,000, while others put it at 50,000 (see Figure 4.1).

Protests and counter-protests continued into the following weeks. On 22 February the opposition organized a 'martyrs' march', in honour of six protesters killed by security forces. Crowds at the protest swelled to 100,000–150,000 people. That evening, King Hamad pardoned 308 people

---

[5] 'Bahrain Trade Union Calls Strike from Sunday', Reuters, 19 February 2011 http://www.reuters.com/article/2011/02/19/us-bahrain-strike-idUSTRE71I1IX20110219. See also 'Trade Unions Call for Strike', *Gulf Daily News*, Manama, 20 February 2011 http://www.gulf-daily-news.com/NewsDetails.aspx?storyid=300036.

[6] Justin Gengler, 'Bahrain's Sunni Awakening', Middle East Research and Information Project, 17 January 2012 www.merip.org/mero/mero011712.

Figure 4.1. As anti-government strikes and protests spread in Bahrain in early 2011 there were some rival events on the streets. On 21 February thousands gathered in support of the royal family for a counter-demonstration in favour of 'national unity and reform' outside the al-Fateh mosque in central Manama.

© *John Moore/Getty Images*

convicted of state security crimes, including a number of exiled political figures. He subsequently announced a limited political reshuffle, replacing four cabinet ministers who were unpopular with the opposition.

In the following weeks, a series of pivotal steps shaped the direction of events on the ground and prospects for a negotiated solution. The first was the return of exiled politician Hassan Mushaima to Bahrain on 26 February.[7] A former member of al-Wefaq, Mushaima had broken with the society in 2006 following its decision to reverse its boycott of parliamentary elections—a boycott initiated in protest against the 2002 constitution. Along with other former members of al-Wefaq and a leftist group, the National Democratic Action Society (Waad), Mushaima established the al-Haq Movement for Liberty and Democracy, a radical new splinter group, which announced it would operate outside the system and mobilize the power of the street through mass rallies and civil disobedience as a means of pressurizing the regime to reform.

Following his return to Bahrain, Mushaima and representatives from two smaller organizations announced the establishment of a 'coalition for the

---

[7] 'Bahrain Unrest: Shi'a Dissident Hassan Mushaima Returns', *BBC News*, 26 February 2011 www.bbc.co.uk/news/world-middle-east-12587902.

republic' on 7 March, openly declaring their aim to topple Bahrain's monarchy and establish a republic in its place. Mushaima's call for the downfall of the regime largely reflected existing calls voiced by the February 14 Movement, which had begun demanding an end to Al-Khalifa rule following the raid on the roundabout.[8] Mushaima declared that this could be achieved through mass civil disobedience and resistance. His announcement caused a further rift within the opposition leadership, which had thus far united around a series of political demands as the basis for a political settlement with the government.[9] The call for a republic heightened anxiety among the loyalist community that the protest movement was adopting radical positions and seeking to impose an Iranian-style republic in Bahrain.[10]

Also significant was the second demonstration organized by the National Unity Gathering on 3 March. At this gathering, al-Mahmoud adopted an increasingly pro-government stance by affirming the legitimacy of the existing leadership and calling for those who disrupted public services by going on strike to be held accountable.

Representatives of the Crown Prince continued to meet the opposition, who demanded the implementation of several reforms, including the resignation of the government and constitutional reform as preconditions to dialogue.

As political leaders consolidated their positions, the direction of grass-roots protests and demonstrations also continued to evolve, with hundreds of protests taking place in areas of symbolic significance. On 27 February protesters formed a human chain around the Bahrain National Assembly, calling for the resignation of the government. On the same day, approximately 200 vehicles parked on a central highway, shutting down traffic. On 4 March more than 10,000 people protested outside the Information Affairs Authority, condemning its one-sided coverage of events in the country and blaming state-owned media for 'inciting sectarianism and civil discord'.[11] That day, tens of thousands also protested outside the Council of Ministers, calling for the resignation of the cabinet. Deliberately seeking to challenge accusations that the movement was sectarian, on 5 March protesters also formed a human chain between al-Fateh mosque and the Pearl Roundabout, the respective sites of the pro-regime and anti-regime demonstrations, emphasizing the unity of the Bahraini people. On 6 March more than 10,000 demonstrators gathered outside one of the king's palaces, demanding the resignation of the prime

---

[8] Toby C. Jones, 'Bahrain's Revolutionaries Speak: An Exclusive Interview with Bahrain's Coalition of February 14th Youth', *Jadaliyya*, 22 March 2012 http://www.jadaliyya.com/pages/index/4777/bahrains-revolutionaries-speak_an-exclusive-interv.

[9] National Democratic Action Society, 'The Roadmap for the Constitutional Exit from the Political Crisis', Manama, 1 March 2011.

[10] BICI, *Report*, 164, 383–4.

[11] Gregg Carlstrom, 'Bahrain Youth March on State TV', Al Jazeera, 4 March 2011 www.aljazeera.com/news/middleeast/2011/03/201134183528970309.

minister and the cabinet. In one of the most symbolic acts of defiance, hundreds of demonstrators marched from the Pearl Roundabout to the site of a billion-dollar financial development, the Bahrain Financial Harbour, on 7 March, brandishing one-dinar notes. The march followed the release of documents days earlier by the secretary-general of al-Wefaq, which purportedly showed the transfer of public land, on which the Bahrain Financial Harbour was built, to the prime minister for just one dinar ($2.67). The march symbolized popular outrage at corruption and nepotism, particularly in land developments.[12] As protesters began to camp out at the Bahrain Financial Harbour, a small flotilla of thirty fishing vessels sailed from a harbour in the north of the country, as a sign of support for demonstrators there.

Labour activists and students also played a role in spearheading demonstrations. On 27 and 28 February groups of several hundred high school and university students left their places of education and joined protests in various parts of the country. On 1 March 800 students protested outside the Ministry of Education, calling for the removal of the minister. A similar protest was held on 3 March, when more than 2,000 students and teachers gathered outside the ministry to protest against deteriorating education standards. That week, a group of professional athletes marched to the Pearl Roundabout in solidarity with protesters, calling for the resignation of the prime minister. Similar protests were organized by professional organizations including teachers, engineers, and lawyers.

Rifts began to emerge around the direction of the protests themselves. On 11 March SMS text messages began to circulate, inviting demonstrators to march to the royal palace in Riffa, an area populated by many members of the ruling family and the heartland of political power. The political opposition societies urged people not to take part in this demonstration, calling on them instead to attend a demonstration in the capital, Manama, which called for the abrogation of the constitution. The Ministry of Interior declared the planned march to Riffa 'an act that threatens security and civil peace'.

On the afternoon of 11 March the two protests took place in parallel. As protesters marched through Manama without incident, riot police erected a barbed wire fence across an empty plot of land leading up to Riffa, preventing groups of hundreds of demonstrators from accessing the area. Several hundred metres away, on the opposite side of the fence, plain-clothes men brandishing batons and sticks had also gathered, promising to defend Riffa from the demonstrators. Independent monitors present at the protest claim to have received reports indicating tacit cooperation between members of the security forces and plain-clothes armed men. According to one monitor, a civilian present in Riffa ahead of the protests claimed to have been dragged out of his car by armed men, and beaten on the floor. After escaping the scene, the civilian

---

[12] Simeon Kerr and Robin Wigglesworth, 'Protesters Draw Bahrain Closer to a Reckoning', *Financial Times*, London, 7 March 2011.

claimed that he gave information about the incident to the police, who advised him to leave the area and who did not take steps to ask who had attacked him or clear the area of such groups. According to the source, the police also made no effort to prevent these groups from hurling rocks at demonstrators gathered on the opposite side of the fence.[13] The demonstration was eventually dispersed after police fired tear gas and rubber bullets at protesters to clear the area.

By mid-March, the rise in popular activism had also begun to mark a corresponding rise in sectarian and vigilante violence. The first reported incidents of sectarian violence broke out on 3 March, between a group of Shi'a students and a group of teenagers from naturalized Sunni families. On 10 March clashes between pro- and anti-government students again broke out at a girls' school, leaving eight students injured. By 12 March a general deteriorating security situation led to the outbreak of numerous acts of vandalism and the erection of civilian checkpoints across various parts of the country. On 13 March residents of a middle-class residential neighbourhood in Manama, Um al-Hassam, reported that unidentified groups brandishing knives and wooden planks were roaming the streets, attacking vehicles and destroying public property.[14] Attacks on private property and commercial establishments continued into the following days, as did attacks against expatriate workers of South Asian origin, who occupy many lower positions in the security agencies.

On 13 March the Crown Prince issued a statement offering 'seven principles' as the basis for a national dialogue: a parliament with full authority, a more representative form of government, a discussion of political naturalization (referring to the reported practice by the government of offering expedited citizenship to foreigners from Sunni backgrounds aimed at diluting the power of the Shi'a population), fair voting districts, and efforts to address problems of corruption, sectarian tension, and appropriation of state property (a reference to illegal practices by high-level government officials of appropriating, and selling off, public coastal lands to private investors). However, at a meeting held that day between Ali Salman, the head of al-Wefaq, and representatives of the Crown Prince, Salman said the solution to the crisis should be the election of a Constituent Assembly to draft a new constitution, without the need for dialogue. Salman's rejection of the Crown Prince's invitation to dialogue marked the end of the phase of negotiations between the government and the opposition, signalling the advent of a security crackdown against opposition leaders and their supporters. On the same day, following a blockade of a central highway by demonstrators, members of the Council of Representatives issued a statement calling on King Hamad to deploy the

---

[13] Author interview, 19 February 2013.   [14] BICI, *Report*, 126.

Figure 4.2. Before the crackdown. Thousands of protesters gathered at the Pearl Roundabout in Manama on 14 March 2011, the same day that GCC troops began entering Bahrain.

Figure 4.3. After the crackdown. The regime entirely demolished the Pearl Roundabout. Here on 29 March 2011 work was underway to convert it into a traffic junction.

Bahrain Defence Force to restore order in the country. The GFBTU announced a general strike for 14–23 March, citing growing incidents of assaults on workers at civilian and military checkpoints, and called on the government and political societies to reach an immediate agreement.

On 14 March the first units from the GCC Jazeera Shield Force, consisting of hundreds of Saudi troops, arrived in Bahrain. That day, security forces killed two civilians in a sweep of the island of Sitra, a hotbed of opposition support. One police officer was killed after being run over by a private vehicle during clashes between police and opposition supporters on the island.

On 15 March King Hamad issued Royal Decree No. 18 of 2011, declaring a three-month 'state of national safety'. That evening, the USA dispatched Assistant Secretary for Near-Eastern Affairs Jeffrey Feltman to examine the potential for an agreement between the two sides. On 16 March six civilians died of shotgun wounds. The following day, security forces arrested many prominent political leaders, including Ibrahim Sharif, Hassan Mushaima, and Abdulhadi Khawaja, in a series of violent pre-dawn raids on their homes. Then on 18 March security forces tore down the Pearl monument and demolished the Pearl Roundabout, the symbolic heart of the movement (see Figures 4.2 and 4.3).

THE LEAD-UP TO THE PROTESTS: BAHRAIN'S POLITICAL SCENE

Bahrain was conquered by a group of Arab tribes, led by the Al-Khalifa, in 1783. In conquering the island, the Al-Khalifa drove out the Al-Madhkur, who had loosely governed Bahrain as a dependency of the Persian Empire. In 1861 Bahrain became party to the Perpetual Treaty of Peace, whereby the Emir pledged to abstain from the 'prosecution of war, piracy, and slavery at sea' in exchange for British protection. The exclusive agreements of 1880 and 1892 secured Bahrain's status as a protectorate, with the ruler agreeing to let Britain control foreign relations and defence, and to accept British 'advice' on issues of succession, customs, and port facilities.[15] In reality, British influence extended well beyond these matters. This system lasted until official British withdrawal from Bahrain in 1971—foreign powers exercising rule over the country being an enduring theme in its history. There is a long history of Iranian claims to Bahrain: an informal consultation held in 1970 by an envoy

---

[15] Fuad Khuri, *Tribe and State in Bahrain: The Transformation of Social and Political Authority in an Arab State* (Chicago: University of Chicago Press, 1980), 24 and 86.

of the UN Secretary-General signalled the desire of many Bahrainis not to become part of Iran. This did not entirely eradicate fears that Bahrain might be nonetheless subject to pressure from its larger neighbour.

Bahrain is diverse in its ethnic and sectarian composition. Its population includes communities of Sunni Arabs who migrated to Bahrain from the Arabian Peninsula, some who played a role in the initial conquest alongside the Al-Khalifa, and Sunni Arabs originating from the Eastern shores of the Gulf (Hawala). It also includes a population of indigenous Shi'a Arabs, traditionally farmers (Baharna), and Shi'a of Persian origin (Ajam). There are no official records of Bahrain's sectarian distribution, but estimates place the percentage of Shi'a at 55–65 per cent, and the corresponding percentage of Sunnis at 35–45 per cent.

Sectarian and tribal politics have historically played an important role as determinants of resource distribution and political power in Bahrain. While political allegiances have often therefore emerged along sectarian lines, ideological tides in the broader Middle East have been equally significant in framing and driving local movements in Bahrain. The rise of early tides of Arab nationalism in the 1930s and 1950s, for example, fuelled the corresponding rise of leftist nationalist politics in Bahrain.

Following independence in 1971, Bahrain's Emir held elections for a committee to draft the country's first constitution, and elections for its first parliament. The experiment in constitutional rule proved short-lived after the parliament had exercised its authority to question Emiri powers, prompting the ruler to suspend the constitution and declare a state of emergency that lasted between 1975 and 2000. Transnational political currents deeply influenced the form and character of political movements during this period. The strengthening of regional Shi'a Islamist politics following the 1979 Iranian revolution led to the emergence of underground radical Shi'a Islamist groups that attempted to overthrow the regime. Sunni Islamist currents, with ties to the Muslim Brotherhood and Salafists, also grew increasingly popular among the country's Sunnis. Sectarian politics grew particularly dominant in the aftermath of the Iraq invasion of 2003, a reflection of broader trends in the Arab world. Perhaps unsurprisingly, the Arab Spring in 2011 re-energized existing calls for change frequently made by Bahrain's own political opposition.

The most recent chapter in Bahrain's political history began a decade prior to the Arab Spring, with the promulgation in 2001 of a document titled the National Action Charter, by the current king, Hamad bin Isa Al-Khalifa. The document promised to end twenty-five years of national emergency and to reinstate the country's constitution and elected parliament. When put to a referendum, the National Action Charter gained the approval of 98.4 per cent of voting citizens and an outpouring of support for the king.

Instead of reinstating Bahrain's constitution as promised, the king imposed a new constitution, which was written behind closed doors and whose parameters were different from the 1973 constitution that had been approved through popular consultation. Key changes included replacing the country's unicameral parliament with a bicameral legislature in which an upper chamber, appointed by the king, shared equal law-making powers with a lower, popularly elected chamber. Oversight of government spending was delegated to the Royal Court, a body under the direct authority of the king. New electoral districts were also drawn up along sectarian lines, providing voters in Sunni-majority areas with relatively greater representation than their counterparts in larger Shi'a-dominated districts. Media restrictions were loosened. A sweeping amnesty law provided immunity for government officials implicated in abuses and for opposition figures in exile and in detention, who had been accused by the government of security-related crimes.

Although political parties remained banned, new political societies, mainly led by established political figures, began to form in the wake of these reforms. These included populist bloc al-Wefaq, a society headed by Shi'a cleric Ali Salman. The society derives its spiritual leadership from Sheikh Isa Qassim, a Qom-educated cleric. The religious clout of Qassim coupled with the youthful charisma of Salman have earned the society tens of thousands of primarily Shi'a supporters since its establishment in 2001, and it remains among the most influential political forces in the country.

Other organizations were created out of the remnants of formerly revolutionary and underground movements. These included al-Amal Islamic Society, a Shi'a-Islamist bloc whose leadership includes former leaders of the Islamist Front for the Liberation of Bahrain, a militant organization that launched a failed coup in Bahrain in 1981, attempting to install Iraqi Ayatollah Hadi al-Modarresi as the spiritual leader of a theocratic state. It enjoys a small base of supporters, mainly followers of the late Islamic philosopher Ayatollah Mohammed Hussein Shirazi, who are referred to as 'Shirazis'. Al-Amal holds an uneasy relationship with al-Wefaq, which al-Amal accuses of attempting to marginalize it. Its licence was briefly suspended in 2005 after it had organized a rally celebrating those imprisoned by the government for their involvement in the attempted coup.

New leftist societies also developed from former revolutionary movements. These include the National Democratic Action Society (Waad), a leftist group founded in 2001 by former leaders of the Popular Front for the Liberation of Bahrain (PFLB), a national offshoot of the broader Arab nationalist movement, which, in the late 1960s, advocated armed struggle as a means of overthrowing sheikhdoms in Oman, Bahrain, and the Trucial States. Waad was founded and headed by Abdulrahman al-Noaimi, a Sunni from an influential merchant family. Following his death in 2010, former banker Ibrahim Sharif assumed leadership of the society. A second leftist society, al-Menbar Progressive Democratic Tribune (al-Menbar Progressive), was founded in 2001 by former leaders of the National Liberation Front, a former communist movement set up in 1955 with ties to the Iranian Tudeh Party and the Communist Party of Iraq. Together with al-Wefaq and other smaller blocs, these opposition societies formed a coalition that united around the need for deeper political reforms through the reinstatement of Bahrain's 1973 constitution.

Abdulhadi al-Khawaja, a leader of the Islamic Front for the Liberation of Bahrain during the 1980s, also returned from exile in 2001 to form the Bahrain Center for Human Rights, a new organization that adopted the discourse of human rights to question the legitimacy of the ruling regime, and highlight government corruption and abuses. Authorities arrested al-Khawaja in 2009, accusing him of giving sectarian legitimacy to the potentially violent over-throw of the government, after he had given a speech during the Shi'a religious mourning of Ashura titled: 'Let's bring down the ruling gang.' The speech connected the political struggle of Bahrain's Shi'a to events during the Umay-yad Dynasty in the seventh century CE, when Imam Hussain, whose death is commemorated at Ashura, was killed.[16] The authorities released al-Khawaja months later, following a royal pardon by the king. A cable released by Wikileaks cited a prominent Shi'a newspaper editor as having described al-Khawaja as '(an opportunist) having no interest in democratic reform', and his strategies as designed specifically to 'provoke the government into aggressive responses' in order to achieve political aims.[17]

Also in 2001, Sunni leaders formed a number of Sunni political blocs, including al-Menbar Islamic Society, a bloc with ties to the Egyptian Muslim Brotherhood movement, and al-Asala Islamic Society, a Salafist organization.

The first and second rounds of parliamentary elections in 2002 and 2006 consolidated the various positions of Bahrain's political societies. The majority of the new opposition societies boycotted the first round of elections, in protest against the new constitution, which they viewed as illegitimate. A decision by these societies to reverse this boycott in 2006 led to a split within their ranks and the formation of a new, rejectionist society, al-Haq Movement for Liberty and Democracy. The new movement was headed by Hassan Mushaima, and included former members of al-Wefaq and Waad from both sects. During these rounds, Sunni Islamists largely avoided confronting the regime on political terms, but engaged in several campaigns to challenge its social policy, perceiving it as too liberal and Western.

A number of scandals rocked the precarious political balance. The most damaging of these took place in 2006, when a former consultant at the Cabinet Affairs Ministry, Dr Salah al-Bandar, leaked a trove of documents implicating top officials in a plot to forge the upcoming election results. The report

---

[16] Cecily Hilleary, 'Bahrain, Who is the Real Abdulhadi al-Khawaja?', *Middle East Voices*, 6 June 2012 http://middleeastvoices.voanews.com/2012/06/bahrain-who-is-the-real-abdulhadi-al-khawaja-41136.

[17] Confidential message of US Ambassador William T. Monroe, 'Reform in Bahrain: Leading Shia Editor Highlights the Challenges', 29 June 2005, released in 2010–11 by Wikileaks https://wikileaks.org/cable/2005/06/05MANAMA922.html.

provided details of a plan, spearheaded by the head of Bahrain's Central Informatics Organization, to change the country's demographic balance by naturalizing tens of thousands of Sunnis from neighbouring states including Pakistan, Jordan, and Yemen. According to al-Bandar, the Central Informatics Organization paid five main operatives a total of more than $2.7 million to run secret intelligence cells to spy on prominent Shi'a figures, and also to run Internet forums that fomented sectarian hatred. He also reportedly paid operatives to subsidize 'new converts' from Shi'a to Sunni Islam. News of the report contributed to an existing sense of marginalization among the country's Shi'a, who are under-represented in its security agencies. It also fuelled similar anger among sections of the Sunni population, who opposed political naturalization as a threat to the country's national and Arab identity.

Relations between the government and the political opposition grew increasingly strained following the arrest of 250 Shi'a citizens in 2010 on accusations of plotting to overthrow the government. Issues of voting irregularity came to the fore that year, following allegations by Ali Salman that at least 890 voters in Shi'a districts had been prevented from casting their ballot. Moreover, opposition societies also criticized the government's creation of general polling stations, which were polling booths set up outside normal voting districts and outside the framework of regular oversight, for allowing swathes of newly naturalized citizens to participate illegally in the elections. Indeed, the two candidates fielded by Waad won the elections in their districts but lost as a result of votes cast in the general polling stations. During this round of elections, as previously, voting patterns largely reflected existing sectarian demographic distributions, with al-Wefaq gaining nineteen out of a total of forty seats. Baqer al-Najjar, sociology professor at the University of Bahrain, commented on the electoral results: 'The way the media handled the security situation which prevailed prior to the elections unexpectedly raised al-Wefaq's shares . . . Shiites felt that they were targeted so they voted intensely for Al-Wefaq despite their restlessness with its performance throughout the past four years.'[18]

BEYOND MARCH 2011: RETRIBUTION

The collapse of negotiations between the Crown Prince and Ali Salman in March 2011 heralded the beginning of a period of widespread retribution against opposition leaders and sympathizers encompassing the dismissal of

---

[18] Taieb Mahjoub, 'Bahrain's Shiites Make Slender Gains in Polls', AFP report, 25 October 2010 http://www.dailystar.com.lb/News/Middle-East/2010/Oct-25/87741-bahrains-shiites-make-slender-gains-in-polls.ashx.

thousands from their workplaces, the detention of thousands, and harassment campaigns by state-run media against targeted segments of the population.

Following the declaration of a state of national safety on 15 March, security forces ramped up the arrests, detaining thousands.[19] Many arrests were carried out between 1 a.m. and 3 a.m. by hooded individuals who raided homes and intentionally broke down doors, a practice often accompanied by sectarian and verbal insults.[20] Security forces also set up checkpoints across the country, where individuals from mostly Shi'a backgrounds were stopped and searched to determine whether they had participated in anti-government demonstrations. People arrested at checkpoints were also subject to various forms of mistreatment, including kicking, beating with batons, and sectarian abuse.[21]

Security forces also adopted measures to quash continued political protests, firing tear gas and rubber bullets at protesters, sometimes into private homes, in an 'unnecessary, disproportionate, and indiscriminate' manner.[22] In some cases, security forces fired shotgun rounds as a weapon of first resort against protesters, leading to fatal injuries. Rubber bullets were also fired at close range, causing permanent injuries and in some cases a partial or total loss of sight.[23] Authorities also razed a number of Shi'a mosques to the ground, on the basis that they were unlicensed structures that violated zoning laws.[24]

Injured protesters in many instances did not seek medical care, fearing arrest in hospital. Indeed, security forces transformed a ward in the country's main hospital into a de facto detention facility, where masked guards maintained a close watch on patients who had sustained protest-related injuries, subjecting a number to incommunicado detention, regular beatings, torture, and other forms of mistreatment. In other incidents, security forces arrested patients checking into hospitals who had sustained shotgun pellet injuries, transferring them to detention facilities before they could seek treatment.[25] Prison visits by an independent investigation team subsequently confirmed dozens of injured protesters were held in detention, some with numerous shotgun pellets still lodged inside their bodies.

Retribution also took place against large segments of the workforce, particularly against individuals and trade unionists deemed to have participated in demonstrations. A total of 2,464 workers in the private sector and 2,075 workers in the public sector were dismissed or suspended from their employment, with the most common causes cited by employers including involvement in

---

[19] BICI, *Report*, 270.   [20] BICI, *Report*, 280.   [21] BICI, *Report*, 150.
[22] BICI, *Report*, 268.   [23] BICI, *Report*, 261.
[24] 'Demolishing Unlicensed Buildings is not Sectarian-Driven, Says Justice Minister', Bahrain News Agency, Manama, 22 April 2011 http://bna.bh/portal/en/news/453868.
[25] Human Rights Watch, 'Bahrain: Systematic Attacks on Medical Providers', HRW, New York, 18 July 2011 www.hrw.org/news/2011/07/18/bahrain-systematic-attacks-medical-providers.

demonstrations and failure to appear at work. According to reports submitted by employees, a single corporation, Aluminium Bahrain, is alleged to have dismissed 399 employees, amounting to 14 per cent of the company's total workforce.[26]

MEDIA AND SOCIAL MEDIA

Beginning in mid-February 2011, Bahrain's main television station, BTV, launched a series of talk shows whose sole purpose appears to have been the incitement of public opinion against opposition sympathizers. During these programmes, talk show hosts described protesters as 'terrorists', 'foreign agents', and 'thugs'. In several instances, state media appeared to act in tacit complicity with intelligence agencies, calling for retribution against identified individuals, some of whom security forces subsequently arrested. BTV also broadcast a series of televised confessions, in one instance by a detainee who had died days earlier in detention.

On a live programme on 4 April, news anchors telephoned athletes who had participated in anti-government protests, demanding that they apologize to the leadership. Security forces arrested a number of athletes who had appeared on the programme the day after it was broadcast, including stars of the national football team, Alaa and Mohammed Hubail. In the following months, a military court sentenced Mohammed Hubail to two years in prison, and charged up to sixty-two other athletes with 'illegal congregation' and 'incitement of hatred against Bahrain's political system'.[27] Up to 150 athletes, including the two brothers, were subsequently fired from national sports teams. In another segment, BTV broadcast photos of demonstrators, their faces circled in red, and called on the public to identify them. Days later, security forces again arrested and detained a number of those who had appeared in the segment.

In other instances, state television launched character attacks against individuals awaiting trial in detention. On 17 April BTV described teachers and educators involved in the unrest as foreign agents engaged in a sectarian conspiracy against the country. Security forces had weeks earlier arrested the president and vice president of the Bahrain Teachers' Society and then dissolved the association just days before the programme went on air.[28]

---

[26] BICI, *Report*, 344.
[27] James M. Dorsey, 'Bahrain Sentences 3 Athletes for Anti-Government Protests', *Hurriyet Daily News*, Istanbul, 8 December 2011 www.hurriyetdailynews.com/bahrain-sentences-3-ath letes-for-anti-government-protests.aspx?pageID=238&nID=8765&NewsCatID=364.
[28] Human Rights Watch, 'Interfere, Restrict, Control: Restraints on Freedom of Association in Bahrain', HRW, New York, June 2013.

A similar segment was broadcast on 11 April, in which the acting health minister accused detained medical professionals of fabricating protestors' wounds in order to tarnish the reputation of the country.[29]

An account on the social media networking site Twitter, under the name 7areghum and which had more than 70,000 followers, also openly harassed and defamed opposition supporters, in some instances revealing their places of work and their home addresses. A number of those named by 7areghum were later dismissed from their jobs.[30]

Pro-government websites and newspapers also targeted American diplomats for allegedly interfering in the country's internal affairs, including by supporting the right of its citizens to engage in peaceful protests. On 7 May an anonymous posting on a pro-government website included links to photographs of the US embassy's human-rights officer, Ludovic Hood, and information on where he and his family lived, accusing him of 'training and provoking demonstrations' and working in cooperation with Hezbollah. Pro-government groups, sponsored 'to varying extents by the Royal Court', launched the campaign against Hood after he had been photographed weeks earlier handing out doughnuts to demonstrators outside the US embassy in Bahrain.[31] The US government withdrew Hood from Bahrain on 30 May 2011. Similar campaigns in newspapers and online forums against US officials, including the US ambassador, continued in the following months. In 2013 Bahrain lawmakers in the lower chamber of parliament urged their government to stop the US ambassador from 'interfering in domestic affairs' and attending 'meetings with those who inspire sedition', in reference to meetings he had held with opposition supporters. In July 2014 Bahrain expelled the United States Assistant Secretary of State for Democracy, Human Rights, and Labor after he had met members of Al-Wefaq, a move that the Foreign Ministry said 'intervened in the country's domestic affairs'.[32] Later that year, Tom Malinowski was permitted to return to Bahrain. Editorials in pro-government newspapers continued to accuse the US ambassador of acting in allegiance with Iran and Hezbollah, against Bahrain's government.

By contrast, Britain's softer stance towards the regime's policy earned it praise in state media and from government leaders. At a security conference

---

[29] 'Al Rased: wizarat al-sihha wa-l-salmaniyya' ('The Observer: The Ministry of Health and Salmaniya Hospital'), Bahrain Television, 11 April 2011 www.youtube.com/watch?v=BCO-BL_6swU.

[30] 'Bahrain Government Continues Confrontation with Media', Project on Middle East Democracy, Washington, 7 May 2012 http://pomed.org/reform/bahrain-government-continues-fighting-with-media/#.UqgvyY2yNQV.

[31] Justin Gengler, 'Is US Ambassador Krajeski the New Ludo Hood?', *Religion and Politics in Bahrain*, blog, 30 May 2013 http://bahrainipolitics.blogspot.co.uk/2013/05/is-ambassador-krajeski-next-ludo-hood.html.

[32] 'US Diplomat Tom Malinowski Expelled from Bahrain', *BBC News*, 7 July 2014 http://www.bbc.co.uk/news/world-us-canada-28204511.

held in December 2012, Crown Prince Salman praised British policy towards Bahrain, thanking Her Majesty's Government for standing 'head and shoulders above all others' in support of Bahrain. He made little mention of the USA in the same speech. British diplomats in Bahrain also expressly lent support to government policy. On 26 March 2013 British Ambassador Iain Lindsey gave an interview to a local newspaper, describing some of the protesters as 'terrorists, full stop', and referring to a report by Human Rights Watch on Bahrain as 'unhelpful, condescending, and patronizing', noting: 'British companies should be able to pick up a billion pounds of business in Bahrain in the next 5–10 years.'[33] The British embassy also came under fire from free-speech activists for publishing on World Press Freedom Day two editorials on its website that advocated censorship and appeared to support the imprisonment of activists. On 11 October 2012 the two countries signed a defence cooperation agreement to promote intelligence-sharing and technical cooperation. On 6 December 2014 UK Foreign Secretary Philip Hammond announced plans to establish a permanent British military base in Bahrain, the first of its kind since Great Britain withdrew from the region in 1971. Presented as part of a broader cooperation between Gulf and Western States in the fight against Islamic State, the announcement nonetheless generated anger within Bahrain, with many lamenting the symbolic significance of a former colonial power reasserting itself on the sovereign soil of a former protectorate. On 20 January 2015, days after the arrest of prominent human-rights activist Nabeel Rajab for a tweet, Philip Hammond praised Bahrain as 'a country which is travelling in the right direction (and) making significant reform'. Both the United States and United Kingdom have stopped the sale of tear gas to Bahrain citing human-rights concerns, but continue to supply billions of dollars' worth of other weaponry to the kingdom. A desire by both states to secure cooperation from the Bahraini regime in the fight against ISIS appears to have eased any earlier pressure exerted by these states for human-rights and political reforms.

GROWING UNREST: DEMONSTRATIONS CONTINUE

As lawful avenues for the expression of political grievances narrowed following the declaration of a state of national emergency, demonstrators continued to use methods of civil resistance, sometimes in innovative forms, while

---

[33] Andy McSmith, 'Is the Foreign Office Facing Both Ways over the Troubles in Bahrain?', *Independent Blogs,* 28 March 2013 http://blogs.independent.co.uk/2013/03/28/is-the-foreing-office-facing-both-ways-over-the-troubles-in-bahrain.

sections of the February 14 Movement simultaneously began adopting a series of violent tactics in confrontations with security forces.

Although authorities banned protests during the period of national safety, political demonstrations continued, with funerals of deceased protesters evolving into demonstrations against the regime. On 19 March 2011, for example, thousands gathered in the village of Sitra to commemorate the funeral of Ahmed Farhan, a student shot and killed by security forces. The procession developed into a demonstration, with thousands chanting 'peaceful, peaceful', and: 'With our lives, our blood, we will sacrifice for our martyr.' As with many other gatherings of its kind, the funeral ended with security forces firing tear gas and rubber bullets to disperse the mourners.

Demonstrators also defied the ban against protests with a variety of creative methods. During the state of national emergency, residents of villages across the country appeared on their rooftops at coordinated times, twice a day, chanting 'God is Great' in unison. The chants provided a vocal and powerful way of circumventing the ban on public gatherings.[34] On 9 September, activists invited motorists to participate in a 'dignity belt', by parking their cars on a central highway and obstructing traffic. That day, traffic extended for several kilometres across the capital, essentially shutting down movement in and out of Manama. Opposition activists repeated their call for participation in the 'dignity belt' on 26, 27, and 28 September, eliciting anger from members of the business community, who complained that demonstrators were preventing people from accessing their workplaces and further damaging the economy.

Activists also engaged in campaigns to claim and sometimes reclaim symbols of the movement. Beginning in late March, protesters in villages including Deraz, Sitra, and A'ali fashioned replicas of the Pearl monument out of plastic, and erected them in central spaces within villages. Numerous videos subsequently surfaced showing security forces destroying and confiscating these monuments. On 23 March 2011 demonstrators in the village of Saar attached photographs of deceased demonstrators to helium balloons, and released them into the sky.[35]

Following a decision by the Central Bank of Bahrain in May 2011 to withdraw the 500 fils coin, which depicted the Pearl monument, activists began to collect the coins, transforming them into commemorative key rings and necklaces. A video that gained popularity on the social networking site YouTube provided instructions on how to transform birdshot pellets and tear-

---

[34] Simeon Kerr and Robin Wigglesworth, 'Bahrain Crackdown Spreads to Villages', *Financial Times*, 20 March 2011.

[35] Marc Owen Jones, 'Creative Resistance in Bahrain', video feature, 21 January 2012 http://www.enduringamerica.com/home/2012/1/21/bahrain-video-feature-celebrating-creative-resistance-owen-j.html.

gas canisters fired by security forces into household items, such as prayer beads and slippers.

Graffiti also functioned as a major outlet for political activists. Popular slogans including 'Down with the regime' and 'We will not forget our martyrs', in addition to stencilled images of opposition leaders, became a common sight on walls within villages across the country. On public highways, pro- and anti-government activists competed for space, with layers of different graffiti on the same surfaces. Authorities expended considerable effort covering anti-government graffiti with paint, which often lasted only a matter of hours or days before being covered again with slogans and images of the movement.

At the same time, anti-opposition groups also began to mobilize against anti-government activists. Following the imposition of the state of national emergency, blogs and social media campaigns emerged calling for the boycott of businesses linked to opposition supporters, including a prominent chain of supermarkets, Jawad.[36] Videos later surfaced appearing to show active collusion between police and protesters in ransacking one of the Jawad stores.[37]

Protests also continued in the months following the decision by King Hamad to lift the state of national safety early, on 1 June 2011. On 8 February 2012 Abdulhadi al-Khawaja began a hunger strike in prison until 'freedom or death'.[38] On 12 April hundreds of demonstrators wearing masks in the image of al-Khawaja protested for his release. After 110 days, interrupted by episodes of force-feeding, al-Khawaja ended his hunger strike, saying that, although he had not been released, he had still achieved his 'overall goal of shedding light on the ongoing human rights situation in Bahrain'.[39]

International events taking place in Bahrain emerged as major targets for the opposition movement. In January 2012 protests took place against the Bahrain International Airshow, a three-day event that included shows by American and British military jets. Protesters burned tyres around the capital Manama, sending plumes of black smoke into the air.[40] On 28 March 2012 a video uploaded by the February 14 Movement titled 'warning operation' showed masked youths setting fire to a car and included text warning authorities against

---

[36] 'A Friendly Guide to Boycotting Jawad!', *The Mushaima Diaries*, blog, 24 July 2011 http://hassanmushaima.blogspot.co.uk/2011/07/friendly-guide-to-boycotting-jawad.html. See also 'A Bahrain Boycott on Sectarian Lines', Al Jazeera, 2 May 2011 http://stream.aljazeera.com/story/201105021839-001568; and 'Boycotting Jawad', *Twitter is Not Enough!*, blog, 18 February 2012 www.life4bh.blogspot.co.uk/2012/02/boycotting-jawad.html.

[37] Bahrain Center for Human Rights, 'Thugs Backed up by Police Attacking Jawad 24 Hours Supermarket', BCHR, Manama, 12 April 2012 www.youtube.com/watch?v=IRrsOdhrssc.

[38] Frank Gardner, 'Bahrain Activist Khawaja to Continue Hunger Strike', *BBC News*, 1 May 2012 www.bbc.co.uk/news/world-middle-east-17908449.

[39] Bahrain Center for Human Rights, 'Abdulhadi al-Khawaja's Statement about Ending his Hunger Strike', BCHR, Manama, 28 May 2012 http://bahrainrights.hopto.org/en/node/5296.

[40] 'Protesters Try to Disrupt Showpiece Bahrain Air Show', Reuters, 19 January 2012 www.reuters.com/article/2012/01/19/bahrain-airshow-idUSL6E8CJ3NN20120119.

holding a planned Formula One race in Bahrain; and, in late April 2012, demonstrators also set up barricades of burning tires around Manama, in protest against the authorities' decision to host the race, which activists claimed lent international legitimacy to the regime. The Bahrain International Airshow was held on 19 January 2012, and the Formula One race on 22 April.[41]

More destructive and violent actions against the regime also began to take place, almost entirely by youths affiliated to the February 14 Movement. From its origins as an online campaign, chapter organizations aligning themselves to the broader movement appeared in mostly Shi'a villages, coming together under the broad umbrella of the February 14 Coalition. The earliest videos showing protesters from a chapter group of this movement throwing incendiary devices at police emerged in November 2011. The video spurred a series of copycat operations by other chapters, which often mimicked one another's strategies. The use of such devices has since become a regular occurrence in confrontations between police and demonstrators, causing the death and injury of several police officers. A video posted on YouTube, dated 2 August 2012, shows dozens of masked youths lobbing Molotov cocktails at a police station in the village of Sitra, setting fire to the building.

The descent into violent action by sections of the February 14 Movement appears to have been seen by them as retaliation for the growing number of arrests of its members, and as an open declaration of the movement's aim to bring about the downfall of the regime. The absence of coordinated hierarchy or centralized leadership within the organization contributed to the fracturing of its strategies. While all its supporters now united around the aim of bringing about the downfall of the regime, many also moved towards pursuing strategies of violence as a means to achieve this aim, while some continued to insist that the use of violent methods to do so was strategically misguided.

REFORM AND THE ELUSIVE DIALOGUE

Faced with a growing international outcry following the retributive measures taken against broad segments of Bahrain's civil society, in June 2011 King Hamad announced the establishment of the Bahrain Independent Commission of Inquiry (BICI), tasked with investigating and reporting on events that took place in Bahrain in February and March 2011 and the consequences of those events.[42]

---

[41] 'Vettel Wins Stunning 2012 Gulf Air Bahrain Grand Prix!!!', Bahrain News Agency, Manama, 22 April 2012 http://bna.bh/portal/en/news/505089?date=2012-06-3.

[42] BICI, 'Bahrain Independent Commission of Inquiry Established', BICI, Manama, 29 June 2011 www.bici.org.bh/indexf295.html?news=bahrain-independent-commission-of-inquiry-established.

King Hamad appointed renowned international law expert Cherif Bassiouni to head the commission, which released its final report on 23 November 2011. The report detailed evidence of a range of abuses committed by security forces and a lack of accountability within security agencies leading to a 'systematic culture of impunity'. The report also identified thirty-five deaths that had taken place between 14 February and 15 April 2011 in connection with the unrest: thirty civilians and five security personnel.[43] The commission released the final report at a ceremony at the king's palace, where King Hamad pledged to 'take to heart' the report's findings and implement its recommendations.

Supporters of the February 14 Movement, who continued to refuse all forms of dialogue with the regime, greeted the release of the report with scepticism. Representatives of opposition political societies welcomed the recommendations and pressed the government to enact the reforms. The government responded by establishing a national commission to institute the reforms and by passing a series of changes, which included revoking the powers of the National Security Apparatus, after the report had found a 'systematic practice of physical and psychological mistreatment, which in many cases amounted to torture'. It also created an 'ombudsman' within the Ministry of Interior, tasked with receiving and investigating complaints from civilians against the agency. The government also implemented legislative amendments expanding the definition of torture under domestic law, and lifted the time limits for the prosecution of cases of torture. The government rebuilt some Shi'a houses of worship destroyed during the crackdown and established a tripartite commission under the supervision of the International Labour Organization (ILO) to review the cases of all dismissed workers.[44] According to its reports, the tripartite commission reinstated thousands of workers, including more than 1,500 workers in state-owned corporations who had been illegally sacked.

Activists and human-rights organizations insist that the reforms do not go far enough, citing the continued detention of top political opposition leaders, including Ali Salman and a group of fourteen others, and the absence of high-level accountability. In particular, activists point to the non-implementation of recommendation 1716, which calls for 'a national independent and impartial mechanism to determine the accountability of those in government who have committed unlawful or negligent acts resulting in deaths, torture, and mistreatment of civilians', as evidence of the insincerity of the reform process. The recommendation is linked to the commission's finding that abuses 'could not have happened without the knowledge of higher echelons of the command

---

[43] BICI, *Report*, 219.
[44] Kristian Ulrichsen and Elham Fakhro, 'Post-BICI Bahrain: Between Reform and Stagnation', openDemocracy, 19 January 2012 www.opendemocracy.net/kristian-coates-ulrichsen-elham-fakhro/post-bici-bahrain-between-reform-and-stagnation.

structure' of the security forces. Indeed, only four low-ranking officers and one first lieutenant have been convicted in the deaths of two protesters and serious injury to a third. Reinstatement of workers also remains a concern. According to the GFBTU, more than 400 remain suspended or dismissed from their jobs in the private and public sector as of early 2015.

Legislative developments since 2011 directly target the ability of civil society to mobilize and develop independent associations. New trade-union legislation introduces greater limitations on the right of workers to strike, and allows employers to dismiss workers who strike illegally, without compensation.[45] It also allows the formation of multiple unions in the same professional organization, and grants the Ministry of Labour the right to decide which of these unions should represent workers in collective bargaining with employers at the national level, and in international forums.[46] While the earlier laws provided a comprehensive list of public areas that were off-limits to striking workers,[47] the new laws leave those areas to be defined by the prime minister. The new law also allows for the formation of multiple unions within the same professional industry, replacing earlier requirements that allowed only one union per industry and per professional organization. Labour activists from the GFBTU assert that measures that allow plurality have in fact been used to dilute the power of the country's labour movement, and that a federation of trade unions that includes unions formed under the new law, the Bahrain Labour Union Free Federation (BLUFF), is a government front that is working to obstruct the efforts of unionists campaigning for workers' rights, including the reinstatement of more than 500 dismissed workers.[48] On 25 March 2013 a representative of BLUFF, stating that 'the issue has since been resolved with royal orders', petitioned the ILO to dismiss complaints lodged on behalf of dismissed workers by the International Trade Union Confederation (ITUC).[49] The ITUC had expressed concern over what it called 'the failure of employers, largely in state-owned companies, to reinstate many wrongfully dismissed workers, or to rehire the workers only under completely unacceptable conditions'. It also expressed concern that reinstated union leaders had to agree not to carry out any further union activity as a precondition of reinstatement, and that others continue to face criminal prosecution.[50] These include Mahdi Abu Deeb, president of the Bahrain Teachers' Society, who in 2011–12 was given a

---

[45] Decree no. 49 of 2006 and Law no. 36 of 2012.   [46] Decree no. 35 of 2011.
[47] Decree no. 49 of 2006.   [48] Author interview, 20 September 2013.
[49] Basma Mohammed, 'ILO Urged to Reject Sackings Complaint', *Gulf Daily News*, 25 March 2013 www.gulf-daily-news.com/NewsDetails.aspx?storyid=350037.
[50] International Trade Union Confederation, 'Bahrain: ITUC Denounces the Ongoing Failure to Reinstate Workers', ITUC, Brussels, 31 January 2012 www.ituc-csi.org/bahrain-ituc-denounces-the-ongoing,10546?lang=en. See also ITUC, *Countries at Risk: Violations of Trade Union Rights 2013* (Brussels: ITUC, 10 June 2013) www.ituc-csi.org/countries-at-risk-2013-report-on.

five-year prison sentence on charges including 'halting the educational process, and inciting hatred of the regime'.[51] The ITUC is the world's largest
trade-union federation, representing 315 national affiliates. The BLUFF includes new unions from a range of public-sector and state organizations,
including Aluminium Bahrain (Alba), the largest aluminium smelter in the
Middle East, Gulf Air, and Gulf Petrochemicals Industries. On 7 October 2012
a delegation from the ILO visited Bahrain to secure a final agreement on the
reinstatement of the workers. Local newspapers reported that the prime
minister intervened by insisting that the cabinet's legal department approve
the deal, even though many aspects of it related to workers in the private
sector.[52]

New laws also include a draft law of association under consideration since
2013, which would grant the Ministry of Social Development sweeping powers
to regulate and shut down independent associations.[53] The law allows the
ministry to deny an organization's request to register if 'society does not need
its services or if there are other associations that fulfil the society's need'. It also
prohibits groups from inviting non-Bahrainis for meetings without prior
permission from the Ministry of Social Development. According to Human
Rights Watch, in April 2011 the Ministry dissolved the Bahrain Teachers'
Society and replaced the Bahrain Medical Society's board members with a pro-
government board.[54] In an interview with the leadership of one of Bahrain's
largest civil-society NGOs, the director claimed that the organization had lost
nearly all sources of funding from abroad as a result of a new crackdown by
the ministry, and that the organization risked shutting down as a result of lack
of funds.[55] New ministerial orders continue to target civil society organizations. On 3 September 2013 the justice minister introduced a new requirement
forcing political groups to obtain permission from the Ministry of Justice
before meeting foreign diplomats. The order also 'requires political groups
to obtain authorization to meet international organizations outside Bahrain,

---

[51] In December 2011 Mahdi Abu Deeb was sentenced to ten years' imprisonment and in
September 2012 his sentence was reduced by an appeals court to five years. Amnesty International USA, 'Urgent Action: Release of Prisoner of Conscience Denied', AI, Washington, 4 July
2013 http://www.amnestyusa.org/sites/default/files/uaa22711_8.pdf.

[52] Basma Mohamed, 'Jobs Deal for Sacked Soon', *Gulf Daily News*, 10 October 2013 http://
www.gulf-daily-news.com/NewsDetails.aspx?storyid=362654; and Basma Mohammed, 'ILO
Urged to Reject Sackings Complaint', *Gulf Daily News*, 25 March 2013 www.gulf-daily-news.
com/NewsDetails.aspx?storyid=350037.

[53] Human Rights Watch, 'Bahrain: No Progress on Reform', HRW, New York, 28 February
2013 www.hrw.org/news/2013/02/28/bahrain-no-progress-reform.

[54] Human Rights Watch, 'Bahrain: New Associations Law Spells Repression', HRW, New
York, 20 June 2013 www.hrw.org/news/2013/06/20/bahrain-new-associations-law-spells-
repression.

[55] Author interview, 5 January 2015.

and to have a government official at all approved meetings'.[56] A new anti-terrorism law also requires judges to withdraw nationality from persons found guilty of terrorist crimes. In November 2012, the interior ministry issued an order revoking citizenship from thirty-one citizens, including two former parliamentarians, for security reasons.[57] In February 2015 the government released the names of seventy-two Bahrainis whose citizenship it chose to revoke, including Shi'a opposition supporters and supporters of the Islamic State on the same list. Commenting on the decision, an activist stated: 'The message has never been clearer: the government of Bahrain views us, who advocate for democracy, human rights and change in Bahrain, as equals to the Jihadi-terrorists of Isis.'[58]

Anniversaries of key events in 2011 continue to be met with street demonstrations. The second anniversary of the uprising, on 14 February 2013, sparked widespread protests, leading to the killing of a teenager by shotgun fire during a protest in the village of al-Daih and the death of a police officer, who was hit by an incendiary device thrown by protesters.[59] In April 2013 a small explosion was detonated inside a car parked outside the Bahrain Financial Harbour. Members of the February 14th group claimed responsibility for the attack. Authorities have also continued to arrest political activists. Members of the Bahrain Centre for Human Rights, including Nabeel Rajab and Zainab al-Khawaja, were imprisoned, released, and rearrested in 2013 and 2014 for inciting hatred against the regime. Activists continue to document evidence of excessive use of tear gas during protests and in residential areas, which they claim has caused the death and injury of dozens since the November 2011 BICI report.

On 23 January 2012 King Hamad announced a series of constitutional reforms, based on the recommendations of a national dialogue held in July 2011. The new changes require the king to consult with the heads of the upper and lower parliamentary chambers before dissolving the legislature. They also grant the elected lower house of parliament the right to vote to withhold cooperation from the prime minister and refer its decision to the king, who acts as the final arbiter on whether to dismiss the prime minister or keep him in his post.[60] Opposition groups criticized the steps for failing to address their

---

[56] Associated Press, 'Bahrain: Order Curbs Political Groups', *New York Times*, 3 September 2013 www.nytimes.com/2013/09/04/world/middleeast/bahrain-order-curbs-political-groups.html.

[57] 'Bahrain Revokes Nationality of 31 Opposition Members', *Al Monitor*, 9 November 2012 www.al-monitor.com/pulse/politics/2012/11/bahrain-revokes-citizenship-khalaf.html.

[58] 'We Are Human Rights Defenders but Bahrain Says We're Terrorists', *Guardian*, London, 9 February 2015 http://www.theguardian.com/commentisfree/2015/feb/09/human-rights-defenders-bahrain-says-terrorists.

[59] 'Deaths Reported after Bahrain Protests', Al Jazeera, 15 February 2013 www.aljazeera.com/news/middleeast/2013/02/201321472234468101.html.

[60] 'Bahrain King Enacts Parliamentary Reforms', Al Jazeera, 3 May 2012 www.aljazeera.com/news/middleeast/2012/05/201253171926431856.html.

key demands, which include broader powers for the elected chamber of parliament and the introduction of limits on the terms of ministerial posts.[61] The dialogue itself was widely dismissed by opposition supporters from the outset for granting just 35 out of a total 300 seats to opposition groups. In the aftermath of the dialogue, the US State Department and a number of international actors stressed the need for Bahrain to embark on a 'meaningful and inclusive' national dialogue, which could pave the way for further reforms.

A second national dialogue, titled the National Consensus Dialogue, began in February 2013, at the invitation of King Hamad. The dialogue included eight representatives of opposition societies, eight representatives of the 'nationalist' and largely loyalist political societies, and eight representatives from both chambers of parliament, in addition to three ministers.[62] In late January the representatives of the opposition political societies addressed a letter to the justice minister outlining a series of demands, including the presence of a representative of the king in the dialogue, stating that the current government was the source of many of their grievances and could not be seen as an independent mediator in the dialogue. The minister did not agree. Over the course of twenty-four sessions between February and September 2013, participants wrangled over the mechanism governing the dialogue, with opposition groups insisting any recommendations agreed to by the parties should be put to a popular referendum, and then submitted to parliament for implementation. This was rejected by the other participants, causing a prolonged stalemate.[63]

The National Consensus Dialogue was suspended on 9 January 2014, following a decision by opposition societies to suspend their participation in it following the arrest of the deputy leader of al-Wefaq a day earlier, on charges including inciting and advocating terrorism, and using his leadership position in a legally organized political society to incite crimes. In November 2014 Bahrain held its fourth round of parliamentary elections, which were boycotted by opposition groups. With an official voter turnout rate of 51.5 per cent—disputed by the opposition—the government has championed the affair as a political victory. The subsequent arrest of Ali Salman further deepened Bahrain's political quagmire and led to protests demanding his release, mostly

---

[61] Gregg Carlstrom, 'Little Optimism over Promised Bahrain Reforms', Al Jazeera, 16 January 2012 www.aljazeera.com/news/middleeast/2012/01/20121159958662428.html.

[62] 'National Dialogue Participants—First Session', National Dialogue, Manama, 10 February 2013 www.nd.bh/en/index.php/dialogue/participants/first-round/sessions1-10/session1 (website under maintenance as of May 2015). On 24 September 2011 parliamentary by-elections were held to replace the members of al-Wefaq who had resigned from parliament. The seats were largely won by independents and government supporters, amid a boycott of the elections by opposition supporters.

[63] Author interview with participant in the dialogue, 25 September 2013.

within villages across the country. Four years after it had erupted in 2011, the crisis remained unresolved both at the negotiating table and in the streets.

CONCLUSION

To what extent could the opposition have achieved more from the start, had it been capable of remaining united under the single banner of constitutional reform and had it accepted dialogue with the regime on this basis? Fracturing on this crucial point made it easier for the regime to present its adversaries in a hostile light and to drive a counter-revolution: both in the form of its own actions against opposition supporters and in energizing an existing loyalist base against any kind of reform. The impact of the regime's disproportionate use of violence against protesters in the early days of the movement cannot be discounted and played a major role in radicalizing elements of the opposition. The regime's history of backtracking on political promises also cannot be ignored: it generated scepticism towards calls by the Crown Prince for dialogue, and contributed to the visible lack of trust between the opposition and the government that for many years has hindered dialogue. The government's immediate strategy of supporting pro-government populist groups was not without long-term consequences, as these groups began to develop into a separate constituency that needed to be negotiated with, further complicating prospects for a negotiated solution. Indeed, strategies of shoring up loyalist groups against regime critics are by no means novel in Bahrain's history: for example, similar strategies were adopted during the 1950s, when the rulers created a committee of Shi'a notables to counteract reformist demands being pushed by a cross-sectarian political committee driven primarily by Arab nationalist and Sunni merchant leaders.

Power political considerations, including Saudi Arabia's fear of Iranian influence, effectively shielded the government from internal political pressures while providing new incentives for the government to impose a security solution in the short term. The need for a political settlement in the form of a more permanent resolution of the crisis remains critical.

The future of the tiny Gulf nation remains dependent on whether talks at the bargaining table can resume following numerous failures, and lead to further reforms and, ultimately, a meaningful settlement between its political actors. The continued absence of such a settlement has empowered radicals at both ends of the political spectrum and fuelled the emergence of a cadre of leaders who stand to benefit from continued unrest in the country. An increasingly violent street movement is competing with established political societies, whose leaders are imprisoned or on trial, for control of the street, while a hardened and vocal loyalist base, mobilized by the regime during the unrest, continues to press the government to adopt tougher measures against violent and non-violent sections of the opposition. The use of violence by sections of the February 14 Movement has also made it easier for the regime and loyalist constituencies to avoid confronting any legitimate calls for reform. Simultaneously, fears of the growing influence of the Islamic State across the region have spiked some initial fears over the impact of Sunni radicalization in Bahrain. As irreconcilable political positions become further entrenched, avenues for a long-term political settlement remain on the table but will become increasingly elusive.

Bahrain's internal politics are increasingly entangled with the growth of sectarian politics across the region. As distrust and frustration continue to deepen, growing extremism and the absence of a negotiated settlement continue to unsettle Bahrain's key allies, including the USA and Saudi Arabia. Credible sources assert in private that high-level Saudi officials played a role in pressuring the king into launching the National Consensus Dialogue round of talks in 2013, indicating serious concern among Bahrain's neighbours over the potential for the country's stalemate to affect regional stability. The USA is also increasingly concerned about the future of the island, with the odd official hinting that the US Navy's Fifth Fleet did not have to remain stationed in Bahrain. Within the country, the USA also remains a target of domestic political frustrations: pro-government groups accuse it of meddling in internal affairs, and anti-government groups accuse it of failing to press the government to make necessary reforms. Overall, Bahrain's uprising has led to a reversal in many of the fundamental rights and freedoms of its people and to a sustained rise in sectarian tensions that increasingly threatens the region's precarious political balance.

5

Civil Resistance in Libya during the Arab Spring

George Joffé

This chapter explores the changing nature of political resistance under the Gaddafi regime, which eventually culminated in the civil war in 2011. It also comments on the evolution of civil resistance after the civil war, as Libya struggles to restore centralized control to the new state, despite what is still, at the end of May 2015, a chaotic security situation. The basic argument is that, despite the autocratic nature of the Gaddafi regime, its control of the 'stateless state' (the *Jamahiriya*) that it had created was, in practice, increasingly challenged, particularly in Cyrenaica, Libya's eastern province,[1] by popular opposition—social movements, in effect—utilizing peaceful methods.[2] Faced with very violent repression, parts of the opposition resorted to armed struggle. The conditions of widespread popular opposition and incipient civil war eventually created the conditions in which, with international support through the United Nations, the regime itself and the state it had created finally collapsed. The subsequent reconstruction of the state has, however, proved to be a major challenge, which, even now, more than four years after the civil war, is still not complete.

---

[1] Libya traditionally comprises three provinces: to the west, Tripolitania, dominated by Tripoli on the coast, with the Jefara plain and the Jabal Nafusa behind it; to the east, Cyrenaica, with its coastal city of Benghazi to the north of the Jabal al-Akhdar; and, in the south, the Fezzan, containing a group of oases and the towns of Murzuk and Sebha.

[2] *Jamahiriya*: 'state of the masses'—the political system created by the Gaddafi regime in which sovereignty was said to reside in the Libyan people, who exercised full authority over the stateless state through direct popular democracy. See M. Al-Qathafi, *The Green Book* (Tripoli: Public Establishment for Publishing, Printing and Advertising, n.d.). The Green Book is amplified by Colonel Gaddafi's dicta, which have been collected in annual volumes as *al-Sijill al-Qawmi*, and specifically religious discourses are available as *Khutab wa-Ahadith al-Qa'id al-Dinyah*. A very early (and now rare) source is to be found in M. O. Ansell and I. B. al-Arif, *The Libyan Revolution: A Sourcebook of Legal and Historical Documents* (Harrow: Oleander Press, 1972).

For forty-two years, from the Great September Revolution on 1 September 1969 up to 17 February 2011, when the Libyan civil war broke out, Libya was dominated by a political vision that formally denied both the possibility and the right of Libyans to civil activism of any kind outside that sanctioned by the Gaddafi regime. Resistance to the regime, its objectives, and policies was rigidly excluded, and those who manifested it, in any form, faced unlimited imprisonment and death.[3] Civil resistance, in the sense in which the term is used in this book—'political action that relies on the use of non-violent methods'[4]—had, therefore, no place, in theory at least, within the political and social ambit of the *Jamahiriya*. In reality, however, particularly during the last two decades of the *Jamahiriya*, acts of resistance—initially violent but subsequently transformed into non-violent civil resistance—became an expanding reality within Libya's social and political life.

With the disappearance of the Gaddafi regime in October 2011, the constraints on civil activism of all kinds disappeared. Libya then offered the panorama of a chaotic interplay between state and citizen: the parameters of protest and political order were painfully explored alongside government attempts to establish a legitimate monopoly of violence within the emerging Libyan state.[5] Yet this new arena for political activism was also, in part, a consequence of the evolution of the Gaddafi regime and of the wider grievances that it had concealed. This chapter, therefore, will begin with a consideration of the status of civil resistance and disobedience in the Gaddafi era before briefly examining subsequent developments.

CIVIL RESISTANCE AND DISOBEDIENCE BEFORE 2011

Libya under the Gaddafi regime was not merely a rigid autocracy in which individual rights were suppressed; it was a state in which image and reality were mirror-image inversions of each other; a state that was not a state and a society conforming to an impeccable ideal that purported to be the only true democracy. The most important corollary of this antiphonal dialectic of

---

[3] The atmosphere of Libya, certainly in the 1970s and 1980s, is brilliantly evoked in Hisham Matar, *In the Country of Men* (New York: Viking, 2006).

[4] Adam Roberts, 'Introduction', in Adam Roberts and Timothy Garton Ash (eds), *Civil Resistance and Power Politics: The Experience of Non-Violent Action from Gandhi to the Present* (Oxford: Oxford University Press, 2009), 2.

[5] 'A state is a human community that (successfully) claims the monopoly of the legitimate use of physical force within a given territory' (Max Weber, 'Politics as a Vocation' (lecture to the Free Students Society at Munich University, 1918), in H. H. Gerth and C. Wright Mills (trans. and eds), *From Max Weber: Essays in Sociology* (Oxford and New York: Oxford University Press, 1946), 78).

opposites was that its political hegemony could not be questioned; dissent, in short, was a criminal betrayal of the ideal.[6] In such an environment, it followed that civil society, as a device for limiting and controlling the potential excesses of governance, was not only unnecessary but was itself an illicit challenge to the democratic ideal embodied in the *Jamahiriya*.

Such baleful perfection in the political and social spheres was buttressed by law; all significant challenges to the state were countered with the threat of execution. Law 71 of 1972 was quite explicit in respect of the consequences of such challenges, for it provided the capital penalty for political dissenters. This law actually condemned any form of group activity based on a political ideology that challenged the principles of the 'al-Fateh revolution': Article 3 provided the death sentence for joining or supporting any group prohibited by law. This law was backed up by a series of provisions in the Penal Code: Article 206 (Law 48 of 1976) provided for the death penalty for membership of a proscribed organization, Article 208 banned forming or joining an international organization, Article 178 provided life imprisonment for disseminating information that 'tarnished' Libya's reputation abroad, and Article 207 provided for the death sentence for any challenge to the basic principles of the Libyan state or for any attempt to overthrow it.

In view of such a battery of legal protection, the *Jamahiriya*, not surprisingly, actively discouraged autonomous political organization. In addition to Law 71 of 1972, non-governmental associations were regulated by Law 19 of 2001. Only after thirty-two years of Gaddafi's regime had passed was it felt necessary to regulate such bodies! According to Human Rights Watch, the law required a 'political body' to approve all such associations, denied an appeal against withheld approvals, and provided for continuous governmental interference in their operation, once permitted. Licences, once granted, could be revoked at any time without formal justification.[7]

Given such constraints, it is hardly surprising that there had been only twenty-two such organizations authorized during the Gaddafi regime's period in office and that none of them had ever criticized the regime. Indeed, the regime had gone out of its way in the very early days of its accession to power to eliminate civil society organizations; either, as happened with professional organizations and trade unions, by incorporating them into its new political structures or by simply banning them outright.[8] As a result, the majority of the

---

[6] Alia Brahimi, 'Libya's Revolution', in George Joffé (ed.), *North Africa's Arab Spring* (London: Routledge, 2013), 105–7.

[7] Human Rights Watch, *Truth and Justice Can't Wait: Human Rights Developments in Libya amid Institutional Obstacles* (New York: HRW, December 2009), 3 http://www.hrw.org/reports/2009/12/12/truth-and-justice-can-t-wait-0.

[8] 'From the retailers associations to the sports clubs, from the suqs to the cafes, the regime has shut down the institutions and places where people might gather outside government supervision' (Lisa Anderson, 'Qadhdhafi and his Opposition', *Middle East Journal*, 40/2 (Spring 1986), 228).

few organizations that were left were semi-official charitable organizations. Independent organizations—of journalists and lawyers, for example—were simply banned. Others, which were allowed to continue, were associations connected with Libya's revolutionary past, such as the Association of Free Officers, which brought together the Colonel's comrades, both military and civilian, in the Great September Revolution, although the Scouts, having originated during the Sanusi monarchy that had pre-dated the Revolution, maintained a precarious existence. According to one source, the Libyan chapter of the Red Crescent was one of the very few organizations that could carry out humanitarian work in the country; other sources have cited two women's organizations in Tripoli in a similar position.[9]

Human Rights Watch has claimed that there were no independent non-governmental organizations and that only organizations with a personal affiliation to the regime could act in the most sensitive field of all—human rights. It mentioned three organizations in this regard: the al-Gaddafi International Charity and Development Foundation (human rights), Waatasemu (women's rights), and the International Organization for Peace, Care, and Relief. It is notable that the first organization was chaired by Saif al-Islam Gaddafi, the second son of the Libyan ruler; the second by Aisha Gaddafi, his daughter; and the third by Khalid Hamaydi, the son of a leading member of the Revolutionary Command Council—thus justifying Human Rights Watch's claim![10]

Such a history suggests that the Gaddafi regime maintained a rigid and absolute control over the socio-political scene in Libya in which no concessions were ever made or felt to be necessary. For example, as late as 2008 an attempt by lawyers and journalists to set up two organizations dealing with human rights and democracy was blocked by the intelligence services after an initial official approval.[11] Thus, despite constant and increasing pressure for liberalization and reform from outside powers—the European Union and the United States, for example, particularly after 1986[12]—there was apparently no

---

[9] The Governance Network and Mercy Corps, *Beyond Gaddafi: Libya's Governance Context* (August 2011) http://www.mercycorps.org.uk/research-resources/beyong-gaddafi-libyas-governance-context.

[10] Human Rights Watch, *Truth and Justice Can't Wait*, 28–9. The Revolutionary Command Council was the body originally set up to act as the executive of the Libyan revolution in 1969. In 1975 it was disbanded as the *jamahiri* system was introduced. The five remaining members of the Council, by then largely deprived of formal political power, became part of a powerful but informal advisory group to the Libyan leader, Colonel Gaddafi, the so-called *rijal al-khaima* ('the men of the tent'—Gaddafi's famous Bedouin tent). The role of informal power was key to the operations of the Libyan state—Gaddafi himself had no formal role within it, even though he was its unquestioned master.

[11] Human Rights Watch, *Truth and Justice Can't Wait*, 32.

[12] The year in which the Reagan administration launched bombing raids (24 March 1986) on missile batteries in Sirte in *Operation Attain Document III*, and subsequently (15 April) on Tripoli and Benghazi in *Operation Eldorado Canyon* in response to Libya's alleged support for

recourse to the model adopted by other autocracies in the Middle East and North Africa, that of the liberalized autocracy. Here, autocratic states under pressure to liberalize their political structures created strictly controlled autonomous political arenas for carefully monitored civil society activities, not as moves preparatory to genuine liberalization but as a means of reducing external pressure and perpetuating autocratic regimes.[13] Libya, however, rather like Syria, clearly felt no need to adopt such a model, thus enhancing its image as an impenetrable and permanent dictatorship.

Regime Vulnerability

The image, however, was deceptive and the Gaddafian state towards the end of its life proved to be increasingly prone to the fragmentation of its autocratic façade. Indeed, it could be argued that the emergence of Law 19 as late as 2001 was an indication of that vulnerability, for it had clearly not been thought necessary beforehand. Up to the beginning of the twenty-first century, all signs of dissidence had been ruthlessly crushed—whether an abortive coup from within the regime in 1975 (the Meheishi coup), tribal dissidence in 1993 at Bani Walid, clandestine religious factionalism from Muslim Brotherhood cells from 1973 onwards, or open violence from a salafi–jihadi opposition in Cyrenaica in the second half of the 1990s. Indeed, the violent dissidence in Cyrenaica after 1995 was, perhaps, the first really serious threat to the Gaddafi regime in the wake of the 1986 bombings of Tripoli and Benghazi by the United States.

The violence in Cyrenaica was carried out by a Libyan group that had formed in Afghanistan during the campaign in the 1980s against the Soviet presence there, which had also spawned al-Qaeda. The group concerned, the Libyan Islamic Fighting Group, distinguished itself from al-Qaeda by adopting a purely nationalist agenda, seeking solely to remove the Gaddafi regime from power in Libya.[14] Its armed campaign was confined to Cyrenaica, however, and was eventually brutally suppressed by Libyan security forces in 1998, with

international terrorism. See Joseph T. Stanik, *El Dorado Canyon: Reagan's Undeclared War with Qaddafi* (Annapolis, MA: Naval Institute Press, 2003), 133–6. This was followed by the 1992 UN sanctions on Libya for its alleged involvement in the destruction of PanAm Flight 103 over the Scottish town of Lockerbie in December 1988. See Ronald Bruce St John, *Libya and the United States: Two Centuries of Strife* (Philadelphia, PA: University of Pennsylvania Press, 2002), 136–7.

[13] Daniel Brumberg, 'The Trap of Liberalized Autocracy', *Journal of Democracy*, 13/4 (October 2002), 56–68; and his *Democratization versus Liberalization in the Arab World: Dilemmas and Challenges for US Foreign Policy* (Carlisle, PA: Strategic Studies Institute, SSI Monographs, July 2005).

[14] See Gary Gambill, 'The Libyan Islamic Fighting Group (LIFG)', *Terrorism Monitor*, 3/6 (Washington: Jamestown Foundation, 5 May 2005), 3, 6 http://www.jamestown.org/single/?no_cache=1&tx_ttnews[tt_news]=308.

several hundreds of its militants being captured and imprisoned. They were held in Abu Salim prison in Tripoli—a prison specifically for political prisoners and controlled by the security services—where eventually the group recanted its belief in violent jihad in a major theological publication, *The Jihad Code*.[15] The result was that the regime then released those it had captured, ironically enough just a few short months before it itself collapsed.

Despite its defeat, however, the activities of the Libyan Islamic Fighting Group underlined the unpopularity of the regime, particularly in Cyrenaica, which had been the birthplace of the monarchy (displaced by Gaddafi in 1969) and which had always resented its subsequent marginalization. Colonel Gaddafi, therefore, was extremely sensitive about disaffection in Cyrenaica, and, despite his regime's suppression of dissidence there, recognized the autonomous power of the Cyrenaican Sa'adi tribes on which the Sanusi monarchy had depended for support. That recognition, in itself, implied that the regime was not as impervious as it appeared to be. Indeed, tribalism, particularly in Cyrenaica, was to become one aspect of a process of slow fragmentation of authority that was to create the basis for the emergence of civil resistance before the civil war began in 2011.

Ironically enough, the regime had always been aware of its vulnerability to the vagaries of tribalism. Its own powerbase had depended on the tribes of Sirtica in central Libya, formerly subservient to those of Cyrenaica. The 1969 revolution was, therefore, in one sense, a reversal of a tribal order in that the formerly dominant Sa'adi tribes were now subordinated to their former vassals. In recognition of this, the regime had, early on in the 1970s, tried to neutralize tribal power outside its own client tribes of the Warfalla, Qadhadhfa, and Maghraha by creating a new system of rural administration that deliberately ignored tribal boundaries and tribal leaders.[16] The experiment failed within a decade and, by 1986 in the wake of the American bombings of Tripoli and Benghazi, it was reversed, with tribal leaderships now being asked to guarantee the loyalty of tribal members to the regime. The new policy was formalized by a committee bringing tribal leaders together in the Popular Social Leadership, under a national coordinator.[17]

Yet, in reality, this provided tribal leaderships with the opportunity to withhold their support, if they felt so inclined, as happened in the aftermath of the Bani Walid coup in 1993, when the leadership of the Warfalla refused the regime's request to punish the coup ringleaders, all members of the tribe.[18] There were similar murmurings of resentment among the Berber tribes of the

[15] Brahimi, 'Libya's Revolution', 112.
[16] Omar I. El Fathaly et al., *Political Development and Bureaucracy in Libya* (Lexington, MA: Lexington Books, 1977), 92.
[17] Amal Obeidi, *Political Culture in Libya* (Richmond, Surrey: Curzon Press, 2001), 119–20.
[18] Lisa Anderson, 'Qadhafi's Legacy: An Evaluation of a Political Experiment', in Dirk Vandewalle (ed.), *Gaddafi's Libya, 1969–1994* (New York: St Martin's Press, 1995), 233–5.

Jabal Nafusa and the Touareg of the Central Sahara, for the Gaddafi regime, given its Arab nationalist origins, refused to recognize the growing sentiments of Amazigh identity in both Libya and elsewhere in North Africa that began to emerge at the end of the 1990s. They mirrored the long-standing, if barely expressed, resentments of religious elements—the Gaddafi regime had expropriated *waqf* property and cowed the *ulema* in 1978, and treated any manifestation of religious belief outside its control as heretical, brutally suppressing movements such as the Muslim Brotherhood after they had appeared in Libya in the 1960s.[19]

Most of the major challenges to the authority of the regime, however, occurred at a crucial moment, when it had had to make a series of concessions to popular sentiment as a result of the antagonism directed at it by Western states. Timid initial measures of political liberalization emerged after 1987, with the removal of restrictions on foreign travel, the liberation of political prisoners, and a human-rights charter, while attempts to liberalize the economy faced the combined opposition of the leadership and the Revolutionary Committee Movement.[20] At the same time, the Libyan regime began to make half-hearted attempts to persuade Libyan exiles abroad to return, to revitalize the economy.[21] Those who did return began to construct a private-sector economy with reluctant regime acquiescence and implicitly, thereby, became another potential pole of resistance to the regime's hegemonic control.

The 1990s, therefore, in addition to seeing major dissidence in Cyrenaica, also witnessed a general fragmentation of regime authority as a result of internal political failure and external diplomatic challenge, even though the fiction of regime control was preserved. At the same time, the gap between the regime's self-image of the *jamahiri* ideal and the reality of its growing weakness was becoming all too apparent, despite its refusal to acknowledge its deficiencies. A new generation was also emerging in a country now dominated

---

[19] Alia Brahimi, 'Islam in Libya', in George Joffé (ed.), *Islamist Radicalisation in North Africa: Politics and Process* (London: Routledge, 2012), 10–19.

[20] Zahi Mogherbi, 'Social Change, Regime Performance and the Radicalisation of Politics: The Case of Libya', in Joffé (ed.), *Islamist Radicalisation in North Africa*, 39–41. The Revolutionary Committee Movement had been created in 1979 as a vehicle for galvanizing the political process and ensuring that Colonel Gaddafi could directly intervene in the political direction of the *Jamahiriya*. Hanspeter Mattes regards this as the inauguration of the dual nature of the Libyan state into an institutional sector, where the Gaddafi leadership had no formal control, that being the duty of the 'people's authority', and the revolutionary sector, legally unregulated and under the regime's direct authority: Hanspeter Mattes, 'Formal and Informal Authority in Libya since 1969', in Dirk Vandewalle (ed.), *Libya since 1969: Qadhafi's Revolution Revisited* (Basingstoke and New York: Palgrave Macmillan, 2008), 58.

[21] Many Libyans had fled abroad after the 1973–9 restructuring of politics and the economy. Although some became absorbed into the multifarious opposition movements to the regime abroad, many more—professionals and businessmen—sought to restore their fortunes in the countries that gave them asylum. Needless to say, those associated with formal opposition movements were not encouraged to return!

by the urban conurbations of Tripoli and Benghazi, in a population transformed by universal education, with tertiary education often gained abroad. It
was increasingly clear that the rigid simplicities of the *jamahiri* system were
ill-adapted to these new domestic and diplomatic environments and that,
despite entrenched resistance from the ideological allies of the colonel-leader,
it would have to evolve to survive.[22]

The most obvious agent for change, not surprisingly, was to emerge from
within the Gaddafi family itself. By the beginning of the twenty-first century,
Colonel Gaddafi's children had begun to come of age and had begun to exploit
the family inheritance that Libya seemed to them to represent. For most of
them, this meant the wilful abuse of commercial and personal opportunity
generated by the untrammelled power derived from their father. However,
Colonel Gaddafi's second son—his first son by his second marriage—Saif
al-Islam, had political pretensions as well. From his position as head of the
al-Gaddafi International Charity and Development Foundation, he began to
suggest cautiously that Libya needed a more structured political system in
which the violence and abuses of the Revolutionary Committee Movement
and the security services could be contained, alongside a more viable economic
system.[23]

Of course, his proposals, as they emerged during the subsequent decade,
were contingent on his father's approval, and it was notable that their prominence in Libyan public life ebbed and flowed with the Colonel's own hesita-
tions about tampering with his political creation. Eventually, of course, when
the civil war erupted in February 2011, Saif al-Islam, abandoning his liberal
pretensions, fell into line behind his father in rejecting the rebellion's explicit
rejection of the *Jamahiriya*.[24] Nonetheless, during those ten years, he had
contributed towards creating an environment in which new, often dissident,

---

[22] In Libya, Colonel Gaddafi was the 'Qa'id'—Leader—of the Libyan Revolution and thus
politically dominant, despite his lack of formal power.

[23] George Joffé, 'Civil Activism and the Roots of the 2011 Uprisings', in Jason Pack (ed.), *The
2011 Libyan Uprisings and the Struggle for the Post-Qadhafi Future* (London and New York:
Palgrave Macmillan, 2013), 31–5.

[24] The reasons for this are still a mystery, particularly as Saif al-Islam seems initially to have
seen the insurgency in Benghazi as an opportunity for positive change. It has been suggested that
it was the insurgents' refusal to accord a formal role for his father in the new Libya that radically
and so rapidly changed his position. However, this is quite inadequate to explain the ferocity of
the commitment he voiced towards his father's regime and against the insurgency in his
television address on 20 February 2011, which marked the abandonment of his urbane image
as reformer and liberal. Indeed, shortly before he actually made the speech, he had talked to a
contact in Britain, expressing his belief that his moment for reform had arrived. On the other
hand, he was always intimidated by his father, and the latter's adamant refusal to tolerate
compromise may have psychologically forced Saif al-Islam to adopt an equally intransigent
position. See Philippe Sands, 'The Accomplice', *Vanity Fair*, 22 August 2011 http://www.
vanityfair.com/politics/features/2011/08/qaddafi-201108.

ideas could emerge—thus underlining the increasing lack of credibility enjoyed by the *jamahiri* vision among Libya's new intelligentsia.

More importantly, by creating a new space for public discussion—and among Saif al-Islam's initiatives were two private daily newspapers, *Oea* and *Quryna*, created in August 2007, together with a satellite television channel, al-Libeyya[25]—a space was also created for open organized public dissidence, particularly in Cyrenaica. This was stimulated, first, by formal discussions, at the University of Gar Younis in Benghazi, of alternative political paradigms for Libya and, second, by the commissioning of an economic development plan from American consultants in Boston by the National Development Board, a formal institution of the Libyan state run by Mahmoud Jibril, a colleague of Saif al-Islam's and the founder, in 2012, of Libya's largest political party, the National Forces Alliance. All these developments contributed towards a sense that a political thaw had begun.

The Crisis in Cyrenaica

There was, however, a series of quite specific issues that played into the regime's apparent lack of self-confidence, as it prepared to accommodate to Western pressure for reform and compliance over the Lockerbie affair, and to growing domestic perceptions that a political thaw was underway. Interestingly enough, they all occurred in Cyrenaica, and each of them undermined the regime's sense of invulnerability, thus preparing the way for civil resistance. The first was the crisis over the Abu Salim prison massacre in 1996, the second the HIV/AIDS scandal in Benghazi, which became public in November 1998, and the third a demonstration in front of the Italian consulate in Benghazi in 2006. Each of them engendered public protest, which became increasingly organized as time went by, and they were to culminate in the demonstrations that ushered in the civil war in February 2011.

The Abu Salim prison massacre occurred on 28–29 June 1996, when, after a demonstration about prison conditions, the prison and security authorities killed up to 1,200 prisoners and buried them in the precincts of the prison in Tripoli. The precise numbers involved are unknown, although the al-Gaddafi Charitable Foundation published a figure of 1,167 deaths on 10 August 2009. The massacre was first admitted by Colonel Gaddafi in a speech in April 2004. It was confirmed in late July 2008 in a speech by his son, Saif al-Islam, who

---

[25] Human Rights Watch, *Truth and Justice Can't Wait*, 2, 20–1. A new state-run terrestrial channel, al-Wasat, was also founded at the same time. Eventually, his father took fright at such uncontrolled media activity and had the newspapers shut down and the television channel taken over by the state in 2010. Committee to Protect Journalists, *Libya Press, under Harassment, Shuts down in Tripoli* (New York: CPJ, 9 December 2010) www.cpj.org/2010/12/libya-press-under-harassment-shuts-down-in-tripoli.php.

stated that an internal investigation had been completed. All results of the investigation were kept secret, apparently because of resistance from the internal security services.[26] The official response, in short, clearly showed an internally divided administration, confused about what the nature of its reaction to the massacre should be.

As a result, in March 2007, thirty families filed a civil claim in the North Benghazi Court (most of the victims appeared to come from Cyrenaica) to force a coherent government response. Although the suit was initially rejected, the court accepted it in June 2008, calling on the government to inform the families of what had happened, and, in December 2008, the Justice Secretary, Mustafa Abdeljalil, called on the General Peoples Committee—Libya's equivalent of a ministerial cabinet—to fulfil the court's decision. By April of the following year, the families of 800–820 of the victims had been given death certificates and those of a further 350–400 victims awaited proper acknowledgement of what had occurred. The government also offered compensation, eventually reaching LD200,000 ($165,000) per victim, provided the families concerned abandoned further attempts at legal redress. On 10 August 2009 the al-Gaddafi Charitable Foundation announced that 569 families had accepted the compensation terms, but that 598 families had refused them, either on principle or because the sums offered were too small—the families of the American victims of the Lockerbie disaster, they pointed out, had been offered $10 million per victim.[27]

By this time, the court delays had emboldened the families into creating an action committee: in April 2008 they formed a Coordination Committee of the Families of the Victims and tried to register it—unsuccessfully, given security service opposition—as a non-governmental organization under Law 19 (2001). The committee organized demonstrations—despite the fact that demonstrations were banned in Libya—beginning in Benghazi in June 2008 and repeating them every two months. The numbers involved were small but swelled to 150 participants by the end of November of that year, despite the official intimidation they faced. It was also clear that they benefited from official embarrassment about what had happened, with different reactions coming from the Libyan leader, his son, and the security services.[28]

The pressure on the authorities was further increased when, in March 2009, the committee published a list of demands on Libyan websites abroad, demanding, inter alia, that the full truth of what had happened at Abu Salim should be revealed, those responsible should be prosecuted, an official public apology should be made, and that compensation up to the level of that paid to settle the Lockerbie affair should be provided. Surprisingly, the first official

---

[26] Human Rights Watch, *Truth and Justice Can't Wait*, 46–51.
[27] Human Rights Watch, *Truth and Justice Can't Wait*, 55–6.
[28] Human Rights Watch, *Truth and Justice Can't Wait*, 56–9.

response was to negotiate, with the security chief, Abdullah Senussi, and the Justice Secretary (later to become head of the National Transitional Council, the effective government of Libya after the civil war) meeting the committee's officials. However, since they refused any question of prosecutions, the negotiations were broken off and a more normal official reaction ensued. At the end of March, five committee members, including Fathi Terbil, a lawyer, were arrested, being accused of 'inciting violence' by the internal security head, Khalid al-Tohamy.[29]

The five were released four days later, after Saif al-Islam had intervened. Not surprisingly, the demonstrations then spread to other cities, in particular Derna and al-Beida, and now targeted the offices of the internal security services, with the numbers involved rising to 200 on 29 June 2009. The antiphonal interplay of demonstration and official response highlighted the ambivalence and weakness of the regime and, more importantly, marked the beginning of organized civil resistance in Libya, despite the continued presence of the repressive institutions of the Gaddafian stateless state. Its success and its legitimacy as a vehicle of dissent were implicitly confirmed when the Justice Secretary Mustafa Abdeljalil made it clear that the administration would accept the judgment of the court over the Abu Salim massacre.

The weakness of the regime in the way in which it reacted to public anger over the Abu Salim massacre was to be exploited in the next scandal that revealed a quite frightening degree of popular vengefulness, which the regime skilfully used to divert public blame from itself. This was the HIV/AIDS crisis that erupted in Benghazi in November 1998, when news that many children in Benghazi's al-Fatih general children's hospital had been infected with the disease. The eventual total reached 426 victims, although the initial report in *La* magazine had mentioned only 60 children who were infected.[30] Twenty-six Bulgarian medical staff at the hospital were investigated, and, in March 1999, five Bulgarian nurses and a Palestinian doctor were accused of being responsible for deliberately infecting the children concerned, even though many of the infections had occurred before those accused had even arrived to work in Libya. Although no clear motive for their actions ever emerged, Colonel Gaddafi eventually hinted at conspiracies by the CIA and Mossad as being at the root of the problem.

The accused were tortured in detention, then tried and condemned to death. After an intervention by Saif al-Islam, the case was remanded to the appeal court and then the supreme court, where the death sentence was

---

[29] Human Rights Watch, *Truth and Justice Can't Wait*, 58.

[30] *La* ('No!') magazine was a monthly, published in Tripoli, and, in its November 1998 issue, no. 78, it published an interview with the health minister in which the details of the AIDS epidemic appeared. The magazine was subsequently shut down, although the article is still available www.webcitation.org/5Mem2Kvyz.

confirmed in a subsequent trial in July 2007, despite scientific reports from international experts, including two pioneers of HIV/AIDS, Luc Montagnier and Vittorio Colizzi, that the cause of the infections was almost certainly the appalling hygiene standards in the hospital.[31] Following the international outcry over the issue, the death sentences were eventually commuted to life imprisonment, and then, through European Union mediation and a late French intervention, the prisoners were extradited to Bulgaria in late July 2007, where, amid considerable Libyan anger, they were pardoned by the Bulgarian president, Georgi Parvanov.

The interesting dimension of this crisis is that, unlike the Abu Salim prison massacre, the issue in Benghazi was driven by public opinion, to which the regime accommodated itself. It did not attempt to conceal information about the issue, nor did it threaten the families of those involved to dissuade them from persisting with their demands for 'justice'. Indeed, it could be argued that it allowed itself to be co-opted by the protestors into endorsing their demands, only turning against them at the end of the crisis when it sought a way out from the outcome it had itself allowed to develop—the death sentences that so outraged the international community.

Two factors seem to explain this acquiescence of the authorities in a narrative that they must have realized quite quickly was false. The first is that the Gaddafi regime was very sensitive about its support base in Cyrenaica, which it perceived to be weak; and the second is that it had already begun to learn how difficult it was to block knowledge of scandals from the public disquiet that had begun to emerge, particularly in Cyrenaica, over the Abu Salim prison massacre affair. Both reasons point to the weakness of the regime in maintaining its hold over the population, especially in the eastern part of the country, a feature that is supported by a third factor that has been rarely adduced in this context—profound popular prejudice.

Bulgaria had long supplied medical staff to Libya; during the Cold War, this was done on a country-to-country basis, and, after the Cold War was over, a commercial Bulgarian company took over the supply process. The system was not popular in Libya itself, for Bulgarian medical staff were generally considered to treat their Libyan patients with some contempt. Palestinians, too, were disliked and distrusted by the regime, and the small Palestinian community in the country found itself increasingly victimized after the Oslo Accords between the Palestine Liberation Organization and Israel had been signed in 1993. As a result, when the crisis broke in Benghazi at the end of 1998, the Bulgarian and Palestinian medical staff at the al-Fatih hospital were convenient and obvious targets for popular anger, which the regime was too weak to

---

[31] Elisabeth Rosenthal, 'HIV Injustice in Libya—Scapegoating Foreign Medical Professionals', *New England Journal of Medicine,* 355/24 (14 December 2006), 2505 http://www.nejm.org/toc/nejm/355/24.

counter and which, instead, it therefore humoured. This included tolerating repeated demonstrations by the families of the victims and threats of legal action for compensation as the crisis deepened.

Finally, on 17 February 2006, public anger at the antics of an Italian cabinet minister on satellite television led to a demonstration outside the Italian consulate in Benghazi—satellite television from Italy can be accessed easily in Libya. The minister had provocatively revealed to the camera a T-shirt he was wearing, which was emblazoned with a series of cartoons produced in Denmark the previous year lampooning Islam and the Prophet Muhammad. The reaction in Benghazi revealed both the depth of Islamist sentiment in the city and the sense of immunity that had developed in Cyrenaica towards the regime. The police in the city reacted violently, and, in the ensuing melee, at least ten people were killed. This, in turn, led to further resentment and demands for compensation, which further reinforced the roles of the lawyers who were already representing families concerned over the prison massacre and the HIV/AIDS scandal. Their protests were bolstered by the fact that the Gaddafi regime, in a gesture towards public sentiment, suspended the interior minister because of police over-reaction.[32]

Thus, by the end of the first decade of the twenty-first century, the Gaddafi regime's image of absolute control of an allegedly perfected political system had been badly dented by civil disobedience and resistance, particularly in Cyrenaica. Its image of perfection, too, had been challenged by new models of political organization tentatively proposed by the intelligentsia around the Colonel's second son, Saif al-Islam, also mainly located in Cyrenaica. Nor had civil disobedience and violent dissidence been confined solely to Cyrenaica: at the beginning of the decade, Colonel Gaddafi's decision to switch his allegiance from Arab to African unity because of his disgust with the lack of support offered to Libya by the Arab world had created another major challenge to the state as well.

A very large group of sub-Saharan Africans entered Libya at the end of the 1990s, in the wake of the regime's decision to espouse the cause of African, rather than Arab, unity and its removal of administrative barriers to inward sub-Saharan African immigration. Their numbers were not known, but estimates ranged between two million and three million—a massive burden for a country with a total population estimated in 2000 at 5.1 million.[33] The Libyan economy, despite its dependence on migrant labour, traditionally supplied mainly by Egypt or Tunisia, with a minor component from the Sahel states to the south, was not able to absorb this influx, mainly from West Africa. Furthermore, the sudden arrival of such migrants, located in large shanty

---

[32] AP report, 'Libya Suspends Interior Minister after Cartoon Riots', *Guardian*, 18 February 2006 http://www.theguardian.com/world/2006/feb/18/muhammadcartoons.libya1.

[33] Charles P. Trumbull (ed.), *Britannica Book of the Year: 2001* (Chicago: Encyclopaedia Britannica, 2001), 658.

towns around the major coastal settlements in Tripolitania, meant a sudden increase in crime and crime-related activities, such as drug-smuggling.

In September 2000 the tensions arising from this led to severe rioting in Zawiya and Tripoli, in which up to eighty persons died (official accounts suggested that only six had died). The rioting was stimulated by the fact that Libyans, like many North Africans, are profoundly prejudiced against sub-Saharan Africans—slavery, traditionally supplied from sub-Saharan Africa, was widespread throughout the Ottoman Empire, of which Libya was a part until 1911. In the wake of the rioting, more than 300 persons—Libyans and African migrants—were put on trial, and, in late May 2001, seven of them were sentenced to death for their involvement.

Popular anger about both the issue of migration and the regime's ill-considered foreign policies remained intense, however, thus further sapping the regime's credibility. While Libyans had shared a strong sense of communality with the Arab world—the Gaddafi regime's original regional diplomatic alignment—they deeply resented the regime's switch to an exclusive identity with Africa after 1997. They also deeply resented the regime's interpretation of what the switch would mean—unrestricted and unregulated inward migration to Libya, particularly to Tripolitania. African irritation with the Gaddafi regime resulted in its marginalization in the new pan-African organization, the African Union, which in 2001–2 had replaced the ineffective Organization of African Unity, an organizational change in which Libya had, ironically enough, been instrumental.

THE STRUGGLE FOR A POLITICAL ALTERNATIVE

The upshot was that, by the end of the decade, the Gaddafi regime had lost much of its credibility; it could certainly still repress those opposed to it, but organized dissent was tacitly tolerated provided it did not directly threaten the regime. Although, unlike its fellows in North Africa, it never adopted the 'liberalized autocracy' solution, it had come to accept what was to prove to be an even more dangerous alternative, informal civil resistance. And this had been allowed to come to the fore in that part of the country where Gaddafi's writ had never been fully accepted—Cyrenaica. Once the regime realized the import of its oversight in this respect, of course, it attempted to respond with brutal repression, as Colonel Gaddafi's son, Saif al-Islam, made clear in a televised speech on 20 February 2011—a decision that eventually entailed the regime's own destruction.[34] These adjustments were to prove crucial when the popular uprisings in Tunisia and Egypt found their echo in Libya in mid-February 2011.

[34] Sands, 'The Accomplice'.

The civil war in Libya did not erupt through a generalized demand for an end to the Gaddafi regime, as had occurred elsewhere. Instead, despite regime fears of sympathy demonstrations and warnings of repressive action if they occurred, the immediate catalyst for the civil war was a demonstration planned in support of the families of the victims of the 2006 cartoon demonstrations. However, Libyan exiled groups and the very small community of Libyan resident internauts had, for several days, been circulating calls for a nationwide 'Day of Rage' on 17 February against the Gaddafi regime as well—which undoubtedly echoed around the wider dissident community inside Cyrenaica.[35] One of them, Jamil al-Hajji, was arrested in Tripoli on 1 February by the Libyan police, allegedly for a car accident but in reality for his appeal to civil resistance, despite Colonel Gaddafi's public warnings of the consequences.[36]

In Benghazi on 15 February 2011, in a pre-emptive move against calls for the 'Day of Rage' demonstrations two days later—the anniversary of the demonstration in 2006 that had caused ten deaths—the authorities arrested the lawyer, Fathi Terbil, who had been instrumental in aiding the 2006 protestors as well as the Abu Salim families in their demands for legal compensation from the Gaddafi regime, and a writer, Idris al-Mesmari, who had given an interview to the Al Jazeera satellite television channel about the proposed protests.[37] That evening a small demonstration against the arrests took place outside the police headquarters in Benghazi, and the police responded brutally. On the following days, the demonstrations spread from Benghazi, to Derna and Beida and, in Tripolitania, to Zintan. The police reaction caused several deaths, especially on 17 February (see Figure 5.1).

By then the demonstrations, generally called the 'February 17 Movement', had become massive.[38] Police and army units in Benghazi and Beida were withdrawn during the following two days as the demonstrations were transformed into violent dissidence in reaction to police and army brutality, and the civil war began in earnest. It was also at this moment that defections from the Gaddafi regime began, led by Mustafa Abdeljalil, the former justice minister and a native of Benghazi, together with the head of the National Development Board, Mahmoud Jibril. They were soon joined by the Libyan interior minister,

---

[35] George Joffé, 'Libya Faces its "Day of Rage"', in Alvaro de Vasconcelos (ed.), *The Arab Democratic Wave: How the EU can Seize the Moment* (Paris: European Union Institute for Security Studies, Report No. 9, March 2011), 20 http://www.iss.europa.eu/publications/reports.

[36] Amnesty International, 'Libyan Writer Detained after Protest Call', Amnesty, London, 8 February 2011 http://www.amnesty.org.uk/press-releases/libya-writer-detained-after-protest-call.

[37] News report from Al Jazeera and agencies, 'Libyan Police Stations Torched', Al Jazeera, 16 February 2011 www.aljazeera.com/news/africa/2011/02/20112167051422444.html.

[38] For well-informed accounts of these events in Libya, including the demonstrations in Benghazi and Tripoli, see Peter Cole and Brian McQuinn (eds), *The Libyan Revolution and its Aftermath* (London: Hurst, 2015). In particular see ch. 2, Peter Bartu, 'The Corridor of Uncertainty: The National Transitional Council's Battle for Legitimacy and Recognition' (pp. 31–55); and ch. 3, Peter Cole and Umar Khan, 'The Fall of Tripoli: Part 1' (pp. 55–81).

Figure 5.1. In a demonstration in Benghazi, in eastern Libya, on 24 February 2011, el-Faitory Meftah el-Bouras holds up a portrait of his son Fathig, one of many thousands of political prisoners killed by Libyan security forces under the Gaddafi regime. The Libyan protests had begun in Benghazi nine days earlier, on 15 February. By the time of this demonstration they had spread to other parts of the country, and in face of the regime's repression there had also been the beginnings of civil war.

© *John Moore/Getty Images*

also an Easterner, Abdelfattah Yunis al-Obidi, who would lead the resistance forces until his mysterious assassination in July 2011. Libyan diplomats abroad also began to abandon the regime, as the rebellion quickly took hold of Cyrenaica. There were also significant defections from the Libyan army based in Benghazi, sparked off by the massive popular demonstrations.

However, the picture of the Libyan opposition in February 2011 as a pure case of civil (i.e. non-violent) resistance is a simplification. The International Crisis Group highlighted this in a report in June 2011:

> At the same time, much Western media coverage has from the outset presented a very one-sided view of the logic of events, portraying the protest movement as entirely peaceful and repeatedly suggesting that the regime's security forces were unaccountably massacring unarmed demonstrators who presented no real security challenge. This version would appear to ignore evidence that the protest movement exhibited a violent aspect from very early on. While there is no doubt that many and quite probably a large majority of the people mobilised in the early demonstrations were indeed intent on demonstrating peacefully, there is

also evidence that, as the regime claimed, the demonstrations were infiltrated by violent elements.[39]

The regime, too, did much to provoke the opposition's reliance on violence. On 22 February Gaddafi, with his grip on the country weakening daily, made a televised speech in which, quite typically, he blamed the unrest on foreign powers, brainwashing, drug-dealers, and regional turmoil, and then called for demonstrators to be executed and for loyalists to 'cleanse Libya house by house'.[40] Unlike the past, however, on this occasion his speech, and the ruthless pro-regime shootings in Tripoli on the same day, had a major effect in mobilizing opinion and action against him throughout Libya. Libyans had, in short, lost their fear of the regime, despite its brutal reputation, largely because of its failure to hold down dissent in Cyrenaica. The speech also had a significant impact internationally, contributing to the hard line taken by the UN Security Council four days later.

The sheer violence of the repression (including of unarmed demonstrators), and of Gaddafi's rhetoric, made it improbable that any resistance, if it were to continue openly on the streets, could have confined itself to non-violent forms of action. A particular consideration was that, in areas (mainly in Cyrenaica) that had freed themselves from Gaddafi's control, there was an understandable concern to have some means of defence against a threatened reimposition by the regime. Yet, despite the increasing trend towards violence, the principles of non-violent civil resistance manifested themselves in three important ways in the course of events in Libya. First, despite the growth in popular violence directed against the regime, as manifested particularly in the sudden emergence of armed militias to oppose it, in the early stages peaceful, unarmed protest demonstrations took place throughout the country until official repression made them far too risky. Secondly, as the chaos of war progressed, disrupting communal and distribution services, spontaneous committees began to emerge that took over municipal and communal responsibilities.[41] And, thirdly, the process of creating new, albeit temporary, governance structures was, too, a consequence of civil resistance.

The National Transitional Council (NTC), formed on 27 February 2011, as a new governance structure, was, perhaps, the Libyan revolution's key achievement, as it provided a vehicle through which the Libyan revolution could reach out to the international community, particularly after the UN Security Council had intervened, declaring, on 26 February, an assets freeze and arms embargo, and then, in mid-March, a no-fly zone over Libya combined with an

---

[39] International Crisis Group, *Popular Protest in North Africa and the Middle East (V): Making Sense of Libya* (Brussels: ICG, Middle East/North Africa Report no. 107, 6 June 2011), 4 http://www.crisisgroup.org/en/publication-type/media-releases/2011/making-sense-of-Libya.aspx, citing several sources, including reports by Amnesty International and Agence France Presse.

[40] Reuters report from Tripoli, 'Defiant Gaddafi Vows to Die as Martyr, Fight Revolt', 22 February 2011 http://www.reuters.com/article/2011/02/22/us-libya-protests-idUSTRE71G0A620110222.

[41] Integrated Regional Information Networks, *Libya: Civil Society Breaks Through* (Geneva: UN Office for the Coordination of Humanitarian Affairs, 16 August 2011) www.irinnews.org/Report/93513/Libya.

authorization to NATO to use force.[42] Talks to form a council to act as an interim administration had begun three days before the date on which the council was formally announced, in Beida, between politicians, former military officers, tribal leaders, academics, and businessmen. The meeting and the council that it formed were chaired by the former justice secretary, Mustafa Abdeljalil and an executive was eventually created by Mahmoud Jibril, the former head of the National Development Board.

The council's success, therefore, was partly predicated on the actions of the UN, and it certainly sought to encourage the international body's active involvement in the struggle now emerging inside Libya. This was particularly the case with the UN Security Council resolution of 17 March authorizing a no-fly zone over the country, an issue over which the Gaddafi regime also proved to be its own worst enemy. The Council's resolution highlighted the fact that the Gaddafi regime had antagonized the Arab League, the African Union, and the Organisation of the Islamic Conference, all of which had issued highly condemnatory statements. Indeed, this absence of any significant international support contributed to the regime's undoing. It was only much later, after its fate appeared to have been sealed, that some African states and other observers began to question what had happened.[43] The Council's resolution makes it clear that it was the Libyan regime's own actions that justified the imposition of the no-fly zone and the asset freeze, the most prominent measures it proposed. In its preamble, the resolution explicitly attacked the regime, for it considered that 'the widespread and systematic attacks currently taking place in the Libyan Arab Jamahiriya against the civilian population may amount to crimes against humanity'.[44] Under paragraphs 8 and 9 of the resolution, 'regional organizations' could be responsible for the policing of the no-fly zone, with NATO being subsequently nominated for this role, a decision the NTC enthusiastically endorsed. The US-supported and NATO-led campaign of air strikes and other military support for the rebels in Libya, from 20 March to 31 October 2011, contributed to the defeat of the Gaddafi regime; and a NATO air strike on 20 October triggered the gruesome events that day in which Gaddafi and his fourth son, al-Mu'atassim, were killed.

In domestic terms, in addition to handling day-to-day administration and overseeing the conduct of the civil war, the council subsequently organized elections and finally handed over power to a provisional government and the elected constituent assembly on 8 August 2012. Although it was not able to ensure full governmental control of the security situation, it did, nonetheless, organize a successful and peaceful electoral process in a country where meaningful elections had not taken place for more than four decades. It also

---

[42] SC Res. 1970 of 26 February 2011; SC Res. 1973 of 17 March 2011.
[43] See Hugh Roberts, 'Who said Gaddafi had to Go?', *London Review of Books*, 33/22 (17 November 2011), 8–18 www.lrb.co.uk/v33/n22/hugh-roberts/who-said-gaddafi-had-to-go.
[44] SC Res. 1973 of 17 March 2011.

Figure 5.2. The graffiti artist's revenge. This wall in Tripoli, photographed on 28 September 2011, shows a municipal sign that reads in Arabic: 'Keep your city clean.' Below that is written: 'Libya is free' and on the rubbish bin where Gaddafi is being consigned are the words: 'The garbage of history.' The Libyan leader was captured and killed a month later.

© *AP Photo/Abdel Magid al Fergany*

made sure that the essential administrative structure remained operational, despite the damage wrought by the war and by growing internecine feuds between those who had supported the previous regime and those who opposed it. It was no mean achievement, even if many involved had been active in the administration of the Gaddafi regime itself. Indeed, sustaining its nature as essentially the embodiment of civil resistance in Libya throughout a nine-month-long civil war was a significant achievement in itself (see Figure 5.2).

THE FRAGMENTATION OF THE NEW STATE

One initial by-product of the new era upon which Libya embarked as a consequence of the disappearance of the Gaddafi regime and the constraints it had placed on freedom of expression was an explosion of non-governmental organizations. This began in Benghazi at the start of the civil war but has now spread throughout the country. Thus, by 2013, the European Union's Neighbourhood Info Centre had noted more than 300 registrations of civil society organizations with the new authorities.[45] Indeed, this could well be an under-estimate, for, as early as November 2011, 361 civil society organizations were said to be active in Benghazi and a further 500 in Tripoli, although many of them were not expected to survive for very long![46]

In fact, by May 2012, the Libyan High National Electoral Commission, the body that registered political parties, unions, and associations, suggested that it had registered 374 'political entities', although it believed that there were many more such groups that were unregistered. The total included 100 political parties, of which 63 were represented in the General National Congress. A draft law on associations was also being prepared that would exclude organizations based on race, gender, ethnicity, tribe, or language—thus preventing tribalism from prejudicing non-governmental organizations in future. It also required such organizations to respect democracy, civic values, equality, national law and international convention, human rights, and transparency. There was a strong prejudice against foreign funding for such bodies, although foreign non-governmental organizations would be tolerated.[47] The media sector, on the other hand, proved to be vibrant—by the summer of 2012, there were estimated to be more than 200 newspapers, 20 private television channels, and 200 independent radio stations operating in the country.[48]

The major problem that Libya faced, however, was that, four years after the collapse of the Gaddafi regime, the new authorities had still been unable to ensure security within the country. This has been largely a consequence of the way in which the civil war had developed, in that armed resistance to the regime was based on the spontaneous formation of armed militias on a regional, tribal, and confessional basis. The loyalties of these groups, estimated at more than 350 in number, remained attached to such geographic, ethnic, or sectarian markers, not to the new state that was to emerge. In addition, the fact that such groups were heavily armed, with their own agendas and often criminalized as well, meant that popular protest at their increasing depredations, given the government's inability to control them, was snuffed out. This was underlined by the arrogation of the right and duty of the state to dispense justice as well as security by the militias themselves, as they set up impromptu detention centres around the country for alleged supporters of the previous regime.

[45] EU Neighbourhood Info Centre, *Libya, Showing a New Face to the World* (Feature No. 87, 21 February 2013), 1 http://www.enpi-info.eu/mainmed.php?id=619&id_type=6&lang_id=450.

[46] Foundation for the Future, *Assessing Needs of Civil Society in Libya: An Analysis of the Current Needs and Challenges of the Civil Society in Libya* (Amman, November 2011), 8 http://foundationforfuture.org/en/WebPresence/Publications/ReportsStudies.aspx.

[47] Barah Mikaïl, *Civil Society and Foreign Donors in Libya* (Madrid: FRIDE, 2013), 3–6 http://www.fride.org/publication/1144/civil-society-and-foreign-donors-in-libya.

[48] Libya Media Wiki http://en.libyamediawiki.com/index.php?title=Overview (website no longer operative May 2015). See also Fatima El-Issawi, *Transitional Libyan Media: Free at Last?* (Washington: Carnegie Endowment for International Peace, 14 May 2013) http://carnegieendowment.org/2013/05/14/transitional_Libyan_media_free_at_last/g3dk#.

In short, the fragmentation of authority implied by the behaviour of the militias, whatever their intentions might have been, meant that civil resistance virtually ceased to be a viable means of protest—just as it had been under the Gaddafi regime itself, although now for quite different reasons, as some observers had anticipated.[49] Nonetheless, the tradition still remains, and, in March 2012, activists in Tripoli announced a campaign of civil disobedience to protest against the activities of the militias at border points throughout the country, in the hope that this would galvanize the government into action.[50] In a similar way, the assassination of the American ambassador in Benghazi in September 2012 led to mass demonstrations against the group Ansar al-Sharia, which was held responsible. There have since been other demonstrations in both Benghazi and Tripoli for similar reasons, some of which ended in deaths among the demonstrators, as embattled militias reacted with military force against their unarmed opponents. Sadly, these campaigns achieved nothing, for the hold of the militias over domestic security in Libya was, as of May 2015, as strong as it was then, with no end in sight.

In fact, since 2012, the situation in Libya has significantly worsened, and the country is now divided into two, possibly three, virtually separate segments corresponding to its traditional elements of Tripolitania, Cyrenaica, and the Fezzan. After new legislative elections hurriedly held in June 2014, two mutually antagonistic governments have emerged. One is the rump of the former parliament originally elected in July 2012 but whose mandate expired in February 2014, the General National Congress (GNC), and is based in Tripoli, where it is supported by moderate Islamists and a major militia coalition based on the town of Misurata. The other, the House of Representatives (HoR), based in the Cyrenaican city of Tobruk, was elected to replace the GNC in June 2014, but its make-up was unacceptable to moderate Islamist groups, who sought to preserve the GNC instead. The HoR is supported by secular and nationalist political movements, together with military underpinning from the revived Libyan army under a renegade general, Khalifa Haftar, who has promised to eliminate Islamist influence throughout the country. Each has its patrons abroad—the GNC relies on Qatar and Turkey while the HoR is supported by the United Arab Emirates and Egypt. The Fezzan, meanwhile, is in a state of uncontrolled chaos, as the Tibu and Touareg peoples, and groups sympathetic to the former regime, vie for control. Extremist Islamist movements have emerged as well, including a revived Ansar al-Sharia, which is pro-al-Qaeda, around Benghazi and, latterly, the Islamic State, which is opposed to it, in Derna.

[49] Maria Stephan, 'Libya's Revolution: A Model for the Region?', *Waging Nonviolence*, 29 August 2011 http://wagingnonviolence.org/feature/libyas-revolution-a-model-for-the-region.
[50] 'Civil disobedience campaign planned in Tripoli over militias' presence', *Libya Herald*, Tripoli, 30 March 2012 https://twitter.com/libyaherald/status/185677278720696320.

In such circumstances, the opportunities for meaningful civil society activities, let alone civil resistance, have virtually disappeared, for activists have been increasingly subjected to violent repression from both militias and extremist groups. Despite the threat and the very real dangers involved, however, Libyans do not appear to have lost their appetite for popular engagement. By August 2013, for example, more than 3,000 civil society groups had been registered with the authorities, covering a vast range of activities, many of them openly political in intent and, in the circumstances, increasingly geared towards civil resistance to the de facto authorities, even if their access to government was hindered by militia and extremist action.[51] In Cyrenaica, in particular, they paid a very heavy price, although around Libya at least thirty-five prominent civil activists were killed during 2014.[52] Women in parliament, in particular, were threatened with assassination and some actually paid the price—Salwa Bughaighis, a prominent human-rights lawyer in Benghazi, was murdered on election day in June 2014 in Benghazi and Fariha Berkawi, a member of the GNC, had been killed earlier.[53] Journalists, such as Muftah Buzeid, the editor of *Bernice*, and Cyrenaican political activists, such as Abdulsalam al-Mismari, also died. Perhaps the two most shocking killings, perpetrated it is believed by extremist groups as a deliberate act of intimidation, were the assassinations between 18 and 20 September 2014 of two very committed activists, 18-year-old Tawfik Ben Messaud and 19-year-old Sami Elkawafi in Benghazi, as part of a campaign of assassinations in the city.[54]

THE REASONS FOR FAILURE

In the light of the situation in Libya in May 2015, it would be easy to conclude that civil resistance, as a technique to ensure popular participation in governance without resorting to violence, has failed. On the face of it, this is undeniable—at least, at present—for militia and extremist violence have rendered such techniques of struggle unviable. However, over the longer term, this is unlikely to be the case, for no system of government can maintain itself in being or discharge its essential obligations indefinitely without some

---

[51] Fadil Aliriza, 'Libya's Unarmed Revolutionaries: Civil Society Groups Face an Uphill Battle in a Society Dominated by Militias', *Foreign Policy*, Washington, 16 August 2013 http://foreignpolicy.com/2013/08/16/libyas-unarmed-revolutionaries.

[52] Mat Nashed, 'Militants Target Civil Activists in Libya', *AlMonitor*, 29 October 2014 http://www.al-monitor.com/pulse/originals/2014/10/libya-militias-kidnapping-youth-civil-activists.html.

[53] Christine Petré, 'Civil Society Struggles for Greater Role in Libya's Transition', *Middle East Monitor*, 17 October 2014 https://www.middleeastmonitor.com/articles/africa/14712.

[54] Ayat Mneina, 'Attacks on Youth and Civil Society in Libya', *Muftah*, 10 October 2014 http://muftah.org/attacks-youth-civil-society-libya/#.VO5hA0Jikqc.

kind of popular endorsement or tolerance. Moreover, popular rejection of militia violence has, on occasion, forced both militias and extremists to concede, demonstrating that, in the last analysis, they, too, are sensitive to a lack of public support. Indeed, it could be argued that the history of the collapse of the Gaddafi regime also demonstrated this to be the case and that history could easily be repeated, given the appropriate circumstances.

Yet the key to success for social movements based on civil resistance—and civil resistance is a technique that depends on a social movement to frame its arguments and to provide it with the impetus for success—lies in their ability to generate effective organization. It is here, perhaps, in addition to the dissuasive power of naked violence, that part of the explanation for the apparent failure of civil resistance, at least to date, may lie. Organizational capacity, as explained at the start of this chapter, was a feature that the Gaddafi regime denied to the Libyan body politic by its imposition of the *Jamahiriya*. The irony, of course, was that it was because of that denial, itself enforced through violence, that in the end civil resistance contributed mightily to the destruction of the *Jamahiriya* itself! Other factors contributed as well: the *jamahiri* system fragmented informal social bonds by destroying trust within the family and wider society, as Hisham Matar so graphically describes in his book *In the Country of Men*.[55] The potent social role of the tribe in Libya, which coalesces social cohesion within the tribe but fragments it outside the tribal framework, provided another factor. Social and economic fragmenta-tion, particularly after private-sector activity was reluctantly sanctioned in the 1990s, together with the growth of a privileged elite, intensified the atomiza-tion of society. All such factors contributed towards denying civil resistance, when it appeared, a coherent organizational base through which to articulate effectively its demands and thus to achieve its aims.

Of course, it could also be argued that civil resistance, in itself, generates the kinds of chaos that exist today in Libya because, through the process of political contestation, it undermines the ability of the state to discharge its function as the monopolizer of legitimate violence to order society. Yet, in the parallel case of Tunisia, for example, this did not occur—or, at least, not to the same extent. One of the main reasons for this was that in Tunisia the police and the army remained in being so that the state retained the means by which to ensure public order. In Libya this did not occur, for spontaneous militias arose to challenge and undermine the security organs of the state and then to arrogate their functions to themselves.

Two factors were at work here. One was the intense personalization of power within the *Jamahiriya* around the person and the family of Muammar Gaddafi, so that there was no functioning bureaucracy to maintain the state in

---

[55] Matar, *In the Country of Men*.

being once his guiding hand or those of his sons had been removed. The other was that, unlike Tunisia but in a way very similar to Syria, Libya never adopted the stance of being a 'liberalized autocracy'. In other words, it never coped with civil society initiatives by tolerating them, yet carefully controlling their activities, as a mechanism to ensure the survival of the regime itself.[56] Instead, it persisted in outright suppression of all such movements until it could no longer do so, thereby denying them the opportunity to organize effectively in order to channel their demands and maintain control of the wider quasi-revolutionary situation that emerged in Cyrenaica in 2011. Violent confrontation, in short, was the only weapon available to it.

In the light of the proud tradition of civil resistance created under the most adverse of circumstances in Cyrenaica, this situation was to prove to be a tragedy—the violent chaos in which civil resisters are now mired. It is to be hoped that the eventual restoration of legitimate government authority will create the conditions in which such a tradition of civil resistance, alongside the new development of civil society, could be restored as a mechanism to control future abuses of governance. The task is particularly problematic because, in the absence of an accepted system of government throughout the country, Libya has had great difficulty in preventing various extremist groups from establishing a presence, especially in the southern desert regions where smuggling of arms, people, and drugs is rife.

Yet, in the Libyan case, civil resistance alone would not have been capable of ending the Gaddafi regime. Nor, indeed, could the military forces created by the opposition empowered by the events of mid-February 2011 in Benghazi have done so either. In this respect, NATO's intervention to protect the civilian population was critical, even though the nature of the intervention turned out to be less discriminate than NATO claimed, with significant loss of civilian life.[57] The separate initiatives of Britain, France, and Qatar, too, with

---

[56] Brumberg, 'The Trap of Liberalized Autocracy'.

[57] Independent assessments of numbers of deaths that were due to NATO air strikes have reached broadly similar conclusions. The UN Human Rights Council's report by an International Commission of Inquiry on Libya chaired by M. Cherif Bassiouni and Philippe Kirsch, doc. A/HRC/19/68 of 2 March 2012, p. 17, para. 86 http://www.refworld.org/docid/4ffd19532.html, stated that, among the 20 airstrikes they investigated, 60 civilians were killed and 55 were injured. Ben Barry, writing on 'Libya's Lessons' in *Survival* (London, October–November 2011), pointed out that, while the Gaddafi regime had claimed that 1,100 had been killed and 4,500 had been wounded, the real figures were probably between 5 and 10% of these figures. C. J. Chivers and Eric Schmitt, 'In Strikes on Libya by NATO, an Unspoken Civilian Toll', *New York Times*, 17 December 2011, reported that between 40 and 70 civilians had been killed, including 29 women and children in 9 attacks that its reporters had visited. Human Rights Watch, in its 14 May 2012 report *Unacknowledged Deaths: Civilian Casualties in NATO's Air Campaign in Libya*, reported that there had been 72 civilian deaths, including 20 women and 24 children, in 8 sites that it had visited, of which 7 had had no discernible military use and the eighth had been the home of a military officer; and it stated that NATO had flown 26,000 sorties against almost 6,000 targets during its campaign in Libya. Al Jazeera, in a report entitled 'NATO "Ignoring Civilian Deaths in

their adoption of an explicit agenda to achieve 'regime change', also played a critical role in this respect. And it should be noted that, whereas the UN-inspired intervention was stimulated by genuine concerns for the safety of the civilian population, in view of the Gaddafi regime's threats against it, this was not necessarily the case for those states that encouraged straightforward 'regime change'. Some of these states—Qatar, France, and Britain with tacit support from Turkey and the United States—were prepared to intervene directly in support of one side in the civil war, in what may have been an abusive interpretation of the UN Security Council resolutions, in order to ensure the destruction of the regime. For them, the regime itself was the target, a punishment for its long-standing truculence and open rejection of the conventions of international society, and the aftermath could be left to look after itself. In taking such a short-term view, those powers and, unintention-ally NATO as well, connived at the security crisis that faced Libya in the years after 2011.

Libya"', published on the same day, reported on the Human Rights Watch findings, pointing out that in March Amnesty International had said that there had been 55 deaths, including 16 children and 14 women, in Tripoli, Zliten, Majer, Sirte, and Brega.

6

The Change Squares of Yemen

Civil Resistance in an Unlikely Context

Helen Lackner

Given its reputation as a strongly tribal society, where there are reputed to be twice as many weapons as people, discussions of politics in Yemen are more likely to focus on Islamist terrorism than on peaceful civil action. Despite its population of twenty-six million, its status as the only poor state in the Arabian Peninsula, as well as its geographical and strategic position bordering the Red Sea and controlling the Bab al-Mandab strait, Yemen is receiving less attention from scholars than it merits. Since the late 1990s, the presence of al-Qaeda in any one of its various incarnations has increased outside interest in the country mostly within the narrow confines of the terrorism and counter-terrorism discourse. Since 2011, the frequent US use of drones to attack intended al-Qaeda targets in rural areas has had a significant negative impact on ordinary Yemenis' perception of the USA, as the majority of people abhor not just the strikes but the constant presence of drones frequently flying over their homes. More rarely, Yemen has provided good news stories, such as the comedy film *Salmon Fishing in the Yemen* (which has little, if anything, to do with Yemen) or the award of the Nobel Peace Prize to a young Yemeni woman. The country's unique role in the Arab revolutions of 2011 deserves detailed analysis, given the scope, duration, and unique socio-political characteristics of these events.

The Republic of Yemen, with its capital in Sana'a, was established in 1990 by the merger of the Yemen Arab Republic (YAR), and the People's Democratic Republic of Yemen (PDRY)—commonly described as North and South Yemen respectively.[1] The YAR was established in 1962 after the overthrow of the

---

[1] More details on Yemen's contemporary politics and major challenges are found in Helen Lackner (ed.), *Why Yemen Matters: A Society in Transition* (London: Saqi Books, 2014); on the Saleh regime in Sarah Philips, *Yemen's Democracy Experiment in Regional Perspective* (New York: Palgrave, 2008); on the PDRY in Noel Brehony *Yemen Divided* (London: I. B. Tauris, 2011).

Mutawakkilite Imamate, which had controlled most of its territory for the previous centuries—with interruptions when the Ottoman Empire ruled the capital Sana'a and the more fertile areas of what was known as Arabia Felix. The PDRY was established shortly after independence from Britain in 1967, the area it covered having been previously known as Aden Colony and the Western and Eastern Aden Protectorates. From 1963 to 1967 a war of liberation in what was to become the PDRY involved both a struggle against British colonialism and an internecine struggle between two liberation movements: a Nasserite one emerging from the trade-union movement in Aden and a more radical, more rural one, whose ideological origins were in the socialist and left-wing elements of the Movement of Arab Nationalists. Some of the tensions currently plaguing the country have their origins in the diverse and very different histories of the various entities that preceded the Republic of Yemen.

The civil resistance movements discussed here have included activities in all parts of the current republic. The events of 2011 had a significant constitutional and evolutionary aspect and amounted to a revolution—of a unique kind. The use of the contested term 'revolution' is justified for several reasons. First, the movement reflected a fundamental change in the country's political discourse and, whatever the short-term impact of events, a return to the previous political model is an unlikely outcome. Secondly, the uprising was a mass movement, involving a substantial proportion of the country's population; it was not simply a short duration event carried out by a small minority, let alone military cadres, as were many regime changes in the Arab world since the 1950s, whether military coups in the YAR or factional party disputes in the PDRY. Thirdly, it involved broad sections of Yemeni society, overcoming traditional regional and social divisions: participants came from all social groups and socio-economic strata, including ordinary poor people, the lower middle class, intellectuals, rural and urban men and women, people from strongly tribal areas, and others from areas where tribalism is of little relevance. Fourthly, the movement had political objectives that, although ill-defined, called for a fundamental transformation of the country's political system and, for many, of its economic and social structures, way beyond mere change of individuals at the top. Finally, despite having achieved in 2011 one of its main stated objectives—the *irhal*, or removal, of President Ali Abdullah Saleh—the movement continued well beyond his resignation. Weekly demonstrations and street encampments persisted well into 2013.

This chapter focuses on the role and nature of the civil peaceful anti-regime movement in the 'Change Squares' of 2011–13. While elsewhere the popular movements focused on Liberation Squares (*midan al-Tahrir*), this could not be done in Sana'a, as President Saleh cunningly pre-empted the revolutionaries and filled Sana'a's own Liberation Square with his supporters in large military tents. The youth therefore settled in an area around the main gates of the university, which they renamed 'Change Square' (*midan al-taghyeer*, which sounds similar). Some knowledge of Yemeni culture and of the history of peaceful movements in the country is necessary to understand better the reasons why, despite expectations of widespread violence, the movement remained peaceful. I will start with a discussion of the history of non-violent political action in the country as a whole. Finally, I will try to assess the convergences and divergences of the Yemeni situation with the broader questions raised by this book.

CIVIL RESISTANCE IN YEMEN PRIOR TO THE 1960s

There were no civil society or other political citizen movements to speak of in the Mutawakkilite Imamate in the twentieth century:[2] attempts to overthrow Imams Yahya and Ahmed took the form of, mostly failed, coups. Development efforts were those of community-based groups of migrants who organized themselves in the countries where they worked to finance social infrastructures at home. They expanded and grew massively after the 1962 revolution until the 1970s, when these activities developed into a major movement in the YAR.[3] During the colonial period in Aden, northern exiles formed associations, which operated with either explicit or covert agreement of the British authorities; most of these had political objectives and were mainly involved in publication of broad educational and anti-imam newspapers and other publications.[4]

Organizations concerned with the situation in Aden and the Protectorates also existed from the 1930s onwards,[5] mostly in Aden but also, to a lesser extent, in the main Hadhrami towns of Mukalla and Seiyun.[6] They were carefully monitored by the authorities: only those considered politically harmless or whose objectives coincided with those of the authorities were allowed to operate. Particularly in Aden, the most prominent were charitable

---

[2] J. Leigh Douglas, *The Free Yemeni Movement 1935–1962* (Beirut: AUB, 1987).

[3] The imamate was overthrown on 26 September 1962 by what is officially described throughout Yemen as a revolution. Although this does not fit into the definition of a revolution, the term must be used here, as it is a generally accepted description in and out of Yemen.

[4] Douglas, *The Free Yemeni Movement*, 69–108, 163–74.

[5] Sharon Beatty, Ahmed No'man al Madhaji, and Renaud Detalle, *Yemeni NGOs and Quasi-NGOs: Analysis and Directory* (Sanaʿa: Royal Netherlands Embassy, 1996), 13–14; Fred Halliday, *Arabia wihout Sultans* (Harmondsworth: Penguin, 1974), 179–80; Helen Lackner, *PDRYemen: Outpost of Socialist Development in Arabia* (London: Ithaca Press, 1985), 27–8; Vitaly Naumkin, *Red Wolves of Yemen* (Cambridge: Oleander Press, 2004), 25–30.

[6] Hadhramaut is the main eastern populated region of Yemen. Its main cities are Mukalla on the coast and Seiyun in the famous wadi of the same name. The adjective relating to Hadhramaut is Hadhrami and the people are also known as Hadhrami.

organizations run by British and Indian women; there were also literary and
language clubs, which included some political discussion beyond their official
remit. From the 1950s onwards, a few attempted to have directly political aims
and consequently operated in a more underground manner. Political movements in Aden Colony and Protectorates were then very divided, in particular
between those who regarded Aden city itself as a clearly separate entity from
the protectorates and those who wanted to integrate the two.

A pioneering example of civil resistance, which is still remembered by older
people, was the 1958 demonstrations in Ghayl Bawazeer, in a private boarding
school set up in coastal Hadhramaut, where many men who later became prominent political leaders studied. The headmaster dismissed a teacher who had
publicly praised the establishment of the United Arab Republic (UAR), the brief
political union of Egypt and Syria. The school authorities then found themselves
facing a mass demonstration of students assembled for a football match. They
responded by bringing in armed government security personnel to end the
demonstration, closing the school, and sending the students home. This tactic
turned out to be counterproductive, as it had the unexpected result of widely
publicizing the establishment of the UAR throughout the Eastern Protectorate, as
well as ensuring that the local youth and population as a whole broadly supported
it—certainly not the outcome the colonial authorities had wanted.[7]

Throughout Aden and the Protectorates, the main civil peaceful popular
movements that could broadly be described as political were the trades unions.
The earliest ones were established in Aden and composed primarily of Adenis
and migrants from what was then the imamate, with a far smaller membership
of Protectorates inhabitants, and of course almost exclusively male in composition. Their actions were often met with repression from the authorities,
though significant concessions were also won through strikes and other labour
action organized by Aden Trade Union Congress and the organizations that
preceded its foundation in 1956.[8]

THE YEMEN ARAB REPUBLIC AND THE
PEOPLE'S DEMOCRATIC REPUBLIC
OF YEMEN: THE 1970s AND 1980s

During the socialist period in the PDRY (1967–90) very few non-
governmental organizations were allowed to operate, whether local or international, and only when they had clearly no political objectives. The country

---

[7] Sheila Carapico, *Civil Society in Yemen: The Political Economy of Activism in Modern Arabia*
(Cambridge: Cambridge University Press, 1998), 96–7.
[8] Halliday, *Arabia without Sultans*, 180–4.

had a law on cooperatives (no. 20 of 1979) but none for NGOs, an indicator of the regime's attitude towards organizations lacking official sponsorship. The only international NGO that was allowed to have a full-time office was the Swedish Save the Children Fund, though other humanitarian organizations were invited temporarily after natural disasters and emergencies such as floods. Local NGOs were in fact officially sponsored mass organizations, such as the Women's Union and the regime-supported trades unions, whose freedom of manœuvre was limited. The only independent association, and the only one that jointly covered the YAR and the PDRY, was the Yemeni Writers' Union, which successfully operated throughout the country. It had joint meetings and managed to manœuvre its way through the limiting hoops of both regimes thanks to a membership of widely respected but independent intellectuals and thinkers. Migrants' organizations outside the country continued to operate and to finance social development infrastructures in their villages; they were also channels for political discussions of the situation in the PDRY for its emigrant citizens.

In the YAR the situation was similar, with trades unions being carefully controlled and monitored by the regime though not officially part of its organizations. By contrast, numerous mostly religious charitable associations were allowed to operate; their activities focused on the distribution of assistance to the poor on religious occasions and after natural disasters and crises. The main independent 'development' movement was the Local Development Associations, which started as an array of genuine village-level organizations, investing the savings of their male out-migrants in the construction of basic development investments, roads, water schemes, schools, health centres, and sometimes even electricity networks. They occasionally also paid for the training and fees of teachers and others operating the facilities. However, this movement was considered a threat by political regimes, which felt the need to control it, and it was gradually emasculated and turned into a centrally appointed local administration in the early 1980s, shortly after Ali Abdullah Saleh had become president.[9]

In neither regime were independent political parties allowed, though some continued to exist underground, and armed resistance against each regime was sponsored by the other during much of that period, except during the three years when Ibrahim al-Hamdi was president of the YAR (1974–7). Despite having relatively authoritarian regimes, the decade of the 1970s was one during which there was a great broadening of experience and of knowledge of the outside world throughout Yemen. A modern education system spread throughout the country, modelled on the Egyptian system in the YAR and a combination of Egyptian and Socialist systems in the PDRY; in the latter it

---

[9] It is discussed in detail in a variety of publications, including Carapico, *Civil Society in Yemen*, ch. 5.

reached the remotest parts of the country, but few girls studied beyond primary level. Illiteracy remained widespread, particularly in the YAR, where the ratio of schools to population was much lower. In the PDRY regular adult literacy campaigns had a notable impact on reducing illiteracy.

Another very effective means through which the outside world penetrated Yemen was the media. TV and radio became commonplace. Information about the outside world was accessible and played a major role in changing people's world views, not just through news bulletins and current affairs programmes (however monotonous and lacking in analysis), but also through Arab soaps, which presented social problems among the wealthy. Most importantly, migrants returning from the Gulf, Europe, or the USA informed their friends and relatives about life elsewhere and brought back stories, images, and sometimes even books. In addition, even in remote rural areas, people had some contact with other countries through teachers from Palestine, Egypt, and Sudan. Although such contacts were very limited by comparison with the role of social media and satellite TV in the 1990s and 2000s, this was a major change from the period prior to 1970, when most ordinary Yemenis had barely any knowledge of the world beyond their village or town and migrants returned only very rarely.

YEMENI UNIFICATION AND THE RISE OF CIVIL AND CITIZEN INITIATIVES: PRECURSORS TO THE LARGE-SCALE UPRISINGS

The early 1990s, the period immediately following the establishment of the Republic of Yemen, were a time when freedom of expression flourished through a variety of media. These years were also marked by unprecedented optimism throughout the country, with widely shared hopes that the new republic would integrate the best of the former states and would fulfil people's dreams of prosperity, happiness, and freedom. The atmosphere in 1991–2 was similar to that in 2011–12, which can be summarized as one of triumph of hope over expectation. Women hoped that the PDRY's family law would prevail. Both men and women hoped the same for the *qat* regulations, while the majority were looking forward to greater economic freedoms, a flourishing private sector, and higher incomes spreading from the former YAR to the rest of the country.[10] All were disappointed. The YAR *qat* and family regulations

---

[10] *Qat* is a mild stimulant drug, which is chewed fresh for a few hours at a time and is prevalent in Yemen and East Africa. In the PDRY its use was allowed at weekends and on holidays in most areas, permitted all the time in growing areas, and forbidden at all times in the areas where it was not traditionally consumed. In the YAR it was consumed daily. While

spread everywhere, while the country entered a major economic crisis within months of its establishment when the regime refused to toe the US line in its response to the Iraqi invasion of Kuwait, leading to the return of more than 800,000 Yemenis from Saudi Arabia and other Gulf states, many of them having lost some or all of their assets en route. In the first years of unity, inflation was rampant and people's living standards dropped considerably, particularly in the southern governorates, where earlier subsidies on basic commodities were cancelled. This impoverishment was the beginning of a trend that was to endure.

The flourishing of dozens of newspapers and political parties was such that, in 1992, when I tried to build up a list of them, I stopped when it reached about forty; according to Beatty and colleagues, the total number reached more than fifty parties in 1994.[11] By 1992 there were 223 NGOs registered in Yemen, 43 per cent of which were charitable organizations.[12]

The early years of the unified republic were marked by a mix of liberal legislation and some constraints, the latter being increasingly used after 1993. As Carapico put it:

After failing to secure the hoped-for popular mandate, power-holders began amending the rules to increase control of elections, economic activity and autonomous organizations. Amidst mounting elite and popular criticism, regimes then imposed higher penalties for transgressions, deployed troops to enforce compliance, and finally suspended the rules, resorting to arbitrary detentions, crude censorship, curfews, expulsions, and torture. Escalating violence and repression culminated in civil war and, eventually, an authoritarian triumph that crushed civic initiatives as well as armed resistance. In each case a new government issued edicts centralizing all significant political, civic, intellectual, and economic projects. Critics and alternative elites were banished.[13]

The initial liberal laws included the 1990 Press Law, the 1991 Constitution, and the 1991 Political Parties Law. All had loopholes, which were later used to restrict the freedoms they addressed. The proposed dismantling of the security apparatus, as Carapico said,

was disingenuous inasmuch as no one imagined the powerful, well-armed security forces could simply be dismissed, even if the political will had existed; and because some now-underemployed security officers were nominated to committees as 'independents' or otherwise interfered in pluralist and civic experiences. It

---

formerly an activity restricted to special events, in recent decades it has become a daily habit for the vast majority of male Yemenis as well as many women. There has long been and still is today considerable support for regulations restricting its use.

[11] Sharon Beatty et al., *Yemeni NGOs and Quasi-NGOs*, 10.
[12] Amani Kandil, *Civil Society in the Arab World* (Washington: Civicus, 1995), 43, 61, 64.
[13] Carapico, *Civil Society in Yemen*, 135.

was nonetheless significant insofar as everyone from petty traders to foreign researchers noticed a short-term diminution of overt security surveillance. Illegal detentions and human rights abuses diminished. As constant security monitoring and occasional harassment had deprived citizens of various political rights and liberties in the past, this was a crucial element in the overall liberalization.[14]

Press liberalization was amazing between 1990 and 1994, but its limits were clear, as all newspapers had to be printed on government presses, which allowed the regime to control what was published when it chose to do so.[15] Later in the 1990s, the appearance and rapid spread of satellite TV and the newly emerging Arab channels played a major role, providing standards and quality of political debate unprecedented in the Arab world. The early years of Al Jazeera, when the channel was openly critical of all regimes, allowed extremely lively political debates between opponents and supporters of most regimes, and often brought the countries to a standstill as everyone watched their regime's resident or exiled opponents arguing (and sometimes physically fighting) over major political issues.[16]

Within two years, the positive aspects started to be overshadowed by the negative, with the postponement of the national parliamentary elections and a series of targeted assassinations of mostly Yemeni Socialist Party (YSP) political leaders: between 1992 and 1993, there were about 150 actual and attempted assassinations.[17] This deterioration soon led to the 1994 civil war, which resulted in a clear victory for the governance system of Ali Abdullah Saleh.

While the role of international media in broadening the political discourse and informing Yemenis of all ages and stripes of new possibilities is evident, the importance of formal NGOs is less clear. For the first ten years of the unified republic, NGO activities were regulated by law no. 11 of 1963, which was widely considered to be inappropriate and restrictive; civil society individuals and organizations worked to have it changed before and after unification. Unification strengthened the movement to achieve a more equitable and permissive set of regulations for the establishment and functioning of NGOs. This was considered a contentious issue by the regime, which resisted attempts to allow civil society organizations to operate freely. Finally law no. 1 of 2001 was issued under pressure from both civil society and foreign aid providers: its

---

[14] Carapico, *Civil Society in Yemen*, 139–40.

[15] Carapico, *Civil Society in Yemen*, 151–4.

[16] Patrice Chevalier, 'Une presse écrite sous tension: Répression et pluralisme', in Laurent Bonnefoy et al., *Yémen: Le Tournant révolutionnaire* (Paris: Karthala et CEFAS, 2012), 326–43; and Benjamin Wiacek, 'L'Émergence de nouveaux médias pour l'expression d'une troisième voix', in Bonnefoy et al., *Yémen: Le Tournant révolutionnaire*, 345–50. Both give clear and brief analyses of the role of the written and audio-visual media in the movement.

[17] Franck Mermier, 'Le Mouvement sudiste', in Bonnefoy et al., *Yémen: Le Tournant révolutionnaire*, 43.

by-laws were issued in 2004.[18] It was broadly criticized for giving the state too much control over NGOs, and the history of drafts and debates around the law parallels that of the short-lived Yemeni spring of the first years of unity, which was followed by the restriction of liberties after 1993. The law also focused on cultural, charitable, and development institutions, and formalized and restricted the freedom of action and movement of all such institutions, thus acting as a brake on political and other collective action and expression, rather than an incentive to develop them.

The years following 1993 were marked by a gradual reduction in civil liberties through laws and mechanisms that were more restrictive than democratic with respect to decentralization and NGOs. In addition, repressive interpretation or distortion of laws or plain physical repression was used to penalize freedom of expression, particularly of the press, outspoken opponents, and human-rights militants, who were attacked and beaten up in the streets, arrested, and detained without charge, and/or had their homes or offices ransacked and robbed.[19] One of the most notorious cases is that of Dr Abu Bakr al-Saqqaf, an independent intellectual activist who was abducted and viciously beaten on a number of occasions in the mid-1990s.[20]

By the beginning of the new century, the whole country was ruled according to the autocratic system that had prevailed in Ali Abdullah Saleh's YAR. Patronage and oppression were the main mechanisms for controlling the population. Alongside other similar systems, this one had a veneer of formal democracy that gave it a good press with the US and European states supporting the regime. These were content with regular parliamentary and local elections, which, thanks to the presence of alternative candidates and a sophisticated rigging system, could be publicly advertised as providing real competition between different parties, particularly as the regime had the wisdom to ensure its victories were within reasonable figures and avoided the 99 per cent positive votes obtained by less sophisticated dictators. This ensured there would be no challenge in the US Congress or elsewhere when military aid and training were proposed to help the Saleh regime in its supposed fight against Islamist terrorists, particularly once the regime had sided with the Bush administration after the events of 2001.

---

[18] Anais Casanova, *Le Droit d'association au Yemen* (Sana'a: CEFAS, 2005), 2.

[19] See *Amnesty International Reports* for different years, which record numerous cases of torture and ill-treatment, as well as extra-judicial killings http://www.amnestyusa.org/our-work/countries/middle-east-and-north-africa/yemen.

[20] Amnesty International, *Amnesty International Report 1996—Yemen*, 1 January 1996 http://www.refworld.org/docid/3ae6aa050.html.

From the mid-1990s onwards, and particularly in 1996, 1998, and again in 2005, implementation of Washington Consensus economic policies led to large-scale popular opposition against price rises and in particular against increases in the price of diesel, a basic commodity for irrigated agriculture as well as for the supply of domestic water to many urban and quite a few rural households. Each time, the initial rise led to demonstrations (described as 'riots' by the official local media), which were repressed with armed force, resulting in the deaths of demonstrators. Similarly, on each occasion this was followed by presidential intervention, which reduced the level of increases, with the end result that the prices rose but less than originally announced and the president claimed to be helping his people. These 'bread and diesel' riots were mere symptoms of the overall crisis and worsening living conditions, as the gap between incomes and prices became ever greater and the level of state-provided services and support smaller. In 1998 the death toll among demonstrators was at least fifty-two; it was as high or even higher in 2005.[21]

With respect to civil society developments, the first decade of this century was marked by the emergence of large numbers of civil society organizations focused on human rights and democratization. This was the result of international funding agencies shifting their focus away from economic and social development and redirecting their financing to governance and civil society activities.[22] NGOs involved in governance issues mushroomed, supported by US agencies such as the National Democratic Institute and the National Endowment for Democracy; for example, over eight years in the late 1990s, Washington spent $6.6 million on the promotion of democracy in Yemen.[23] The EU, the UN, and bilateral funding agencies were also increasingly involved in financing such activities, thus further reducing the funds available for economic and social investments. This support for democratization was tolerated by the regime for two reasons. First, it was seen as the price to pay for continued financial and military support from the West, particularly the US and EU states. Second, given the formal democracy of the regime, it was (possibly wrongly, given later developments) not seen to be a major threat, as the influence of these NGOs was limited to a small group of 'middle-class' educated urban younger people.

---

[21] Marta Colburn, *The Republic of Yemen: Development Challenges in the 21st Century* (London: Stacey International, 2002), 51.

[22] Sheila Carapico, *Political Aid and Arab Activism: Democracy Promotion, Justice, and Representation* (Cambridge: Cambridge University Press, 2014), discusses the role of North Atlantic state agencies in the development of governance-related NGOs throughout the region, including many examples from Yemen.

[23] *Deepening our Understanding of the Effects of US Foreign Assistance on Democracy Building* (Washington: USAID, 28 January 2008), 70 http://www.pitt.edu/~politics/democracy/democracy.html.

THE SOUTHERN MILITARY RETIREES, PEACEFUL
DEMONSTRATIONS, AND THE EMERGENCE OF
THE SOUTHERN SEPARATIST MOVEMENT

Peaceful resistance to the regime emerged again in a surprising way as an indirect consequence of the 1994 civil war. The war was followed by the dismissal of more than 86,000 military and security personnel from the Southern Governorates (former PDRY) most of whom returned to their rural homes and found that the pensions they received were increasingly worthless, owing to inflation and increased cost of living; moreover they were not paid regularly.[24] The regime justified their forcible retirement under the excuse that these people had sided with what it regarded as secessionist southern rebels in 1994, but this was rarely the case. The retirees had mostly remained either neutral or been in units or locations that supported unity: hence the decision to exclude them was an attempt more to remove and isolate a potential perceived threat rather than to address a real one.

After a decade of frustration and worsening relations with the regime, in 2007 a group of retired southern army officers started a peaceful movement of demonstrations in their home areas (mostly Habilayn and surrounding areas in Lahej governorate) to demand compensation, reintegration into their previous positions, or adequate pensions. From the beginning they asserted their determination to remain peaceful: 'We call on the people of the south to actively participate in this event...while holding dear their civil values and civilized manners and peaceful means in changing opinion.'[25] Their decision to be peaceful was both tactical and strategic. There is no doubt that, like all other Yemenis, they had easy access to small weapons, though they did not have the equipment to resist a major assault. However, resorting to arms would basically have meant they were yet another anti-regime rebellion, whereas initially their demands were not directly political. They gave the regime the benefit of the doubt by providing it with the opportunity to correct unjust decisions and restore their civil rights. They maintained their resistance peacefully through unarmed demonstrations, despite the fact that the regime responded with violence. By using civil and peaceful means, they also wanted to demonstrate higher moral and cultural values than those of the 'northern' regime.

The movement rapidly spread beyond the retirees and became broader, explicitly demanding southern rights and even separatism on the grounds that the South (defined as within the borders of the former PDRY) was, in their

---

[24] Mermier, 'Le Mouvement sudiste', 51.
[25] Nasir Nuba in November 2008, quoted in Human Rights Watch, *In the Name of Unity: The Yemeni Government's Brutal Response to Southern Movement Protests* (New York: HRW, December 2009), 17 http://www.hrw.org/reports/2009/12/15/name-unity.

view, oppressed and 'occupied' by the North. Overall the Southern demonstrators remained largely peaceful. In 2009 a leader stated: 'We have faced a lot of violence from the state. Whenever there is a major rally, people are killed. But people in the movement are peaceful—and this is a historical development in a tribal society where everyone is armed. Most of the protesters have legal weapons at home, and they know how to use them, but we prefer to be peaceful.'[26]

As this quotation indicates, Southern demonstrations were met with force, which included armed attacks on demonstrators, with hundreds killed and wounded in the following years, some in genuine armed clashes with groups that did not subscribe to the peaceful approach, but the overwhelming majority during street demonstrations, when the only violence came from official government forces. These situations cannot be described as clashes, given that only one party was armed and attacking the other, which was unarmed and did not respond in kind. While the Southern separatist movement continued and escalated in the coming years, and its objectives were increasingly focused on separatism, its methods, if not its objectives, certainly served as a model for the revolutionary uprisings that emerged on a mass scale in 2011.

THE 2011 MASS UPRISINGS: CHANGE SQUARES

As discussed, a significant mass opposition movement had taken to the city streets and was also active in rural areas in the second half of the first decade of the twenty-first century in the south of the country. In addition, there was an intermittent civil war going on in the extreme north of the country between the Huthis and the state. The Huthi movement, a Zaydi (Shi'a) revivalist movement, rose up in opposition to the regime in the early 2000s as a result of general neglect of their home area, Sa'ada governorate, with respect to development, as well as political manipulations by the Saleh regime. But it also opposed what many believed to be Saleh's plan for his son Ahmed to succeed him as president. In 2004–10 there were six Huthi wars.[27]

Throughout the rest of the country, there was periodic unrest, which often took the form of inter- or intra-tribal disputes. Fundamentally, this was caused by the worsening economic situation and increasing political frustration. There were also some particularly striking injustices, such as the case of the people from Ja'ashin in Ibb governorate, where a whole village was deprived of its land, which had been appropriated by an unscrupulous sheikh supported

---

[26] Nasir Bahabib in July 2009, quoted in Human Rights Watch, *In the Name of Unity*, 17.

[27] The Huthi movement was initially mainly active in the far north of the country, and based in Sa'ada governorate, bordering Saudi Arabia, where these wars took place.

by the president, who liked his poetry. The villagers demonstrated for months and finally settled down in a street encampment in Sana'a, with support from various people, including Tawakul Karman, who later received the Nobel Peace Prize for her role in the 2011 uprising.[28]

By early 2011 the country was ready to explode. Not only were people's living conditions continuing to deteriorate, employment opportunities scarce, and oil running out, but Ali Abdullah Saleh then, yet again, tried to change the constitution so he could run for a further presidential term, which would have left him in position until his son was old enough to replace him at the following election.[29] He had already unilaterally postponed the parliamentary elections due to take place in 2009, as the Joint Meeting Parties (JMP) official opposition had rejected his proposals.[30] This constitutional change was about to be forced upon the parliament, causing further anger and despair throughout Yemen.

Saleh's attempt to remain in power beyond 2013, worsening socio-economic conditions, and anger at the corrupt regime, combined with the vision that change was possible, were the sparks that brought about the long-awaited popular explosion. People's patience had finally run out. Seeing the success of the then peaceful and successful popular demonstrations in Egypt and Tunisia, from February 2011 onwards the youth expanded their existing small demonstrations in Sana'a into full-time encampments with regular street demonstrations. The movement had a broad range of objectives, including ending the conflict with the Huthis in Sa'ada, economic reform, preventing the presidency from becoming hereditary, responding to southern grievances, establishing a more genuine democracy with clean elections, and generally addressing some of the country's major problems of governance and corruption—basically changing the regime. The slogan that brought everyone together and kept the largest numbers out in the streets was '*irhal*' (roughly translated as 'get out'), directed at President Saleh, but it implied not just getting rid of him personally but getting rid of the whole corrupt and nepotistic structures around him. From the very first, the social composition of the movement was inclusive and broad (see Figure 6.1).

---

[28] The 2011 Nobel Peace Prize, announced in Oslo on 7 October 2011, was awarded jointly to Ellen Johnson Sirleaf, Leymah Gbowee, and Tawakul Karman http://www.nobelprize.org/nobel_prizes/peace/laureates/2011/press.html.

[29] Article 106 of the constitution states that a presidential candidate must be at least 40 years old.

[30] The Joint Meeting Parties was formed in 2005 as a coalition of opposition parties, bringing together the partly Islamist Islah Party (officially the Yemeni Congregation for Reform), the Yemeni Socialist Party, Hizb Al-Haq (a Zaydi party), the Unionist party, and the Popular Forces Union party—the last two small Nasserist organizations. The coalition survived in 2013, despite the widely different programmes of its members.

Figure 6.1. Protests in early 2011 in Sana'a brought together people from different areas, tribes, and social and educational status. Here a female protester chants slogans demanding the resignation of President Ali Abdullah Saleh on 12 March 2011. Earlier that day police had stormed a nearby square filled with protest tents and killed at least one demonstrator.

©*AP Photo/Muhammed Muheisen*

In Sana'a, the anti-regime demonstrators settled in tents and created large meeting and living areas. Different political and regional groups had their own tents, and much time was spent in discussion and debate, both within the tents and on the official platform built around the plinth of an obelisk outside the main entrance of the university, which was rigged with sound equipment. The area had physically separate zones for men and women, and security was strict at the entrance, with sex-segregated body searches to ensure that no weapons were brought into the area. The movement is usually described as youthful, hardly surprisingly, as 80 per cent of the country's population is under 35.[31]

The respective roles of independent groups and political parties remained a major issue between 2011 and 2013. Youth from the different opposition political parties were active and participated in the movement from the earliest days. Islah, often seen as the Yemeni version of the Muslim Brotherhood, was present from the beginning and both organized and financed the movement from February onwards. Early on it played a major role in limiting discourse and debate by controlling the locations where these happened. The Huthis were also present from the earliest stages, but at that time did not have the political weight they later achieved. Other parties, such as the Yemeni Socialist Party, had a smaller role based on their overall political influence. Although

---

[31] Although the UN system defines youth as those under 35, in Yemen the definition has been extended to 40, making it the overwhelming demographic group.

independent demonstrators were very important—particularly in introducing ideas, offering new types of thinking, and representing a variety of views—they were a numerical minority throughout.

The mass movement developed and increased in size in the early months of 2011 and remained peaceful, despite considerable provocation. Certain moments became famous, in particular the killings in Sanaʿa on 18 March 2011, known as the Friday of Dignity, when 'dozens of men wearing civilian clothes and armed with military assault rifles... opened fire. Over the course of three hours, the gunmen killed at least 45 protestors... and wounded 200, while state security forces made no serious effort to stop the carnage.'[32] This massacre outraged the country and led to the largest set of defections from the governing party (ministers, members of parliament, ambassadors, and others) as well as that of a significant section of the army, which changed sides and swore to protect the demonstrators. Similarly, the main official opposition movement, including the strong tribal federation of the Hashed and its leaders, then declared its allegiance to the revolution.[33] The 18 March events also marked a fundamental change in the character of the movement, as, once the peaceful and unarmed protestors were under the protection of a major military faction and the main militarized tribes, they were less likely to be physically attacked by the regime's forces. This 'protection' also limited their independence.

Further significant attacks and killings occurred in Sanaʿa on 27 April (12 killed, 210 injured, 80 disappeared) and on 21 May (6 killed, dozens injured, and 40 disappeared). Outside Sanaʿa the main killings took place during the night of 29 May, when Change Square in Taʿiz was attacked and set on fire by similar 'unknown' forces probably composed of tribal provocateurs and security forces personnel.

In Sanaʿa, soon after 18 March, territories between the two competing groups were roughly defined. The area around the university was under the control of the anti-regime groups and within the 'zone of influence' of the First Armoured Brigade, which had sided with the revolutionary movement after the killings of 18 March and whose HQ was nearby. The areas around the presidential palace and the main parade ground were used by pro-regime forces for their demonstrations. Within the city centre, the area around Tahrir Square was controlled by pro-regime forces. The anti-regime forces were allowed to remain around the university, but, whenever they attempted to get close to the prime minister's office (opposite the radio station and the Ministry of Information), they were repelled.

---

[32] Human Rights Watch, *Unpunished Massacre: Yemen's Failed Response to the 'Friday of Dignity' Killings* (New York: HRW, February 2013), 1 http://www.hrw.org/node/113213/section/2.

[33] The Hashed is the most powerful tribal confederation in Yemen, based north of Sanaʿa. Its leaders have played important political roles since the establishment of the republic. After the death of Shaykh Abdallah bin Husayn al Ahmar in 2007, relations between his sons and the Saleh regime deteriorated. The Islah party represents two major and sometimes quite distinct forces: the Hashed confederation and its leadership, on the one hand, and Islamists, on the other.

After 18 March, support from the country's major northern tribal leaders, who were also the president's main rivals, meant that the squares were not just filled with students and other youth from tribal and non-tribal backgrounds, but that large numbers of ordinary tribesmen joined them (see Figure 6.2).

However, throughout the period, most women demonstrators were from more educated, urban, and liberal social groups. This broad participation had, among others, the effect of transforming the protest movement into an entity likely to bring about long-term fundamental social change: people from different areas, tribes, and social and educational status all shared similar tough living conditions (tents were mostly without water, toilets, or other basic facilities). They exchanged ideas, came together with a common objective, discussed the country's future, and, for the first time, took an active part in a major social and political event. Many found that they had a lot in common with people whom they had previously regarded as totally different. Conversations and relationships developed between people who previously considered each other totally alien—for example, young, educated, middle-class women from Ta'iz discussed openly with older conventional tribesmen from Mareb.

For two years, starting in early 2011, there were weekly mass demonstrations by regime opponents following Friday prayers held in the open in Sana'a

Figure 6.2. The sit-in became an important act of resistance. Here Yemeni tribesmen sit inside one of the tents erected in the heart of Sana'a as they demand the removal of President Ali Abdullah Saleh. A month later Saleh agreed to step down. This photo was taken on 13 October 2011.

© *Marwan Naamani/AFP/Getty Images*

and other cities.[34] In Sana'a they took place along Sixty Metre Road (a six-lane ring road, which goes past both the presidential palace and the university) and were by far the largest in the country. In the early months, demonstrations were also held on other days when the occasion arose, and these involved opposition attempts to show their strength in other parts of the city. Within weeks similar Change Squares and weekly demonstrations were held in most of the major cities of the country, including Ta'iz, Ibb, Aden, Hodeida, and Mukalla, and also in the smaller capitals of other governorates, including Dhamar, Hajja, Lahej, Al Ghaydah, and Mareb. Many of them included encampments, where people lived for a number of months.

In the early months, the regime organized counter-demonstrations in Sana'a on Fridays around the parade area near the presidential palace and the grandiose al-Saleh mosque built in the first decade of the twenty-first century. In addition to bussing in loyal supporters for these demonstrations, the regime relied on the occupants of the tents in Tahrir Square, who were kept there with regular supplies of meals and *qat*. The pro-regime demonstrators included both civilian supporters of the regime from different parts of the country and military and security personnel wearing civilian clothes following a tactic often used by the regime over the years.

As well as running counter-demonstrations, the regime also acted against the demonstrators through both provocations and standard crowd-control methods by armed security and military personnel backed up by the threat of water cannon. These were generally located at crossroads in areas that the regime had deemed to be off-limits to anti-regime demonstrators, and they were used whenever the demonstrators attempted to cross these known lines in the city of Sana'a. In addition to these official forces, the regime also provided some of its supporters with sticks and hidden firearms. These unofficial forces were known as *baltagia*, a name adopted from the Egyptian anti-revolutionary militias, and acted mainly as agents provocateurs, doing their best to force the anti-regime demonstrators out of their peaceful approach. The word is of Turkish origin and, in Yemen, covered security personnel operating incognito and thugs who attacked the demonstrators either because they opposed change or were paid to do so.

While the movement was largely a popular one throughout, its impact on political transformation changed after the 18 March killings, with a clear shift favouring the mainstream opposition Yemeni political forces (namely, parties, powerful tribes, and formally recognized civil society including religious groups) in the internal balance of power following their military and political

---

[34] Nabil Subay, 'Un peuple en quête de convergence: La Révolution yéménite face à un pays fragmenté', in Bonnefoy et al., *Yémen: Le Tournant révolutionnaire*, 149–61, which describes the early period of the uprisings from the point of view of participants not aligned with any of the existing political parties or factions.

defections from the regime. By April it was clear to international actors that President Saleh's control over the country was unlikely to be restored: this led to calls for a peaceful transition. The USA—which had, up till then, accepted Saleh's argument that he was the only alternative to al-Qaeda-sponsored chaos—started calling for his departure. Despite the *fin de règne* atmosphere in Riyadh in the final months of King Abdullah's reign, Saudi Arabia became more actively involved, prompted by its long-term policy of keeping Yemen sufficiently stable to avoid chaos spilling over the border and sufficiently unstable to reduce its perceived threat. Saudi Arabia has a multiplicity of policies concerning its relations with Yemen, each led by a different senior member of the Al-Saud ruling family. International involvement produced what became known as the Gulf Cooperation Council (GCC) Initiative as it was sponsored by the GCC states, and supported by the other major states involved in Yemen—the USA, Britain, France, and Germany—although its main elements were the fruit of the work of senior Yemeni politicians. On a number of occasions, Saleh failed to sign it, each time finding a spurious last-minute excuse. On one occasion, 22 May 2011, he even arranged for his supporters to lay siege to the UAE embassy where the GCC representatives and other ambassadors were waiting together to travel to his palace to attend the signature ceremony.[35] They had to be helicoptered out! This was probably a tactical error, as it strengthened the determination of the GCC states and other major international players to work for a transfer of power.

On 3 June 2011, in an event that was certainly not planned by Saleh himself, a massive explosion in his palace mosque seriously wounded him and killed many. Despite initially claiming that he would not leave the country, his medical condition and international pressure forced him to accept the hospitality of Saudi Arabia, where he was treated during the following months, while his vice-president, Abdo Rabbo Mansour Hadi, officially became acting president, though Saleh's sons did not even allow him into the large official presidential palace, an indication of his lack of real authority at the time. On 23 September Saleh successfully tricked his hosts and returned to Yemen, to widespread dismay. His return, alongside the worsening situation with increasingly frequent and serious military clashes in various parts of the country, added to Saleh's earlier dallying about signing the deal, encouraged the GCC and other ambassadors seeking a solution to raise the threat of UN sanctions.

The UN Security Council had already discussed the issue in April, when Jamal Benomar had started work as Special Adviser. However, it was only in October 2011 that the Security Council adopted Resolution 2014, calling for the immediate implementation of the GCC Initiative and for regular reports on progress thereafter. (It also supported 'the legitimate demands and

---

[35] *Al Arabiya News* (English-language web service of Al Arabiya News Channel), 22 May 2011.

aspirations of the Yemeni people for change', and condemned 'the excessive use of force against peaceful protestors'.) Saleh finally signed the agreement on 23 November 2011, and on 21 February 2012 handed over the presidency to his former vice-president, Abdo Rabbo Mansour Hadi, who had been elected unopposed in a national election. The extremely high turnout at this uncontested election was a strong show of popular support for change and for an end to the Saleh era. The additional UN Security Council Resolution 2051 in June 2012 and the regular reports and discussions of Yemen at the Council initially helped the transitional process.[36] However, their weakness failed to prevent what the UN calls 'obstructionists', primarily Saleh and his supporters, from undermining the process, despite Resolution 2140 of February 2014, which agreed sanctions on a number of individuals to be named by a committee.[37]

This international support for Saleh's departure, while partly influenced by the demonstrations in Yemen, did not represent a sudden conversion to the political demands of the revolutionary youth in the Change Squares. Neither the GCC states, which had sent their armies to terminate the Bahraini revolutionary movement in March 2011, nor the USA and EU, were seeking fundamental social, economic, or political change in Yemen. None of these is known to support either Muslim fundamentalists or anti-capitalist revolutionaries. All are motivated primarily by a counter-terrorism agenda, something that Saleh exploited when in power and continued to do so in the following years in his efforts to demonstrate his value and the error of their ways in dumping him.[38] Because of all these factors, international support during the transition gave a very strong hand to formal opposition political parties. At the same time, these international actors are concerned about the 'Muslim Brotherhood' element of Islah, which, in Yemen as elsewhere, has considerable popular support. However, as part of the international community's strategy to counter the strength of the fundamentalists, it also helped the new forces of youth and women to increase their influence in national politics, mainly through the National Dialogue Conference (NDC). The fact that none of the 2011 revolutionaries challenged the neo-liberal political or economic agenda certainly facilitated this support, though, in the view of this writer, confronting the neo-liberal agenda is essential to address successfully the country's fundamental problems of poverty and inequitable distribution of resources.

---

[36] SC Res. 2014 of 21 October 2011, and SC Res. 2051 of 12 June 2012.

[37] SC Res. 2140 of 26 February 2014, paras 11 ff.

[38] While, outside Yemen, al-Qaeda is assumed to be the instigator of all armed attacks, most Yemenis consider that Saleh and his associates are actively involved in many, if not all of them. In addition, for the past two decades or so there has been a close (and complex) relationship between Saleh's security organizations and armed aggressive Islamists, regardless of their label. See 'Final report of the Panel of Experts on Yemen established pursuant to Security Council Committee resolution 2140 (2014)', UN doc. S/2015/125 of 20 February 2015, 19–21.

The live-ins in the squares persisted until mid-2013, probably the longest time anywhere in the Arab world. Although the tents were not all fully occupied at all times and it is difficult to estimate the numbers involved in the encampments, Friday demonstrations took place until April 2013, with residents of the squares and others joining them. After his election, the new president initially encouraged the youth to remain in the squares and continue to be a political force through their presence. They thus strengthened his limited power base, given that he lacked support from powerful tribes. By mid-2014, although the weekly demonstrations had ceased, some tents were still occupied mostly by Huthi supporters as well as a few independents in Sana'a city.

THE NATIONAL DIALOGUE CONFERENCE AND THE RISE OF THE HUTHIS

The National Dialogue Conference was one of the main elements of the GCC transition agreement and was designed to bring together all Yemeni political forces, including the traditional parties and personalities from the opposition and the ruling group, as well as new ones emerging from the 2011 popular uprisings, including women, youth, and civil society. Despite many problems such as its delayed start and longer duration, the sometimes questionable selection mechanism and therefore representativity for its membership, this was a major political event in which young people, women, and civil society elements were able fully to participate and express unorthodox views. Older influential 'traditional' leaders were compelled to engage with them as equals, something that some of them probably resented. The NDC, which met in Sana'a between March 2013 and January 2014, produced more than 1,800 decisions. Owing to fundamental political disagreements, it was unable to agree solutions to the southern question or decide the number of regions to be included in a federal state.

The NDC was the focus of political activism, replacing Change Squares as the main site for frequent protests and demonstrations both by some of its members and by others. Causes included a range of demands for political and economic reform, protests at killings and, above all, calls for the cancellation of the immunity granted (by parliament as part of the GCC deal) to Saleh and his closest associates, and demands that he should face justice for killings and extortions throughout his reign.

The peaceful street movement certainly contributed to ensuring that the NDC took place with Huthi participation, and that civil war did not break out at that time. Like all other attempts, it failed to bring some southern secessionist leaders into the debate, but that was because of these leaders' inability or unwillingness to give priority to the welfare of Yemenis as a whole, regardless of where they live, over their personal political ambitions, however unrealistic. Most important, the NDC was the first occasion in Yemen when women and youth were included as recognized political constituencies.

During the unrest of 2011 and beyond, political and military attacks continued. The worst explosions killed hundreds of people, including 120 young security graduates on 21 May 2012 at a parade rehearsal, 65 people at the military hospital on 5 December 2013, 35 graduates on 7 January 2015 near the police club in Sana'a, and 137 people in 2 mosque attacks on 20 March. The perpetrators were never identified, let alone brought to justice. These attacks were attributed to aggressive Islamist organizations, though there was widespread suspicion that Saleh was not totally unconnected with at least some of them.

While these shocks contributed to the creation of an atmosphere of fear and instability, the main political development during this period was the rise of the Huthis, which was considerably facilitated by their alliance with Saleh and therefore access to military/security forces still loyal to him.[39] Having taken control of their home area (Sa'ada governorate in the far north of the country) in the course of 2011, they expanded their area of control during 2012 and 2013, but 2014 saw their power rise dramatically, culminating with the bloodless takeover of Sana'a on 21 September 2014. Since then, their attempt to take full control of the country has led first to the resignation and house arrest of the president and government, and then to unsuccessful efforts by the UN and others to find an agreement between the Huthis and other political parties. On 21 February 2015 Hadi escaped to Aden, where he resumed his responsibilities as president, but he was soon driven out by the Huthi–Saleh military forces.

The takeover of increasing parts of the country in 2015 has clearly demonstrated that so-called Huthi military forces are mainly those of the well-armed, well-trained, and well-equipped units that remain loyal to Saleh. They came close to full control of the major cities of Aden and Ta'iz by end March 2015. Unwilling to accept a Huthi–Saleh-dominated Yemen, the new rulers of Saudi Arabia, a younger self-confident generation led by Crown Prince Mohammed bin Nayef and his cousin, Minister of Defence Mohammed bin Salman, alongside the other GCC states (with the notable and 'usual' exception of Oman), launched the *Decisive Storm*[40] air offensive on 26 March, with the

---

[39] This is very much an 'alliance against nature', as there is no love lost between them, Saleh having been the initiator of the six anti-Huthi wars and the killing of their original leader, Hussein al Huthi.

[40] On 22 April this was renamed *Restore Hope*, but little changed in its activities other than a possible reduction in the number of daily sorties.

participation of allies/vassals from the region and beyond. While their stated aim is to restore the legitimate government of President Hadi to power, they also intend to demonstrate Saudi Arabia's power in the region and its willingness to take initiatives independently of the USA, and to confront Iran, which it claims is behind Huthi successes, regardless of the fact that Iran supported the Huthis only after they had become powerful. They also want to ensure that any regime in Yemen rules within a socio-political framework acceptable to them.

Since that date, hundreds of strikes have destroyed much of Yemen's infrastructure as well as significant weaponry, but, as an activist in Sana'a put it: 'We are stuck in the middle. Both sides are terrorizing people and there's no chance to even express that because you're under threat as to what they can possibly do.' This witness also said the Saudi-led coalition was 'destroying the chance for the emergence of a popular resistance to Huthi rule'.[41] With the explicit involvement of Saleh alongside the Huthis and the formal support of Iran, the struggle became a 'proxy' Iran–Saudi Arabia conflict, a very unfortunate innovation. This internationalization of Yemen's power struggle is reminiscent of the Lebanese Civil War of the 1970s–80s, ensuring that the struggle is longer, more destructive, and more difficult to resolve than if it had remained an internal Yemeni issue. The story is by no means complete, but it is clear that the 'new' Yemen that young democrats, women, and the majority were seeking in 2011 is further away than ever.

The rise of the Huthis has not remained unopposed. While they successfully mobilized the 'street' in August 2014 to oppose the increase in fuel prices, which the Washington Consensus institutions had been demanding for a long time, the population promptly turned against them after their 'slow coup' in early 2015, with mass demonstrations taking place almost daily in many Yemeni cities and towns (Sana'a, Ta'iz, Aden, Dhamar, and Hodeida).[42] The Huthis repressed these demonstrations with beatings and shootings in the areas under their control. This revival of the popular movement, including involvement by the unaligned progressive 'modernist' elements, demonstrates that, despite being demobilized and demoralized in the face of the apparent dominance of traditional formal political forces during the NDC, it remains active and likely to develop its thinking and initiatives in search of new politics in the future.

---

[41] Kareem Shaheen, 'Air Strike on Refugee Camp in Yemen Kills 45 as Saudi Planes Target Rebels', *Guardian*, London, 31 March 2015, p. 16.

[42] Stephen Zunes and Noor Al-Haidary 'Powerful Nonviolent Resistance to Armed Conflict in Yemen', openDemocracy, 11 April 2015 https://www.opendemocracy.net/author/stephen-zunes. This article gives a useful list of the many civil peaceful resistance and opposition demonstrations to the different armed factions, even after fighting in Yemen had reached the stage of full-scale war.

CHARACTERISTICS OF THE PEACEFUL
MOVEMENT FOR CHANGE

The Change Squares movement in Yemen had a number of characteristics that both reflect and challenge widespread assumptions and beliefs about the country. Some of these are worth discussing here.

Why did the demonstrators decide to remain peaceful? Yemen has a history of armed struggle. In the 1960s armed struggle ended colonialism in the south and failed to destroy the republican regime in the north. Armed tribal revolts are frequent occurrences. In the early days there was considerable discussion about the likelihood of a similar armed movement developing in Yemen. Much of that discussion revolved around the issue of weapons. Many feared that anti-regime action would rapidly degenerate into armed confrontation in view of the widespread availability of weapons. Until a few years ago, most Yemeni men, particularly tribesmen, would not leave home without a gun, as this was considered part of their normal attire: just as women generally carry handbags, men carry their Kalashnikovs. It is only since 2000 that the regime has been able to prevent the bearing of weapons, at least in the cities. People were therefore very fearful that there would be massive bloodshed on both sides. Many thought that the population as a whole would bring out their weapons, and there would be a full-scale civil war rather than popular demonstrations in the streets. Moreover, in the country's tribal system, killings are liable to result in long-lasting feuds between perpetrating families or tribal groups, thus leading to an endless sequence of murders. This concern contributed to the movement's decision to remain peaceful. The provocations of the regime and its supporters were intended to split the movement and encourage armed confrontations, which would have led to the sequences described. It took considerable mental and psychological strength for participants in the movement to remain peaceful in the face of the many provocations they suffered, mostly in the cities of Sana'a, Aden, and Ta'iz.

The extent of knowledge of other historic non-violent political movements was very limited among ordinary demonstrators, but the examples of non-violence in both the Tunisian and the Egyptian movements of early 2011 definitely contributed to the Yemeni movement participants' decision to remain non-violent. Some knowledge of earlier movements may have been discussed in the tents, but the main factors ensuring the determined peaceful approach in the squares were moral and tactical: people were quite sure that, if they responded to regime provocations with arms, massacres would ensue and the death toll would be horrific. Instead, thanks to the peaceful approach, the number of demonstrators killed in 2011 was limited to 270.[43]

---

[43] Human Rights Watch, *Unpunished Massacre*, 3

The use of agents provocateurs was a clear attempt by the regime to change the balance of power by forcing peaceful demonstrators out of their moral high ground of remaining peaceful despite provocations. Armed attacks against the demonstrators, leading to a significant number of deaths during the two years, were intended as much to split the movement and turn it into a 'traditional' tribal armed uprising, or even an inter-tribal fight, as to suppress it directly. The regime hoped to transform the struggle and turn it into something that fitted within its own modus operandi, thus justifying its use of brute force. However, after 18 March, when both the leaders of the Hashed tribe and the First Armoured Brigade turned against Saleh, the military balance was transformed, and neither side was likely to achieve complete victory. The likelihood of a bloody stalemate contributed to Saleh finally giving into the inevitable, and signing the agreement.

Although Yemen is a genuine national entity whose citizens share clear common cultural characteristics, it is also true that there are significant differences of all kinds: social, between people of different status such as tribes, non-tribal groups and *sada* (descendants of the Prophet), and low status groups; religious, between two different branches of Islam, Shafi'i (Sunni) and Zaydi (Shi'a); regional, as, for example, between Hadhrami and Ta'izzi, which have fairly significant differences in daily culture and customs; finally (and currently unfortunately most significant) geographically, between inhabitants of the former YAR and many of those of the former PDRY, who believe they form a different 'national' entity, which they sometimes describe as 'South Arabian'. There are also clear differences between educated and uneducated people, between men and women in a society that is very strictly sexually segregated, and between younger and older people. The squares were physical and social spaces where people from all these different groups met and exchanged views, shared living conditions, and generally interacted in a largely unprecedented manner. The recourse to non-violence was a major mechanism to allow these groups, some of which clearly distrusted each other, to meet and freely participate in discussions in a way they would not have done had they feared armed response to the expression of their views. This enabled them to discover that they shared common concerns and could seek common solutions. The peaceful nature of the movement and its ability to bring together men and women of completely different social status and background to discuss issues of common national concern in squares throughout the country was a major achievement and an element that will have a long-term impact on Yemeni political development.

Modern media played a key role in the movement, and this role must be assessed at its true level and neither over- nor under-estimated. The media were not the revolution, and the revolution would have happened without them. However, the use of mobile phones to film and photograph incidents and to send that information to colleagues in other cities, as well as to the national and international TV stations and media, was effective in different ways. It prevented regime disinformation strategies from succeeding. Most importantly, it prevented the regime from using worse violence than it did. It ensured that people throughout the country actually knew what was going on and could see the exactions and illegitimate actions of the provocateurs. It spread the news of the revolution to potential supporters. It maintained close contact between demonstrators and their friends and relatives, something that is significant when people are concerned about the safety and condition of their family members. It assisted in organizational matters, allowing rapid mobilization of supporters when and where necessary; and, of course, it played a major role in informing people in Yemen of events elsewhere, partly through the use of the international satellite television channels, but also by direct communication through social media. Finally, it created a link between the cities where the events were happening and the rural areas from which many participants came, thus ensuring that the movement had a fully national scope, an important feature in a country where 70 per cent of the population still live in rural areas, some of them isolated.

The participation of women has been one of the most surprising and hopeful aspects of the Yemeni revolution. Women, fully covered and veiled, played a major role, participating in demonstrations on a weekly basis. A few even lived in segregated tents in 2011, despite both verbal attacks from President Saleh and physical attacks at different times, from religious conservative participants in the movement. This involvement enabled women to achieve a much louder and more effective voice in the post-Saleh regime and in the NDC; although the draft constitution respects the NDC decision to have 30 per cent women in all leading bodies, it remains to be seen what happens in the future, given the role and influence of Islamist parties, including the Huthis, who already impose very restrictive rules on women in the areas they control.

Finally, but most importantly, for the first time in decades, an innovative political discourse and practice is emerging outside the Islamist discourse. Islamists had monopolized the ideological debate in recent decades. Now a new youth movement has developed that is framing the debate around social, political, and economic development within new paradigms, which may include political Islamism, whether based on Zaydi or Shafi' beliefs, but may offer alternatives. After the events of 2011–14, fundamentalist armed Islamists in Yemen can no longer present themselves as the only alternative to the current political regime and system. To counter this, they are claiming connections with the Change Squares movement. Although the revolution did not eliminate their presence, the armed Islamists' appeal is now significantly weaker.

CONCLUSION

The Change Squares movement was a completely new form of political action in Yemen. It triggered the transition from Saleh's rule, thus setting in motion a process that had been long awaited. Its main weaknesses were the absence of a clear political and economic programme, as well as the lack of leadership. Its main achievement was to open up the prospect of a fundamental transformation in the nature of political debate in the country. It brought on to the formal and official political stage young people, women, and others whose political philosophy goes beyond power-seeking and tribal balance. In the long term, Yemeni politics will have to address social concerns, including tribalism, equity, the problems of minorities, and economic issues such as youth unemployment, the limited natural resources (particularly water), and the low educational standards of the population.

The decision of the movement to use non-violent political methods to overthrow the existing regime and bring about a truly democratic regime representing the whole population was made for the following reasons:

- the imminent danger of civil war, which many believed would result from armed opposition;
- a strategic decision to counter the regime's violence with a methodology that would embody an entirely different philosophy—that is, representing a clear alternative to the regime acting as a violent minority oppressing the population and appropriating the country's wealth;
- the wish to demarcate itself from the regime by respecting human rights in its militancy, thus taking the moral high ground;
- the use of non-violent methods as an effective means to undermine the legitimacy and authority of the regime; throughout the country and beyond, people were impressed by the determination of the youth to continue demonstrating peacefully in the face of violent reactions from the regime's official and unofficial forces.

The transformation of the movement after March 2011, when a significant section of the military as well as the main northern tribal confederation officially supported the movement, had a number of consequences. While, on the one hand, it protected the demonstrators from worse violence by the regime and consequently reduced the death toll, on the other, it reduced the political and philosophical freedom of the movement and effectively marginalized the independent male and female youth who, alongside older women, were clearly its most dynamic and innovative elements. Although the opposition parties, including the strongest of them, the largely Islamist Islah, as well as the weaker but important Yemeni Socialist Party, Nasserists, and Baathists, had been involved in the Change Squares from early in the movement, by April 2011 they had become the main participants in the debate between the old regime and mediators seeking a solution, leaving the independent youth somewhat marginalized, though they were included in the NDC.

The street movement could not have overthrown the regime on its own for a number of reasons. It lacked military strength; its support, while considerable, was not overwhelming; and it had neither leadership nor a long-term programme or strategy for running the country. Most important, the traditional elite, whether opposition or regime, was too strong to be overthrown by a disparate group of poorly organized idealists associated with the Change Squares movement.

Despite the many adverse developments from 2014 onwards, it would be a mistake to consider the movement a failure. It has a number of very important achievements to its credit. It will take many more years before fundamental political transformation changes the balance of forces between the wealthy and powerful, on the one hand, and the majority, including the poor, on the other, but that is true everywhere. Meanwhile it has laid a set of bases on which much can be built in coming years. First and foremost, without the Change Squares movement, it is still unclear how or when the regime of Ali Abdullah Saleh would have been brought to a close, despite the sorry state the country had reached by 2011. Second, the new forces of youth and women imposed themselves as actual participants in the transitional government and as a force that had to be included in the national dialogue, thus enabling them to participate in deciding the future of the country. Third, they developed a new form of political discourse among the population at large, and demonstrated that it is possible for rural tribal people to discuss the future of the country with urban intellectuals, for men to debate with women, and for people from different regions to exchange views and share objectives. Fourth, they provided an alternative to armed Islamism for youth seeking solutions to the country's problems. Finally, unlike earlier movements, they recognized that the world is a different place and that the recipes of the twentieth century are no longer appropriate.

Beyond factional political struggles and the deteriorating security situation, the challenges facing Yemen and its people are enormous, given the country's growing population and its limited natural resources, particularly the shortage of water. In the turmoil enveloping the country in 2015 and beyond, the experience of today's young activists is an important step towards a more democratic future. The 2011 events initiated broad and open discussion and dialogue between men and women from totally different socio-economic backgrounds and regions that is an essential basis for the emergence of a 'new' Yemen in which the benefits of modern technology and the material world are at the service of the people as a whole. Their commitment, energy, enthusiasm, and innovative ideas are currently focused on developing strategies for a distant future, but they also respond to events and re-emerged strongly in the streets in early 2015 to oppose the Huthis when the country's political crisis worsened dramatically. However, events in 2015 clearly demonstrate that we still live in an age where the force of arms usually prevails over peaceful civil resistance. While the Yemeni context was a very unlikely and difficult one, the Change Square live-ins created a hopeful precedent for the next generation.[44]

[44] Thanks to the following people for reading and commenting on an earlier version: Mohammed Bahran, John Gittings, Kais al Iryani, Michael Maguire, and Mohammed Qassem al Thawr. Their assistance is greatly appreciated, but they bear no responsibility for the final text.

7

Hirak! Civil Resistance and the Jordan Spring

Jacob Amis

While Jordan's experience of the Arab Spring was not the most dramatic in the region, it was one of the most 'civil'. From January 2011 the kingdom witnessed both an acceleration of existing processes of civil resistance and the emergence of entirely new forms of activism. Directly inspired by events abroad (particularly in Tunisia and Egypt), the increased popular mobilization—known as *hirak*, or 'movement'—was also informed by very local identities and priorities, and a specifically Jordanian historical landscape of resistance. The result was a highly contentious but assiduously non-violent campaign of civic action, from demonstrations and sit-ins to strikes and boycotts. Protests were small in comparison to those seen elsewhere, but were constant, appearing across the country and involving almost all sections of a complex and multi-layered society. Activists' demands were self-limiting, but still taboo-smashing. In turn, a restrained regime response—generally non-lethal if not entirely non-violent—locked both sides in a closely fought and sometimes explosive contest for the 'red lines' of acceptable expression in the post-2011 climate. Although, by early 2015, the *hirak* had not achieved its key reform goals, it nevertheless represented a sea change in opposition discourse, political engagement, and cross-communal cooperation among Jordanians, pointing to the liberating potential of non-violent action.

BEFORE THE SPRING: REBELLION AND RESISTANCE IN JORDAN

Resistance to central government authority, not always 'civil' in nature, has been a significant feature of Jordanian politics since the inception of the

Hashemite–Mandatory state. The birth pangs of the 'Emirate of Transjordan' (1921–46) included an immediate tax revolt in the settled northern population of al-Kura and a full-scale tribal rebellion led by the Adwan of the central Balqa region in 1923.[1] Many of the same actors re-emerged at the Amman General National Congresses (1928–33), a political campaign opposing arbitrary rule and British influence. The high tide of 1950s Arab nationalism introduced massive popular mobilization to Jordanian politics. Demonstrations involved much of the urban population on both the East and West Banks, and were sometimes put down with live fire from the security forces. When a nationalist government swept to power in a free election and proceeded to challenge royal authority, an alleged coup attempt and a temporary breakdown in public order led King Hussein (r. 1953–99) to impose martial law in April 1957.[2]

With political parties banned and constitutional freedoms suspended, the next challenge to the Jordanian state took an armed and absolutist form, in the brief and bloody army-*fedayeen* war of 1970–1. Though not an all-out conflict between the broader Palestinian and East Jordanian populations, the violent insurrection of Palestinian Liberation Organization guerrillas—crushed by a predominantly East Jordanian soldiery—enlivened inter-communal tensions and left Jordan a more divided and fractious society. As we shall see, latent mistrust between East Jordanians and the Palestinian-origin majority, at times encouraged by state policies, came to be a major factor shaping the limits of protest in the kingdom.[3]

Something closer to civil resistance resumed, much as it had begun in the 1920s, in the East Bank hinterland. In April 1989 steep price rises dictated by an IMF austerity package sparked riots and mass protests across the impoverished southern governorates of Ma'an, Kerak, and Tafileh. The disturbances,

---

[1] The 'Balqa Movement' (*harakat al-Balqa*) is still celebrated in local oral history traditions, which often betray a highly ambivalent attitude towards state authority. The rebellion was only the first event to give lie to the caricature of Jordan's East Bank 'tribes' as monolithically and immemorially 'loyal' to the Hashemites. See Andrew Shryock, *Nationalism and the Genealogical Imagination: Oral History and Textual Authority in Tribal Jordan* (Berkeley and Los Angeles: University of California Press, 1997), 88–94.

[2] Joseph Massad, *Colonial Effects: The Making of National Identity in Jordan* (New York: Columbia University Press, 2001).

[3] 'East Jordanian' (*urduni sharqi*) or 'East Bank Jordanian' refers to those Jordanians whose ancestors happened already to be living on the strip of land that became the 'Emirate of Transjordan' in 1921, as distinguished here from Jordanians of Palestinian descent, and especially those who migrated to Jordan in the wake of the 1948 and 1967 Arab–Israeli wars. While 'Jordanian' and 'Palestinian' identities are complicated and fluid, from the 1970s each came to be increasingly pitted against the other, with the numerical 'Palestinian' majority perceiving itself as marginalized at the expense of royally favoured East Jordanian tribes, while voices among the latter saw themselves as the 'original Jordanians' (*urduni asli*), dispossessed by successive waves of refugees. See Adnan Abu-Odeh, *Jordanians, Palestinians, and the Hashemite Kingdom in the Middle East Peace Process* (Washington: United States Institute of Peace, 1999).

which came to be known as *Habbat Nisan*, 'The April Uprising', quickly spread to the north and acquired political demands to which King Hussein acceded, embarking on a 'riot-induced process of limited democratization'.[4] Non-violent forms of political contention honed in the temporary opening proved resilient in the face of an unpopular move towards peace with Israel in the mid-1990s, and the top-down 'deliberalization' with which it was intimately linked. Diverse elements of civil society, drawn from Islamist and Leftist opposition parties, trade unions and professional associations, joined forces to protest peacefully against normalization and the incremental closure of political space.[5] A further round of structural adjustment caused demonstrations across the country in 1996, but this time concessions were not forthcoming. In Kerak, where unrest began and subsequently turned violent, the army was deployed and a curfew imposed.[6]

These trends intensified in the first decade of Abdullah II's reign (r. 1999–), as the kingdom's authoritarian retrenchment continued apace. Renewed mobilization led by political parties and professional associations frequently met with tear gas and police batons.[7] Significantly, the wellspring of activism expanded beyond established oppositional structures. Workers from a range of sectors began to bypass docile trade unions to stage protests, sit-ins, and wildcat strikes. Public-sector schoolteachers and day labourers began to push for better working conditions and the right to unionize. As before, the strongest resistance often appeared at the rough edges of state neo-liberal economic policies: in 2009 a sit-in by thousands of port workers protesting the privatization of the Aqaba Development Corporation ended with a violent crackdown and mass arrests.[8]

Alongside the new labour movement an 'alternative opposition' emerged, operating outside state bureaucratic regulations and at the boundaries of acceptable discourse.[9] Fresher and less cautious than the established parties, movements such as the Social Left (*al-yasar al-ijtima'i*) rallied youth

---

[4] This included the lifting of martial law, the legalization of political parties, and the freest elections since the 1950s. Curtis Ryan, 'Peace, Bread and Riots: Jordan and the International Monetary Fund', *Middle East Policy*, 6/2 (October 1998), 54–66.

[5] Laurie Brand, 'The Effects of the Peace Process on Political Liberalization in Jordan', *Journal of Palestinian Studies*, 28/2 (Winter 1999), 52–67.

[6] Jillian Schwedler and Lamis Andoni, 'Bread Riots in Jordan', *Middle East Research and Information Project*, 26 (Winter 1996), 40–2.

[7] Jillian Schwedler, 'More than a Mob: The Dynamics of Political Demonstrations in Jordan', *Middle East Report*, 226 (Spring 2003), 18–23.

[8] Fida Adely, 'The Emergence of a New Labor Movement in Jordan', *Middle East Report*, 264 (Winter 2012) http://www.merip.org/mer/mer264/emergence-new-labor-movement-jordan.

[9] The term is Hisham Bustani's. See Hisham Bustani, 'The Alternative Opposition in Jordan and the Failure to Understand Lessons of Tunisian and Egyptian Revolutions', *Jadaliyya*, 22 March 2011 www.jadaliyya.com/pages/index/959.

followings around economic and political demands.[10] The ferment extended even to that most privileged keystone of the regime's support base: the armed forces. In May 2010 the National Committee of Retired Servicemen, representing some 140,000 veterans including officers of the highest rank, published an unprecedented attack on King Abdullah's record in rule. Although the communiqué was dominated by an East Jordanian nationalist agenda—the threat of Jordan becoming the de facto 'alternative homeland' (*al-watan al-badil*) of the Palestinians at the expense of East Bank Jordanians—it reflected the wider current of mounting activism, and revealed serious discontent within even this praetorian sector of Jordanian society.[11] It was into this febrile atmosphere that the Arab Spring erupted in January 2011.

BEGINNINGS: FROM DHIBAN TO AMMAN

The origins of Jordan's Arab Spring reflect the complex interaction between broader regional and very local, even parochial, contexts in propelling the new civil resistance. As in other countries, unrest began on the rural periphery, where widely held socio-economic grievances were most sharply felt. Since the onset of privatization in the last decade of King Hussein's reign, East Bank communities such as Dhiban had weathered dramatic reductions in public services and employment opportunities, underdevelopment, and agricultural decline, all compounded by soaring commodity prices in the late 2000s. In the latter period, Dhiban had become a hub of activism associated with the Social Left and the movement for public-sector day-workers' rights. Thus it was in this particular village, a tiny appendage to the town of Madaba, some 50 kilometres south of Amman, that Jordan's Arab Spring began on 7 January 2011.

The small group of activists behind the Dhiban protest had no notion that it would become the founding myth of a nationwide movement. 'When we went out on the first march, we were thinking of daily bread and living standards, nothing more,' recalled Hatem Irsheidat, one of seven individuals who planned the demonstration and initially constituted its sole participants. Yet even at this early stage their socio-economic demands were infused with the

[10] According to former Secretary General Dr Khaled Kalaldeh, the Social Left organized more than sixty demonstrations in the two years before the Arab Spring, despite not being registered as a legal political party. Interview with author, Amman, August 2011.

[11] The declaration received further attention for criticizing Queen Rania's supposed unconstitutional influence in state affairs, but it also articulated grievances regarding corruption and social justice that would recur later. See 'bayan "al-wataniya li-l-mutaqa'idin al-'askiriyin"' ('Declaration of "the National Committee of Retired Servicemen"'), *Ammon News*, 1 May 2010 www.ammonnews.net/print.aspx?articleno=59696.

emerging regional language of revolt: the soon to be ubiquitous call for 'bread, freedom, social justice' was prominent among the slogans. The first ripples of the Tunisian unrest then gathering pace may also account for the wholly unexpected course of events:

> We hadn't planned on mentioning the Prime Minister, let alone the King. Back then this was a red line. We were scared—there were only seven of us, and no one knew what might happen. But to our surprise, others started to join us and take part...before we knew it we were calling for the fall of the Samir Rifa'i government.[12]

This caught the attention of Dr Khaled Kalaldeh, the leader of the Social Left, whose youth members were involved at Dhiban, and planted the idea of a rally in the capital the following Friday. Again the small organizing vanguard found itself overtaken by a new popular receptivity to protest: 'I talked to the youth sector in our movement. I said: "If you can march with 200 people it will be very good." We were 5,000.'[13]

All the ingredients for a surge in civic activism existed in Jordan before the Arab Spring, but the impetus for mobilization was now explicitly Tunisian. It has generally escaped notice that the major demonstration in Amman on 14 January 2011 was the first link beyond Tunisia in the famous chain reaction of emulation, and took place some hours *before* the departure of President Ben Ali later that day. The Amman march was branded on social media as 'The Jordanian Day of Rage', a direct reference to the unrest in Tunisia.[14] 'This told you it was something different, something special,' one participant affirmed. 'It was a transmission, an idea we took from Tunisia.'[15] Conscious emulation of events abroad differentiated the new mobilization from the activism of preceding years, and the protest also replicated the non-partisan and youth-led character of the Tunisian uprising. Established political parties kept their distance as alternative opposition movements and independent activists prepared to mobilize. 'No one was with us, and we approached almost every group in the country,' said one.[16] More importantly, the protesters deliberately placed themselves outside the framework of traditional politics, eschewing all ideological identification: 'It was the best demonstration ever in Jordan. It had no political colour; it was just the people...everybody came and asked for

---

[12] Hatem Irsheidat, Dhiban Popular Movement for Change, interview by author, Amman, February 2013.

[13] Khaled Kalaldeh, former Secretary General, Social Left Movement, interview by author, Amman, August 2011.

[14] The 'About' section of the 'Jordanian Day of Rage' Facebook group read simply: 'If some day the people decide to live, fate must bend to that desire'—a quotation from the Tunisian revolutionary poet Abu al-Qasem al-Shabbi (1909–34).

[15] Mohamed Obaid, Popular Unity Party Youth Section, interview by author, Amman, September 2011.

[16] Kamal Khoury, Social Left Movement, interview by author, Amman, August 2011.

Figure 7.1. Inspired by Tunisian demonstrations, thousands of Jordanians protested rising food prices and unemployment, calling for the cabinet to be sacked. One held aloft a placard with a loaf of flatbread and the words in Arabic: 'Where are you my dear?' at the demonstration on 14 January 2011 in Amman, which coincided with the fall of the Tunisian president later that afternoon. Two weeks later King Abdullah responded by dismissing his government.

© *Khalil Mazraawi/AFP/Getty Images*

fairer taxes, lower prices—universal demands.'[17] Ben Ali fled Tunisia that very day, and a new model of non-violent resistance was cemented (see Figure 7.1).

Symbiosis with regional developments made escalation inevitable. Protests became weekly events, taking place after Friday prayers in towns across the country, and at the second Amman demonstration voices were already calling for a return to the 1952 Constitution, a liberal document promulgated in the brief reign of King Talal (1951–2), which had qualified some of the monarchy's key powers. The third consecutive Friday demonstration in the capital, coming three days after Egyptians had flooded Tahrir Square in their own 'Day of Rage', saw a significant expansion in participation. Traditional opposition parties turned out for the first time, including the powerful Islamist movement, the Muslim Brotherhood, and its formal party, the Islamic Action Front, whose followers alone almost doubled the size of the crowd. Having failed to stem the tide with increased fuel and food subsidies, on 1 February 2011 King Abdullah dismissed the government, a time honoured shock-absorption

---

[17] Mothana Gharaibeh, National Progressive Current activist and March 24 Youth organizer, interview by author, Amman, September 2011.

tactic that only added to the sense of momentum.[18] The following month, an amendment to the Public Gatherings Law bowed to the fait accompli of regular mobilization, legalizing demonstrations without prior approval, and the new government announced the historic concession of an independent teachers' union. 'With Rifa'i gone, the regime thought the movement would end,' one activist stated. 'But it increased.'[19]

Beyond a steady street presence, the protest movement quickly gained organizational depth across diverse sections of society. Even as established political parties and trade unions joined the fray, bringing with them urban and largely Palestinian-origin followings, new reformist alliances were emerging with grassroots connections to the towns and villages of the East Bank. Building on increased cooperation over the previous decade, an array of non-party-based reform movements came together as the Jordanian Campaign for Change, also known as *Jayeen* ('We're Coming'). This included Leftist groups, activists of the labour movement, and the National Committee of Retired Servicemen. In addition, a specific role for tribally identifying reform coalitions was announced with an open letter to the king, signed by thirty-six dignitaries of prominent tribes, calling for urgent political reform lest 'the Tunisian and Egyptian deluge come to Jordan sooner or later'.[20] While this mixture of societal forces did not immediately unite behind a coherent platform, the simultaneous flush of anger very much resembled what Curtis Ryan has called 'a kind of *de facto* national "street coalition" for change'.[21] Since the 1970s, Jordanians of Palestinian and East Bank heritage had all too often vented their frustrations with the state separately—and with one eye over their shoulder. Now they were marching at the same time, if not quite with one voice.

Participants in the early protests recall the sense of invulnerability provided by the seemingly unstoppable march of events abroad. Jordanian protesters felt tightly intertwined with their counterparts elsewhere:

> We were protected by the Arab Spring. When the king changed the government, Egyptian friends called me from Tahrir Square and said: 'Hey, you should thank us! We just knocked down your government!' And in a way that's what happened—Egypt knocked down our government.[22]

Activists who had been engaged in contentious politics for years with limited returns now found themselves filmed by Al Jazeera, quoted by international

---

[18] One historical parallel that did not escape the notice of protesters was the sacking of Zayd al-Rifa'i, Samir Rifa'i's father, to defuse popular discontent during *Habbat Nisan* in 1989.

[19] Mohamed Obaid, interview by author, Amman, September 2011.

[20] Arabic text of the declaration, 'bayan li-shakhsiyat wataniya yutalib bi-islahat siyasiya haqiqiya ba'idan 'an istihlak al-istilahat' ('Declaration of patriotic figures demands real political reforms rather than meaningless rhetoric'), *Sahafi*, 6 February 2011, www.sahafi.jo/files/9368188b03e65b600dca224dc0eb905cb18aa91e.html.

[21] Curtis Ryan, 'Political Opposition and Reform Coalitions in Jordan', *British Journal of Middle Eastern Studies*, 38/3 (2011), 382.

[22] Mothana Gharaibeh, interview by author, Amman, September 2011.

media, and joined by fellow citizens in spontaneous acts of defiance. Manifest success, at home and abroad, was an electrifying new dynamic: 'The roots of the Jordanian movement were there before the Arab Spring, but the Arab Spring gave it strength.'[23]

At the same time, the need for consensus between assorted and potentially competing protest camps led Jordanian demonstrators to mark themselves off from the Arab Spring in important ways. Keenly aware of societal divisions, and the potential for instability and communal rivalry in a situation of drastic upheaval, activists made clear from the start that they did not seek revolution. Protesters carried Jordanian flags to convey national unity, and professed a commitment to change within the framework of Hashemite rule: popular anger and ridicule was directed at appointed ministers, not the royal personage at the apex of the political system. If protesters challenged monarchical authorities, they did so indirectly and in strongly legalist terms, calling for the restoration of civil and democratic rights constitutionally enshrined but subsequently eroded. The singular nature of what came to be known as the 'Jordan Spring' (*al-rabi'a al-urduni*), both intimately connected to and distinct from the broader regional drama, was encapsulated early on by an adaptation of its most iconic slogan: 'The people want the *reform* of the regime.' At a stroke, this emphasis on the terms, rather than the fact, of Hashemite monarchy radically diminished the potential for violence, whether from the state or its resisters. As if to confirm that the Jordanian case would be different, protests were greeted by a vast but initially cordial security presence: far from firing on the crowds, police handed out refreshments.

Beneath the veneer of orderliness, however, the situation was extremely fragile. Although the mobilization was attracting organized and experienced adherents, it remained improvised and energized by youth. Oppositional discourse, for all its moderation and constitutional ceiling, was nonetheless encroaching on previously taboo subjects. More seasoned observers saw danger in the concentric expansion of demands should the protection of the Arab Spring prove limited or illusory. As one veteran oppositionist and participant in the early protests noted:

> At the first march in Amman there were only a few slogans—and the youth stuck to them. By the second protest they start to talk about the constitution— immediately. Why? Are we powerful enough yet to talk about these things? We don't know! This was only the second week, and already they want to raise the slogans.[24]

The optimism of the early period would be severely tested in the coming phase.

---

[23] Mohamed Obaid, interview by author, Amman, September 2011.

[24] Interview by author, Amman, August 2011.

TOUCHING THE 'RED LINES'

With the abdication of President Hosni Mubarak on 11 February 2011, the Arab Spring claimed its greatest prize, and expectations of change rose across the region. 'History will not be made on this couch', wrote the Jordanian poet and activist Hisham Bustani. In a work dedicated 'to the revolutionaries of Egypt who left their couches and set the television ablaze', Bustani captured the Egyptian revolution's mingled effect of inspiration and frustration among its spellbound audience of young Jordanians:

> The television is burning, and history isn't being made on this couch.
> The television is burning, and the remote control doesn't change history.
> The television is burning, and I am here, in front of it.[25]

Events elsewhere further suggested that the window of historical opportunity might be closing. On 17 February, Bahraini security forces cleared the Pearl Roundabout in a dawn raid, killing several protesters. In mid-March, martial law was declared as Gulf Cooperation Council (GCC) troops entered the island kingdom; scores of Yemeni protesters were killed in a sudden government crackdown; similar violence was reported from the Syrian city of Dara'a; and Libya was deep in civil war.

It was at this moment that a coalition of reform-minded Jordanian youth staged a daring new initiative. Breaking with the pattern of transient weekly demonstrations, the 'March 24 Youth' emerged on Facebook calling for *i'tisam maftuh*, 'an open-ended sit-in', at Gamal Abdel Nasser Circle, a transport hub in central Amman known as *Duwwar Dakhiliyya* ('Interior Ministry Circle') because of its proximity to the building. The movement described itself as 'a mixture of free Jordanian young men and women tired of delays and promises of reform, who see the spread of corruption, the deteriorating economic situation, the regression of political life, the erasure of freedoms and dissolution of the social fabric'. Though they clearly sought to replicate the logic of Tahrir Square through the occupation of public space, their political aims were still limited. Under the consensus banner of 'The people want the reform of the regime', the March 24 Youth staked out seven broad demands: a representative parliament, elected government, 'real' constitutional reforms, corruption prosecutions, tax reform, 'lifting of the security grip', and 'realization of national unity'.[26]

Sure enough, on 24 March 2011 a substantial crowd assembled at the Circle, replete with tents, stocks of food, a sound system, and an array of recording equipment including a live Internet stream. Participants were predominantly

---

[25] Hisham Bustani, *Ara al-Ma'na* ('The Perception of Meaning') (Beirut: Dar al-Adab, 2012), 129–32.
[26] See www.facebook.com/shbab.march.24/info.

young but diverse, coming from all communities and walks of life—both Palestinian-origin and East Jordanian—with perhaps the majority made up by 'independents' unaffiliated with any particular political party or trend. As the crowd settled, women and children appeared and prominent civil society figures gave speeches. In a further nod to the civic ethic displayed at Tahrir Square, teams of volunteers kept the area organized and tidy. Into the night, protesters sang patriotic songs and waved Jordanian flags beneath a large portrait of the king. They also called for the resignation of the new prime minister and the director of General Intelligence, mentioning the latter by name.[27]

What followed revealed much about the limits of free expression in Jordan, and the scale of the challenges faced by the advocates of reform. Gradually over the course of the night, a crowd of counter-protesters formed beyond the police perimeter surrounding the March 24 Youth. Amid intermittent stone-throwing, the chanting of the new arrivals cast the original protesters as divisive outsiders: Palestinian Islamists, or Shia Muslims sent by Iran. Occasional attempts by the self-described *baltajiyya*, 'thugs',[28] to break through the police line were dutifully parried, to cheers from the reformists, who greeted each volley of missiles with chants of *silmiya*, 'peaceful'. On Friday, 25 March, the pro-reform camp was bolstered significantly as word spread of the unfolding stand-off. In the early evening, however, the atmosphere changed. Nearby streets were closed off. The security presence grew in size and adopted an intimidating posture. Forces were assembled on a bridge overlooking the Circle, and at around 4 p.m. the police gave a formal warning to the protesters over a loud speaker: 'Leave now.' When the crowd refused, a convoy of vehicles arrived and unloaded counter-protesters, who began showering the demonstration with rocks and masonry from the bridge above. Riot police and *baltajiyya* then cleared the Circle in force, leaving one protester dead and more than 100 wounded.[29] After the melee, uniformed police and plain-clothes thugs were seen openly celebrating together, chanting royalist slogans. That

---

[27] The following account is based on interviews with March 24 Youth organizers and participants conducted during August–October 2011, December 2011, September 2012, and January–February 2013. See also the eyewitness account of blogger Naseem Tarawnah, 'The Quick Death of Shabab March 24 and what it Means for Jordan', *The Black Iris of Jordan*, blog, 26 March 2011 http://black-iris.com/2011/03/26/the-quick-death-of-shabab-march-24-and-what-it-means-for-jordan/.

[28] The Jordanian word for such people is *zu'ran*, 'troublemakers'. According to eyewitnesses, however, the counter-protesters actively asserted a *baltajiyya* identity—in emulation of the Egyptian pro-regime thugs who attacked demonstrators in Tahrir Square in February 2011—a reminder that Arab Spring 'mirror-effect' inspiration was also available to anti-reform elements.

[29] Security officials stated that Khairy Jamil suffered a heart attack during the operation to clear the square. His son, who was also attacked by police, claimed he died after being heavily beaten. Among activists Jamil is widely regarded as a martyr. See Ranya Kadri and Ethan Bronner, 'Riot Police in Jordan Clear Camp of Protesters', *New York Times*, 25 March 2011 http://www.nytimes.com/2011/03/26/world/middleeast/26jordan.html.

evening, Prime Minister Marouf al-Bakhit echoed the narrative of the counter-demonstrators in a televised speech, blaming the incident on an externally orchestrated Islamist conspiracy.[30]

Battered but unbowed, the reformulated 'March 24 Coalition' attempted another sit-in on 15 July 2011 at Al Nakheel Square, in what was to be a desperate affair. On this occasion, security forces adopted a policy of pre-emptive violence, dealing out beatings to protesters and journalists on sight.[31] Khalid Kamhawi, an organizer of the sit-in, described the situation:

> As soon as people arrived, the security forces met them with violence—from the start. They didn't want people to consolidate and form a large mass. Lots of people were injured and taken to hospital. What trickled down from this was maybe 500–800 people who managed to meet in the middle of the square, where we were surrounded by police and the roads around us sealed off. Our plan was to stay in place and wait for more people to come and for the whole thing to grow.[32]

Instead, the protest leaders found themselves flanked by men claiming to be *mukhabarat* agents, who followed their every move. One of the men then delivered a threat of lethal violence to the organizers: 'They said there were snipers on the roof, and if we didn't leave within two hours they might start shooting.' After anxious deliberation, the thirteen-member steering group broke off the sit-in to avoid bloodshed. For Kamhawi, who alone voted to continue the protest, this was a fateful decision:

> I still believe it was a mistake. There are certain historical moments which you should capture. These moments, if you don't take them when they come by, it's very difficult to reproduce them. I think it showed the regime that the youth movements, like their elders, are willing to compromise on certain positions... because it was a battle of wills at that point, and whoever flinches first loses. And there was a flinch from the youth movement.[33]

The following day, the Coalition reconvened at Amman's Fourth Circle. Defiant speeches were made, but the crowd was small and the sense of disappointment palpable. 'People were disillusioned with us', said Kamhawi, 'and I think they were right to be so'.

---

[30] Bakhit accused the Jordanian Muslim Brotherhood of 'taking orders from the Muslim Brothers in Egypt and Syria', with 'an agenda to create chaos in the country'. See 'Jordan's Opposition Demands PM's Ouster after Unrest', *al-Arabiya*, 26 March 2011 www.alarabiya.net/articles/2011/03/26/143091.html.

[31] Distinctive media vests had been distributed by the Public Security Directorate to local and international reporters, who nevertheless found themselves singled out for assault. The head of Jordan's Press Association claimed the vests were 'a trap to target journalists'. See Banan Malkawi, 'Downtown Amman: Security Attack Protesters, Journalists in Pro-Reform Demonstration', *Ammon News*, 15 July 2011 http://en.ammonnews.net/article.aspx?articleNO=12876.

[32] Khalid Kamhawi, March 24 Coalition, interview by author, Amman, February 2013.

[33] Khalid Kamhawi, interview by author, Amman, February 2013.

The deft application of targeted, generally non-lethal violence prevented the emergence of the kind of open-ended protest around which events had revolved elsewhere. In effect, the emotive connection to Tahrir Square was severed:

> The occupation of public space is very dangerous for the regime, because through occupation you could raise the notion of liberation. If you occupy a public space and say 'This space designates a space of liberty and freedom, where we can say whatever we want and demand the future we want'—it's as if you're liberating that space from a certain occupier, which is the regime.[34]

In the manner of guerrilla warfare, however, the battlegrounds of protest simply shifted. Even as protesters drew back from the occupation of the capital's landmark squares, they colonized virtual—but no less public—space. Across an increasingly vibrant activist social media enclave, bloggers regularly uploaded evidence of police excesses to 'name and shame' offenders.[35] On the ground, too, new sources of strength came to the fore.

DE-CENTRING PROTEST: VERTICAL AND HORIZONTAL EXPANSION

The Muslim Brotherhood began to take on a more prominent role in the still-evolving *hirak*. Emboldened by the rise of its counterparts in Tunisia and especially Egypt, the Brotherhood sharpened hitherto broadbrush calls for change into a tightly organized push for constitutional reform. In particular, the Islamists focused attention on the unrestricted power of the king to dissolve parliament (Article 34), appoint the prime minister (Article 35) and the entirety of the senate (Article 36), while stepping up pressure for a new election law to empower political parties as opposed to local independent candidates. Drawing on its decades-old grass-roots network and nationwide infrastructure, the Brotherhood became a powerhouse of mobilization, especially in the large urban centres of Amman, Zarqa, and Irbid. The increasingly organized make-up of the *hirak* meant a return to the traditional *masira* ('march'), following a ritual of set routes and speeches, expertly kept in line by Brotherhood organizers in fluorescent vests. Though a world away from the

---

[34] Khalid Kamhawi, interview by author, Amman, February 2013.

[35] One security man unexpectedly shot to fame after footage of his particularly zealous exertions at the 15 July clashes circulated on the Internet. Since his chosen weapon was a barbecue rack (*mangal*) requisitioned from a nearby restaurant, activists christened him 'Abu Mangal', which became a byword for police brutality. Eponymous Facebook pages became dedicated sites for the exposure of such incidents. See www.facebook.com/AbuManqal; www.facebook.com/AbuMan8al.

open-ended protest envisioned by ambitious reformist youth, the rhythm of mobilization lent urgency to the far-reaching demands for structural political change now championed by the kingdom's oldest and most experienced opposition movement.[36]

Meanwhile, the most significant developments were taking place far from Amman, in the towns and villages of the East Bank. The mood of pervasive activism that had extended from Dhiban to all governorates in the early weeks of 2011, initially led by labour movements and the National Committee of Retired Servicemen, began to take further organizational shape in the rise of so-called popular movements (*harakat sha'biyya*), soon to be found in every major settlement in the country. These local activist committees, though diverse and imperfectly understood, represented a new form of collective action in what are usually regarded as conservative and relatively insular communities. In an account mirrored by activists from other governorates, a founding member of a typical *haraka*, the Kerak Popular Youth Movement, described the formative process:

> At the beginning of 2011, a group of youths in the Kerak governorate began to hold meetings together. It was unusual because they involved people from a whole range of perspectives and points of view. Among us were Islamists, Leftists, independents—a mixed group of youths. But the one goal for all of us was to try to save our country from corruption, the loss of freedoms and the rolling back of the power of the people.[37]

Distinguished by cross-ideological collaboration and the participation of youth never before engaged in politics, the movements also followed the existing grain of their local communities, harnessing the solidarity of tribal structures (*al-asha'ir*).[38] Outside the capital, they spearheaded and to a large extent embodied the novel activism now widely known as *hirak*.

The emergence of the popular movements extended the pattern of civil resistance since *Habbat Nisan*, whereby the once 'loyal' towns and tribes of the East Bank had become the kingdom's principal sites of contentious action. Mobilization in places such as Kerak, Ma'an, and Tafileh initially operated at a remove from the debates about the election law and constitutional reform promulgated by the Muslim Brotherhood and traditional opposition forces; rather, it reflected decades of deprivation and moral outrage specific to these communities, and heightened by perceptions of

---

[36] Jacob Amis, 'The Jordanian Brotherhood in the Arab Spring', in Eric Brown, Hillel Fradkin, and Husain Haqqani (eds), *Current Trends in Islamist Ideology*, xiv (Washington: Hudson Institute, December 2012).

[37] Thabit Assaf, Kerak Popular Youth Movement, interview by author, Amman, February 2013.

[38] The Dhiban Popular Movement for Change, for instance, is by default closely integrated with the local Bani Hamida tribe. Other movements, such as the Bani Hassan Gathering for Reform, explicitly assert a tribal identity.

runaway corruption and reckless privatization under King Abdullah II in particular. Unlike their counterparts in Amman, moreover, a constituency of civil resisters drawn from the monarchy's traditional bases of support could not easily be dismissed as foreign-sponsored subversives. Thus provincial activists were able to extend their critique to the very top of the political system and the final red line: the king himself. As an oppositionist from Tafileh observed:

> Southern people—you can't accuse them of being directed from the outside. These are closed communities. If, here in Amman, you start to talk about the king, they will say: 'Oh, it's the Iranians, or the Muslim Brothers, or the Americans.' But in the south, they are loyal all their lives. The royal guards are drawn from Tafileh—and even there they have started to talk about the king.[39]

By the summer of 2011 chants comparing King Abdullah to Hosni Mubarak (and, still more scandalously, Muammar Gaddafi)—and warning him of the same fate—were openly shouted at southern protests, and whispered about in the capital. The ultimate glass ceiling was cracking before everyone's eyes. 'In Amman talking about the king is still a red line. But it's also a tactical thing,' an activist of Palestinian origin from the capital stated at the time. 'Once all the southern cities—Kerak, Tafileh, Ma'an—once they are all talking about the king directly, then we will join them here.'[40]

BUYING TIME AND KILLING MOMENTUM

Like its counterpart in Morocco, the regime attempted to defuse popular pressure and take control of the enhanced opposition discourse by way of a top-down 'reform process'. The decision to introduce amendments to the constitution raised hopes for a decisive reform settlement. 'Even talking about this used to be forbidden—it was a red line even a few months ago,' an activist stated. 'We're talking about the constitution and the king's authorities for the first time.'[41] In September 2011, after an opaque consultation process with no opposition participation, amendments proposed by a small committee of senior officials were reviewed by the government and approved by parliament and the senate. Unlike in Morocco, where the royal reform package was submitted to popular referendum, wider civil society watched from the sidelines.

---

[39] Dr Khaled Kalaldeh, interview by author, Amman, August 2011.
[40] Interview by author, Amman, September 2011.
[41] Mothana Gharaibeh, interview by author, Amman, September 2011.

The resulting amendments established new bodies to monitor elections and legislation, and nominally expanded civil liberties, but did not affect the overall concentration of decision-making power in the hands of the king. Abdullah II remained free to dissolve parliament, ratify and promulgate laws, appoint the prime minister, cabinet, and the entirety of the senate, all while being constitutionally 'immune from any liability and responsibility' (Article 30).[42] Long-awaited reform of the election law proved equally tentative, introducing only 27 out of 150 parliamentary seats for national-level candidates, well short of the 50 per cent allocation demanded by both the Muslim Brotherhood and the National Front for Reform, a broad coalition led by former Prime Minister and latterly oppositionist Ahmed Obaydat.[43] Rather than pre-empting protests with bold concessions, the new reform push repeated in miniature the forlorn experience of the previous ten years of Abdullah's reign: successive committees and initiatives, overseen by a carousel of governments and accompanied by constant verbal encouragement from the king, ultimately delivered little in the way of systemic change.[44]

In any case, subsequent regime policies seemed to contradict the values of free expression and human rights upon which the 'reform process' was rhetorically predicated. The year 2012 began ominously with the detention of an 18-year-old activist on 11 January, for setting fire to an image of the king.[45] Waves of arrests swept the country in a concerted crackdown on newly prevalent criticism of the monarch and royal family. Having legalized protests in 2011, the authorities now rounded up activists for 'undermining royal dignity', punishable under Penal Code Article 195 with up to three years in prison, and 'subverting the system of government' (Article 149). On 31 March demonstrators at Amman's Fourth Circle demanding the release of activists detained in Tafileh were themselves beaten and arrested after chanting 'O Abdullah, O Abdullah, Jordan will not be scorned', in defiance of a police warning not to cross 'red lines'.[46] Peaceful civilian protesters increasingly found themselves before the State Security Court, a military-dominated panel of appointed judges, whose remit the vaunted constitutional reforms

---

[42] Indeed, critics noted that the amendments actually expanded the king's powers, with the 'independent' Constitutional Court set to be headed by a royal appointee.

[43] Taylor Luck, 'Elections Law Amendments "Death Blow" to Jordan's Reform Drive', *Jordan Times*, 11 July 2012.

[44] Marwan Muasher, *A Decade of Struggling Reform Efforts in Jordan: The Resilience of the Rentier System* (Washington: Carnegie Papers, May 2011).

[45] Udai Abu Issa was sentenced to two years' imprisonment, but received a royal pardon in February 2012 after repeated hunger strikes. 'Youth jailed for "Undermining the King's Dignity" Pardoned', *Jordan Times*, 29 February 2012 http://jordantimes.com/youth-jailed-for-undermining-the-kings-dignity-pardoned.

[46] Human Rights Watch, 'Jordan: Demonstrators Beaten in Custody', HRW, Beirut, 3 April 2012.

had specifically restricted to high treason, espionage, and terrorism.[47] Those imprisoned sometimes gained royal pardon through hunger strikes, but reports of abuse and torture while they were in detention were not uncommon.[48]

The security sweep often extended to journalism and political analysis. In April 2012 a writer and also the publisher of the *Gerasa News* website were charged with 'subverting the system of government' for an article on alleged royal intervention in a corruption investigation.[49] Four opposition figures faced the same charge, along with Jordanian MP and *Straight Talk* presenter Rula Hurub, after the weekly talk show aired an over-frank discussion of reform.[50] As if to formalize the backslide into censorship, an August 2012 amendment to the Press and Publications Law dismayed Jordan's vibrant blogosphere and online news sector with new government powers to block websites, and an extension of bureaucratic restrictions on newspapers to broadly defined electronic publications.[51] 'This is the history of free speech in our country,' reflected Naseem Tarawnah, blogger and co-founder of the citizen-journalism website *7iber* ('Ink'). 'The security apparatus allows the pressure on the cooker to be relieved, it allows people to vent, then it slowly clamps down.... The only difference is that the Arab Spring bought more time—the window of opportunity was never open for this long—but now it's slowly closing again.'[52]

CIVIL RESISTANCE BETWEEN THE TRANSNATIONAL AND THE SUBNATIONAL

With the ground disappearing beneath their feet, disparate strands of the *hirak* started to come together. Popular movements merged at the local level and

[47] Human Rights Watch, which has extensively documented the constriction of free speech in Jordan since the Arab Spring, called the arrests 'a concerted move by security and judicial authorities against opposition groups' (Human Rights Watch, 'Jordan: Arrest Wave Signals Growing Intolerance for Dissent', HRW, Beirut, 14 September 2012 www.hrw.org/news/2012/09/14/jordan-arrest-wave-signals-growing-intolerance-dissent.

[48] See Mohamed al-Najjar, 'itihamat li-l-amn al-urduni bi-ta'dhib mu'taqalin' ('Jordanian Security Faces Accusations of Torturing Detainees'), *Al Jazeera Net*, 21 November 2012 www.aljazeera.net/news/pages/ab2b67f9-2a91-419c-b661-464fb063c248.

[49] According to the defendants, the military prosecutor at the State Security Court told them that King Abdullah was at the forefront of the fight against corruption and it was forbidden to imply otherwise. Human Rights Watch, 'Jordan: Publisher, Journalist Charged in State Security Court', HRW, Beirut, 25 April 2012 www.hrw.org/news/2012/04/25/jordan-publisher-journalist-charged-state-security-court.

[50] Human Rights Watch, 'Jordan: A Move to Censor Online Expression', HRW, Beirut, 10 September 2012 www.hrw.org/news/2012/09/10/jordan-move-censor-online-expression.

[51] Daoud Kuttab, 'Freedom in Jordan Does not Extend to Information', *Washington Post*, 5 October 2012.

[52] Naseem Tarawnah, interview by author, Amman, February 2013.

developed cooperative relationships with their counterparts in other regions. Even in towns where social media had scarcely featured before the Arab Spring, it became a vital tool for increasingly outward-looking East Bank reformist groups: according to Mohamed al-Dabbas, a regional coordinator for popular movements, 'Facebook brought the *hirakiin* together'.[53] In July 2012 representatives from thirty-five popular movements and tribal coalitions from across Jordan convened at the Muslim Brotherhood's Amman head-quarters, alongside the National Front for Reform, and union and political party figures, to call for genuine constitutional and electoral reform and announce a united boycott of forthcoming parliamentary elections.[54]

The quest for unity had to contend, however, with a campaign of violence and propaganda intent on inflaming multiple fault lines in Jordanian society, sometimes with the complicity of elements of officialdom and the security forces. The *baltajiyya* narrative that painted often predominantly East Jordanian reformist youth as a dangerous 'Other' ('Palestinian', 'Islamist', and 'Shia/ Iranian'), which emerged at *Dakhaliyya* on 25 March—and received apparent official sanction via the intervention of gendarmes on the streets and the prime minister on national television—resurfaced in a steady drumbeat of intimidation. More than once, security forces stood by as peaceful marches organized by the Muslim Brotherhood in conjunction with popular move-ments and tribally based committees came under vicious assault. Such tactics often seemed designed to prevent the Muslim Brotherhood, as a notable representative of Palestinian-origin Jordanians, from building reformist alli-ances in the East Bank heartlands. They also appeared to play on tribal segmentations within East Jordanian communities.

On 15 October 2011 a pro-reform gathering took place in the village of Salhub, featuring the Muslim Brotherhood and National Front for Reform, under the auspices of representatives from an array of prominent Jordanian tribes. The event came to an abrupt end, however, when assailants fired gunshots into the air and threw rocks at speakers and audience members before violently dispersing the crowd. A Public Security Directorate spokes-person later claimed the attackers were tribesmen who objected to the Muslim Brotherhood's presence, adding that security forces were unwilling to interfere in a tribal dispute. Similarly, in December 2011, a reformist march in the northern town of Mafraq, organized by the Muslim Brotherhood in conjunc-tion with local youth and tribally based committees, came under a prolonged attack that left dozens of activists injured and the local Brotherhood and IAF

---

[53] Mohamed al-Dabbas, Coordination Council for Popular Hirak in Salt and Al Balqa, interview by author, Salt, February 2013.
[54] 'liqa al-islamiyin wa-l-harakat: tuwafuq 'amm 'ala muqata'at al-intikhabat' ('Meeting of Islamists and Movements: General Agreement on Election Boycott'), *Amman Net*, 11 July 2012 http://ar.ammannet.net/news/163664#.UCvYrqmPWa8.

headquarters burned to the ground. As an International Crisis Group report noted: 'While the lack of transparent investigation into these incidents makes it difficult to attribute authorship, they were well organized and almost certainly intended to inflame existing tensions and associate protests with the threat of communal violence.'[55] Local activists tended to be less equivocal: 'The regime sponsors these aggressors, the *baltajiyya* and *zu'ran*. These people beat protesters and throw stones in the name of the king while carrying his portrait.'[56]

The greatest deterrent to Jordanian mobilization, however, came from the very source that powered its initial surge. The 'mirror effect' of the Arab Spring darkened as civil resistance in neighbouring countries gave way to brutal war and increasingly problematic transitions. Above all, the Syrian crisis played into the hands of those eager to posit an inevitable connection between civil resistance and civil war: 'The more the contrast between stability here and the lack of it in Syria grows, the more people are inclined to stay home and not protest. The state knows this and they play on it often.'[57] In addition, the conflict drove a wedge between the Muslim Brotherhood, which strongly backed the Syrian Uprising, and Leftist and Arab Nationalist opposition elements (not least the two Jordanian cognates of the Ba'ath Party), which remained supportive of the regime in Damascus. The paralysing effect of both regional and communal conflict suggested depressing comparisons. 'Jordan is like Lebanon,' Bustani lamented, 'inherently designed to be void of any context for independence and sovereignty'.[58]

Other international forces certainly worked to shelter the regime against calls for reform. As a resource-poor monarchy teetering on the Gulf's near periphery, Jordan became a focal point of an activist post-Arab Spring GCC foreign policy. Though talk of imminent Jordanian and Moroccan accession proved premature, in December 2011 Saudi Arabia, the UAE, Kuwait, and Qatar unveiled a $5 billion fund to support the would-be members.[59] For activists, the closing of ranks with monarchies characterized by a more vigorous absolutism, and still less in the way of elected representation and

---

[55] International Crisis Group, *Popular Protest in North Africa and the Middle East (IX): Dallying with Reform in a Divided Jordan* (Amman/Brussels: International Crisis Group, Middle East/North Africa Report no. 118, 12 March 2012), 23–5. For a further discussion of identity politics in Jordan and its role in the Jordan Spring, see Curtis Ryan, 'Identity Politics, Reform, and Protest in Jordan', *Studies in Ethnicity and Nationalism*, 11/3 (December 2011), 564–78.

[56] Thabit Assaf, interview by author, Amman, February 2013. Ironically, the conviction that such incidents represented a deliberate regime strategy to divide the *hirak* became a point of agreement among activists, repeatedly voiced in interviews with opposition actors of all stripes.

[57] Naseem Tarawnah, interview by author, Amman, February 2013.

[58] Hisham Bustani, 'Jordan: A Failed Uprising and a Re-Emerging Regime', *Your Middle East*, 8 January 2013 www.yourmiddleeast.com/opinion/hisham-bustani-jordan-a-failed-uprising-and-a-reemerging-regime_12178.

[59] 'Gulf Leaders Set up $5b Fund to Support Jordan, Morocco', *Jordan Times*, 21 December 2011.

institutional checks and balances, did not bode well for a genuine process of democratization. Nor were they impressed by a ramping-up of US aid when combined with fulsome praise for reforms widely regarded as superficial.[60] In the event, however, Gulf funding trickled through only gradually and, like US financial support, was tied to specific development projects rather than directly mitigating the burgeoning state deficit.[61] If the backing of powerful outsiders appeared to endorse the status quo, it did not make it sustainable, and could not avert a $2 billion IMF loan conditional on commodity price rises and cuts to public subsidies.[62] With poor economic prospects and shrinking political freedoms, pressure on Jordanians continued to build.

HABBAT TISHREEN

In November 2012 the bubble burst. A sudden cut in government subsidies on oil derivatives led to overnight price increases of more than 30 per cent for transport and heating fuel, and more than 50 per cent for cooking gas. Within an hour of the announcement, Jordanians took to the streets, beginning four consecutive days of mass protest and unrest now popularly known as *Habbat Tishreen*, 'The November Uprising'. As in 1989, the ferment saw the mobilization of the 'silent majority', unconnected to and beyond the control of organized political forces, and a significant slide into violence. Across the country, protesters blocked roads with burning tyres and threw rocks at security forces, who responded with tear gas, water cannon, and baton charges.[63] 'The *hirak* became a small elite in this moment', as one activist put it, 'and we found that it was more moderate than the mass of the people' (see Figure 7.2).[64]

---

[60] 'Jordan, US Sign Grant Deals Worth $356.9 Million', *Jordan Times*, 1 October 2012. Far from prodding their ally towards further reforms, public comments by US (and EU) diplomats and statesmen tended to express unqualified admiration for steps already taken. Following an Oval Office meeting with King Abdullah in January 2012, President Obama hailed 'the extraordinary efforts that have been made by His Majesty...in guiding political reform inside of Jordan', which had placed him 'ahead of the curve in trying to respond to the legitimate concerns and aspirations...of the Jordanian population' www.whitehouse.gov/the-press-office/2012/01/17/remarks-president-obama-and-his-majesty-king-abdullah-jordan.

[61] Omar Obeidat, 'Jordan Reaches out to Wealthy Arab States for Urgent Financial Aid', *Jordan Times*, 18 September 2012.

[62] 'Jordan Gets $2.0 Billion IMF Loan to Support Economy', *IMF Survey Online*, 3 August 2012 www.imf.org/external/pubs/ft/survey/so/2012/int080312a.htm.

[63] The Public Security Directorate recorded more than 100 separate 'riots' in the first seventy-two hours of nationwide protests, which saw government buildings and police stations stormed as well as acts of looting. See Taylor Luck, 'Fuel Price Riots Enter Third Straight Day', *Jordan Times*, 15 November 2012.

[64] Hatem Irsheidat, interview by author, Amman, February 2013.

Figure 7.2. The dignity and courage of non-violence. Riot police were brought in to stop renewed protests, this time against rising oil prices, at Gamal Abdel Nasser Circle in Amman on 14 November 2012 following a sudden cut in government subsidies. The four consecutive days of mass protest were known as the November Uprising.
© *Jordan Pix/Getty Images*

Even where non-violent tactics prevailed, the language of protest shifted dramatically, as traditions of deference towards the monarchy evaporated in a manner unprecedented in the history of Jordan. In Amman, people spontaneously gravitated towards *Duwwar Dakhiliyya*—where an attempted sit-in was once again broken up by riot police—and raised chants against the king of a kind previously restricted to the most strident southern protests.[65] On Friday, 16 November, a peaceful rhythm of protest was largely restored, with mass rallies organized by popular movements and traditional opposition forces in nine of the kingdom's twelve governorates, to be backed up by union strikes the following week. The radicalized discourse persisted, however, as cries of 'the people want the *fall* of the regime' rang out from Kerak to Amman, where riot police had to be deployed to stop protesters marching on the Royal Court.[66] Just as they had

---

[65] 'al-urdun: quwat al-amn tafad i'tisaman fi 'amman ihtijajan 'ala ziyadat as'ar al-wuqud' ('Jordan: Security Forces Disperse Amman Sit-in Protesting Fuel Price Increase'), *BBC Arabic*, 14 November 2012 www.bbc.co.uk/arabic/middleeast/2012/11/121114_jordan_demos_police.shtml.

[66] 'suwar – i'tisam amama al-husayni wa mana' al-tuwajuh ila al-diwan al-malaki' ('Pictures—Sit-in in Front of al-Husseini Mosque and Sealing off of the Royal Court'), *Amman Net*, 16 November 2012 http://ar.ammannet.net/news/177984#.UKZQROSNtlE; see

roundly condemned the use of violence, opposition leaders distanced themselves from the calls for regime change.[67] But, in those few days in November, ordinary Jordanians threw down a gauntlet to their ruler as never before.

A number of factors, recurrent throughout the Jordan Spring, ensured once more that no tipping point was reached. The discipline with which police and gendarmes avoided the use of lethal force was probably decisive in preventing a more sustained violent reaction from the population.[68] It found its mirror image in the moderation, even timidity, with which organized opposition elements responded to the transformed dynamics of resistance, actively working to isolate and condemn hints of revolutionary sentiment. At the same time, carefully controlled coercive tactics enforced the familiar red lines: sit-ins were broken up when protesters attempted to hold ground, and a tightly meshed security net descended on those deemed to have trodden too brazenly on royal toes.[69] For now, the regime's skilful combination of permissive and punitive responses— and the opposition's reluctance to provoke a potentially divisive and destabilizing situation of all-out change—appeared to bring the country back from the brink.

SUCCESS OR FAILURE? ASSESSING THE HIRAK

Four years on from the outbreak of the Arab Spring, the Jordanian *hirak* had not realized any of its most widely articulated demands. The process of top-down reform it had helped to initiate did not alter fundamental power relations between the monarch, the appointed government and senate, and the elected representatives of the people. Institutional imbalances aside, one could point to the abiding influence of the security apparatus, ongoing civilian

---

also 'al-karak: nahna al-sh'ab al-khat al-ahmar' ('Kerak: We Are the Red Line People'), *Amman Net*, 16 November 2012 http://ar.ammannet.net/news/178018#.UKeEueSNtIE.

[67] Tellingly, the language of regime change was denounced not only by the Muslim Brotherhood and National Front for Reform, but also by alternative opposition movements such as the Social Left: Khaled Neimat, 'Opposition Groups Say they Want Regime Reform not "Downfall"', *Jordan Times*, 17 November 2012.

[68] The only citizen killed by security forces during the November Uprising was apparently one of an armed band that attacked a police station near Irbid. See Taylor Luck, 'Fuel Price Riots Enter Third Straight Day', *Jordan Times*, 15 November 2012.

[69] Some 300 citizens were arrested in connection with the protests, of whom 107 were detained for an extended period and referred to the State Security Court on a number of charges, including 'subverting the system of government' and 'insulting the King'. See Human Rights Watch, 'Jordan: End Protester Trials in State Security Court', HRW, Beirut, 30 November 2012 www.hrw.org/news/2012/11/30/jordan-end-protester-trials-state-security-courts. Although the bulk of the detainees were subsequently freed by royal pardon, many were recalled by the SSC to face charges in 2013. See Ahmad Abu Hamad, 'amn al-dawla tu'awada ist'ida mu'taqali habbat tishreen' ('State Security Resumes Summons of Habbat Tishreen Detainees], *Amman Net*, 30 January 2013 http://ar.ammannet.net/news/186147.

trials at the State Security Court, and the lack even of a thoroughgoing anti-corruption drive, and conclude that the movement for reform had failed. For activist and writer Labib Kamhawi, the record of the Jordan Spring revealed a 'bitter truth'. Jordanians had hopes and grievances nearly identical to those of others in the region, and distinguished themselves with a clear commitment to peaceful reform, but their uniquely moderate Spring did not bear fruit. Rather, Kamhawi argued, it was exploited and thwarted by an intransigent regime.[70]

The January 2013 parliamentary elections were a showcase of surface changes amid structural continuity that typified the march of official reform. Overseen by the newly established Independent Electoral Commission and international monitors, the polls displayed a number of procedural improvements: though abuses and irregularities were reported, they did not match the allegations of widespread rigging that blighted elections in 2007 and 2010. Of course, with the 'one vote' election law still operative for 108 of 150 parliamentary seats, and the opposition absent through boycott, the regime risked little: even the novel quota of 27 seats for 'national lists' was more a contest of social ties and tribal affiliations than political platforms.[71] Turnout was modest, at less than 40 per cent of eligible voters, a significant slip on 52 per cent in 2010, but officials snatched victory from the jaws of defeat by publicizing the figure of 56 per cent, calculated from the total *registered* voters, as a putative increase in participation. The elections were successfully marketed as a rejection of the opposition and a ringing popular endorsement of palace-led reform, all the while reproducing a parliament every bit as parochial, loyalist, and royalist as its predecessor.[72] Counter-intuitively, and in contrast to historical civil resistance campaigns, free (if not necessarily fair) elections here dealt another blow to the aspirations of Jordanian civil resisters.

The changing regional picture also had its impact. King Abdullah II was quick to support the July 2013 military takeover in Cairo by Abdel Fattah el-Sisi, and promptly arranged a royal visit to endorse the new regime. Regional alliances, with Egypt but also with the United Arab Emirates and Saudi Arabia, became so important as to impinge directly on the Jordanian political opposition: in December 2014 the deputy head of the Muslim

---

[70] Labib Kamhawi, 'al-urduniun: al-haqiqa al-murra' ('Jordanians: The Bitter Truth'), *Al Quds Al Arabi*, 1 October 2012 www.alquds.co.uk/index.asp?fname=data%5C2012%5C10% 5C10-01%5C01qpt989.htm.

[71] Danya Greenfield, 'Optimism after Jordan's Election', *Foreign Policy*, 25 January 2013 http://mideast.foreignpolicy.com/posts/2013/01/25/optimism_after_jordans_election.

[72] Ziad Abu Rish, 'Romancing the Throne: The New York Times and the Endorsement of Authoritarianism in Jordan', *Jadaliyya*, 3 February 2013. On 13 February 2013 US Secretary of State John Kerry described the elections as an 'important milestone' with a 'very, very significant outcome', noting 'the record level of turnout, notwithstanding one group's decision to boycott – [participation] was higher than any time previously...' www.state.gov/secretary/remarks/2013/02/204560.htm.

Brotherhood was jailed for a Facebook post critical of the Emirati regime.[73] Jordan's decision to play a public role in the fight against ISIS in Syria, deploying its own fighter jets, raised concerns among some in the kingdom of the risk of incurring retaliation, particularly after the brutal killing of a captured Jordanian pilot in early 2015. However, the swift execution of two convicted death-row prisoners and the king's promise of a redoubled effort against ISIS again seemed, at least initially, to strengthen the position of the monarchy and to dampen the cause of political reform at home.[74]

Yet, for all the disillusion and lack of progress in formal politics, it would be wrong to conclude that the *hirak* had failed. Rather, the deadlock at the state level was shown up by a profound societal transformation witnessed in two years of constant mobilization. Political engagement and participation, albeit in particular contentious forms, had rarely been higher among Jordanians. In the run-up to the elections, opposition parties, the Muslim Brotherhood, and local popular movements came together for a succession of 'centralized actions' in Amman, not least the October 2012 'Friday of National Salvation', widely acknowledged as the largest demonstration seen in the kingdom for decades.[75] More significant than any one protest, however, was the panorama of concurrent mobilizations that took place on a weekly basis, cumulatively revealing thousands of resisters in diverse locations throughout the country. Though the definition remained fluid and contested, it was this climate of protest, as well as the specific grass-roots associations it produced, that the term *hirak* primarily described:

> Before the Arab Spring people used to talk about 'opposition' [*mu'arida*], or 'the political opposition' [*al-mu'arida al-siyasiya*], and this referred to formal parties and the elite. But the word *hirak* has a different meaning, closer to 'revolution' [*thawra*]—that is to say a revolutionary condition [*halat thawriya*] that exists among the people.[76]

At least for a time, it changed the nature of politics in Jordan: 'They managed to create a situation where people saw something different...These new movements—young movements, tribal movements, non-Amman-based—the

---

[73] Rana Sweis, 'Brotherhood Leader's Arrest in Jordan Is Seen as a Warning from Monarchy', *New York Times*, 7 December 2014 www.nytimes.com/2014/12/08/world/brotherhood-leaders-arrest-in-jordan-is-seen-as-warning-from-monarchy.html.

[74] Rod Nordland and David Kirkpatrick, 'Jordan's King Abdullah II Returns Home to Cheers after Swift Executions', *New York Times*, 4 February 2015 www.nytimes.com/2015/02/05/world/middleeast/jordans-king-abdullah-ii-returns-home-to-cheers-after-swift-executions.html.

[75] Taylor Luck, 'Over 70 Political Groups Vow to Hold Jordan's "Largest Ever" Pro-reform Protest', *Jordan Times*, 30 September 2012 http://jordantimes.com/over-70-political-groups-vow-to-hold-jordans-largest-ever-pro-reform-protest.

[76] Thabit Assaf, interview by author, Amman, February 2013.

meaning of opposition is being reformed just by the existence of these groups, just by them going out and doing what they do.'[77]

Despite a rearguard action from the state, two years of sustained protest necessarily entailed an extraordinary expansion in public expression and debate. All close observers and actors, from Islamists to Leftists to tribal and youth activists in the governorates, described a deep psychological change among the Jordanian public. In particular, Jordanians now openly discussed the royal elephant in the room: 'We were able to shift the narrative. We changed the concepts that people were thinking about, we pushed the slogans ahead. Before, people never used to declare the root of all our problems: it was taboo to say that the king and his decisions and his cronies are the reason.'[78] The willingness to question the core terms of Hashemite rule was not confined to firebrands among the popular movements, but could be found in the top ranks of Jordan's established and historically cautious opposition. 'We can't go on living under a form of rule that goes back to the Middle Ages, whereby one person exercises all the power without accountability,' stated Dr Ruhayil Gharaibeh, a leading light of the Muslim Brotherhood at the time. 'Absolute power is absolute corruption; this is a well-known rule of politics.'[79]

There were also indications that the new civil resistance could transcend the ideological, regional, and communal fault lines that have sometimes divided Jordanian society. The unifying potential so memorably demonstrated on 24 March 2011 was quietly reproduced in broad reform coalitions and countless protest actions involving Jordanians of all backgrounds and political stripes. Something akin to a distinct *hirak* culture emerged, full of political possibility, flexible enough to accommodate Islamist, Leftist, tribal, and local identities, and in which 'coordination' (*tansiqia*) and 'cooperation' (*ta'awun*) were prized values. It could even cross the kingdom's greatest communal divide, as a popular movement leader in the Balqa, a quintessentially 'tribal' East Jordanian region home to a large Palestinian refugee camp, made clear: 'There are people in the *hirak* in Salt [a town in the west-central region of Jordan] from the Baqa'a camp. They are here, and we are hand in hand for reform. The corruption in Jordan doesn't differentiate between Jordanian and Palestinian; the corrupt ones are united against the people, so we must be united against them.'[80] To be sure, internal frictions asserted themselves against the appealing but traditionally fraught notion of societal consensus on change and reform. Yet the new mobilization was nonetheless marked by a consistent unifying impulse, expressed in a shared vocabulary of resistance among

---

[77] Naseem Tarawnah, interview by author, Amman, February 2013.

[78] Khalid Kamhawi, interview by author, Amman, February 2013.

[79] Dr Ruhayil Gharaibeh, former Head of IAF political office, interview by author, Amman, October 2011.

[80] Mohamed al-Dabbas, interview by author, Salt, February 2013.

al-hirakiin ('the movers') that consciously suggested something greater than the sum of its parts. Crucially, its most significant 'Other' was no longer a neighbour of different tribal or regional origin or ideological persuasion, but the regime and its favoured satellites. We were left once more with *sha'ab* ('people') and *nizam* ('regime').

Four years on, the *hirak* had not created sufficient popular pressure to force through a substantial top-down liberalization of the political system—a genuine 'refolution'—but it did build space at the societal level that could one day underwrite such change.[81] At the height of the Arab Spring, Hamid Dabashi argued that the events had ushered in a new genre of revolution. What we were witnessing, Dabashi contended, were 'open-ended' not 'total' revolutions, in which abrupt changes to regime and state formation were overshadowed by 'the expansive unfolding of the public space and the consolidation of social justice from the ground up'.[82] It was this kind of success, gradual and inconclusive, that coexisted in the Jordanian case, unlike so many others, with non-violence. 'Believe in the people, and you will find them,' one activist concluded. 'But it's not a two-day job. It's a long march.'[83]

---

[81] The term 'refolution' was coined by Timothy Garton Ash to describe the mixture of reform and revolution experienced in Poland and Hungary in 1989, where mobilization 'from below' helped to induce enlightened political liberalization 'from above'. See his 'Refolution: The Springtime of Two Nations', *New York Review of Books*, 15 June 1989.

[82] Hamid Dabashi, *The Arab Spring: The End of Postcolonialism* (London: Zed Books, 2012), 247.

[83] Mothana Gharaibeh, interview by author, Amman, September 2011.

8

Morocco

Obedience, Civil Resistance, and Dispersed Solidarities

Driss Maghraoui

Morocco is a country that has been more stable politically than most other Arab countries. With a current population (2014 census) of more than thirty-three million with a 99.1 per cent Muslim majority, the Moroccan state has a long history and is one of the oldest established monarchies in the world. The monarchy dates back to the seventeenth century, when the Alaoui dynasty took power in 1666 and gradually established its authority in the face of various social, economic, military, and political challenges both within and outside its territory. After independence from France in 1956, the monarchy, under the effective political manœuvring of King Hassan II, established a parliamentary constitutional monarchy and a multi-party system in which the king remained the prime holder of political power and the arbiter over increasingly weak political parties. This political context, in which the king has dominant political power, was essentially the work of Hassan II, who ultimately facilitated a smooth transition of power to his son, Mohammed VI, who came to the throne in 1999. While the constitution currently in force, that of July 2011, provides for a monarchy with a parliament, and a head of government drawn from the political party that won the most seats in the parliamentary elections, it is the king who retains the main executive powers. A constant characteristic of modern Moroccan politics since independence has, therefore, been the hegemonic powers of the king vis-à-vis political parties and other political forces.

Achieving this dominant position for the monarchy did not come without major confrontations, continuous struggles, and civil resistance on the part of different social and political forces, which have been important factors in the shaping and reshaping of the political system up to the twenty-first century.

Indeed, as different countries started to witness waves of uprisings in the Arab Spring, the Moroccan regime was faced with a similar social uprising, which came to be known as the February 20 Movement. The movement was initiated in January 2011 by a small number of young Moroccans through Facebook groups, the most important of which was called 'Moroccans converse with the king'. The group became an uncontrolled public sphere in which a number of Moroccans started to debate political matters and issues and attributed direct responsibility to the monarchy for the problems society faced. The events in Tunisia and the ousting of Zine El Abidine Ben Ali, as well as the subsequent mood of the Arab uprisings, had a clear effect on young Moroccans, who started to question the political status quo and the very nature of the Moroccan political system. More and more Moroccans started to call for constitutional reforms. This initial cyberspace activism would soon turn into actual street protests, when members called for a nationwide march on 20 February 2011.

This movement was behind the organization of several consecutive protests in 2011 and called, among other things, for constitutional reforms to reduce the powers of King Mohammed VI and to increase freedom of speech, make economic opportunities more equal, end corruption, expand human and cultural rights, and establish an independent justice system. The February 20 Movement was the result of a short-lived political synergy between different ideological forces, including Islamists, liberals, leftists, and activists for cultural and women's rights, who were united mainly by their opposition to the autocratic system of government. The movement was spearheaded by the young, but people of all ages joined the demonstrations in the streets of major cities. Most of the young people did not associate themselves with any political party or association and preferred not to claim any form of ideology or to have a formal leadership. They organized themselves through so-called *tansiqiyat* (literally 'coordinations') committees headed by young activists responsible for coordinating political actions and protests.

This chapter examines the relationship between civil society in Morocco and the emergence of new forms of civil resistance in the context of a hegemonic monarchical institution and fragmented political parties. It gives a historical dimension to the phenomenon of civil resistance, which has evolved in diverse ways. The argument begins with the observation that the growing role of civil society actors in the 1980s and the rise of the February 20 Movement in the context of the Arab Spring was symptomatic of the weakness of political parties vis-à-vis the dominant role of the monarchy. It is further argued that the rise of civil society actors and the eventual rise of the February 20 Movement as a subaltern form of politics were part of what I call 'dispersed solidarities', which encouraged the regime to make some reforms but which did not push it onto a clear and meaningful democratic path. By subaltern politics, I mean a form of politics from below, outside formal political parties

and in confrontation with the authoritarian structures of rule and the hegemonic position of the monarchy. This domain of politics went beyond formal
institutions and the official media in order to express new political and
cultural dynamics of resistance. For example, Moroccan youth found in social
media new 'social spaces of relative autonomy', without fixed viewpoints, and
where authoritarian power found it more difficult to crowd out their views or
deprive them of freedom of speech and various forms and symbolic acts of
resistance.[1] Subaltern politics in this sense were part of an autonomous space
in which critical expressions and freedom of speech were more possible,
obedience to the ruler was rejected, and insubordination was nurtured. By
dispersed solidarity I mean that social activism focused on a variety of
different causes without a sense of relating these causes to structural political
obstacles. The notion of dispersal has also an ideological connotation because
these emerging social forces did not necessarily rely on a coherent ideology
and were united by what they opposed, not what they proposed. Finally, the
dispersed aspect of these solidarities is meant in a geographical and temporal
sense: sit-ins and social resistance took place in different cities and at different
intervals of time.

This chapter examines the role of civil society in Morocco, focusing on the
three decades from the 1980s to 2011. The 1980s saw the expansion of the
peaceful role of civil society in the public sphere, but its activism and ability to
mobilize remained rooted in specific and separate issues such as human rights,
gender rights, or cultural rights. They were thus devoid of a vision that
connected these concerns to structural and systemic political issues, and to
the imbalanced relationships of power between the monarchy and the different political actors. Nonetheless, because of the role played by civil society
actors, the 1980s and the 1990s saw an increasing challenge to the regime's
hegemonic position at least in relation to these issues. This showed not only
the value of social activism, but also its structural limitations. This means that
the regime reacted positively to the pressure of civil society actors, but this
pressure was often perceived by the monarchy as having accommodating and
not threatening goals. In the long term these accommodating goals ironically
proved to be politically more in favour of the monarchy because it managed to
develop different strategies of adaptation to constant pressures. As the internal
divisions among political parties continued to segment and eventually delegitimize them, many Moroccans, and the youth in particular, started to look for
other forms of social mobilization and new forms of political participation
outside formal political parties. The continuing quiescence and fracture of the
political elite gradually channelled social activism into a new public sphere,
where a broad and politically heterogeneous subaltern opposition was formed

---

[1] James C. Scott, *Domination and the Arts of Resistance: Hidden Transcripts* (New Haven and
London: Yale University Press, 1990), 118.

to contest both the political and the economic status quo. As will be shown later, while the February 20 Movement was able to put constitutional reforms on the regime's agenda, it was not able to operate effectively because it was ideologically diverse and because of the unfavourable internal political conditions, not least fragmented political parties and coercive and intimidating regime strategies. Implicit in my argument here is that it is impossible to analyse the nature and place of civil resistance in Morocco if we do not take into account the nature of the regime, the factors of power relationships, and the specific political context within which the different social and political actors operated. In comparison with other Arab countries, the Moroccan case presents us with a scenario that is very much rooted in history and embedded in the political culture of a system that is essentially allergic to any form of criticism or civil resistance. It is to this context and political culture that I now turn.

THE POLITICAL CULTURE OF
OBEDIENCE IN MOROCCO

Any discussion about the nature of political participation and civil resistance in Morocco should start with a few clarifications about the nature of the political system. Since independence, the regime has set clear limits on the meaningful political participation of actors in the public sphere. The monarchy remained the main component of the political system and the centre around which all political parties revolved. Even though there was a multi-party system, liberal democratic institutions were merely a veneer for a semi-autocratic regime making use of a kind of controlled liberalism. Hassan II managed changing situations and political challenges through the use of repression, co-optation, and consensus. But the king was able to ensure the stability and continuity of the regime without completely closing the public space to some form of political participation, which at times allowed for peaceful demonstrations. Mohammed VI maintained if not reinforced the centrality of the monarchy through a more liberal style, thus guaranteeing his predominance in politics. But, under his reign, there began to be more tolerance for different forms of protests and civil resistance as long as they were directed against veneer institutions such as the government or the parliament. In fact, the majority of the protests that took place in the capital Rabat happened in front of the parliament, while no demonstrations were ever allowed in the vicinity of the heavily guarded palace.

Moroccan political culture has historically been shaped by an entrenched authoritarian rule around the central power of what is called the *makhzan*—that is, the monarchy and its hegemonic state apparatus.[2] The French sociologist Édouard Michaux-Bellaire called this brand of rule a 'despotic authority' that aspires to a certain social disorder in order to maintain its own power to arbitrate. Since then a number of other scholars have looked at how the *makhzan* has metamorphosed without ever losing its dominant hold on power.[3] Other political scientists and anthropologists have analysed the notion of the *makhzan* by relying on cultural explanations or from the perspective of political economy, and the results always converge on the centrality of the monarchy, whether in terms of monopolizing the cultural production of legitimacy or the economic and coercive systems of power for keeping its political authority unchallenged.[4] To survive, this kind of authority has sustained a set of allegiances and has succeeded, over the years, in converting allegiance into submission by creating a culture of obedience: it has stigmatized not only any form of political dissent from the political elite, but also civil resistance and social movements involving trade union and party members. In the politico-cultural sphere, Hassan II instrumentalized Islam and tradition to his advantage in order to sustain a political culture of obedience. Even as Morocco went through constitutional reforms in 2011, this political culture and the political economy that maintained it did not essentially lose their potency, and the remnants of monarchical strategies for control remained ever present.

The very nature of the monarchical system created a political culture and a public sphere where obedience, rather than disobedience or resistance, were so expected by the regime that the parties and the political elite from conservatives to liberal and leftists came to internalize and rationalize the norms of their own obedience and submission by tracing it back to history and the specificities of the Moroccan state. The performative aspects of this political

---

[2] The literal meaning of *makhzan* is 'storage'. It was used historically to refer to the sultan's court and retinue, the regional and provincial administration, the army, and all persons linking these institutions to the general population. The *makhzan*'s task was the collection of taxes, and, when certain groups resisted, it turned to coercive measures. The notion of *makhzan* and its meaning have changed over time. It has also been variously used to refer to the state apparatus; the services that the state provides to its citizens, such as education, health care, and other forms of economic and social development; and all persons in the service of the central power (the monarchy) and with official and unofficial (religious, military, economic, or political) authority.

[3] See Rachida Chérifi, *Le Makhzen politique au Maroc: Hier & aujourd'hui* (Casablanca: Afrique Orient, 1988).

[4] On these different perspectives, see Clement M. Henry, *The Mediterranean Debt Crescent: Money and Power in Algeria, Egypt, Morocco, Tunisia and Turkey* (Gainesville, FL: University Press of Florida, 1996); André Bank, 'Rents, Cooptation, and Economized Discourse: Three Dimensions of Political Rule in Jordan, Morocco and Syria', *Journal of Mediterranean Studies*, 14/1–2 (2004), 155–79; Abdallah Hammoudi, *Master and Disciple: The Cultural Foundations of Moroccan Authoritarianism* (Chicago: University of Chicago Press, 1997); Rahma Bourquia and Susan Gilson Miller (eds), *In the Shadow of the Sultan: Culture, Power, and Politics in Morocco* (Cambridge, MA: Harvard University Press, 1999); and Henry Munson, *Religion and Power in Morocco* (New Haven: Yale University Press, 1993).

culture are best captured in the so-called ritual of *bay'a* or allegiance.[5] The *bay'a* was the most highly symbolic act and the cultural basis upon which the king acquired what one observer called a 'supra-legal' authority.[6] Throughout Moroccan history the *bay'a* remained a very important instrument for the legitimization of power.[7] After the last referendum for a new constitution on 1 July 2011, officials and dignitaries, once again, lined up to bow to the monarch in the classic ritual of the *bay'a*, which turned out to be one of the most symbolic acts of servitude. The kissing of the hands of the king was a regular feature of official events involving the monarch and was regularly performed on public television in front of millions. It was, therefore, a characteristic of the political system that social disobedience and resistance were not accepted, and the cultural basis for it was concocted from the lexicon of a religious Islamic principle known otherwise as *ta'a*, which means literally 'submission'. Hence, it was common for the ministry of religious affairs to mobilize Islam by using the concept of *ta'a* in order to warn against any form of civil resistance or disobedience. In the official religious lexicon, Moroccan subjects had a duty to obey the ruler and, if they engaged in civil resistance, then it was to be seen as *fitna*, another historically based politico-religious concept that refers to the disorder and anarchy that emerged after the death of the Prophet Muhammad and the subsequent divisions that followed in the early Muslim community in Arabia. Following a number of social protests in Morocco, Hassan II never hesitated to make reference to these concepts in order to associate various protests with religiously negative connotations and thus delegitimize them.

The nature of political culture in Morocco was such that the monarchy consistently considered itself the primary, incontestable actor. This political culture created an atmosphere in which critics, dissidents, and potential political challengers, via formal elections or social activism, were often controlled, muted, or considered as subversive, a situation that clearly contributed to making political participation by different political and social actors much more constrained. Meanwhile, the monarchy played an important role in the perpetuation of elite stasis while at the same time creating a clientelist network in which economic self-interest and the mere search for prestigious government positions became part of political parties' shared values.[8] Even the most

---

[5] See M. Elaine Combs-Schilling, *Sacred Performances: Islam, Sexuality, and Sacrifice* (New York: Columbia University Press, 1989).

[6] Mohamed Tozy, *Monarchie et islam politique au Maroc* (Paris: Presses de la Fondation Nationale des Sciences Politiques, 1999).

[7] Bettina Dennerlein, 'Legitimate Bounds and Bound Legitimacy: The Act of Allegiance to the Ruler (Bai'a) in 19th Century Morocco', *Die Welt des Islams*, 41/3 (2001), 287–310.

[8] On the lack of ideology and the shared value of economic interest, see Mark Tessler, 'Morocco: Institutional Pluralism and Monarchical Dominance', in I. William Zartman et al. (eds), *Political Elites in Arab North Africa* (New York and London: Longman, 1982), 72.

democratically oriented elite from the political left gradually fell back on a culture of passivity and political apathy.

We can, therefore, notice the gradual emergence of a normatively informed *makhzanian* political culture, where allegiance had to be made to values that were clearly in tune with the monarchy's position. The majority of political parties were gradually attuned to accept a consensus imposed from above, in which there was no space for polemic, criticism, or acts of resistance. Formal government institutions and the main political parties lost the clout and political stamina to question the structural supremacy of the monarchy in the decision-making process. It was this form of imposed consensus that was an essential part of the monarchical mechanism of control over the nature of political participation by the elite.[9] It is in the context of this political culture, which has not been in favour of establishing the appropriate rules of fair political participation, that we can situate and historically trace the role and place of different civil society actors and ultimately the rise of the February 20 Movement in 2011 as a new form of civil resistance.

CIVIL RESISTANCE: A HISTORICAL OVERVIEW

Different forms of resistance punctuated much of Moroccan history during the pre-colonial period when the *ulema* (religious scholars), sufi brotherhoods, and tribes offered a permanent challenge to the *makhzan* mainly because of the search for new religious legitimacy, imposed taxes, or other political and economic factors. Resistance to colonial rule in both rural and urban areas was similarly typical of the ways in which different social forces reacted to colonial intrusion in its economic, political, and cultural dimensions. From independence in 1956, cities such as Hoceima and Nador in north-east Morocco saw various forms of civil resistance that were typical of the decolonization period and of the challenges faced by newly emerging states. Civil resistance by trade-union workers, left-wing political parties, and university and high-school students in the 1960s to the late 1980s in major cities such as Casablanca, Fez, Marrakech, and Rabat was a constant challenge to the regime but not a significant threat. The causes of peaceful demonstrations varied from increases in the price of basic commodities and foodstuffs to increased school fees and political demands. It is fair to say that there had regularly been a feeling of resentment among Moroccans from different social classes. Very often this resentment was the result of underlying problems typical of contemporary Moroccan society, including social and economic inequality as well as political

---

[9] Saloua Zerhouni, 'Morocco: Reconciling Continuity and Change', in Volker Perthes (ed.), *Arab Elites: Negotiating the Politics of Change* (Boulder, CO: Lynne Rienner, 2004).

grievances. By the 1990s the issue of the *diplomés chomeurs* (unemployed graduates) as well as poverty and social marginalization, and abuses of human, cultural, and women's rights, were of major concern. In retrospect, it was student activism in the 1960s that represented a peak of civil resistance and that shaped the historical memory of the struggle for progressive social, economic, and political changes in society.

Student political activism did not start in the 1960s: there were many examples of political involvement that indicate broader long-term trends in student politics. Students had, for instance, a long-standing role in the rise of nationalism, and some of the earliest significant student movements were related to the nationalist struggle against European colonial rule, especially among Moroccans in France.[10] In the aftermath of independence, civil resistance became more associated with the activism of student unions. In comparison to other North African and Middle Eastern countries, students in Morocco became an important element in social and political mobilization and a major challenge to the hegemonic power of the monarchy, especially under Hassan II. But the student unions and the youth in general could not be seen at this point as detached from the activities of left-wing political parties that were at the time a significant threat to an autocratic regime that was still in the initial phases of its elaboration. The main organizational basis for students was the Union Nationale des Étudiants Marocains (UNEM), which was established in 1956. The UNEM functioned under the umbrella of the leftist opposition leader Mehdi Ben Barka, who represented at this point a more radical political vision within the nationalist party of *al-Istiqlal*, the most organized opposition force after independence. From its inception, the UNEM was conceived of as a strong oppositional force to the monarchy.

An ideological division within *al-Istiqlal* in 1959 resulted in the establishment of a new left-wing party known as the Union Nationale des Forces Populaires (UNFP), to which the majority of the Moroccan students in the UNEM became attached. In this way it had a major effect on the trajectory of the student movement in Morocco. In retrospect this was the beginning of the division and dispersed political solidarity that marked the initial opposition to the regime. The radicalization of the students' movement was associated with the UNEM's eighth congress in 1963, when it called for the abolition of the regime as a condition for freeing the country from authoritarian rule. That year students started to engage in peaceful acts of defiance against the regime through a series of strikes throughout Morocco and overseas in at least six so-called *occupations* of Moroccan embassies abroad. This became part of a frontal opposition to the nascent regime of Hassan II, which would soon react strongly. From the 1960s student strikes regularly punctuated academic life in

---

[10] See Charles-André Julien, *Le Maroc face aux impérialismes: 1415–1956* (Paris: Éditions JA, 1978).

the main university campus, Université Mohammed V in Rabat. University strikes often spread to high schools in the capital and then affected other universities in Casablanca or Fez. Student demands varied from local and institutional grievances to broader social and political demands for reform of the education and political system.

One of the most substantial instances of civil resistance in Morocco took place in Casablanca in March 1965. It significantly threatened the stability of the regime, which reacted in a brutal manner, suppressing protests and killing hundreds of people.[11] The immediate cause was an attempt by the education ministry to prevent over-age students from enrolling at university, which at a stroke would have excluded a large number of students. To protest this measure, the UNEM organized a week of strikes beginning on 22 March 1965. On the same day, the government closed some schools in several neighbourhoods of Casablanca, where demonstrations had taken place. According to some estimates more than 2,000 students were arrested. There was soon a spillover of student strikes into working-class neighbourhoods, and the strikes turned into major riots and protests by workers and the un-employed. The Casablanca riots were spontaneous, taking the government and even opposition parties and trade unions by surprise. As the Moroccan state tried to put down the riots by imposing a curfew, the protests reached other cities, including Fez and Rabat. The reaction of the regime was ultim-ately very harsh: the army intervened to crush the revolt.

The strategies of the regime towards student mobilizations in the 1960s varied from coercion, to financial control, some forms of reconciliation, and suppression. In 1963 a military tribunal condemned the president of the UNEM to death in absentia, because he showed solidarity with Algeria's socialist government during the Moroccan–Algerian border war of that year. In reaction to a strike in celebration of the first anniversary of the Casablanca demonstrations, the education ministry responded by closing the university campus. Another strategy to limit student activism was the selective applica-tion of a new law introducing universal military conscription.[12] Following this law, most of the members of the UNEM's executive committees were drafted into the army before the union's eleventh congress in July 1966.

The reaction of the Moroccan regime and its harsh response to the political activism of the UNEM did not initially affect the union's popularity or strength in the 1960s. The students' movement was able to gain very good

---

[11] The exact number of people who died in Casablanca remains unknown. In various statements the Equity and Reconciliation Commission, established in 2004, referred to mass graves. e.g. *Follow-up Report on the Implementation of Equity and Reconciliation Commission Recommendations: Main Report* (Rabat: Advisory Council on Human Rights, December 2009), 33–44.

[12] Clement H. Moore and Arlie R. Hochschild, 'Student Unions in North African Politics', *Daedalus*, 97/1 (Winter 1968), 21–50.

organizational experience. In fact, the reaction of the regime contributed to the radicalization of the movement and to the development of a closer alliance with more radical members of the UNFP. By the mid-1960s, the phenomenon of mobilizing students against the monarchy in universities and high schools was at its historical peak. Inspired by Marxist and Leninist ideologies, union members tended to be more interested in the structural constraints against progressive change in Morocco, and their stand on what they perceived as the exploitative nature of modern capitalism was well known among the students.[13] Relying on a Marxist-inspired discourse, the students viewed the regime through lenses that saw the system as reactionary and feudal and the monarch as a despot. In retrospect, the students' movement was one of the most active in North Africa.

Trade unions were also involved in civil resistance against the regime, principally as formal allies of political parties. However, the co-option of the political parties by the monarchy, notably through the nationalist campaign around Morocco's claim to the Western Sahara from the 1970s, weakened their willingness to confront the system. This was further weakened by the results of economic liberalization in the 1980s, associated with structural adjustment programmes induced by the IMF. Important labour unions became divided and incapable of creating common cause around which ordinary people could mobilize and establish a major social movement.[14] Economic hardship contributed to the atomization of society, which led to a gradual weakening of trade unionism. From another angle, the political openness of the regime by the end of the 1990s made it possible for the country to become fertile ground for the emergence of a more vibrant civil society, which numbered more than 30,000 local associations. Nearly 40 per cent of Moroccan associations were concentrated in major cities such as Casablanca, Fez, Rabat, and Tangier.[15] The concentration of civil society associations in large urban centres meant that a different form of political activism was gradually shifting from formal political institutions to civil society organizations, which started to fill the political vacuum left by discredited political parties. Hence civil society became another alternative for political mobilization in large cities, a reality that contributed in the long term to further fragmentation of the social and political forces that could have constituted a more serious challenge to the monarchy.

The fact that the monarchy kept different political and social forces under its control and monopolized the debate in the public sphere did not, however,

---

[13] See Mostafa Bouaziz, *Introduction à l'étude du mouvement marxiste-léniniste marocain (1965-1979)*, mémoire sous la direction de E. M'Bokolo (Paris: École des Hautes Études en Sciences Sociales, 1981).

[14] Mahmoud Jibril, 'Le Syndicalisme en crise', *La Gazette du Maroc*, 4 April 2005.

[15] See James Sater, *Civil Society and Political Change in Morocco* (London: Routledge, 2007).

prevent contesting voices of resistance and a dispersed but constant civil resistance on the part of civil society actors.[16] The political and social context favoured the growing role of what I call here 'dispersed solidarities' and a new kind of civil resistance in which civil society actors started to act outside the orbit of the state, quiescent political parties, and disqualified trade unions, in order to introduce new issues such as human rights, women's rights, and cultural rights into the public sphere. It is to these issues and the role of civil society in raising them that I turn in the next section.

HUMAN-RIGHTS ACTIVISM AND THE ROLE OF CIVIL SOCIETY ACTORS

Since the early 1980s a number of associations have become very active in different fields, including but not limited to human rights, cultural associations, and women's associations. The Association Marocaine des Droits Humains (AMDH) is a very good example of the peaceful form of social and political activism that started in the long term to challenge the regime over human rights. Established in 1979 for the defence of human, individual, and civil rights, it managed to establish itself as one of the most respected human-rights associations and became a major factor in the push for local forms of civil disobedience.[17] The AMDH played a significant role in raising the issue of human-rights abuses in the public sphere and building a human-rights culture that has permeated through all sectors of society. The AMDH owes its popularity and legitimacy to its long-established record of working independently from the discredited political parties. The association encouraged mass action by involving more citizens and has regularly supported the principles and implementation of political, social, and cultural democracy as the basis of society. The AMDH has been at the forefront of the human-rights debate since it started condemning the repressive system of Hassan II. Since the 1980s it has played an important role in taking public positions, exposing human-rights violations, raising awareness about social and economic issues, pressing for justice for victims, and training members of various human-rights associations.

---

[16] See Driss Maghraoui, 'The Dynamics of Civil Society in Morocco', in Ellen Lust-Okar and Saloua Zerhouni (eds), *Political Participation in the Middle East* (Boulder, CO.: Lynne Rienner, 2008).

[17] See Mohamed Mouaquit, 'Le Mouvement des droits humains au Maroc', in Maria-Angels Roque (ed.), *La Société civile au Maroc: L'Émergence de nouveaux acteurs de développement* (Paris: Publisud, Institut Européen de la Méditerranée, 2004).

The other major example of this new kind of social activism is the Organisation Marocaine des Droits Humains (OMDH) and the Forum des Alternatives Maroc (FMAS). The OMDH was created in 1988 and established for itself a strong reputation as a human-rights association.[18] It regularly called on the government to adhere to and comply with international human-rights conventions. The FMAS, a more recent association that was created in June 2003, intended to contribute to the establishment of an autonomous democratic, social, and citizens' movement and identified itself as a civil society organization that defended and promoted economic, civil, political, social, and cultural rights. The FMAS worked with different social actors, including the government, and emphasized the role that civil society could play in promoting democracy. One of the specific characteristics of the FMAS was that it projected itself as a social movement in Morocco but within an international dynamic of globalization in which Moroccan social actors became part of an international movement for peace. The FMAS encouraged what it called 'participative citizenship' by creating a new context for meetings. It organized debates about, and among, the youth and students, civil society associations, trade unions, and political parties in order to encourage initiatives and involve young people in mobilizing collective actions of various kinds.

The AMDH and the OMDH have been relatively influential, especially through their role in resistance and as whistle-blowers over human-rights abuses. Through their connections to international organizations, they have managed to enhance their domestic and international legitimacy and encourage significant participation in small-scale protests and peaceful commemorative activities such as those at former detention centres. However, their influence has often been countered by the regime's strategy of appropriating the language of human rights and making it its own, notably by establishing a ministry of human rights and more latterly the Equity and Reconciliation Commission in 2004.[19] The initiative of the creation of a truth commission was in fact proposed by the Moroccan Forum for Truth and Justice, the AMDH, and the OMDH, but was quickly appropriated and constrained under the umbrella and control of the monarchy. As it constantly attempted to domesticate any emerging political actors, the regime managed to bring under its orbit different civil society activists thereby creating divisions among them. The political sphere has always been dominated by a powerful monarchy, a situation that translates sometimes into dangerous alliances, where political actors are not only appeasing the *makhzan* but allying themselves with it.[20]

---

[18] See the official website of the *Organisation Marocaines des Droits Humains* www.omdh.org.

[19] Susan Slyomovics, 'A Truth Commission for Morocco', *Middle East Report*, 218 (Spring 2001), 18–21.

[20] See Lise Garon, *Dangerous Alliances: Civil Society, the Media and Democratic Transition in North Africa* (London and New York: Zed Books, 2003).

Reliance on strategies of appropriation does not preclude other forms of control of more independent civil society actors. More recently, the Moroccan authorities have started to rely once again on different strategies of intimidation and interdiction to block the activities of the AMDH in different cities.[21] For example, between July 2014 and early 2015 the Ministry of Interior blocked the holding of more than fifteen public meetings, and also several other events and peaceful activities planned by the Moroccan League for Human Rights, Amnesty International, and other organizations.

THE WOMEN'S MOVEMENT

In Morocco, it might be difficult to understand the history of social resistance if we do not systematically incorporate women and gender issues, because they were intricately embedded in the factors that occasionally triggered and sustained social protest. One of the best examples of a long-term and effective form of resistance to the patriarchal structures of Moroccan society was the women's movement. From a historical perspective, women were involved in different forms of social and political activism long before independence. The movement often consisted of an elite form of social organization concerned initially with issues that were specific to women, but in informal ways it also played an important role in the struggle against colonialism. Its main purpose was initially to deal with the question of literacy and social assistance for women and children. Over time the movement evolved and became more focused on probing gender questions and promoting women's political and civil rights. These associations have been able to exemplify the kind of social movements that have striven for reforms by showing a tenacious ability to call for broad-based social and political change. One of the characteristics of the women's movement was that it went beyond gender issues in order to push for political, legal, and educational reforms. Hence, the women's movement became intertwined with other pressing issues, such as human rights, social and economic equality, parliamentary politics, and religious and educational reforms.

The movement brought together women who were activists in the women's sections of political parties and in associations. Their experience within political parties made them aware of their marginalization within what they often perceived as men's clubs. For many years political parties used the pretext of religious and cultural constraints in order to keep women's issues

---

[21] See Human Rights Watch, 'Morocco: Human Rights Gatherings Blocked', HRW, Rabat, 7 November 2014 http://www.hrw.org/news/2014/11/07/morocco-human-rights-gatherings-blocked.

off their political agenda and to limit women's visibility and their impact in public life. Many women started to organize themselves into separate associations within which they could more easily express their points of view, be heard, and defend their common interests. Women's associations started to emerge in the mid-1980s with the aim of developing a gender-based agenda and engaging in actions that defended their specific interests.

The culmination of the success of the Moroccan women's movement was the passing of a new family code in 2004. Known commonly as the *moudawana*, the code in its new form resulted in new reforms meant to improve the roles and relationships between men and women within the family. There had not been much change in the status of women in civil law since the 1957 and 1958 family laws introduced after independence. Under these laws, women had been legally considered as minors and their access to divorce was limited. Under the *moudawana*, they were required to have the consent of their fathers and husbands to open a business or obtain a passport. Women also had only limited property and inheritance rights. From the early 1990s, reform of the legal system became the most important issue for the women's movement. One of the main groups promoting women's rights, the *Union de l'Action Féminine*, organized a campaign to collect one million signatures in order to urge Hassan II to reform the *moudawana*. The women's associations had very specific goals: first, to raise to 18 the minimum marriage age for women; second, to require a judge's authorization for polygamy; third, for women to have the right to divorce their husbands; fourth, for women to have new rights to assets acquired during marriage; and, finally, to reinforce children's rights. Hassan II agreed to hear the women's concerns, and he called on a council of religious leaders to look into the matter. By 1993 the women had gained some success in the reform of the *moudawana*, but it was very limited.[22] The most important effect of the reforms was the fact that the *moudawana* was for the first time open to change and, hence, began to be perceived as something less than a sacred legal text.

Under Mohammed VI the women's movement gained more ground, and the demands for reform of the *moudawana* became more pressing. Women activists were able to make the reforms part of a national debate. On 13 March 2000 some of the more liberal women's NGOs organized a demonstration in Rabat, which drew an estimated 100,000 demonstrators. Such pressure contributed to the eventual formal revision of the code in 2004, introducing most of the demands of the women's movement. In the long term, it is fair to say that the women's rights movement had in its own way contributed to a kind of feminization and democratization of the public space in Morocco, because it

---

[22] The marriage contract now required the consent and signature of the bride.

unleashed a significant change in discourse and more concretely at the legal level with the 2004 Family Law reforms.[23]

The campaign to reform the *moudawana* had, however, highlighted the strength of other actors in society who were also capable of mobilizing large numbers of people. The fact that some of the dispositions in the reform plan touched upon sharia (Islamic law) raised eyebrows in different segments of society. The Islamists, notably those in the new Party of Justice and Development (PJD) and the formally banned *Al-adl wal-Ihsan* (Justice and Charity Movement), organized mass rallies against the planned reforms. These groups organized a large rally in Casablanca on the same day in March 2000 as a rally by the women's association in Rabat. The Islamists brought out approximately 300,000 demonstrators—three times the number attending the Rabat march.[24] This was not the first time Islamist organizations had mounted such a show of strength and support. Justice and Charity had organized significant protests against the prosecution and imprisonment of its leaders in 1990, and Islamists of all shades were heavily present in mass demonstrations in early 1991 against the Gulf War.[25]

CULTURAL RIGHTS: THE AMAZIGH MOVEMENT

The rise of the Amazigh movement since the late 1970s can be considered one of the most important forms of cultural discourse and will probably reshape both the cultural map and politics in Morocco. The term Amazigh refers to the cultural identity of the oldest established inhabitants of the country, and *Imazighen* means literally 'free people' or 'noble people'. The Amazigh label came to replace the word *Berber*, which was seen as pejorative and a colonial construct.[26] Since independence, the social movement seeking to promote aspects of Amazigh identity was more often marginalized if not repressed, because of its perceived challenge to the official identity of the Moroccan state, which was viewed as exclusively Arab. The gradual emergence of civil society in the 1990s, however, gave new life to the movement as a significant expression of identity. More than 100 Amazigh associations emerged, with varying

---

[23] Fatima Sadiqi and Moha Ennaji, 'The Feminization of Public Space: Women's Activism, the Family Law, and Social Change in Morocco', *Journal of Middle East Women's Studies*, 2/2 (Spring 2006), 86–114.

[24] Some observers spoke of the 'one-million march', but there was no exact figure of the number of participants. Overall, the demonstration was considered a success.

[25] Munson, *Religion and Power in Morocco*, 172–3.

[26] When the Romans arrived in North Africa, they met tough resistance and named the inhabitants of the region Barbarians, hence the word *Berber*.

degrees of influence.[27] Although these associations had different focuses and political agendas, they all agreed on the necessity of safeguarding Amazigh culture and defending the linguistic and cultural rights of the Amazigh people.

The monarchy reacted to identity politics in a gradual and calculated way. The initial reaction to the emerging influence of the Amazigh issue came from Hassan II. In a speech on 20 August 1994 the king emphasized the necessity of preserving Amazigh culture and the need to introduce the teaching of the Amazigh language, Tamazight, in schools. Four days after the speech, national television started to broadcast the news in Tamazight three times a day. Mohammed VI continued the same policy of appropriating the Amazigh cause and making it part of his own field of politics.[28] On 17 October 2001 the king created the Institut Royal de la Culture Amazighe Marocaine (IRCAM). In addition to promoting Amazigh culture and art, one of the main goals of the institute was the introduction of the Amazigh language into the Moroccan educational system. In March 2010 a special Amazigh television channel was launched.

As these initiatives came from the royal palace, most of the political actors did not attempt to criticize them and instead supported them. But protests did come from some Amazigh associations, which considered the king's initiative as an effort to domesticate the Amazigh cause. For instance, in 2007 the Confederation of Amazigh Cultural Organizations in Morocco (TADA) strongly denounced the 'hypocrisy of the Moroccan monarchy' in dealing with the demands of the Amazigh movement.[29] For TADA, by introducing the Amazigh language into schools, the monarchy was only trying to 'appropriate, be in control and weaken the cause by emptying it from within'.[30] For the members of this association, the government was not providing the necessary resources and means for the introduction of the Amazigh language, which had already officially started in some schools in September 2003. Despite the appropriation and endorsement of large parts of the Amazigh movement's agenda by the monarchy, there was no mention of the Amazigh and Imazighen in successive constitutions. However, this was resolved in the 2011 constitution, which featured a new article (Article 5) that stated that,

---

[27] For example, l'Association Marocaine de la Recherche et d'Echanges Culturels and the Association Nouvelle pour la Culture et les Arts Populaires. These associations existed in both the countryside and the cities.

[28] In an interview conducted by four Lebanese papers (*Al-Hawadith, la Revue du Liban, Monday Morning*, and *Al-Bairak*) in March 2002, Mohammed VI said: 'Amazigh is the property of all Moroccans. It is a national wealth, a basic component of the national pluralistic identity.'

[29] Mustapha Berhouchi, President of the Bureau of TADA, 'La Confédération TADA des associations culturelles amazighes au Maroc appelle au soutien des détenus politiques du Mouvement culturel Amazigh', Confédération TADA, Goulmima, 16 June 2007 http://www.amazighworld.org/human_rights/index_show.php?id=1069.

[30] July 2003, cited in Berhouchi, 'La Confédération TADA'.

alongside Arabic, the 'Amazigh language is an official language of the state'.[31] Although widely welcomed, this constitutional change was viewed by many members of the Amazigh movement as a further attempt to co-opt the movement and its agenda and weaken the support it gave to the February 20 Movement.

The Amazigh awakening had the capacity significantly to affect the Moroccan political scene at the national level. The movement has been able to strengthen its position, as more transnational associative networks have organized themselves to help defend Amazigh cultural rights. A good example of such a network was the Réseau Amazigh pour la Citoyenneté, which was established in February 2004. The network concentrated on issues around cultural identity, human rights, women's rights, and the environment. One of its main objectives was the promotion of the Amazigh culture and language and the safeguarding and defence of the identity and culture of the Imazighen in Morocco and North Africa in general. The Amazigh movement gradually became one of the most important social movements in Morocco, as it was able to develop a strong regional and international network in North Africa and Western Europe.[32]

SUBALTERN POLITICS AND THE
FEBRUARY 20 MOVEMENT

The February 20 Movement was not the only example of civil resistance in Morocco in 2011. Even prior to 2011, there were different forms of dispersed struggles that were more socio-economic in nature than political. From November 2008 onwards, the emergence of the *soulaliyate* women's movement around the city of Kenitra was an important example of how the public sphere had become more and more a place for peaceful protest and the claiming of rights. The *soulaliyate*, which literally refers to their tribal origin, was a women's movement that claimed the right to collective lands that had been privatized by the Moroccan authorities for the interest of different companies.[33] Mainly from within rural marginalized social classes, the *soulaliyate* have become nationally the symbol of women's struggle, not only against male dominance over the right to use land but also against the unequal

---

[31] Constitution of Morocco, promulgated on 29 July 2011, official French text available from http://www.maroc.ma/en/content/constitution.

[32] Bruce Maddy-Weitzman, 'Ethno-Politics and Globalisation in North Africa: The Berber Culture Movement', *Journal of North African Studies*, 11/1 (2006), 71–83.

[33] Yasmine Berriane, 'Terres collectives et inégalités: Le Combat des soulaliyates', *Economia* (Rabat, May 2014), 28–31 http://economia.ma/fr/numero-20/e-revue/terres-collectives-et-inegalites-le-combat-des-soulaliyates.

distribution of wealth in Morocco. Just a few days before 20 February 2011, there were sit-ins in Tangiers against a water distribution company because of high utility bills. On 21 February in Khouribga a small number of unemployed young people began camping outside the official phosphate mining company demanding jobs, and there were confrontations with police there on 18 March. Putting a twist on the name of the Egyptian square in Cairo, 'maidan al-tahrir', the Moroccan youth called it 'maidan al-tachghuil' (the square of employment).[34] Morocco has the largest share of the world's phosphate, but the local populations of Khouribga felt marginalized from the benefits of its exploitation. Similar forms of civil disobedience between local people and businesses took place in the southern Moroccan city of Sidi Ifni many times before the 20 February protests. Social marginality in Sidi Ifni was at the core of the social unrest in a town that is located next to substantial fishing resources and a fishing industry that is controlled by local notables and military officers. But, while the movements of protest and civil resistance in twenty-first-century Morocco can be seen as part of the persistence of similar economic problems and contradictions witnessed since the 1980s and 1990s, the contradictions were more than before, starting also to touch upon politics and the thorny issues of the structural political dominance of the institution of the monarchy, democracy, transparency, and corruption, all of which were more specifically raised by the February 20 Movement. In order better to understand the movement, it might be useful briefly to locate it in its proper historical context both internally, within a growing dynamic of social protest and the political vacuum that was left as a result of discredited political parties, and regionally, as a movement that was inspired by the revolts that swept across the Middle East.

From the historical perspective outlined above, it is clear that, since the 1980s, the processes of economic liberalization associated with the programmes of structural adjustment imposed by the IMF and the World Bank had eventually weakened the role of the state in terms of generating jobs and providing services for ordinary people.[35] Poverty increased in both major urban centres and villages in the countryside. Marginalized social groups in Casablanca, Rabat, Fez, Meknes, and other cities grew, and Morocco still recorded some of the highest levels of poverty and unemployment in the Arab world. While economic liberalization in Morocco was able to open new opportunities for some, it paradoxically widened the gap between the wealthy and the working poor and subsequently created a greater sense of

---

[34] See Koenraad Bogaert, 'The Revolt of Small Towns: The Meaning of Morocco's History and the Geography of Social Protests', *Review of African Political Economy*, 42/143: 124–40, published online 24 September 2014.

[35] See Thierry Desrues and Eduardo Moyano, 'Social Change and Political Transition in Morocco', *Mediterranean Politics*, 6/1 (2001), 21–47.

social alienation and hopelessness among both the marginalized social classes and the middle class.[36] A growing phenomenon was what were commonly called 'the boats of death', in which young Moroccans seeking a better future and work in Europe died trying to cross the Mediterranean. While the youth were looking for other horizons for their future, a new category of workers was also emerging as part of the working poor. Meanwhile the working class became more disillusioned with its labour unions. The largest union organizations in Morocco, Union Marocaine du Travail (UMT), Confédération Démocratique du Travail (CDT), Union Générale des Travailleurs du Maroc (UGTM), and Fédération Démocratique du Travail (FDT), witnessed serious internal divisions and were unable to face up to the challenges of neo-liberalism.[37] Trade unions lost the political stamina to mobilize the people. In addition, the main political parties in Morocco gradually lost their credibility and became discredited in the eyes of the population. It was this context that favoured the growing role of a more active civil society and the emergence of what I call 'subaltern politics'—that is, political activity outside the control and orbit of the authoritarian state and quiescent political parties, whose generally corrupt and co-optable leadership willingly engaged in the politics of obedience discussed above or in what Étienne de la Boétie called in the sixteenth century 'voluntary servitude'.[38]

Following Alain Badiou, I locate these subaltern politics in a public space where we need constantly to be aware of social and political events where the forgotten people can declare and affirm their existence. This is a form of politics that is outside the realm of the technocratic state associated with administration officials or political parties. It is part of an autonomous politics of the politically marginalized and more progressive voices. Badiou's philosophical position speaks of 'a politics without a party', a reality in the postmodern condition that is both necessary and very difficult to achieve. I argue that the February 20 Movement, like its counterparts elsewhere in the Middle East, seemed to fall within this category of politics that has erupted in spontaneous ways within an interstitial space between corrupt and politically impotent parties and an undemocratic state. The February 20 Movement was, therefore, part of an unplanned, non-institutionalized political venture seeking what Badiou called the *champs du possible*, the 'realm of possibility'.[39] Moroccan political parties had gradually come within the orbit of the *makhzanian*

---

[36] See Shana Cohen, 'Alienation and Globalization in Morocco: Addressing the Social and Political Impact of Market Integration', *Comparative Studies in Society and History*, 45/1 (2003), 168–89.

[37] Jibril, 'Le Syndicalisme en crise'.

[38] Étienne de La Boétie, *Discours de la Servitude Volontaire* ('Discourse on Voluntary Servitude'), written in 1552/3 and first published in 1576.

[39] For a discussion of some of these issues, see Alain Badiou, *Conditions* (Paris: Éditions du Seuil, 1992), or Badiou, *Peut-on penser la politique?* (Paris: Éditions du Seuil, 1985).

state and were part of the politics of ideological consensus: they could no longer challenge the monarchy or propose democratic alternatives. But the February 20 Movement was outside this orbit and instead a manifestation of subaltern politics, in the Gramscian sense of a form of 'politics of the people' and 'from below'.[40]

It was, therefore, against the context of highly discredited Moroccan political parties and labour unions that the February 20 Movement was able to lead calls for nationwide protests calling for major political change, including reform of the existing and extensively criticized constitution, which had come into force in 1996. The movement acquired its name because on 20 February 2011 approximately 150,000–200,000 Moroccans in 53 cities and towns marched for democracy and change, symbolized by the popular call: 'al-sha'ab yurid udusturan jadid' ('the people want a new constitution'). Moroccans used the famous revolutionary phrase that had become popular throughout the Arab world, but twisted it in a way that implied that the protestors were calling not for the downfall of the monarchy but rather for its transformation into a constitutional monarchy. From the start this political agenda distinguished Moroccan social protests as reformist rather than revolutionary in nature. Inspired by the revolts in Tunisia and Egypt, and aided by Internet connections and technology such as Facebook, thousands of young people joined the movement and became active in the protests. However, the February 20 Movement cannot be seen as simply a result of the Arab Spring. In the Moroccan context, a dynamic civil society had already been active since the 1980s.[41] What the Arab Spring clearly did was provide stamina to a movement that had already begun to energize a political landscape that since the late 1990s had been substantially depoliticized in the sense that Morocco's problems were no longer seen as political but rather as technical in nature and thus the solutions were to be found by technocrats.[42]

Like most social movements that swept across the Middle East and North Africa, the February 20 Movement was a mishmash of different ideological stripes united only by their opposition to authoritarian rule in all its different manifestations. Many young people did not associate themselves with any political party or association, and the movement emphasized that it did not want to claim any form of ideology. The movement was not well organized and had no formal leadership, but it managed to put together the *tansiqiyat*, which coordinated political actions and protests. While the movement was the

---

[40] See Antonio Gramsci, *Selections from the Prison Notebooks of Antonio Gramsci*, trans. Quintin Hoare and Geoffrey Nowell Smith (New York: International Publishers, 1971).

[41] See Driss Maghraoui, 'Dynamics of Civil Society in Morocco'.

[42] Abdeslam Maghraoui, 'Depoliticization in Morocco', *Journal of Democracy*, 13/4 (2002), 24–32.

Figure 8.1. As so often across the Arab Spring, it was a youth-led movement that came to the fore in Morocco. Here members of the Moroccan activist group the February 20 Movement call for reform at a press conference in Rabat on 2 June 2011. A month later a nationwide referendum was held to approve constitutional reforms in which the king relinquished some of his powers and promised early elections.
© *Abdelhak Senna/AFP/Getty Images*

initiative of the young, it quickly was able to attract a wider range of supporters (see Figure 8.1).

It would be very misleading to think of the February 20 Movement as mainly the outcome of economic problems and unemployment or as a movement that was in continuity with the so-called bread riots of the 1980s.[43] While the 2011 protesters called for more social equality and access to social welfare services in the fields of health, education and housing, their demands were more generally focused on political issues. What united the movement was a set of grievances that spoke clearly to some of the major problems that marked the Moroccan political system since its inception. Some of these demands related to the classical liberal principle of installing a more democratic constitution that established popular sovereignty as the basis of rule, created an independent judiciary, and respected the notion of the separation of powers.[44] As far as the power of the king was concerned, popular

[43] The social movements in the MENA region had long since gone beyond the *khubziste* (bread-seeker) demands and logic of earlier periods. See Larbi Sadiki, 'Popular Uprisings and Arab Democratization', *International Journal of Middle East Studies*, 32/1 (2000), 71–95.

[44] See 'Harakat shabab 20 fibrayar—bayan' (February 20 Youth Movement—Communiqué), 16 February 2011 http://al-manshour.org/node/195.

ambition was captured by the slogan 'The king who reigns but should not rule'. The protesters also called for the freedom of the press and independent media. More immediate and specific concerns related to the dismissal of the serving government and the creation of a transitional administration. Prominent among the demands was the call for an end to the system of corruption and for the prosecution of key officials alleged to be involved in the mismanagement of public funds.

One of the major issues that was constantly raised was the close connection that had been established between business and royal circles. The February 20 Movement was in many ways the expression of the growing public concern over corruption and a Moroccan political system that had sustained itself over the years by providing power and privilege to those who were willing to serve its interests. More specifically targeted were close advisers and friends of the monarch himself. Naturally the slogans targeted the then prime minister, Abbas el-Fassi, who was seen as someone lacking charisma and leadership and who, on his appointment in 2007, had openly declared that his government's programme would be drawn from the speeches of the king.[45] Moreover, el-Fassi came from a large elite family that had held many high positions in government and that had become associated with nepotism and inefficiency. The slogans also called for an end to torture and condemned violations of human rights that had taken place under the reign of Mohammed VI. From a cultural perspective, the recognition of Amazigh as an official language was one of the most prominent demands. The banners of the demonstrators also called for freedom of speech, the release of political prisoners, and the trial of all those responsible for arbitrary arrests and torture. All these demands indicated the heterogeneous political ideologies of the people who joined the movement.

The movement was joined by the largest informal Islamic opposition group, Justice and Charity, and by the two human-rights groups AMDH and OMDH. The movement was also able to gain the solidarity of small segments of left-wing political parties and labour unions, including the Unified Socialist Party (PSU), An-Nahaj Ad-Dimocrati (The Democratic Path), and the Party of the Democratic and Socialist Vanguard (PADS). In some cases, even members of the mainstream parties of the political consensus, such as a group calling itself the '20 February *ittihadis*' (the youth of the Union Socialiste des Forces Populaires), joined the movement, demonstrating the disillusion of the young with the political choices and orientations within their own parties. Finally, a number of Amazigh associations found in the movement new opportunities to press for change on cultural and identity issues.

While the slogans of the February 20 Movement were revealing about the heterogeneous ideological orientations of its activists, they nevertheless seemed able to establish common ground in terms of what they wanted to

---

[45] Karim Boukhari, 'Tous, sauf Abbas!', *Tel Quel*, Casablanca, 15–21 September 2007, p. 32.

see changed. As far as the 1996 constitution was concerned, many slogans called for the repeal of Article 19, which stated:

> the King, Amir al-Muminin (Commander of the Faithful), shall be the Supreme Representative of the Nation and the Symbol of the unity thereof. He shall be the guarantor of the perpetuation and the continuity of the State. As Defender of the Faith, He shall ensure the respect for the Constitution. He shall be the protector of the rights and liberties of the citizens, social groups and organizations.

The protesters also called for the end to the 'sacred' character of the king enshrined in Article 23. Several constitutional articles, including Articles 19 and 23, along with Articles 24, 27, and 30, gave the king unlimited powers. The basic principle of separation of powers was generally not respected in the 1996 constitution.[46] As will be shown, this principle was still not respected in the new constitution of 2011.

While in general the protesters did not raise slogans against the king in person, his closest entourage was the target of much criticism. Specifically, protesters called for the resignation of two close friends and advisers, Mohamed Mounir Majidi and Fouad Ali el-Himma. Majidi was the private secretary of the king and official manager of the royal holding companies Omnium Nord-Africain (ONA) and Société Nationale d'Investissement (SNI). For many, he symbolized the growing connection between royal political power and business. While in the popular imagination the king had originally been associated with the poor, he had gradually accumulated more wealth since he took the throne in 1999.[47] Many business leaders saw those in the royal entourage as using their position to benefit from economic transactions and using political power to do business. Many of the slogans called, therefore, for an end to the privileges granted to the close circles of the monarchy and demanded the establishment of the principle of social justice and a better distribution of wealth. The other figure of concern to the protesters was Fouad Ali el-Himma, a close friend of the king and the founder of one of the main royalist political parties—the Party of Authenticity and Modernity (PAM).[48] The proximity of El Himma to the king had enticed a number of opportunist politicians

---

[46] These articles of the 1996 constitution gave the monarch his key powers. Article 23: 'The person of the King is sacred and inviolable.' Article 24: 'The King shall appoint the Prime Minister. Upon the Prime Minister's recommendation, the King shall appoint the other Cabinet members as he may terminate their services. The King shall terminate the services of the Government either on his own initiative or because of their resignation.' Article 27: 'The King may dissolve the two Houses of Parliament or one thereof by Royal Decree, in accordance with the conditions prescribed in Articles 71 and 73.' Article 30: 'The King is the Commander-in-Chief of the Royal Armed Forces. He shall make civil and military appointments and shall reserve the right to delegate this power.'

[47] As a prince he was popularly known for his support for the poor, and, when he became king, he was called 'King of the poor'.

[48] See Farid Boussaid, 'The Rise of the PAM in Morocco: Trampling the Political Scene or Stumbling into It?', *Mediterranean Politics*, 14/3 (2009), 413–19.

Figure 8.2. At times peaceful protest took the form of political street theatre. Here in Casablanca on 20 November 2011 activists mocked the coming parliamentary elections, portraying an overweight politician marked with the word 'corruption' as a senior official paraded around him with a wad of banknotes. Elections went ahead later that month and for the first time were won by the moderate Islamist Party for Justice and Development.
©*AP Photo/Abdeljalil Bounhar*

to leave their own parties and join the PAM on its creation, highlighting for many the mediocre and clientelist realities of political parties and the greedy and unprincipled nature of politicians. While the close royal economic entourage was severely criticized and while El Himma could not have created a new party without the blessing of the palace, it is interesting that the persona of the king and his responsibility and accountability as head of the state were at this point not evoked or made explicitly part of the equation in the slogans by the protesters (see Figure 8.2).

One important aspect of the relative success in the organization and communication style of the movement was the use it made of the Internet. The Internet has gradually emerged as the epicentre of a growing public sphere in which informed Moroccans debate highly contested issues regarding social justice, democracy, and cultural and gender rights.[49] The Internet

---

[49] An important theme of the February 20 Movement was related to gender issues, which connected it with the women's movement. See on this issue Houda Abadi, 'Gendering the February 20th Movement: Moroccan Women Redefining: Boundaries, Identities and Resistances', *CyberOrient*, 8/1 (2014) http://www.cyberorient.net/article.do?articleId=8817.

became a site where the Moroccan regime was symbolically and discursively delegitimized. While we cannot reduce the phenomenon of civil resistance mainly to the existence of the Internet, for the February 20 Movement it became an important tool for gathering momentum for protest. Following the examples of the other social movements in Tunisia and Egypt, young Moroccans used social networking websites such as Twitter, Facebook, and YouTube as well as various news outlets regularly to call for action and demonstrations, and to express their views about reforms. The initial protest, which took place on Sunday, 20 February 2011, was called for via these networks. All the subsequent calls for demonstrations followed in the same way. The *tansiqiyat* published their press releases and statements mainly on Facebook. The February 20 Movement often complained that the official media covered their activities and rallies in a biased way by presenting the activists as a source of instability for the country or as inexperienced youth who were unaware of Morocco's problems. Movement members said official TV channels would manipulate or falsify statements by the protesters and not report accurately the numbers taking part in the protests. In one statement, a movement activist said: 'Although the state TV has covered the March 20 protestors, it adopts the same misleading strategy based on the orders they receive.'[50] The movement therefore resorted to an interstitial autonomous space, using alternative media outside the control of the Moroccan state. It was in this context that they established *Mamfakinch*, a news portal site made by a group of Moroccan activists and bloggers who supported major democratic change in Morocco and who constantly presented a counter-discourse to the dominant politics of consensus.[51] As a form of uncontrolled politics, *Mamfakinch*, which literally means 'We are not going to let go' in Moroccan colloquial Arabic, became a space for independent political opinion and analysis, and coverage of events and regular protests. The blog was regularly updated with the latest information from different *tansiqiyat*. It also included live blogs that involved a network of correspondents and activists in different Moroccan cities and small towns. *Mamfakinch* made use of different languages, including Arabic, English, French, and Tamazight. It became an impressive tool for communication at the international level, as it was able to connect Moroccans residing in different countries, and it gathered thousands of online sympathizers. However, while social media were an important component of the February 20 Movement, ultimately it was the protests on the streets that most concerned the Moroccan authorities.

It was also outside the politics of consensus and from within this interstitial autonomous space that the February 20 Movement viewed the proposals for constitutional reforms that came from the royal palace as not constituting real

---

[50] See Hisham Almiraat, 'Maroc: Le Mouvement du 20 Février raconté en 20 vidéos', *GlobalVoices*, 29 December 2011 http://fr.globalvoicesonline.org/2011/12/29/92778.
[51] See https://www.mamfakinch.com. See also 'Shabab al faysbook', *al Mashhad*, 65 (25 February–3 March 2011).

and structural democratic change. In a speech on 9 March 2011, in a clear if not acknowledged response to the protests of the February 20 Movement, the king promised major constitutional reforms.[52] However, the movement saw the reform commission established by the king after his speech, the Constitutional Reform Advisory Commission, as made up of individuals under royal appointment who were ultimately working within structural constraints. While the royal commission met representatives from different political parties and civil society organizations, there were no rational rules that could function as a guarantee to respect the propositions presented by these political forces. The result was that the constitution had to be reworked and validated within the royal cabinet in order for it to be presented to a referendum. The final constitutional text was not, in fact, effectively debated but simply presented and then promoted by the state-run media when it was put to a referendum on 1 July 2011. The referendum passed with an overwhelming 98.5 per cent of the vote.

It was within this context and these constraints that the February 20 Movement considered the *makhzan* approach structurally and essentially flawed and saw the resulting constitution as 'al-destour al-mamnuh' ('the granted constitution'). It was no accident that the movement had declined the invitation to come up with propositions before the royal commission, given that, for many activists, it lacked legitimacy as a body and did not respect the principle of popular sovereignty. The movement therefore condemned the process leading up to the reforms and called for a boycott of the referendum, whose outcome it viewed as predetermined. The protesters believed that the new constitutional reforms were merely cosmetic and did not challenge a political system that remained structurally authoritarian.[53] In a number of statements on Facebook and other Internet sites, the movement clearly showed its rejection of what they called a 'political game' constantly controlled by the monarchy.

The state's reaction to the peaceful protests alternated between accommodating tolerance, occasionally threatening violence, and imposing strategies of intimidation.[54] The authorities initially allowed demonstrations to take place and then gradually changed their approach to them. Ironically, four days after the king's speech of 9 March, in which he had declared to the people that Morocco would engage in constitutional reforms to establish democracy and the rule of law, the police used violence to disperse demonstrators in Casablanca. Violence was then abandoned until the middle of May, when the

---

[52] 'Morocco's King Promises Constitutional Reforms', *BBC News*, 10 March 2011 www.bbc.com/news/world-africa-12695902.

[53] For an analysis of the changes in the 2011 constitution and the February 20 Movement's reaction to it, see Michael J. Willis, 'Evolution not Revolution? Morocco and the Arab Spring', in Larbi Sadiki (ed.), *Routledge Handbook of the Arab Spring: Rethinking Democratization* (Abingdon and New York: Routledge, 2015), 440–2.

[54] See Noureddine Meftah, 'Sultawiya am tasadi li iskat annisam' ('Authoritarianism or Putting a Lid on 'Down with the Regime'), *al-Ayam*, 14 June 2011, pp. 14–16, and 'Khalfiyyat al harb ala harakat 20 fibryar' ('The Implications of the War on the February 20 Movement'), *Akbar al-yawm*, 5 June 2011.

authorities started to resume a more violent response. It seemed that the Moroccan authorities were setting the limits of demonstrations. On 29 March, when the movement called for a sit-in in front of what was commonly identified as a clandestine detention centre in Temara, outside Rabat, the police stopped the march, violently intervened in the demonstration, and chased away the protesters. Between 20 February and August, police violence was repeated in other cities such as Casablanca, Tangier, Agadir, and Safi, leaving dozens injured and many arrested. Kamal el-Omari, an activist from the city of Safi, died in May 2011 as a result of head injuries inflicted by the security forces, and his death became a symbol of police brutality. In addition to violent police repression, there were other cases of intimidation against well-known activists of the February 20 Movement. Under the pretext of supporting the king and maintaining stability, the authorities used pro-regime supporters to intimidate protesters, particularly during the referendum for the new constitution in July 2011.

A notable feature of the February 20 Movement and its protests was the absence of calls to bring down the regime, which were a prominent feature of protest movements in other parts of the region. This prompts the question of what would have happened in Morocco if the February 20 Movement called for the downfall of the regime. This is a particularly relevant question, because it highlights the fact that the movement emphatically stressed the point that the call for reforms was made with the monarchy and not against it. It spoke very clearly about the reformist outlook of the movement. This was most noticeably symbolized by the protesters' signs that always read 'Down with Corruption' ('isqat al-fasad' in Arabic) and not 'Down with the Regime' ('isqat al-nizam'). It was exactly this reformist stand by the protesters that played an important role in terms of framing the way in which the monarchy reacted to the demands of the movement. However, the constitutional reforms that resulted were in the end orchestrated and controlled by the monarchy, and the political stamina of the February 20 Movement was sapped after the 2011 elections. As the Islamist association Justice and Charity withdrew its support in December 2011, the number of protesters in the streets started to dwindle. The ideological incoherence of the movement, its relative spontaneity, the absence of a clear leadership, the lack of an organizational structure, and the slow and sustained strategies of the regime were all factors for the subsequent failure of the movement in the long term.

With all the limits associated with the constitutional reforms in Morocco, the reactions of international actors were, however, more positive than critical. Historically, neither Europe nor the USA was ever seriously engaged in the promotion of real democratic change in the Middle East or Morocco: the stability paradigm remained the most important framework for dealing with the region as a whole. As Europe and the USA enjoyed very good diplomatic relations with the most autocratic regimes, they gave only lip service to the promotion of democracy in the region. In the context of revolutionary upheavals and violent outcomes in a number of Arab countries, Morocco was in fact seen through a favourable diplomatic lens by both European and US officials. First, the constitutional reforms, and the constructed international image of a 'democratically' self-constituting people, contrasted with what had been happening in Egypt, Yemen, and Syria. Achieving a new constitution that had been voted in by the people served to cast an image of Morocco not only as a country where popular sovereignty was exercised but also as a model for other Arab states. Outside observers compared the process of constitutional reforms to the violent changes elsewhere. The reforms were viewed by the European Union as part of 'a clear commitment to democracy'.[55] US Secretary of State Hillary Clinton gave her support by declaring on 23 March 2011 that the plans for reforms by the king 'hold great promise' and were part of a 'comprehensive approach'.[56] International actors did not hesitate to view the constitutional reforms as part of 'a peaceful democratic transition in Morocco [that] would provide a powerful model that the monarchies of the Gulf might potentially be forced to follow'.[57]

CONCLUSION

This chapter examined the relationship between civil society and the emergence of new forms of civil resistance in a Moroccan context where the monarchy had the political upper hand. To what extent have civil resistance, civil society activism, and subaltern politics transformed the Moroccan regime? I argued here that, while the political system had to engage in different reforms as a result of societal pressure, the weakness of political parties and the dispersed nature of social solidarities did not yet create sufficient pressure to reverse the structural political supremacy of the monarchy. There is no doubt that the constitutional reforms that took place in 2011 were the consequences of the pressures of the February 20 Movement. But the constitutional outcome was disappointing. Although he delegated some of his powers to the head of government, the king, as the Supreme Commander and Chief of Staff of the Royal Armed Forces, still held an exclusive monopoly over appointments to the

---

[55] 'Joint statement by High Representative/Vice-President Catherine Ashton and Commissioner Štefan Füle on the Announcement of the New Constitution of Morocco', European Commission Press Release, Brussels, 19 June 2011 http://www.europa.eu/rapid/press-release_MEMO-11-424_en.htm?locale=en.

[56] 'Remarks with Moroccan Foreign Minister Taieb Fassi Fihri', US State Department, Washington, 23 March 2011 www.state.gov/secretary/20092013clinton/rm/2011/03/158895.htm.

[57] James Traub, 'Game of Thrones', *Foreign Policy*, 10 June 2011 http://foreignpolicy.com/2011/06/10/game-of-thrones.

military. The newly created Supreme Security Council was also chaired by the king. In addition, the king retained the power to declare a state of exception, akin to a state of emergency. The king is still the head of the Constitutional Council, which was set up under the 2011 constitution as an initial step towards the creation of a constitutional court, and appoints half of its members.[58]

I argued that the growing role of civil society actors in the 1980s and the rise of the February 20 Movement in the context of the Arab Spring were symptomatic of the weakness of political parties vis-à-vis the dominant role of the monarchy. But the rise of civil society actors or subaltern forms of politics and resistance could not replace formal institutions such as parties, which should normally be an important basis for social mobilization and one of the main forces that ought to trigger more significant and consistent processes of democratization. Although they had the ability to press for reforms, civil society actors did not have the political leverage or probably the will to be critical of the overall political supremacy of the monarchy and its undemocratic system. Since 2013 civil resistance in Morocco has involved mainly small-scale and scattered struggles as a means to initiate more localistic socio-economic changes, but these struggles lack a broad-based coordination and the synergy to translate them into a major force capable of transforming the political system and the institutional structures as a whole.

The use of peaceful methods of struggle was generally positive for the February 20 Movement, helping it to gain support both within Morocco and internationally. More significantly the movement has made it possible for different segments of the marginalized classes, whether in urban or remote rural areas, no longer to be afraid to voice their grievances and to protest in the public sphere. Yet four years on from 2011, the February 20 Movement itself seemed out of the picture, reduced to a small hard core of a few hundred protesters who continued to be harassed by the authorities. The Islamist Justice and Charity organization, which had initially supported the movement, formally left it in early 2012. This was symptomatic of the ideological dispersion of a movement that was never able to present a coherent ideology and programme. But, even without a coherent ideology and without a structural vision of change, all these social and political forces—from civil society actors, dispersed struggles, and subaltern forms of politics—could yet, in a time of a major crisis of governance, converge in a scenario where peaceful forms of social resistance could turn from a more accommodationist, reformist, and evolutionist approach into a more threatening and revolutionary logic against the regime. This was exactly what happened—but with very different outcomes—in certain other countries, especially Tunisia and Egypt.

---

[58] See Mohamed Madani, Driss Maghraoui, and Saloua Zerhouni, 'The 2011 Moroccan Constitution: A Critical Analysis', International Institute for Democracy and Electoral Assistance, 2012 www.idea.int/publications/the_2011_moroccan_constitution.

9

Civil Resistance in the Syrian Uprising

From Peaceful Protest to Sectarian Civil War

*Raymond Hinnebusch, Omar Imady,
and Tina Zintl*

This chapter examines civil resistance during the Syrian Uprising that began in March 2011, looking both at its consequences for the power struggle unleashed by the revolt and the long-term effect on citizen participation in Syria. In the civil resistance paradigm, non-violent resistance can force an end to authoritarian governance. In the Syrian case, unprecedented large-scale peaceful protests broke out in 2011 and quickly destabilized the regime of President Bashar al-Assad. However, not only did a peaceful transition to a more inclusive regime fail to take place, but in 2012 the country descended into armed civil war.

This chapter analyses why mass mobilization took place and why, instead of precipitating democratic transition, it led to escalating conflict that degenerated into sectarian violence. We also examine how peaceful civil resistance brought about associational activity, which survived the initial descent into violence and may still have permanent positive consequences in a post-Assad Syria. In the process, we consider the implications of the Syrian case for the non-violent resistance paradigm.

UPGRADING THE NON-VIOLENT RESISTANCE PARADIGM

A study of 323 cases of resistance—both civil and violent—from 1900 to 2006 by Stephan and Chenoweth[1] finds that non-violent campaigns succeed if they

---

[1] Maria J. Stephan and Erica Chenoweth, 'Why Civil Resistance Works: The Strategic Logic of Nonviolent Conflict', *International Security*, 33/1 (Summer 2008), 7–44.

can mobilize active and sustained participation by just 3.5 per cent of the population.[2] Yet the authors also argue that this dynamic operates by inducing a split in the regime, especially defections from the security forces. Since it is, therefore, not mass mobilization alone but the *interaction* between it and regime (elite) behaviour that matters, the civil resistance paradigm could benefit from the more explicit connections proposed in democratization studies' *transition paradigm*: a peaceful transition to democracy is facilitated by a *pact* between moderates in the ruling elite and among the opposition, wherein the latter would not threaten the vital interests of incumbents, who, in return, would concede a pluralization of the political system.[3] Such a scenario is more likely when non-violent resistance encourages moderates within the regime to push for reform and/or withdraw their support from hard-line authoritarians and less likely when rebels make maximalist demands or resort to violence, thereby empowering hardliners against the moderates. Below we use this 'upgraded' synthetic framework as a guide to understanding the Syrian conflict and in the conclusion we summarize the implications of the Syrian case for the framework.

CIVIL RESISTANCE TO AUTHORITARIAN RULE IN SYRIA

Obstacles to Regime Change

Syria's Ba'ath regime was long thought to be a robust authoritarian regime combining many mechanisms of co-optation and corporatism as well as a pervasive *mukhabarat* (intelligence) network that debilitated any independent civil society. It had long effectively managed opposition and had demonstrated a willingness to repress resistance harshly and successfully over many decades.

Bassam Haddad pointed to several factors that in Syria would work against regime change through non-violent resistance.[4] Unlike in Egypt and Tunisia,

---

[2] Erica Chenoweth, 'The Dissident's Toolkit', *Foreign Policy*, 25 October 2013, p. 2 http://www.foreignpolicy.com/articles/2013/10/24/the_dissidents_toolkit.

[3] Guillermo O'Donnell and Philippe Schmitter, *Transitions from Authoritarian Rule: Tentative Conclusions about Uncertain Democracies, Part 4* (Baltimore, MD: Johns Hopkins University Press, 1986). For Middle East applications of the pact notion, see John Waterbury, 'Democracy without Democrats? The Potential for Political Liberalization in the Middle East', in Ghassan Salamé (ed.), *Democracy without Democrats: The Renewal of Politics in the Muslim World* (London: I. B. Tauris, 1994), 23–47; and Jean Leca, 'Democratization in the Arab World: Uncertainty, Vulnerability and Legitimacy', also in Salamé, *Democracy without Democrats*, 49–53.

[4] Bassam Haddad, 'Why Syria Is Unlikely to be Next…for Now', *Sada* (online journal of Carnegie Endowment for International Peace, Middle East Programme), 9 March 2011 http://carnegieendowment.org/2011/03/09/why-syria-is-unlikely-to-be-next-.-.-.-for-now/6bhl.

where the departure of the president, who came to be seen as a liability, did not threaten the establishment, in Syria the cohesion and societal linkages of the regime meant many more interests would be threatened in such a scenario. The dense links between Bashar al-Assad and the regime core prevented elites' abandonment of the president; at the same time, thicker state–society relations in Syria prevented a Libya-style social isolation of the top leadership. While the regime was cohesive, the heterogeneity of Syrian society had long undermined collective action among the opposition. Assad's regime also enjoyed some nationalist legitimacy from decades of opposition to Israel and Western imperialism, in sharp contrast to the other Arab presidents. Many Syrians valued stability and feared a return to the sectarian violence that racked Syria in the early 1980s, the costs of which had recently been demonstrated again in Syria's neighbours, Lebanon and Iraq. Although these factors did not prevent the Syrian Uprising, they did shape its pathway and, specifically, made for the extremely violent stalemate that has distinguished it from the uprisings in some other Arab states.

Grievances and the Opportunity Structure of Mass Protest

Why after three decades of quiescence was mass civil resistance to the regime mobilized in 2011? First, the accumulation of grievances could be said to have reached a tipping point. Observers had long pointed to a population bomb: high birth rates combined with free education produced a rapid growth of unemployed educated youth that the economy could not absorb. In rural areas, population growth on fixed land resources, which left peasant youth without land, combined with severe drought (described by the UN as the worst in four decades) to prompt an exodus to urban slums that would be the tinderboxes of the uprising. In parallel, the regime's economic liberalization policies privileged investors and enriched the well connected, notably in the main cities of Damascus and Aleppo, where conspicuous consumption for the new rich burgeoned. At the same time, the regime's withdrawal from its former populist 'social contract' meant an insufficient safety net for the victims of neo-liberal economic 'reforms': 30 per cent fell under the poverty line and 11.4 per cent below subsistence, according to a UN Development Programme report.[5] Corruption was a long-standing grievance, but, as social mobility stalled for the majority while a visible few enriched themselves, it became even less tolerable. The arbitrariness of the security forces was another

---

[5] Heba El-Laithy and Khalid Abu-Ismail, *Poverty in Syria: 1996–2004—Diagnosis and Pro-Poor Policy Considerations* (UNDP Syria, 2005), 1 www.undp.org/content/rbas/en/home/library/poverty_reduction.html.

long-standing grievance, with continuing instances of arbitrary arrest and torture underlining the absence of rule of law and protection of human rights.

At the same time, the 'opportunity structure' of political mobilization, in the parlance of social movement theory, improved in the late 2000s.[6] Several previous instances of civil society mobilization, such as the Damascus Spring (2000–1) and the Damascus Declaration (2005), even though repressed by the regime, provided experience and models for dissent. As part of the regime's 'modernization', the spread of the Internet and mobile phones acquired a critical mass in the latter part of the 2000s. This helped overcome the atom-ization of society, while activists also started to get experience in circumvent-ing regime controls over such media. In parallel, the deliberate enervation of the Ba'ath party and its corporatist auxiliaries, which Bashar saw as obstacles to his market reforms, debilitated incorporation of the regime's traditional constituencies, especially in rural areas, once the regime's stronghold; this left the inhabitants of rural areas 'available' for anti-regime mobilization. There was also a certain loss of fear as, under Bashar, repression became more selective: this loss of fear was especially felt among the new generation, which had not experienced the 1980s suppression of an Islamist uprising in Hama and other northern cities.[7] The success of uprisings in other Arab states encouraged people to believe that even repressive authoritarian regimes could be driven from power.[8]

The Precipitants of Non-Violent Resistance

The Syrian Uprising began on 15 March 2011, but as early as 18 January a Facebook page had been created by Syrian youth in exile entitled 'The Syrian Revolution against Bashar al-Assad' that called for a 'Day of Rage' to be held on 5 February; the event, however, attracted only small numbers, who were quickly dispersed or arrested. This was a sign that, prior to the Syrian Uprising, youth organizers, including Syrian exiles aggrieved at the regime, were preparing to use social media, which had become popular among Internet-connected Syrian youth. Facebook rapidly became an effective in-strument to mobilize protests, and also to focus internal and external attention on the regime's excessively violent response, thereby giving protests a multi-plier effect.

[6] The notion of opportunity structure is explored in David S. Meyer, 'Protest and Political Opportunities', *Annual Review of Sociology*, 30 (2004), 125–45.

[7] Referring to the government's 1982 sack of Hama, where the Muslim Brotherhood had mounted an insurgency and where more than 20,000 people were reputedly killed.

[8] Empirical evidence on the roots and early dynamic of the uprising is from Raymond Hinnebusch, 'Syria: From Authoritarian Upgrading to Revolution?', *International Affairs*, 88/1 (January 2012), 95–113.

On 17 February the first precursor of the uprising took place in Damascus. An argument with a traffic policeman in Hariqa, in the old city, evolved into one of the first spontaneous protests by Damascenes since the early 1970s. As preserved video recordings show, the protesters chanted: 'The Syrian people cannot be humiliated.'[9] This did not, however, escalate into confrontation, because, wisely, the interior minister arrived on the scene to placate the protesters; had the regime continued to respond to protest in such a measured way, the course of subsequent events might have been significantly different. Also during this early period, there were several attempts in Damascus to hold demonstrations and vigils in front of the Ministry of Interior, the Egyptian embassy, and the Libyan embassy: these demonstrations included the intellectuals of the Damascus Declaration period, such as Tayyeb Tizini, and political activists such as Suhair Atassi.

At the same time, the seeds of another spontaneous protest were being planted. Anger against the business dealings of Rami Makhlouf, the president's cousin and head of a financial network, led to anti-Assad slogans being sprayed on walls in the southern town of Dara'a by several schoolchildren, who were arrested and tortured. The visit of Dara'a notables to the office of Atef Najib, a cousin of the president and head of the Political Security Directorate in the town, not only failed to secure the release of the children, but was met with an insulting response, sparking the first protests. The harsh response by the security forces led to a rapid escalation of protest across the country.[10]

The failure of the Syrian government to come to terms with what might be called the psychological dimension of the Syrian Uprising can be seen clearly from this early phase. TV footage of how popular protests had overthrown dictators in Tunisia and Egypt created a sense of empowerment in Syria, giving a dimension to the protests that was over and above economic and political grievances. The failure of the regime to diagnose accurately the phenomenon it was confronting can be seen in its efforts to mitigate it through

---

[9] See 'Dimashq: Tazahura ba'da 'itida' al-shurta 'ala shab bil-darb' ('Damascus: A Demonstration after Police Assault a Young Man'), *BBC Arabic*, 19 February 2011 http://www.youtube.com/watch?v=qAHcgwJP7uI.

[10] This story was reported (with various elaborations) on numerous websites, and was corroborated by visitors of Bashar al-Assad, who, according to them, confirmed its basic elements. See 'Dimashq tamna' ahad aqriba' al-asad wa-muhafizan sabiqan min mughadarat al-aradi al-suriyah' ('Damascus Prohibits a Relative of the President and an Ex-Governor from Leaving Syria'), *Al-Sharq Al-Awsat*, 14 June 2011 www.aawsat.com/details.asp?section=4&article=626456&issueno=11886 - .UsAOGv3APfY; 'At the Birthplace of the Revolution, One Year Later', *'Ukaz*, 17 March 2012 www.okaz.com.sa/new/Issues/20120317/Con20120317486572.htm; Samar Yazbik, 'Kanat tihmati anani min 'ailat aba zaid' ('My Charge Was that I Was from the Family of Aba Zaid'), *Al-Hayat*, 16 August 2011 http://all4syria.info/Archive/23235; Jim Muir, 'Syria: Setting the Country Alight?', *BBC News*, 24 March 2011 www.bbc.co.uk/news/world-middle-east-12814530; 'Shaikh mujahidin hums' ('The Leader of the Mujahidin of Homs'), *Suriya al-Mustaqbal*, 29 February 2012 http://defense-arab.com/vb/threads/53732/.

concessions such as higher salaries, and vague promises of lifting the state of emergency, which was a long-standing opposition demand. To address effectively the protesters' sense of empowerment would have required that the government change its traditional repressive attitude towards dissent and take seriously the demand of the people that they be treated with dignity. Yet, in his speech to parliament on 30 March, Assad, instead of addressing the peaceful protesters and their concrete demands, blamed the unrest on foreign conspirators. Had the president driven to Dara'a, met the families of the children who had been arrested, and promised to punish his cousin Atef Najib, as many had hoped and anticipated, rather than stand in parliament and laughingly dismiss the significance of the protests, many analysts believe that the Syrian Uprising could have been largely pre-empted. For during the initial protests the president still enjoyed some legitimacy: protests did not target him and urged him to respond positively and even lead a democratic transition. Arguably, had he opted to lead the reform process, becoming the solution rather than the problem, the legitimacy windfall might have enabled him to win a free election and hence legitimize his office and regime. Instead, protest was met by violence from the security forces, and the claim of an international conspiracy against Syria became pervasive in government discourse. It was the failure of the regime to respond positively to the demand for reform that was the catalyst that would spread civil resistance and escalate its demand to calling for the fall of the regime.

Mobilization took place on two levels: at the local level, coordinating committees in mosques planned day-to-day protests, while cyber activists used the Internet to share information, coordinate and publicize their protests, keep the momentum going, and convey a sense of national-level solidarity.[11] Syria's Internet penetration level was actually fairly low, but there were enough youth in all areas who were electronically connected and acted as focal points, linked by the Internet to each other across the country and also by more traditional means to their local communities. The Syrian Uprising was as virtual as it was actual, in the sense that it would often create a momentum online before it was translated into something tangible on the ground. A key tactic was documenting acts of resistance against the government and government overreactions to them, usually in the form of short video clips or news items that would subsequently be posted on the Internet. Frequently, short protests would take place for the sole purpose of publishing a video clip that was meant to show that Syrians did indeed have the courage to confront the regime, if only for a few minutes, then dispersing before the security forces arrived—so-called flying demonstrations that gave a multiplier effect to protests.

---

[11] Kim Ghattas, 'Syria's Spontaneously Organised Protests', *BBC News*, 22 April 2011 www.bbc.co.uk/news/world-middle-east-13168276.

In the Syrian case, the demonstrations on the scale of millions mobilized in Egypt and concentrated at the centre of power failed to materialise—especially after it became clear, as early as March 2011, that the government was willing to use lethal force against protesters. In contrast to Egypt, protests proliferated in the periphery. Their origins in Daraʿa were in part because the regime was less vigilant in an area of traditional Baʿath support, yet strong tribal links and cross-border linkages via labour migration and smuggling were instrumental in enabling rapid mobilization of protests.[12] At the same time, despite repression, a mass movement rapidly spread from Daraʿa, concentrated in provincial towns such as Idlib and Deir ez-Zor and in medium-sized cities such as Homs and Hama. This was all the more remarkable given the communal heterogeneity of the population and the debilitation of civil society, which tended to stunt habits of association, at least beyond the local area. Filling this vacuum, mosques became centres of protest, especially around Friday prayers, while social media created virtual networks. Throughout 2011 and into 2012, the numbers of demonstrators ran into the tens of thousands: major protests took place without respite in virtually every Syrian town and city except Damascus and Aleppo, such that, even though unarmed, they posed a serious threat to the regime's survival.

The Initial Peacefulness of Protest

Why did the uprising take a peaceful form for so long, by contrast, for example, to the 1980s Islamist insurgency and in spite of excessive violence used by the regime to repress it? There was a previous tradition of non-violent opposition: in 2000–1 the 'Damascus Spring' opposition mounted non-violent petitions and staged peaceful indoor assemblies for limited demands such as an end to the emergency law and restraints on the *mukhabarat*. Over seventy political salons, *muntadayat*, were founded during this period, including the Jamal Atassi Forum founded by Suhair Atassi, and the Tartous Forum founded by Habib Saleh. In 2005, in the Damascus Declaration, a broad coalition of opposition factions inclusive in its narrative, involving Alawites and reaching out to Kurds, petitioned for democratization. Among the notable co-signers of the Declaration were Michel Kilo, a Christian human-rights activist, who was imprisoned several times for his political activities; and Riad Seif, a prominent businessman and member of parliament who founded a political salon known as the Forum for National Dialogue in 2000, and who later asked for a formal investigation into how Syria's first cellular contracts were awarded, a stand

---

[12] Reinoud Leenders and Steven Heydemann, 'Popular Mobilization in Syria: Opportunity and Threat, and the Social Networks of the Early Risers', *Mediterranean Politics*, 17/2 (2012), 139–59.

that was followed by his arrest. Riyad al-Turk founded the 'Political Bureau', or the branch of the Syrian Communist Party, which in essence refused to be tamed by the Hafiz al-Assad regime. In 1980, when al-Turk failed to condemn the violence of the Muslim Brotherhood, he was arrested and imprisoned, in harsh and isolated conditions, until 1998. He was rearrested in September 2001 after stating during an interview with al-Jazeera that the 'dictator had died' (in reference to Hafiz al-Assad), and remained in prison until November 2002. In parallel, the mobilization of an Islamic civil society had advanced for two decades and especially in the 2000s under Bashar al-Assad, as the regime fostered a peaceful non-political Islam in order to marginalize the radicals.[13] Charities, schools, and mosques proliferated, but were predominantly Sufi and peaceful in orientation. Also the Muslim Brotherhood had converted to non-violent resistance, a function of the high costs of its 1980s violent insurgency. This actually meant a return to its historical modus operandi of peaceful political participation; and, in parallel, the Brotherhood now also embraced democracy and minority rights. As a result of this, it was slow to turn towards violent resistance throughout 2011, in spite of regime violence against pro-testers.[14] This was congruent with one trend in Islamic discourse across the Arab world that had come to reject political violence; indeed, Syrian religious scholar Jawdat Said had long argued that Muslims should not seek power through violence and that repression should be countered by non-violent resistance. Said had signed the 2005 Damascus declaration and re-emphasized his principle of non-violent resistance in a speech delivered to a large dem-onstration held in Dara'a province on 8 April 2011.[15] In this tradition, attempts were explicitly made in the early days of the uprising—famously in the Damascene suburb Daraya by the activist Ghuyath Mater, later murdered—to use Gandhi-like tactics to win over the army at demonstrations by talking with and distributing water bottles and flowers to the soldiers.

But it was the scenes of thousands of peaceful protesters bringing down two of the most repressive regimes in the Middle East that was primarily respon-sible for perpetuating peaceful protests in Syria even after they had been met by a brutal response. After all, if it worked in Tunisia and Egypt, why—as protesters argued on social media sites during 2011—should it not work in Syria as well? In the first months of the uprising, its leaders were careful to insist on peaceful protest and also to promote a cross-sectarian narrative meant to be inclusive of minorities, including the politically dominant

---

[13] Line Khatib, *Islamic Revivalism in Syria: The Rise and Fall of Ba'thist Secularism* (London: Routledge, 2011).

[14] Rafaël Lefèvre, *Ashes of Hama: The Muslim Brotherhood in Syria* (London: Hurst, 2013), 181–200.

[15] Jawdat Said, *The Doctrine of the First Son of Adam: The Problem of Violence in the Islamic World* (no publisher indicated, 1964). For Said's Dara'a speech, see 'Jadwat Said, Jasim, Dara'a', *Ziwar Majeed*, 9 April 2011 www.youtube.com/watch?v=dOSwF8kWkkU.

Alawites. Protesters were, from the outset, addressing outside audiences, not simply the regime or the Syrian public: hence the narrative of peaceful non-violent protest was essential to get international sympathy and impose pressure on the regime to restrain its response.

FROM FAILED DEMOCRATIC TRANSITION TO CIVIL WAR: WHAT WENT WRONG?

Yet non-violent mass protest failed to precipitate a transition to democracy. It led to escalating violence and polarization, empowering hardliners on both sides rather than enabling a convergence between soft-liners among elites and counter-elites. Polarization led not to revolution and regime collapse but to stalemate. Multiple complex factors explain this.

The immediate origin of the escalation of violence was the regime's 'security solution' to the mass protests. Initially, the regime appeared to exercise restraint, but, reportedly, a security committee had judged that rebellion had ousted presidents in Tunisia and Egypt because regimes had used insufficient repression.[16] There may have been deliberate efforts by radical elements among the protesters to provoke the regime, and it fell into the trap. Once the government had responded to demonstrations and attacks on public buildings with excessive force, a tit-for-tat process of escalation began, which rapidly expanded the protests from their start in Dara'a to other towns and suburbs where the deprived or aggrieved were concentrated. The regime's forces, lacking training and experience in crowd or riot control, continued to respond with excessive violence, multiplying regime enemies, and making funerals occasions for more confrontation. Although initially the protests largely took a peaceful form, as the protesters turned from demanding reform to demanding the fall of the regime and escalated their resistance via ever-larger mass demonstrations, the threat to the survival of the regime became significant. As the regime failed to contain the protests at one level of violence, it increased the level—thereby killing many peaceful protesters and even bystanders and stimulating a desire for revenge.[17] Many protesters started to believe that the regime's unlimited ruthlessness justified armed

---

[16] Carsten Wieland, *Syria: A Decade of Lost Chances: Repression and Revolution from Damascus Spring to Arab Spring* (Seattle, WA: Cune Press, 2012), 17–27.

[17] Yet, as Maciej Bartkowski and Mohja Kahf point out, the regime was not uniquely brutal in its response: 'The Shah of Iran killed 600 nonviolent demonstrators in Tehran on one day alone, September 8, 1978 and . . . Mubarak's police . . . hesitated little before gunning down 900 protesters during 17 days of demonstrations in 2011—more than twice the casualties in Syria during the first two and a half weeks of nonviolent protests' (Maciej Bartkowski and Mohja Kahf, 'The Syrian Resistance: A Tale of Two Struggles', openDemocracy, 23 and 24 September 2013 www.

protection of non-violent protesters and armed rebels began barricading areas against regime troops. Once the opposition was militarized, the regime felt free to vastly increase the use of lethal force, including use of air strikes and artillery. Eventually, the larger part of the opposition abandoned non-violence. The regime may have deliberately encouraged this since it would be easier to legitimize the use of the unrestrained violence against armed rebels. In this sense, it was the opposition that fell into the trap, because once they were seduced into departing from their commitment to non-violence the regime no longer felt the need for restraint.

This shift greatly increased casualties. During the first five months of non-violent civil resistance (mid-March to mid-August 2011), the death toll was 2,019 (figures exclude regime casualties which were also significant) while in a five-month period of predominantly armed resistance (mid-January to mid-June 2012) the death toll soared to 8,195, and thereafter at greater rates yet.[18] Regime forces, and Alawites disproportionately, also suffered casualties, which quickly mounted. Indeed, a turning point toward the regime's use of heavy weapons against whole towns was its attack in June 2011 on the northern town of Jisr ash-Shaghour after the killing of more than a hundred soldiers and policemen stationed there. The spilling of blood happened so quickly on such a significant scale that the negotiation of a transition was soon rejected on both sides.

The strategy of the opposition also had an impact on the escalation of the conflict. It depended on mounting protests on such a scale that the security services would be stretched thin and exhausted. It was prepared, in this way, to provoke the regime into increasing its repression to a level that would turn the majority of the population against it, or that might bring about a split in the regime. The hope was that the army would become an unreliable instrument of repression and even fragment along sectarian lines. As the use of lethal violence increased, military defections occurred, especially among Sunni conscripts. These, however, amounted to individuals and groups rather than whole units. The regime responded by introducing snipers and tanks to reduce contact between soldiers and protesters and by relying on loyalist militias, the infamous *shabiha* (Arabic for 'ghosts'). Hundreds of soldiers were executed for refusing orders to fire on unarmed demonstrators. Assad began using only those three of his army's twelve divisions which were manned by Alawites;[19] this meant, however, that the regime lacked the manpower to control fully Syria's territory, swathes of which fell, in time, into opposition hands or

opendemocracy.net/civilresistance/maciej-bartkowski-mohja-kahf/syrian-resistance-tale-of-two-struggles).

[18] Bartkowski and Kahf, 'The Syrian Resistance', pt two. Their figures for casualties are based on data from the Violations Documentation Center in Syria http://www.vdc-sy.info/index.php/en.

[19] Bartkowski and Kahf, 'The Syrian Resistance', pt one.

became contested regions. Nevertheless, the defections, whether from the army, or, subsequently, from high officials—even a prime minister—did not touch upon the core of the government's power base. Once the opposition was militarized, defections declined, partly since those of doubtful loyalty had already joined the opposition.

Also driving the escalation in violence was that peaceful protests led not to isolation of the regime, as would be needed for them to succeed, but to polarization of society. The opposition had underestimated the level of support for the government in certain segments of the population, not only among the minorities but also the urban middle class and bourgeoisie in Damascus and Aleppo. These societal strata valued stability, had much to lose economically from the disorder, and therefore remained relatively immune to the spread of the uprising. The opposition came to understand that it could not win without breaking the alignment between the regime and the urban elites. At first, the opposition thought that the turmoil would paralyze the economy enough to cause the business elites to desert the regime, while international economic sanctions would sap the regime's revenue base, hence its ability to pay salaries and sustain the loyalties of the state administration. However, an economic collapse did not take place, and the regime proved capable—with the help of external funding from, for example, Iran—of perpetuating itself financially. Non-violent resistance was still attempted in the main cities, but no critical mass could be mobilized. Ultimately, to turn these cities against the regime parts of the opposition sought to demonstrate that the regime could not guarantee stability and turned to bombings and armed infiltrations into urban neighbourhoods; the regime, in turn, used heavy weapons against areas harbouring the insurgents to send the message to populations that such armed groups should not be tolerated in their midst. The conflict also geographically intensified: at first confined to smaller towns and rural areas, its scope dramatically widened when anti-regime fighters entered Aleppo in the summer of 2012, provoking the regime's destruction of large parts of the city (see Figure 9.1).

Also crucial in propelling the violence was the way the possibility of external military intervention shaped both opposition and regime strategies. Many Syrian expatriates, young cosmopolitans who were instrumental in initiating and internationalizing the uprising, believed that external intervention would turn the balance of power in their favour. Encouraged by the Western-promoted 'Responsibility to Protect' (R2P) principle,[20] they expected fear of intervention would restrain the regime's repressive options. External activists told those on the ground, pointing to the Libya no-fly zone, that

---

[20] This principle was incorporated in the UN World Summit Outcome Document of 2005 (UN General Assembly Res. 60/1 of 16 September 2005), and has been the subject of much international controversy since.

Figure 9.1. Amid the divided loyalties of the Syrian people, a mass rally in favour of the regime. Thousands gathered in Damascus on 29 March 2011 to show their support for the Syrian President Bashar al-Assad. Only some months later did the uprising begin to descend into brutal civil war.

© *AP Photo/Bassem Tellawi*

'the international community won't sit and watch you be killed.'[21] They claimed that another Hama was not possible because 'everything is being filmed on YouTube, and there's a lot of international attention on the Middle East.' When this expectation proved illusory, elements of the opposition, in their zeal to provoke Western intervention, exaggerated the bloodshed and found willing partners in the Western and Gulf-owned media keen to discredit the regime.[22] The regime, for its part, initially tried to calibrate its violence within limits that would not trigger an international bandwagon toward intervention. On the other hand, at a certain point, it felt the need to smash resistance quickly so as not to lose control of territory that could be used to

---

[21] Kate Seelye, 'Syria Unrest "Cannot Be Contained"', *Daily Beast*, 28 March 2011 www.thedailybeast.com/articles/2011/03/28/syria-unrest-cannot-be-contained-dissidents-say.html.

[22] William Blum, 'Putting Syria into Some Perspective: The Anti-Empire Report', *Dissident Voice*, blog, 8 April 2012 http://dissidentvoice.org/2012/04/putting-syria-into-some-perspective/; Alastair Crooke, 'Unfolding the Syrian Paradox', *Asia Times Online*, 15 July 2011 http://www.atimes.com/atimes/Middle_East/MG15Ak02.html; Angela Joya, 'Syria and the Arab Spring: The Evolution of the Conflict and the Role of Domestic External and Factors', *Ortadoğu Etütleri*, 4/1 (July 2012), 40–3.

stage an intervention as had happened in Libya. This was crucial in precipitating a transition from the 'security solution' to the 'military solution'.

The regime's near paranoia about foreign conspiracies was also part of the toxic mix. Having survived several decades of international isolation orchestrated by the US, but also involving Europe, it had always seen itself as besieged by foreign enemies. The role played by external exiles and internet activists abroad in provoking or escalating the uprising was congruent with the regime's perceptions of conspiracy and tarnished the indigenous opposition with the suspicion of treasonous dealings with foreign enemies, justifying therefore the resort to repressive violence. It could be said to have been a major mistake of opposition activists, deluded by Western discourse of humanitarian intervention and international human rights, to solicit support from external powers in a region where the struggle against 'Western imperialism' remained so salient. Yet, in contrast to Libya, there was no regional or international consensus for intervention, for reasons which will be examined later.

When, during the second year of the uprising, the opposition realized non-violence would not dislodge the regime and that foreign intervention was not coming, regime opponents had to decide between armed struggle for total victory and a compromise political settlement. It decided on the former for several reasons. While the regime had conceded reforms, which, in principle, achieved demands the opposition had been making throughout the previous decade,[23] its failure to change its discourse that in essence the Syrian Uprising was a foreign conspiracy, and its continued use of violence made it impossible for anyone in the opposition to embrace these reforms without losing their credibility in the process. Besides the moral outrage at the killings perpetuated by the government and the belief of many that the government's offers of dialogue were not sincere, opposition activists believed that they could only be safe if the regime was totally destroyed since if it survived it would be certain to seek retribution. The regime, for its part, also believed that an opposition willing to call for intervention by Syria's historic enemies in the West was a fifth column that had to be eliminated. These dynamics gave the uprising a self-perpetuating momentum.

Red lines around the use of particular weapons systems were overstepped one by one: a spiral of violence leading from bullets to bombs and from snipers to sarin was set in motion. As civilians on both sides were targeted the security dilemma gave the conflict an additional dimension: each side, to feel secure, created armed groups that made all less secure.[24] Proponents of non-violent struggle were not only marginalized but also, like vast parts of the initially uninvolved civilian

---

[23] These reforms included the cancellation of the state of emergency, which had continued since 1963; several general amnesties; new laws covering the media, demonstrations, parties, and elections respectively; as well as drafting a new constitution, which was adopted after a referendum—with disputed fairness—in early 2012.

[24] Barry Posen, 'The Security Dilemma and Ethnic Conflict', *Survival*, 35/1 (Spring 1993), 27–47.

population, driven out of their homes, injured or killed, with many going into exile to escape the violence, leaving the field to the armed factions.

There were, to be sure, attempts to reverse the escalation of violence. Several external efforts were made by the Arab League and the UN, with Kofi Annan and then Lakhdar Brahimi serving as special envoys to Syria. Internally, third parties who tried to mediate were squeezed out, notably the traditional opposition organized in the National Coordination Committee (NCC), whose members were much older and more urban than younger demonstrators stemming from suburbs or the countryside. However, neither side was ready to negotiate. Any effort to do so would run up against the daunting reality that there were no reliable interlocutors on either side. In particular, the opposition was leaderless or lacked credible leaders, exactly because parts of it had given up on peaceful civil resistance; the regime's moderates such as Vice-President and former Minister of Foreign Affairs Farouq Sharaa and Presidential Adviser Bouthaina Shaaban, who spoke the language of reconciliation, seemed to lack power, which was in the hands of the hardliners, such as Maher al-Assad, the president's brother and commander of the elite 4th Armoured Division.[25]

Thus, even when it became apparent that there was no easy victory for either side without inflicting unacceptable costs on the whole society, no de-escalation took place. From the outset, the hardliners had dominated on both sides, each more interested in destroying the other than in a peaceful transition. The opposition, particularly the hard-line aggrieved expatriates amongst it, was prepared to challenge the vital interests of regime elites; the regime, also dominated by hardliners, resorted almost immediately to brutal and unnecessary coercion. Each side, unable to win at one level of conflict escalated the violence, only resulting, however, in stalemates which both then sought to break by means of further escalation, relying on resources provided by external backers. The polarizing policies followed by both sides marginalized the 'moderates' in both camps, preventing a transition pact. Nor could any third party break the cycle of escalation.

DISSECTING THE TURN TO SECTARIAN CIVIL WAR

The Vulnerabilities of a Fragmented Society

Syria's Uprising had not only turned increasingly violent but also, by its second year, had the clear features of a sectarian civil war. The descent into sectarian violence was, however, by no means inevitable and requires

---

[25] Peter Harling, 'Syria's Race against the Clock', *Foreign Policy*, 11 April 2011 http://mideast. foreignpolicy.com/posts/2011/04/11/syrias_race_against_the_clock.

explanation. Syria is, to be sure, a 'mosaic' society with a multitude of minorities that, in the 1980s, had experienced localized sectarian violence; it was also always potentially vulnerable to the spread across its borders of the 'disease' of sectarian violence that had afflicted Lebanon and Iraq in recent decades. For this very reason, however, Syria was thought to be immunized: the 1980s experience of the Muslim Brotherhood's revolt, which culminated in the Hama massacre of 1982, had made Syrians wary of political violence and many valued the regime-delivered stability that had spared them the fate of their neighbours. The minorities had been integrated into society to a substantial extent. Wieland recounts a widely accepted narrative of Syria as an island of civility amid violent sectarian conflict.[26] There were widespread norms of tolerance. Christians enjoyed greater freedoms, such as the right to build churches, than in other Muslim countries. Minorities fleeing sectarian violence in Iraq had largely been welcomed and integrated into Syrian society. The regime, in some ways a coalition of minorities, posed as protector of the latter and mediator between them and the Sunni majority.

To be sure, there were signs that all was not well. Sectarian mistrust was rife under the surface and, as a taboo subject, could not be faced and dealt with openly. The Ba'athist narrative of Arabism integrated the Arabic-speaking minorities but marginalized other identities. The privileges of the Alawite elites were resented by the Sunni majority, many of whom believed that sectarian connections governed access to opportunity. The decline of secular ideologies, including Arab nationalism and, after 1990, socialism, left an identity vacuum that was filled by religion, above all Sunni Islam, which in turn provoked a defensive, solidarity among the minorities, although many held to the unifying narrative of secularism. In parallel, money from the Gulf was funding a Salafist revival that would morph into jihadism under the conditions provided by the uprising. The regime appears to have retained a sense of how vulnerable the country was to sectarian fragmentation—though obviously playing with this risk (for example, by demonizing the initially peaceful opposition)—but many of the opposition youth appear to have been surprised at the Pandora's Box they inadvertently helped to open.

Sectarian Civil War as a Self-Fulfilling Regime Prophecy

Actors' choices provide a first, obvious explanation for the descent into sectarian violence. The regime, despite the high risks, deliberately sought to rally the solidarity of its minority base, particularly the Alawite-dominated security forces, by sectarianizing the issue, accusing the opposition of Islamist terrorism, and framing the alternatives as stability and social peace versus

---

[26] Wieland, *Syria: A Decade of Lost Chances*, 79–87.

jihadi violence. A particularly sectarian caste was imparted by the regime's recruitment and use of mostly Alawite militias, the so-called *shabiha*, made up primarily of violent thugs. The government's success in infusing the conflict with a strong sectarian dimension and, in turn, securing the support of those minorities that could expect retribution if the regime fell served only to mobilize further the majority Sunnis against it, especially in rural areas. At the same time, allegations of the kidnapping and killing of Alawites by Sunni Islamists increased as the Alawites, facing a security dilemma, were driven into solidarity with the regime and were seen to be complicit in its repressive actions.

The opposition initially sought to win over minorities with the rhetoric of civic inclusion. However, as the balance of power shifted to Islamist hard-liners, empowered by money and guns from the Gulf, parts of the opposition did adopt a (Sunni) sectarian identity. Their incentive to sectarianize the conflict increased, since, to the extent it became framed in sectarian terms, a regime of minorities would be vulnerable to the potential of the Sunni-led opposition to mobilize the Sunni majority community against the regime.[27]

Also driving sectarianization were international jihadists and al-Qaeda, who arrived on the scene because they saw a failing state as a perfect arena in which to recover the momentum they had lost when the Arab Spring made it appear that non-violent protests could produce democratic transitions. Some of these were veterans of the early 1980s armed Islamic insurgency in Syria, members of the radical 'Fighting Vanguard of the Islamic Revolution', who had, after the failure of their insurgency in Syria, morphed into transnational jihadists and travelled to Afghanistan, where their guerrilla skills were valued and where they played a role, with Egyptian counterparts, in the formation of al-Qaeda. One, Abu al-Mus'ab al-Suri, joined Bin Laden and became a theorist of decentralized transnational jihad. Then, a new generation of Syrian jihadists got their battle credentials in Iraq after their transit there had been facilitated by the Syrian regime in an effort to divert potential domestic opponents into jihad against the American occupation.[28] Now they flowed back into Syria and were joined by transnational contingents of jihadists from around the region and further afield, many generously funded and armed by Gulf donors. On Salafi and jihadi Internet networks, and on satellite TV including Saudi and Qatari stations, Gulf-funded preachers painted the Syrian struggle in sectarian terms. Thus, the regime prophecy of 'armed groups' came true with the militarization and sectarianization of the conflict. This phase of the uprising began in the summer of 2012, when the battles over Aleppo, particularly in the

---

[27] Of course, many Sunnis were secular, and hence would not normally mobilize on the basis of Sunni identity. This figure also included the Kurds (7–10% of the total population), whose separate ethnic identity overrode their Sunnism.

[28] Lefèvre, *Ashes of Hama*, 137–60.

Salaheddine neighbourhood of the city, drew increasing numbers of jihadist fighters.

Meanwhile, the processes that led to and fostered sectarian strife fed into an apparent drive for the establishment of 'sectarian-cleansed' regions secure from the threat of the 'other', raising the possibility of post-war fragmentation of Syrian territory along confessional lines. The battle for the town of Qusayr, meant to secure a link between the capital Damascus and the coastal region, which is predominantly inhabited by Alawites—together with rumours that several massacres, like those at Houla in spring 2012 or at Baida, near Baniyas, in spring 2013, were motivated by 'cleansing' of Sunni villages or neighbourhoods—suggested Assad aimed at consolidation of a rump state in western Syria. At the same time, allegations of the kidnapping and killing of Alawites by Sunni Islamists abounded. In parallel, Sunni Islamists consolidated control of eastern regions bordering Iraq and Jordan, and of northern regions bordering Turkey, raising the spectre of state boundaries being re-drawn along sectarian and/or ethnic lines. Thus, militarization and sectarianization proved to be mutually reinforcing.

THE INTERNATIONALIZATION OF THE CONFLICT

In parallel, a broader internationalization of the conflict took place, giving it greater durability than would otherwise probably have been the case. In the region, a new 'struggle for Syria', with high stakes for the whole regional balance of power, drew in Turkish, Saudi, and Qatari support for the opposition, which was countered by Iranian, Hezbollah, and Iraqi support for the regime, with increasingly sectarian discourses on both sides deepening sectarian animosity at all levels of Syrian society.

At the same time, Western countries, some of which had long been engaged in democracy promotion in the Middle East, as well as a majority of Arab countries, took a stance against regime repression. In April 2011 Western powers implemented, and later expanded, sanctions against Syrian institutions and regime officials, criticized Assad's hard line against the protesters, and, in time, urged him to step down from the presidency. At the same time, Russia, and to a lesser degree China, supported the regime, and vetoed some UN Security Council resolutions critical of the Syrian regime, justifying their stance as a defence of Syria's sovereignty against external meddling. These external involvements, each blocking the other, not only contributed to a stalemate in the conflict but also helped fuel the fight, through the resources they supplied to the warring sides, or even—as in the case of the opposition, which got most of its weapons through the Arab Gulf states—changed its direction in the favour of hardliners. Moreover, the national, regional, and international links in the Syrian conflict made it harder to constrain and abate than a civil war with fewer cross-border alliances.

The sectarianization of the civil war tended to shift the international narrative away from a conflict involving democratization and sovereignty. Especially given rising levels of jihadist involvement, the West became less concerned with the 'responsibility to protect' principle than with the 'international war on terror'. Paradoxically, Western states' fear of increasing jihadism indirectly contributed to its rapid spread: as Western powers declined to deliver lethal aid to the Syrian opposition, rebel fighters saw themselves increasingly dependent on Islamist or jihadist sources of funding and equipment. This facilitated the sectarian turn of the uprising and further sidelined advocates of cross-sectarian, non-violent protests. Both local and externally based opposition groups, such as the Syrian National Coalition, saw themselves caught in a dilemma: either they declined radical Islamist sources of funding and thus were not able to provide defence provisions for the Syrian people; or they procured supplies from such sources and thus became vulnerable to accusations of furthering sectarian strife. Different sections of the opposition arrived at different decisions in this dilemma, thus further splitting the armed opposition into those accepting and those declining foreign allies with a religious agenda. These cleavages helped to reinforce and perpetuate the civil war, as the opposition increasingly fragmented into often feuding groups, competing for arms and money and promoting rival ideological agendas.

A new layer of external intervention was precipitated when a large-scale chemical attack on the suburbs of Damascus in autumn 2013 almost led to military intervention by the USA, Britain, and France, but then made such an intervention all the more distant an option. A deal brokered by Russia and the USA and implemented by the Organisation for the Prohibition of Chemical Weapons (OPCW) stipulated that Syria hand over its chemical arsenal and have it destroyed; this meant that Assad gained credibility as an international negotiating partner.

Paradoxically, over the course of the uprising, while the regime at first lost legitimacy as it used excessive violence to quell resistance, it later regained a degree of credibility (but not legitimacy) because its narrative of an armed and extremist foreign-backed opposition—which had been a rather baseless accusation at the time Assad first mentioned it publicly in March 2011—slowly became a reality. Thus, some credence was acquired by Assad's warning that Syria was 'the fault line in the Middle East [that] ... when you play with it, you will have [an] earthquake that is going to affect the whole region'.[29]

---

[29] 'Interview with Bashar al-Assad', *ABC News*, 7 December 2011.

NON-VIOLENT RESISTANCE BETWEEN
REGIME AND ISLAMIC STATE

When peaceful protesters decided to take up arms to defend themselves and—as they hoped—increase their leverage, their struggle instead forfeited its main advantage—that is, its peaceful character, through its escalation into an armed and increasingly sectarian civil war. Yet, it would be premature to dismiss the enduring and long-term effects of the peaceful resistance and activism for Syria's future. It would be equally premature to dismiss the role that non-violent organizations may be destined to play once the fighting comes to a halt. The uprising gave rise to an extensive network of *tansiqiyat* or Local Coordination Committees (LCCs), composed chiefly of self-selected local activists who may never have previously been involved in political activity. The committees served as mechanisms of mobilization—for example, inviting individuals to protest at a specific time and place. Many of the members of these early committees were identified by the government and arrested. By July 2012 those members with the most advanced survival skills had managed to perpetuate approximately eighty-three coordination committees. They had no specific leadership and operated in what might be described as a fluid virtual/actual sphere. There were several attempts to bring together these committees under some kind of umbrella—including the Union of the Syrian Uprising Coordination Committees, the Syrian Revolution General Commission, and the Local Coordination Committees—to synchronize some of their activities.

Peaceful activism continued in parallel with violent uprising. Even as the uprising morphed into a violent civil war, non-violent protesters still tried to tip the balance against the regime in urban areas that had remained under regime control. In December 2011 and January 2012 activists mounted *Idrab al karama*—'dignity' general strikes and coordinated sit-ins—although these failed to reach a critical mass or to drive a wedge between the regime and its supporters.[30] Alawite activists made behind-the-scenes efforts at conflict resolution among Alawite and Sunni villages and city neighbourhoods. The Syrian Revolutionary Youth group, active in Homs and Damascus, was launched in May 2012 to rebut claims that the military struggle had marginalized peaceful protests. Certainly, this powerful tradition of activism, manifest at its height in the millions of people in the streets in scores of towns and cities across the country, will not be easily reversed by any subsequent regime. Sinjab noted an unprecedented sense of solidarity as people shared homes, clothes, and food amid the millions displaced by the fighting.[31] The sense of freedom was

---

[30] Donatella Della Ratta, 'Syria: The Virtue of Civil Disobedience', Al Jazeera, 6 April 2012 http://www.aljazeera.com/indepth/opinion/2012/04/20124283638298672.html.
[31] Lina Sinjab, 'Syria Conflict: From Peaceful Protest to Civil War', *BBC News*, 15 March 2013 http://www.bbc.co.uk/news/world-middle-east-21797661.

Figure 9.2. The Syrian Uprising more than any other in the Arab Spring was marked by a devastating toll of civilian death and injury. Here in Aleppo on 14 September 2012 a man runs past sniper fire near a checkpoint manned by the Free Syrian Army.
© *Marco Longari/AFP/Getty Images*

palpable, with more than thirty new online publications promoting democracy, despite the crackdown.

Also, the uprising, in removing or weakening the highly intrusive hand of the government, which had never had much tolerance for any aspect of civil society it could not control, spurred and unleashed citizen associations. As government services and security broke down in many areas, local neighbourhoods organized an alternative local governance set-up, including self-defence groups, an underground clinic system, schools, media, and transportation services. With the intensification of the armed conflict, local committees became active in humanitarian relief. For a while some managed to preserve their civility, openness, and accountability before, increasingly, Islamist and jihadist groups proved they were also capable of providing these services (see Figure 9.2).[32]

After mid-2012, once the regime had lost total control over wide parts of the north and east of the country, the external-led opposition attempted to set up new institutions to replace defunct regime ones. According to Baczko et al., these included new municipal and district councils in charge of health and education; courts, made up of fighters, clerics, and 'free' lawyers, and a

---

[32] Anand Gopal, 'Welcome to Free Syria: Meeting the Rebel Government of an Embattled Country', *Harper's Magazine* (August 2012) http://harpers.org/archive/2012/08/welcome-to-free-syria/.

substitute police force.[33] Later, at the governorate level, councils were established to link local communities to the externally based Syrian National Council (SNC, founded in August 2011 in Istanbul) and the Syrian National Coalition (founded in November 2012 in Doha), which used their foreign funding to establish client links with 'liberated' territory.

Yet these networks were contested. In some places government civil servants and teachers continued to be paid by Damascus, allowing dual or overlapping service networks. As the opposition fragmented, groups under no unified command and not accountable to any civilian political body proliferated and increasingly morphed into warlord-led factions living off a war economy. Elsewhere, rival networks were established that did not recognize the mainstream opposition leadership. The al-Qaeda-inspired Jabhat al-Nusra, which had assumed a leading role in the fighting on the ground, established control in Raqqa and managed the supply of flour and fuel in the north and east, while the Democratic Unionist Party (PYD), the Syrian affiliate of the radical anti-Turkish Kurdish party, the PKK, took over in Syria's Kurdish areas after regime forces had withdrawn from them. Before long, opposition groups were fighting each other as much as the regime, fragmenting governance in the opposition-controlled territories.

As the uprising took on the form of armed struggle, with increasing sectarian overtones, those advocating continued non-violent resistance were caught between the 'for us' or 'against us' mentalities of both sides. As one activist stated: 'Now everyone in Syria is armed, and weapons bring out the worst in people.... Weapons and power are addictive.' With the armed conflict in numerous cities, predatory practices, criminal activity, and warlordism became commonplace. In reaction, a grass-roots youth campaign, 'Syria First', proclaimed a 'revolution within the revolution' that attempted to defend what its activists considered the core values of the revolution, dignity and freedom for all citizens, regardless of sect. They condemned not only regime repression but also the excesses of the rebels, and assumed the mission of monitoring the revolution to keep it on the right path and work against new forms of repressive power in liberated areas. This brought them into clashes with Jabhat al-Nusra, which was intolerant of these moderate voices within the opposition.[34]

The rise of IS (formerly known as ISIS, Islamic State in Iraq and al-Sham region) was symptomatic of the declining space for non-violent civil activism

---

[33] Adam Baczko, Gilles Dorronsoro, and Arthur Quesnay, *Building a Syrian State in a Time of Civil War*, Carnegie Endowment for International Peace, 16 April 2013 http://carnegieendowment.org/2013/04/16/building-syrian-state-in-time-of-civil-war/fzrk.

[34] Line Zouhour, 'Whither the Peaceful Movement in Syria?', *Jadaliyya*, 18 March 2013 www.jadaliyya.com/pages/index/10616/whither-the-peaceful-movement-in-syria; Serene Assir, 'Activists Struggle to be Heard amid Roar of Syria Violence', *Daily Star*, Beirut, 30 October 2012 http://www.dailystar.com.lb/News/Middle-East/2012/Oct-30/193205-activists-struggle-to-be-heard-amid-roar-of-syria-violence.ashx.

in Syria. It was partly a response to the militarization and sectarianization of the conflict initiated by the regime, and partly a function of the vacuum left by state failure in Syria and Iraq. Other contributing causes were the deployment of sectarian identities in the regional power struggle by, notably, Turkey, Iran, and the Gulf Arab monarchies; the security dilemma that enhanced in-group solidarity at the grass-roots level; and the war economy, wherein IS showed its great capacity to use plundered state resources and external support to provide services or pay recruits. The attraction of IS for non-Syrian Muslims from around the world demonstrated an increased global credibility of jihadist discourse, partly provoked by the Syrian crisis. The rise of IS was paralleled by a counter-mobilization of Shi'a groups on the side of the Syrian regime, not only Hezbollah, but also Iraqi Shi'a fighters, further sectarianizing the conflict. IS assaults on minorities deepened sectarianization and increased the adhesion of the latter to the Assad regime, although some of the regime's failures effectively to counter IS attacks undermined their faith in its ability to protect them. Assad's international standing benefited from the priority given by the US-led coalition to fighting IS, a war in which Iran and the Syrian regime were inevitably tacit allies of the West.

The result was further to squeeze out both secularists and moderate Islamists who were committed to non-violence, with many exiting Syria or else joining more militant Islamist groups, many of which were gradually absorbed by IS and al-Qaeda avatar Jabhat al-Nusra. Non-violent resistance depends on a modicum of social order and tolerance of dissent, and the militia-ization of both sides of the regime–opposition divide left little room for overt peaceful opposition. Of the original peaceful opposition groups in the regime controlled areas, only the barely tolerated National Coordinating Committee of leftist and Kurdish parties remained semi-active inside the country, participating notably in the early 2015 Cairo and Moscow conferences exploring a negotiated settlement. In non-regime controlled areas, ISIS represented a counter-state that eschewed both civility and non-violence. With the two main armed statelike contenders being the regime and IS, the chances of a democratic reconstruction of Syria dwindled. Any national-level political settlement would face the challenge not only of incorporating the remnants of regime institutions and disparate opposition networks into a transitional regime but also, at the same time, defeating IS's rival state-building project.

CONCLUSION

The Syrian Uprising began, similarly to its immediate precursors in Tunisia and Egypt, with non-violent civil resistance. Syrian civil resistance was strong enough to bring about massive protests that the regime could not quickly suppress and that put it very much on the defensive. Yet, while civil resistance withstood militarization and sectarianization for a remarkably long time, it did not stimulate a transition to a more politically inclusive political order and led instead to the partial collapse of the country into mutually exclusive and contested zones of control. The non-violent struggle was gradually undermined by the Syrian regime's disproportionate use of force, by its self-fulfilling sectarian rhetoric, and by the opposition's turn to armed struggle. As in Tunisia and Egypt, this opened the door to competing forces, in this case, trans-state radical Islamists, to 'steal' the putative democratic revolution even while it was still underway. Although, four years after the uprising began in March 2011, the outcome is still open, the spiral of violence and sectarian strife is certain to leave an immense long-term negative legacy for Syria and its people.

The Syrian experience suggests that the conditions and mechanisms by which non-violent resistance can lead to peaceful political change, avoiding both extreme repression and extreme disorder, are under-theorized. First, the claim of the civil resistance paradigm that non-violent resistance can lead elites to concede political reform because, unlike violent rebellion, it does not threaten the lives or well-being of members of the target regime is contestable. Peaceful resistance is, after all, an instrument in a struggle for power that may well threaten not only the vital interests of ruling elites but also wider social forces, especially when massive scale protests adopt maximalist demands for the overthrow of the regime, as happened in Syria.

That non-violent resistance can put regimes under intense pressure is incontestable, but the paradigm does not tell us how they can be brought to allow a peaceful transition to a more inclusive political order rather than responding with violent repression. In this respect, the transition paradigm's coalition between soft-liners in the regime and opposition combining to marginalize the hardliner is part of the answer; where this obtains, the outcome can be the departure of authoritarian leaders with a minimum of bloodshed, as happened in Egypt and Tunisia in 2011. The peaceful resistance paradigm argues that this depends on the opposition remaining non-violent. The transition paradigm tells us this happens if the moderates marginalize the hardliners on *both* sides, and each side accepts the legitimacy of the other; if hardliners remain dominant, however, transition fails, with the outcome being authoritarian resilience, violent revolution, or a collapse into civil war.

In the Syrian case, the soft-liners were marginalized on both sides by the regime's use of violence but also by the maximalist demands of the opposition. In this respect, several analysts argued that the mistake of the Syrian protest movement was its 'rush to confrontation' with the regime prior to the latter's thorough ideological de-legitimation.[35] While al-Assad's regime was de-legitimized among a significant part of the population, for others its Arab nationalist legitimacy and promotion of the interests of the new urban middle and upper classes gave its discourse some credibility among at least a third of society. Yet, the hardline opposition insisted on the fall of the regime. Under these conditions, the soft-liners in the regime were unlikely to marginalize the hardliners.

Nevertheless, based on the assumption that non-violent protest is *qualitatively different* from violent rebellion, Stephan and Chenoweth argue that, *even if* the regime refuses protesters' demands and uses violence against them, this is likely to *backfire*, stimulating wider anti-regime mobilization, precipitating international sanctions and support for the opposition, and, most importantly, causing defections in the security forces, which will be reluctant to use violence against fellow citizens who are not themselves using violence. Yet, according to their own statistical evidence, resistance methods have *insignificant* effects on security force defections, and regime violence has *no statistical impact* on the outcome of non-violent resistance, suggesting that *regime violence may not backfire*.[36] It might not if the regime has some legitimacy and can discredit the opposition (for example, if it allegedly collaborates with foreign enemies) or if society is so polarized that the opposition can be constructed as the 'other', not part of 'us', among the regime's constituency.

In Syria's case, the regime's use of lethal force against non-violent protesters *did* alienate wide swathes of the public. For others, however, the regime's claim to defend order against the disruption unleashed by the uprising may not have legitimized its violence but did cause a significant segment of Syrians to acquiesce in it as the lesser of two evils. This was all the more the case once radical Islamists, and especially al-Qaeda-linked jihadists, assumed a high profile within the opposition and as the opposition itself fragmented into warring camps. Moreover, while regime violence did escalate protests to the numbers claimed by Stephan and Chenoweth to be enough to prevail and did precipitate some defections from the security forces, these were not enough to cause regime collapse and rather led to the militarization of the opposition and civil war. This suggests that a blind spot in studies of non-violent resistance may be their failure sufficiently to differentiate *kinds* of authoritarianism, and, in particular, to take into account those that are capable of surviving significant defections within the army and the executive without disintegrating in the process. In particular, states constructed in fragmented societies around a

---

[35] Stephen Zunes and Jack DuVall, 'Ruthless Regimes not Impervious to Civil Resistance: A Reply to Maged Mandour', openDemocracy, 1 November 2013 www.opendemocracy.net/civil resistance/stephen-zunes-jack-duvall/ruthless-regimes-not-impervious-to-civil-resistance-reply-; Maged Mandour, 'Beyond Civil Resistance: The Case of Syria', openDemocracy, 26 October 2013 www. opendemocracy.net/arab-awakening/maged-mandour/beyond-civil-resistance-case-of-syria.

[36] Stephan and Chenoweth, 'Why Civil Resistance Works', 20–1.

cohesive communal and armed core may be far less susceptible to non-violent resistance regardless of its magnitude and duration.

The lessons of Syria suggest that the belief of advocates of non-violent resistance that once enough anti-regime protesters have been mobilized they are likely to prevail over regimes seems over-optimistic. In Syria, civil resistance not only failed to achieve its initial objectives despite mass mobilization, but also set in motion a scenario under which it became highly unlikely that either the regime or the opposition could assert full control over all of Syria, resulting in a failed state and vast refugee flows: by mid-2015, some 4 million of its 2010 population of 21.5 million had left Syria, posing a major challenge to countries in the region and then also to the European Union's members. Syria's experience, therefore, points to the need for more appreciation among the advocates and practitioners of civil resistance of the complex requisites of success and, if these do not obtain, its potentially high costs in fragmented societies where the security dilemma is liable to be unleashed by any break-down in order. The civil resistance model assumes low costs because it imagines a robust society confronting a vulnerable and isolated regime; where the opposite is the case, as in Syria, the costs may well be exorbitant—for both sides.

10

Palestine and the Arab Uprisings

Wendy Pearlman

Would the Arab Spring spark a 'Palestinian Spring' or 'Third Intifada'? As a revolutionary wave swept through other countries in the Middle East and North Africa in 2011, many commentators speculated about whether it would reach the Palestinian territories as well. Though other uprisings targeted domestic despots rather than foreign occupation, the values and sentiments that animated them—calls for freedom, justice, and dignity, as well as a sense of being fed up with a status quo that seemed both intolerable and unending— echoed those of the Palestinian struggle. Palestinians strongly identified with their brethren who took to the streets elsewhere in the Arab world. A March 2011 poll found that 92 per cent of Palestinians described themselves as sympathetic with demonstrators in Tunisia, Egypt, and Libya.[1]

Some outside observers and Palestinians themselves judged that a new Palestinian uprising was imminent.[2] Advisers to the Israeli prime minister, comparing conditions in the Palestinian territories to those preceding prior intifadas, came to similar conclusions.[3] This chapter explores why this new Palestinian uprising did not occur then. It sets this exploration in its historical context. Though their use of armed means has often gained more attention, Palestinians' tradition of engagement in non-violent resistance is as long as

---

[1] Palestinian Center for Policy and Survey Research (PSR), *Poll No. 39*, 17–19 March 2011, p. 19 http://www.pcpsr.org/en/node/214.

[2] Nathan Thrall, 'The Third Intifada Is Inevitable', *New York Times*, 22 June 2012 www.nytimes.com/2012/06/24/opinion/sunday/the-third-intifada-is-inevitable.html; Gideon Levy, 'The Specter of a Third Intifada', *Haaretz*, 29 September 2012 www.haaretz.com/weekend/twilight-zone/the-specter-of-a-third-intifada-1.467279; Nassif Hitti, 'Is This a Palestinian Spring, or a Coming Third Intifada?', *Al-Monitor*, 3 October 2012 http://www.al-monitor.com/pulse/politics/2012/10/new-palestinian-intifada.html.

[3] Amir Oren, 'Israel's Settlement Policy Could Trigger a Third Intifada, Experts Warn Netanyahu', *Haaretz*, 10 June 2012 www.haaretz.com/print-edition/news/israel-s-settlement-policy-could-trigger-a-third-intifada-experts-warn-netanyahu.premium-1.435377.

their struggle for self-determination itself.[4] No understanding of Palestinians' response to the Arab Spring is complete without taking this past into account.

A SHORT HISTORY OF PALESTINIAN CIVIL RESISTANCE

Many Palestinians would say that their lives since the 1948 war, which created the state of Israel and resulted in Palestinians' dispersion and statelessness, has been one in which everyday life is a form of civil resistance. This is captured in the concept of *sumud*, or steadfastness. *Sumud* refers to Palestinians' struggles, despite the odds, to maintain a presence on the land of their ancestors, empower local communities, and sustain the vibrancy of their national identity, culture, traditions, folklore, and collective memory. Apart from ongoing and everyday forms of resistance, the Palestinian national movement has also given rise to dramatic shows of mass defiance more akin to the uprisings that shook the Arab world in 2010–11. Three major popular revolts stand as landmarks in Palestinian national history.

The first was directed against the British Mandate in Palestine and its commitment to the 1917 Balfour Declaration in which the British government endorsed the establishment in Palestine of a Jewish national home. Representing the approximately 90 per cent of the Palestinian population that was Muslim and Christian Arab, a leadership of traditional Arab notables undertook political and non-violent means to protest against what they understood as a violation of their own national rights. Their petitions, delegations, speeches, articles, leaflets, and episodic demonstrations failed to forestall Jewish immigration, land purchases, and institutional development.[5] Grass-roots frustration with the failure of such strategies fuelled violent riots in 1920, 1921, and 1929.

By the 1930s, several developments increased prospects for mass rebellion. On the one hand, expansion of education, urbanization, print culture, and professional and social associations enhanced Arabs' political awareness and tools for mobilization.[6] On the other, rising Jewish immigration and land purchases indicated the advance of the Jewish national project on the ground. Nationalist achievements in neighbouring countries stirred Palestinian Arab

[4] See, inter alia, Mary E. King, *A Quiet Revolution: The First Palestinian Intifada and Nonviolent Resistance* (New York: Nation Books, 2007); Maxine Kaufman-Lacusta, *Refusing to be Enemies: Palestinian and Israeli Nonviolent Resistance to the Israeli Occupation* (Reading: Ithaca Press, 2011); Wendy Pearlman, *Violence, Nonviolence, and the Palestinian National Movement* (New York: Cambridge University Press, 2011); Mazin B. Qumsiyeh, *Popular Resistance in Palestine: A History of Hope and Empowerment* (London: Pluto Press, 2011).

[5] Yehoshua Porath, 'The Political Organization of the Palestinian Arabs under the British Mandate', in Moshe Ma'oz (ed.), *Palestinian Arab Politics* (Jerusalem: Jerusalem Academic Press, 1975), 1–20; Ann Mosely Lesch, *Arab Politics in Palestine, 1917–1939: The Frustration of a Nationalist Movement* (Ithaca, NY, and London: Cornell University, 1977), ch. 4.

[6] Lesch, *Arab Politics*, 61–4, 106–8.

opinion, as did frustration with infighting and self-interest among aristocratic leaders. In 1935 the discovery of ammunition smuggled to a Jewish business-man heightened suspicions that the Jewish community was preparing for war. A Muslim preacher named Shaykh Iz al-Din al-Qassam called for armed struggle, and his death in battle against British troops inspired an outpouring of sympathy. Meanwhile, Arab elites' last hope for political resistance against a seemingly imminent Jewish state, a proposal for a legislative council encom-passing all of Palestine's inhabitants, was rejected by Britain's Parliament.[7]

Palestinian Arab society was gripped by the sense that they were soon to be made strangers in their own homeland. In April 1936 a roadside incident provided the spark channelling that sentiment into what became the three-year 'Grand Arab Rebellion'. Arab gunmen stopped a car and shot Jewish travellers, and a Jewish paramilitary responded by shooting two Arabs. As rumours spread, Arabs rioted and attacked Jews. Arab activist professionals and merchants in major towns used the tension as a springboard for the organization of a grass-roots protest effort. They called public meetings, formed popular committees, and announced the commencement of a general strike.[8] These nationalists sought to seize the momentum to mobilize more radical opposition to British policies, yet also to obtain a measure of discipline to prevent events from spilling out of control.[9] Within days, committees had emerged throughout the country. A countrywide general strike took hold, and the press responded with praise and calls for national unity behind the protest.

As the rebellion cascaded across the country, different sectors of society participated, using non-violent means at their disposal.[10] The Arab Car Owners' and Drivers' Association halted transport facilities, merchants and city labourers stayed home, prisoners refused to perform penal labour, and schools and factories closed. People participated in public demonstrations and boycotted Jewish firms and products. Boy scouts and urban young men enforced compliance with the strike and boycott at the neighbourhood level. Although Arab civil servants did not go on strike, they donated a percentage of their salaries and submitted a memorandum to the government explaining Arab grievances and claims. Intellectuals demanded 'no taxation without

---

[7] Yehoshua Porath, *The Palestinian–Arab National Movement, from Riots to Rebellion 1929–1939* (London: Cass, 1977), 157–8.

[8] Akram Zu'aytir, *Yawmiyat Akram Zu'aytir: Al-harakah al-wataniyah al-Filastiniyah, 1935–1939* ('Diary of Akram Zu'aytir: The Palestinian National Struggle, 1935–1939') (Beirut: Institute of Palestine Studies, 1980), 60–1.

[9] Lesch, *Arab Politics*, 217.

[10] For details, see Porath, *Palestinian–Arab National Movement*, 166–73; Muhammad 'Izzat Darwazah, *Mudhakkirat Muhammad 'Izzat Darwazah, 1305 H–1404/1887 M–1984: Sijill hafil bi-masirat al-harakah al-'Arabiyah wa al-qadiyah al-Filastiniyah khilala qarn min al-zaman* ('Autobiography of Muhammad 'Izzat Darwazah: Registrations alongside Arab Movements and the Palestinian Cause over a Century of History'), ii (Beirut: Dar al-Gharb al-Islami, 1993), 20–2.

representation'. The strike appeared to inspire a new popular unity among the Palestinian Arab population.[11] This pushed hesitant elite politicians to form a coalition leadership body to lead the strike. They announced that protest would continue until the government established a representative national government in Palestine, ended Jewish immigration, and banned the transfer of land from Arabs to Jews.

Although the 1936 strike marked a new achievement in civil resistance, some participation was coerced, and the strike was also accompanied by violence. Arabs carried out dozens of attacks on Jewish people and property, which increased as Britain refused to accommodate the strike's demands. The government sought to quell the rebellion with countermeasures that included the deportation and arrest of Arab activists, search and arrest without warrant, imposition of collective fines and curfew, and demolition of entire neighbour-hoods.[12] As authorities cracked down, popular participation in civic protest receded, and bands of armed rebels formed in the countryside to carry out sniping and sabotage.[13] After six months the Arab leadership called off the strike, and the rebellion entered a hiatus. It resumed in autumn 1937 in reaction to the British Peel Commission's recommendation to partition Palestine. The second phase of rebellion was a more dramatically and exclusively violent battle between rebel bands and British troops. An estimated 5,000 Palestinian Arabs were killed, many in internecine fighting, before the revolt was defeated in 1939.[14]

In 1947 Britain announced the end of the Mandate. The Arab–Israeli War of 1948–9 ended in the establishment of the State of Israel and Palestinians' dispersion under different state powers. Israel's capture of the West Bank and Gaza in the 1967 war and subsequent annexation of Jerusalem spurred protest manifestos and strikes.[15] In the years that followed, Israel curtailed Palestinian nationalist activism through means of both repression and co-optation. The movement's centre of gravity solidified with the Palestine Liberation Organization (PLO) in exile.

Still, nationalist activity was never dormant in the Occupied Territories. The 1970s and 1980s saw the increasing transformation of the peasantry into a

---

[11] Robert John and Sami Hadawi, *The Palestine Diary*, i (Beirut: Palestine Research Center, 1970), 259.

[12] Matthew Hughes, 'From Law and Order to Pacification: Britain's Suppression of the Arab Revolt in Palestine, 1936–39', *Journal of Palestine Studies*, 39/2 (Winter 2010), 6–22.

[13] Yuval Arnon-Ohanna, 'The Bands in the Palestinian Arab Revolt, 1936–1939: Structure and Organization', *Asian and African Studies*, 15/2 (July 1981), 230–3.

[14] Walid Khalidi (ed.), *From Haven to Conquest: The Origins and the Development of the Palestine Problem* (Beirut: Institute for Palestine Studies, 1971), 848–9.

[15] Ann Mosley Lesch, *Political Perceptions of the Palestinians on the West Bank and the Gaza Strip* (Washington: Middle East Institute, 1980), 32; Ibrahim Dakkak, 'Back to Square One: A Study in the Re-Emergence of the Palestinian Identity in the West Bank, 1967–1980', in Alexander Scholch (ed.), *Palestinians over the Green Line: Studies on the Relations between Palestinians on Both Sides of the 1949 Armistice Line since 1967* (London: Ithaca Press, 1983), 70–3; Emile Sahliyeh, *In Search of Leadership: West Bank Politics since 1967* (Washington: Brookings Institution, 1988), 22–4.

working class, the opening of new universities, and the spread of underground political factions and mass organizations. As in the 1930s, these developments politicized new sectors of society and created an organizational infrastructure for mass action.[16] Still, the Israeli occupation entered its twentieth year with no end in sight. As economic downturn compounded daily hardships, confrontations between Palestinian civilians and Israeli soldiers increased. In December 1987 an Israeli truck collided with labourers from Gaza, leaving dead and injured. Riots ensued, and the Israeli army's violent response helped them spread across the Gaza Strip and West Bank. Palestinians dubbed the unrest an 'intifada', literally a 'shaking-off' of the occupation.

The intifada became a popular uprising in which people of all walks of life sought 'to create a daily series of acts of defiance'.[17] An underground coalition leadership formed to direct the uprising with instructions and encouragement communicated in leaflets distributed in secret. Popular committees formed to implement these directives and organize protest at the local level. These bodies urged tactics that spanned all of Gene Sharp's categories of non-violent protest—namely, the expression of opposition, non-cooperation with authorities, and concerted intervention.[18] Palestinians took part in street demonstrations, defied soldiers on the streets, plastered walls with political graffiti, and displayed banned nationalist symbols such as the Palestinian flag. Youth erected barricades behind which they declared their communities to be liberated zones. Merchants carried out a commercial strike by shutting their doors on designated days and times, thereby setting the rhythm of daily life in sync with the uprising.

Non-violent protest evolved to disengagement, including the boycott of Israeli goods and services and the expansion of local manufacturing and food production in the quest for self-sufficiency.[19] Palestinians tried to minimize their dealings with the Israeli Civil Administration, even though it had come to govern all aspects of life. Public employees resigned en masse, and some residents forwent applying for the licences and permits requisite for an array of essential tasks, sometimes at tremendous personal and financial cost. Families withdrew deposits from Israeli banks and complied with periodic

---

[16] Joost Hiltermann, *Behind the Intifada: Labor and Women's Movements in the Occupied Territories* (Princeton: Princeton University Press, 1991); Glenn E. Robinson, *Building a Palestinian State: The Incomplete Revolution* (Bloomington, IN: Indiana University Press, 1997).

[17] Laetitia Bucaille, *Growing up Palestinian: Israeli Occupation and the Intifada Generation*, trans. Anthony Roberts (Princeton: Princeton University Press, 2004), 18.

[18] Gene Sharp, *The Politics of Nonviolent Action* (Boston, MA: Porter Sargent, 1973).

[19] Zachary Lockman and Joel Beinin (eds), *Intifada: The Palestinian Uprising against Israeli Occupation* (Boston and Washington: Middle East Research and Information Project and South End Press, 1989); Ze'ev Schiff and Ehud Ya'ari, *Intifada: The Palestinian Uprising: Israel's Third Front*, trans. Ina Friedman (New York: Touchstone, 1989); Don Peretz, *Intifada: The Palestinian Uprising* (Boulder, CO: Westview Press, 1990); Jamal R. Nassar and Roger Heacock (eds), Intifada: *Palestine at the Crossroads* (New York: Praeger, 1990); Andrew Rigby, *Living the Intifada* (London: Zed Books, 1991); King, *A Quiet Revolution*.

strikes on labour in Israel. Some refused to pay taxes and fines or to carry Israeli-issued identity cards.

The underground leadership did not rule out the torching of Israeli cars or the throwing of stones and Molotov cocktails. However, Mary King calculates more than 90 per cent of its appeals during the first eighteen months of the uprising encouraged specific non-violent actions.[20] It largely eschewed fire-arms, and the public overwhelmingly backed this strategy.[21] Caches were hidden among the Palestinians, and families possessed light weapons in the thousands.[22] Thus, the upholding of civil resistance rather than armed resist-ance was a result of choice and consensus as much as non-availability.[23]

The scale of the First Intifada was unprecedented in Palestinian history. The Israeli army registered 187,435 incidents of unarmed protest in the West Bank and Gaza Strip between 1987 and 1992, in addition to 904 shooting inci-dents.[24] Though some social sectors played more prominent roles than others,[25] the uprising was distinguished by participation across cleavages of geography and class, as well as by those who had not typically taken part in protest.[26] With this mass character as its main source of strength, the uprising resulted in important achievements. It moved Israelis to debate withdrawal from the Palestinian territories,[27] encouraged the PLO to declare an inde-pendent state of Palestine next to Israel in 1988, and helped to bring about Palestinian attendance at the 1991 Madrid international peace conference.

Nonetheless, the failure of subsequent peace talks to yield results enervated a civil uprising that had already exacted an enormous toll. By the end of 1988, the intifada had claimed 12 Israeli lives, in comparison to 332 Palestinians ones.[28] Israel used bullets, beatings, and tear gas to disperse

---

[20] King, *A Quiet Revolution*, 257–8.

[21] Joe Stork, 'The Significance of Stones: Notes from the Seventh Month', in Lockman and Beinin (eds), *Intifada: The Palestinian Uprising against Israeli Occupation*, 74.

[22] Schiff and Ya'ari, *Intifada: The Palestinian Uprising*, 31; Aryeh Shalev, *The Intifada: Causes and Effects* (Tel Aviv: Jaffee Center for Strategic Studies, Jerusalem Post and Westview Press, 1991), 76; Jerusalem Media and Communication Centre (hereafter cited as JMCC), *The Stone and the Olive Branch: Four Years of the Intifada: From Jabalia to Madrid* (Jerusalem: JMCC, 1991), 19.

[23] Souad Rashed Dajani, *The Intifada* (Amman: University of Jordan Center for Hebraic Studies, 1990), 73; Stork, 'The Significance of Stones', 74.

[24] Pearlman, *Violence, Nonviolence*, 106.

[25] Salim Tamari, 'Limited Rebellion and Civil Society: The Uprising's Dilemma', *Middle East Report*, 164–5 (May–August 1990), 5.

[26] Rashid Khalidi, 'The Palestinian People: Twenty-Two Years after 1967', in Lockman and Beinin, *Intifada: The Palestinian Uprising against Israeli Occupation*, 117–18.

[27] Eitan Y. Alimi, *Israeli Politics and the Palestinian Intifada: Political Opportunities, Framing Processes, and Contentious Politics* (London and New York: Routledge, 2006), ch. 5.

[28] B'Tselem (The Israeli Center for Human Rights in the Occupied Territories), 'Statistics: Fatalities in the First Intifada', B'Tselem, Jerusalem, undated www.btselem.org/statistics/first_intifada_tables.

demonstrations. It also detained some 50,000 Palestinians,[29] and carried out deportations, curfews, closures of schools, and threats to confiscate businesses.[30] As months became years and occupation remained, power struggles intensified between Palestinian political factions and within them. A measure of political parity between Palestinians inside the territories and the PLO leadership in exile gave way to the resurgent domination of the latter.[31] As many Palestinians withdrew in exhaustion, masked men appeared on the streets, militias engaged in gun battles, and attacks on Israelis multiplied.

The 1993 disclosure of a PLO–Israeli agreement ushered in the Oslo peace process. The Palestinian Authority (PA) became a self-governing apparatus in parts of the West Bank and Gaza Strip from which Israel redeployed. Yet seven years of negotiations failed the hopes of Israelis and Palestinians alike. Israel faced traumatic attacks unlike ever before when Palestinian critics of Oslo initiated suicide bombings targeting civilians. Palestinians saw the prospects of independence wane as Israeli checkpoints and settlement expansion fragmented the territory of a future Palestinian state.

Against this backdrop, in September 2000 Palestinians launched what became known as the Second Intifada. Demonstrations began in Jerusalem and areas where Palestinian territory bordered Israeli military deployments in the West Bank and Gaza Strip. Palestinians threw rocks and Molotov cocktails at Israeli soldiers, who responded with tear gas, rubber bullets, and live ammunition. In the first days of unrest alone, Israeli troops reportedly fired a million shots—what a security official later dubbed 'a bullet for every child'.[32] Palestinian gunfire was confirmed on the fourth day, when PA policemen stationed at demonstrations turned their weapons against the Israeli army.[33]

In the weeks that followed, Palestinian activists shot at Israeli military installations, settlements, and roads in the West Bank and Gaza. Israel shelled Palestinian neighbourhoods, bulldozed homes and fields, and blocked movement with hundreds of new checkpoints. Palestinian casualties during the first

---

[29] Mark Tessler, *A History of the Israeli–Palestinian Conflict* (Bloomington, IN: Indiana University Press, 1994), 701.

[30] US Department of State, 'Country Reports on Human Rights Practices for 1988, "The Occupied Territories"', *Journal of Palestine Studies*, 18/3 (Spring 1989), 114–16; Al-Haq (Law in the Service of Man), *Punishing a Nation: Human Rights Violations during the Palestinian Uprising, December 1987–December 1988* (Boston: South End Press, 1990); Schiff and Ya'ari, *Intifada: The Palestinian Uprising*, 150.

[31] Sara M. Roy, 'Gaza: New Dynamics of Civic Disintegration', *Journal of Palestine Studies*, 22/4 (Summer 1993), 23–5; Ziad Abu-Amr, *Islamic Fundamentalism in the West Bank and Gaza: Muslim Brotherhood and Islamic Jihad* (Bloomington, IN: Indiana University Press, 1994), 75.

[32] Ben Kaspit, 'Israel Is Not a Country with an Army, but an Army with an Attached Country', *Maariv*, 6 September 2002, as cited in Foreign Broadcast Information Service, insert, 9 September 2002; Reuven Pedatzur, 'More than a Million Bullets', *Haaretz*, 29 June 2004.

[33] 'Chronology', *Journal of Palestine Studies*, 30/2 (Winter 2001), 198.

three months nearly totalled those of the entire first year of the previous intifada. Palestinian protest became less broad-based and more lethal over time. Palestinian activists engaged in gun battles and shootings at Israeli settlements, roads, and installations in the West Bank and Gaza. A suicide bombing on New Year's Day opened the year 2001. By year's end, Palestinians had carried out more such bombings than they had during the previous seven years combined. Whereas no Israelis were killed in suicide bombings in 2000, eighty-seven were killed in 2001 and seventy-eight were killed in the month of March 2002 alone.

The Second Intifada is regarded as perhaps the bloodiest chapter in the Israeli–Palestinian conflict. Non-violent action during this period remained generally limited, localized, and overshadowed by violent attacks, frequently targeting Israeli civilians. It did not acquire sustained, countrywide scope as a strategy of national liberation that could unify and mobilize Palestinians from across the political spectrum. For most Palestinians, participation in the Second Intifada meant suffering through Israeli repression.

In spring 2002 Israel began a 45-day reoccupation of most West Bank cities, eventually leaving at a toll of 497 Palestinians dead, more than 8,500 arrested, and hundreds of millions of dollars in property destruction.[34] This operation led to a dramatic deceleration of Palestinian attacks, as did the start of construction of a 700-kilometre security fence/wall. Though presented as necessary to protect Israel from suicide bombings, the barrier was built mostly on Palestinian land confiscated from within the West Bank and East Jerusalem.[35]

This threat to Palestinian communities served as an impetus to new forms of civil resistance. Bil'in, Nil'in, Budrus, and other villages in the route of the barrier launched popular struggle campaigns against it.[36] Protests, some carried out every Friday for years, rallied the participation of a swathe of residents and also Israeli and international solidarity activists. To sustain participation and media interest, they frequently used props, costumes, performances, and creative themes as part of the demonstrations. As in the First Intifada, protestors sometimes threw rocks at Israeli soldiers. Israeli soldiers regularly responded with arrests and what Amnesty International judged to be excessive force, including firing tear gas and even bullets (see Figure 10.1).[37]

---

[34] *Report of the Secretary-General Prepared Pursuant to General Assembly Resolution ES-10/10*, 30 July 2002 http://unispal.un.org/unispal.nsf/udc.htm.

[35] International Court of Justice, *Advisory Opinion on Legal Consequences of the Construction of a Wall in the Occupied Palestinian Territory*, 9 July 2004.

[36] Julie M. Norman, *The Second Palestinian Intifada: Civil Resistance* (New York: Routledge, 2010), ch. 3; Qumsiyeh, *Popular Resistance in Palestine*, 188–93; Maia Carter Hallward and Julie M. Norman, *Nonviolent Resistance in the Second Intifada: Activism and Advocacy* (New York: Palgrave Macmillan, 2011).

[37] Amnesty International, *Annual Report 2012* (London: Amnesty International, 2012), 188.

Figure 10.1. Israel's West Bank barrier, begun in the early 2000s, had given impetus to non-violent resistance well before the Arab Spring. A protester carrying a Palestinian flag runs from Israeli troops during a weekly demonstration against the barrier at Bil'in, in the occupied West Bank, on 17 June 2011.

© *Abbas Momani/AFP/Getty Images*

Other forms of civil resistance in these years likewise involved Palestinians together with Israeli and international activists.[38] Founded in 2001, the International Solidarity Movement worked in partnership with Palestinians to carry out non-violence training and direct actions.[39] Beginning in 2006, the 'Free Gaza movement' attempted to sail boats to the Gaza Strip to call attention to and challenge Israel's tightening of the closure on that territory.[40] Meanwhile, Palestinians led a campaign for 'boycott, divestment and sanctions' (BDS) against Israel. Since 2005 more than 170 Palestinian civil society groups have signed a call for people throughout the world to impose boycotts and divestment initiatives against Israel similar to those applied against Apartheid-era South Africa.[41] Though the campaign is yet to gain mass participation, solidarity activists around the globe have taken up the banner of BDS in their communities. Finally, since late 2009, Palestinians, Israeli

---

[38] Hallward and Norman, *Nonviolent Resistance in the Second Intifada*.

[39] Norman, *Second Palestinian Intifada*, 44.

[40] Qumsiyeh, *Popular Resistance in Palestine*, 203–5; interview with Huwaida Arraf and Adam Shapiro, 'The Free Gaza Movement', in Hallward and Norman, *Nonviolent Resistance in the Second Intifada*, 153–62.

[41] Omar Barghouti, *Boycott, Divestment, Sanctions—The Global Struggle for Palestinian Rights* (Chicago: Haymarket Books, 2011).

activists, and others have engaged in demonstrations against Israel's demolition of Palestinian homes and expansion of settlements in East Jerusalem, where there were regular rallies in Sheikh Jarrah and other neighbourhoods. With the exception of occasional stone-throwing and clashes with police, protests were typically peaceful and sometimes attracted thousands of participants.[42]

PATTERNS OF PEOPLE POWER

Several themes emerge across these three major popular uprisings in Palestinian history. All began against a backdrop of political–diplomatic stalemate in the Palestinian quest for self-determination. People rose up when they had lost hope in promises of a solution to their plight, on the part either of foreign powers or of their own official leadership. In addition, young cohorts were the spearheading force behind protest. They were typically critical of Palestinians leaders' failures to realize popular aspirations, if not also their prioritization of personal or factional interests.

Uprisings took shape at junctures when conditions suggested that Palestinians' situation on the ground was getting worse, in terms of economic opportunity, loss of land, and perceived prospects for attaining freedom and sovereignty. They were thus fuelled by a sense of urgency: the status quo was perceived as one of deterioration, and its very continuation undermined the national cause. Under these circumstances, contingent sparks lit a readiness for contentious collective action. Uprisings began with an explosion of optimism that mass defiance could show the world that Palestinians refused to wait indefinitely for meaningful political change. Top-down politics had proved insufficient, and so the grass-roots seized the opportunity to liberate themselves from the bottom up.

From these common beginnings, the unfolding of the uprisings likewise reveals patterns. All began as mass shows of civil resistance in which men, women, and children participated using the protest means available to them— namely, their voices to articulate demands, their bodies to put on the line in demonstrations, their purchasing power to direct towards the domestic economy, and their choice whether to cooperate with authorities. These means often also included low-level or non-lethal violence, such as stone-throwing. In the first and third revolts, they also encompassed bloody attacks on both government targets and civilians. In all three uprisings, the occupying power refused to accommodate the demands of mass-based resistance and instead

---

[42] Nir Hasson, 'Thousands of Protesters Rally against Jewish Presence in East Jerusalem', *Haaretz*, 6 March 2010 www.haaretz.com/news/thousands-of-protesters-rally-against-jewish-presence-in-east-jerusalem-1.264238.

responded with an array of repressive measures. Targeted, indiscriminate, or collective, such repression often struck those who had engaged only in non-violent protest, or perhaps engaged in no protest at all. Repression decreased mass participation in resistance and expanded opportunities for those who advocated violent protest to play a more prominent role. In each uprising—in some cases much earlier than others—violent protest came to outweigh non-violent protest.

PROTEST IN THE WAKE OF THE ARAB UPRISINGS

Some of the conditions that were the backdrop to the revolts of 1936, 1987, and 2000 also obtained in 2011. Most fundamentally, Palestinians' national aspirations remained unfulfilled. Indeed, Sara Roy argues that Palestinian society and polity had been 'dismembered' and 'eroded' more than any time since 1948.[43] Against a backdrop of geographic fragmentation and ongoing settlement expansion, continued Israeli occupation appeared more likely than any diplomatic breakthrough towards a two-state settlement. Political stasis was compounded by economic hardship. In the absence of a serious programme for sustainable development, Palestinian families grappled with high unemployment, high costs of living, low wages, and financial crisis in the PA.[44]

In the aftermath of the Tunisian and Egyptian revolts, these grievances contributed impetus to Palestinians' undertaking of many acts of civil resistance. On the one hand, they continued popular campaigns that had been ongoing since the mid- to late 2000s, such as those against the West Bank barrier and East Jerusalem house demolitions. On the other, they engaged in new acts of protest in part inspired by the revolutionary atmosphere sweeping the Middle East at large. A 'Third Palestinian Intifada' Facebook page, attracting 250,000 subscribers in less than two weeks, bore the mark of this regional context.[45] Connecting online, Palestinians from different parts of the diaspora called for a peaceful march to their homeland on 15 May 2011, the anniversary of the start of the 1948 war that Palestinians remember as the 'Nakba' (the Catastrophe). On the day, thousands of Palestinian refugees in Lebanon, Syria, and Gaza marched to their respective borders with Israel. Those coming from

---

[43] Sara Roy, 'Reconceptualizing the Israeli–Palestinian Conflict: Key Paradigm Shifts', *Journal of Palestine Studies*, 41/3 (Spring 2012), 71–91.

[44] Ashraf al-Ajami, 'As Hard Times Get Harder, Palestinians Start Protests', *Al-Monitor*, 7 September 2012 http://www.al-monitor.com/pulse/tr/politics/2012/09/with-times-harder-than-ever-palestinians-begin-to-protest-their-economic-plight.html#.

[45] Leila Farsakh, 'Searching for the Arab Spring in Ramallah', *Jadaliyya*, 21 February 2012 www.jadaliyya.c.jadaliyya.com/pages/index/4438/searching-for-the-arab-spring-in-ramallah.

Syria, on encouragement from Syrian authorities,[46] breached the border and moved towards the village of Majdal Shams in the Golan Heights. Protesters threw stones. Israeli troops, opening fire on what they considered illegal infiltration, killed thirteen people.[47] The following month, on the anniversary of the 1967 war, Palestinian and Syrian protesters again attempted to scale the fence on the Syrian border. According to Syrian sources, Israel shot and killed some twenty protestors.[48] Civil resistance continued thereafter. April–May 2012 saw a hunger strike by about 2,500 Palestinian prisoners in Israeli jails. Some neared death after refusing food for seventy-seven days. The dramatic act of defiance inspired solidarity demonstrations and protests in the West Bank and Gaza Strip, and also captured international attention. An agreement was hailed as a victory when Israel conceded a number of the strikers' demands.[49]

Against the backdrop of the Arab uprisings, Palestinians also engaged in protest against issues other than the direct conflict with Israel. Discontent with domestic politics was significant. Opinion polls showed that majorities of up to 80 per cent of Palestinians believed there was corruption in governmental institutions, while around two-thirds of Palestinians in both the West Bank and Gaza believed that people could not criticize ruling authorities without fear.[50] The greatest source of frustration with internal politics was the destructive rivalry between Palestinians' two largest political factions. A short but bloody conflict in 2007 led to the effective division between the Fatah-dominated PA in the West Bank and the Hamas-led government in the Gaza Strip. Rashid Khalidi spoke for many Palestinians when he lambasted Fatah and Hamas as 'two feeble and clueless Palestinian political movements . . . fighting like two cocks on a garbage heap'.[51]

Surveys revealed that combined support for the two factions typically hovered around just 50 per cent of the public. About a third of survey respondents said that they supported no political party.[52] When asked which individual leader they most supported, a plurality usually said no one.[53] A March 2011 opinion

[46] Jonathan Steele, 'How Yarmouk Refugee Camp Became the Worst Place in Syria', *Guardian*, London, 5 March 2015 http://www.theguardian.com/news/2015/mar/05/how-yarmouk-refugee-camp-became-worst-place-syria.

[47] Harriet Sherwood, 'Thirteen Killed as Israeli Troops Open Fire on Nakba Day Border Protests', *Guardian*, 15 May 2011 www.theguardian.com/world/2011/may/15/israeli-troops-kill-eight-nakba-protests.

[48] 'Golan: Israel Troops Fire on Pro-Palestinian Protestors', *BBC News*, 5 June 2011 http://www.bbc.com/new/world-middle-east-13660311.

[49] Harriet Sherwood, 'Palestinian Prisoners End Hunger Strike', *Guardian*, 14 May 2012 www.theguardian.com/world/2012/may/14/palestinian-prisoners-end-hunger-strike.

[50] PSR, *Polls Nos 39–42*, March–December 2011 http://www.pcpsr.org/en/node/154.

[51] Rashid Khalidi, 'Palestine: Liberation Deferred', *Nation*, New York, 8 May 2008.

[52] PSR, *Polls Nos 39–42*.

[53] Jerusalem Media Communication Centre, *Polls Nos 73–78* (April 2011–December 2012) www.jmcc.org/polls.aspx.

poll asked Palestinians a series of questions inspired by revolts elsewhere in the region. One asked respondents what they believed to be the single most important slogan to raise in demonstrations. A majority said: 'People want an end to the division'. It was more than twice the percentage that advocated the slogan 'People want an end to occupation'.[54]

This slogan was not the only echo of the other uprisings in the Middle East and North Africa. New actors and modes of organizing resonated, as well. For months prior, Palestinian youth activists had been meeting in discussion groups to debate strategy. They gathered in cafes, Skyped each other between Gaza and the West Bank, and joined Facebook groups addressing domestic and nationalist political priorities.[55] As elsewhere, they worked beyond the confines of partisan affiliation, used social media, and attempted to organize civil resistance by directly engaging with the public.[56] In November 2010 a loose group of such activists had joined with others from progressive political parties and non-governmental organizations to form an umbrella called 'the Independent Youth Movement'.[57]

The new mood of hope and activism sweeping the Arab world offered a promising environment for this network to rally broader involvement. Beginning in February 2011, the group organized weekly sit-ins in Ramallah's central square to demand the end of the schism between Fatah and Hamas.[58] Some engaged in a hunger strike while others set up protest tents in major Palestinian cities.[59] Still other activists decided to try to organize a major demonstration on 15 March. That day, thousands came into the streets of Ramallah and Gaza City to call for national reconciliation. The scenes of Palestinian crowds in two central squares waving their national flag and chanting in unison paralleled scenes recorded throughout the Arab world at the time. The group behind the demonstrations became known as the March 15 Movement (see Figure 10.2).

This show of people power was one of several factors pushing Fatah and Hamas to sign a reconciliation agreement in May 2011. The March 15 Movement petered out shortly thereafter. The incipient movement had appeared to suggest a rebirth of popular resistance in general and a new type of youth-driven street politics, in particular. In the absence of a clear political programme, however, it proved unable to resolve tensions among its constituent groups, defend itself against hostility on the part of both Palestinian authorities, and ultimately mobilize society.[60]

---

[54] PSR, *Poll No. 39*, 17–19 March 2011, p. 23.

[55] Linah Alsaafin, 'Imperfect Revolution: Palestine's 15 March Movement One Year on', *Electronic Intifada*, 23 March 2012 http://electronicintifada.net/content/imperfect-revolution-palestines-15-march-movement-one-year/11092.

[56] Nathan J. Brown, 'Palestine: The Fire Next Time?', *Carnegie Endowment Online*, 6 July 2011 http://carnegieendowment.org/2011/07/06/palestine-fire-next-time/2sh8.

[57] Farsakh, 'Searching for the Arab Spring'; Alsaafin, 'Imperfect Revolution'.

[58] Farsakh, 'Searching for the Arab Spring'.   [59] Alsaafin, 'Imperfect Revolution'.

[60] Alsaafin, 'Imperfect Revolution'.

Figure 10.2. Following other Arab countries, Palestinians went into the streets to express discontent with their political leaders and to make demands for change. Demonstrations were held in the Gaza Strip and the West Bank on 15 March 2011 to call for unity between the two political factions, Hamas and Fatah. Here women in Gaza City demonstrate. Posters behind them read: 'The people want an end to the division'. This was one factor that pushed Hamas and Fatah to sign a reconciliation agreement in May 2011.

© *Said Khatib/AFP/Getty Images*

Signs of a Palestinian grass-roots revival thus remained, in Nathan Brown's words, 'tremors', rather than a 'groundswell'.[61] In the end, protests did not rally the large numbers that gave power to the other revolts of the Arab Spring. Small demonstrations and marches to checkpoints continued to occur periodically in and after 2011. However, protests that in previous years had rallied thousands, such as those on landmark days in the Palestinian national calendar, saw the participation of only dozens.[62] Ultimately, the revolutionary wave sweeping the Middle East and North Africa did not engulf the Palestinian territories.

WHY WAS THERE NO 'PALESTINIAN SPRING'?

Many factors distinguish the Palestinian situation from that of those who launched uprisings in other Arab countries in 2010–11. A few are particularly

---

[61] Brown, 'Palestine: The Fire Next Time?'.
[62] Avi Issacharoff and Amos Harel, 'The Palestinians are not Battling with Israel, but with their Apathy', *Haaretz*, 4 May 2012 http://www.haaretz.com/news/diplomacy-defense/the-palestinians-are-not-battling-with-israel-but-with-their-apathy-1.428312.

relevant in dampening prospects for mass civil resistance. First, spatial dimensions in the Palestinian territories impeded the enactment of tactics that proved critical elsewhere.[63] Space figured prominently in the Egyptian revolt's occupation of Tahrir Square. It was also arguably the most important tactical innovation diffusing from country to country, as uprisings in Yemen and Bahrain quickly occupied central squares, as well.[64] Space played a different role in Tunisia and Libya, where protest began in a far corner of the country and gained power as it moved towards the capital. Such was also the case in Syria, where protest likewise began in the rural periphery and became more threatening to the regime as it closed in on its main commercial and political cities.

The political geography of the Palestinian territories was distinct from that underlying these other uprisings. Israeli checkpoints and other measures severely restricted movement into, out of, and between the West Bank, Gaza Strip, and East Jerusalem.[65] Israel's redeployment from Palestinian towns and villages in the West Bank during the Oslo peace process had divided that territory into Areas 'A', under full PA control, Areas 'B', in which security matters were under joint Palestinian–Israeli control, and Areas 'C', where security matters were under full Israeli control.[66] Israel's building of its barrier in the West Bank created still further spatial divisions within and between Jerusalem and the West Bank. Israel's 2005 removal of settlements and military installations from the Gaza Strip enabled complete freedom of movement within that 139-square-mile rectangle on the Mediterranean coast. Nonetheless, Israel, in cooperation with Egypt, maintained control over movement into and out of the Strip.[67]

This spatial matrix rendered it difficult for Palestinians to make effective some of the forms of civil resistance that had gained prominence in the Arab uprisings. Popular demonstrations in major towns in the West Bank or Gaza Strip that were under Palestinian control would not put pressure on Israel; on the contrary, Israelis would not see them, and would be unlikely to care. Alternatively, Palestinians might undertake marches to Israeli checkpoints or settlements in the West Bank or towards Israel's crossing points into the

---

[63] Social movement scholars give increasing attention to the role of space in contentious politics. See William H. Sewell Jr, 'Space in Contentious Politics', in Ronald R. Aminzade, Jack A. Goldstone, Doug McAdam, Elizabeth J. Perry, William H. Sewell Jr, Sidney Tarrow, and Charles Tilly (eds), *Silence and Voice in the Study of Contentious Politics* (Cambridge: Cambridge University Press, 2001), 51–88.

[64] David Patel, Valerie Bunce, and Sharon Wolchik, 'Diffusion and Demonstration', in Marc Lynch (ed.), *The Arab Uprisings Explained: New Contentious Politics in the Middle East* (New York: Columbia University Press, 2014), 57–74.

[65] Amira Hass, 'Israel's Closure Policy: An Ineffective Strategy of Containment and Repression', *Journal of Palestine Studies*, 31/3 (Spring 2002), 5–20.

[66] Sara Roy, 'Why Peace Failed: An Oslo Autopsy', *Current History*, 100/651 (January 2002), 8–16.

[67] Roy, 'Reconceptualizing the Israeli–Palestinian Conflict'.

Gaza Strip. However, these were militarized spaces. Clashes during and since the Second Intifada showed that demonstrations at Israeli checkpoints and settlements frequently ended in Palestinian civilians throwing stones and Israeli soldiers shooting tear gas and/or bullets. Even should such protests begin peacefully, they were unlikely to conclude that way. The 15 May 2011 marches, by indicating that Israel would respond forcefully to any attempted infiltration of its sovereign territory, confirmed this conclusion. Further complicating matters, security coordination between Israel and the PA obligated the latter to prevent any breaches of the areas controlled by the former. Grass-roots Palestinian action of this type was thus likely to elicit a backlash from the PA police, as indeed it repeatedly had.[68]

Apart from spatial dynamics, Palestinians faced a multifaceted domestic political landscape that inhibited the designation of clear protest objectives. In contrast to countries where uprisings targeted a single regime or autocratic leader, Palestinians were ruled by two competing governments. Most of the Arab revolts fought 'presidents for life', who sat atop ruling parties that had become little more than vehicles for co-optation and patronage.[69] Despite Palestinians' deep criticism of Fatah and Hamas, those factions had roots in society that were much more authentic and meaningful than those of the hollowed-out ruling parties of authoritarian Tunisia and Egypt. Both factions claimed long histories of leading grass-roots resistance, which they could summon when political imperatives required it. Their domination of the nationalist struggle crowded out alternative voices. At the same time, they tapped into genuine national sentiments to rally mass shows for their own political projects.

This carried complicated implications for the prospects of Palestinian civil resistance. Fatah and Hamas might welcome some kinds of popular mobilization as leverage against Israel. Yet they would go to lengths to ensure that it neither slipped from their control nor evolved into a challenge against them. Both Fatah and Hamas thus used violence and detentions to prevent civilians' peaceful protests, including those in solidarity with uprisings elsewhere in the Middle East.[70] They were particularly suspicious of any protest that they perceived might benefit their rival. By late 2012 each faction surprised the public by allowing its rival to organize isolated demonstrations in the territory that it controlled.[71] More commonly, they arbitrarily arrested and harassed each other's supporters in effort to maintain their faction's dominance.

---

[68] Linah Alsaafin, 'West Bank Protests: Waiting for a Tipping Point', *Al-Akbar English Online*, 21 November 2012 http://english.al-akhbar.com/node/14055.

[69] Roger Owen, *The Rise and Fall of Arab Presidents for Life* (Cambridge, MA: Harvard University Press, 2012).

[70] Human Rights Watch, *World Report 2012: Events of 2001* (New York: HRW, 2012), 571–2; Amnesty International, *Annual Report 2012*, 267.

[71] 'After 5 Year Ban, Hamas Holds Rally in West Bank', *Haaretz*, 13 December 2012 www.haaretz.com/news/middle-east/after-5-year-ban-hamas-holds-rally-in-west-bank-1.484743;

The upshot was that no undertaking of popular resistance was immune from the pressure of these contradictory agendas. It was not clear what a mass-scale renewal of Palestinian people power would look like, given its potential to be blocked, influenced, managed, or manipulated by the main political factions. Thus, PA President Mahmoud Abbas encouraged street celebrations supporting his application for a UN seat in September 2011 and again in November 2012, in favour of the UN General Assembly resolution recognizing Palestine as a non-member observer state.[72] Given Abbas's commitment to a political resolution, however, he opposed any civil resistance that might jeopardize the return to meaningful negotiations with Israel. Thus, PA forces used violence to break up popular demonstrations against a visit by Israeli Vice Premier Shaul Mofaz to Ramallah in July 2012.[73] In November 2012 renewed hostilities between the Gaza Strip and Israel triggered protests across the West Bank targeting Israeli checkpoints, settlements, and prisons.[74] PA police forcibly blocked some demonstrations, even beating and arresting participants.[75] Similar patterns for and against popular mobilization unfolded in Gaza. Uniformed and plain-clothes Hamas forces attacked Gaza participants in the 15 March 2011 national unity demonstrations.[76] The Gaza government did not allow demonstrations to mark Abbas's submission of the UN statehood bid. In December 2012, however, Hamas rallied tens of thousands of supporters to celebrate the twenty-fifth anniversary of its founding and pledge defiance against Israel.

A final factor dampening prospects for mass civil resistance in the wake of the Arab Spring was the emotional climate in the Palestinian territories. Other uprisings in the Arab world were propelled by the unleashing of frustrations that had been pent up for decades. Palestinians, on the other hand, had an uprising every generation. In this sense, it is difficult to underestimate the devastating toll of the Second Intifada. Between 2000 and 2005, some 3,135 Palestinians had been killed by Israeli forces and many times that number injured or detained. Millions of dollars' worth of Palestinian houses, fields, trees, and infrastructure had been destroyed.[77] The use of tanks, helicopter

---

Patrick Keddie, 'Gaza Reacts—Somewhat—to the UN Bid for Palestinian Statehood', *Suspect Device*, blog, 30 November 2012 http://patrickkeddie.wordpress.com/2012/11/30/gaza-reacts-somewhat-to-the-un-bid-for-palestinian-statehood.

[72] GA Res. 67/19 of 29 November 2012, 'Status of Palestine in the United Nations' http://www.un.org/en/ga/search/view_doc.asp?symbol=A/RES/67/19.

[73] 'PA Police Crack down on Ramallah Protest of Mofaz Visit', *Jerusalem Post*, 1 July 2012 www.jpost.com/Breaking-News/PA-police-crack-down-on-Ramallah-protest-of-Mofaz-visit.

[74] Alsaafin, 'West Bank Protests: Waiting for a Tipping Point'.

[75] Alsaafin, 'West Bank Protests: Waiting for a Tipping Point'.

[76] Amnesty International, *Annual Report 2012*, 267.

[77] UN-ECOSOC, 'Question of the Violation of Human Rights', 23; Al-Mezan Center for Human Rights, *The Intifada in Figures: Statistics on Israel's Violations of Human Rights in the Occupied Palestinian Territories, September 28, 2000–September 28, 2003* (Gaza: Al-Mezan

gunships, and warplanes to shell civilian neighbourhoods caused civilian casualties, property damage, and trauma, particularly for children.[78] The tightening of closure resulted in enormous economic losses. By 2004, average Palestinian incomes had dropped by more than one-third, a quarter of the workforce was unemployed, and half of all Palestinians lived below the poverty line.[79] By 2010 about 80 per cent of families in Gaza relied on some form of humanitarian aid. Nearly the same percentage of West Bankers in Area C lacked sufficient food.[80]

Palestinians were still arguably recovering from the Second Intifada, therefore, at the time when the Arab world was experiencing a surge of popular optimism about what collective action could achieve. Such optimism had been a crucial part of previous Palestinian uprisings beginning in 1936, 1987, and 2000, as well as the initial surge of the Palestine Liberation Organization in the late 1960s.[81] In 2011 and 2012, however, many Palestinians were sceptical that renewed civil resistance could produce change. Four polls conducted between March and December 2011 asked Palestinians if, in the light of the successful revolts in Egypt and Tunisia, they thought a peaceful popular revolution in the West Bank would be capable of ending occupation or stopping settlements. A plurality ranging from 48 to 52 per cent consistently responded that it would be incapable. Asked if armed confrontations would help achieve Palestinian national rights in ways that negotiations could not, a plurality likewise responded that it would not.[82]

Hence, in contrast to other Arab publics, Palestinians were not alight with the thrill of reclaiming a long-suppressed voice. Rather, many seemed understandably disillusioned from shouting for so long. Residents and close observers described the public mood in the Palestinian territories as one of 'apathy',[83]

Center for Human Rights, 2003); Amnesty International, *Israel and the Occupied Territories: Under the Rubble—House Demolition and Destruction of Land and Property* (London: Amnesty International, 18 May 2004); B'Tselem, *Policy of Destruction: House Demolitions and Destruction of Agricultural Land in the Gaza Strip* (Jerusalem: B'Tselem, January–February 2002); Human Rights Watch, *Razing Rafah: Mass Demolitions in the Gaza Strip* (New York: HRW, October 2004).

[78] B'Tselem, *Excessive Force: Human Rights Violations during IDF Actions in Area A* (Jerusalem: B'Tselem, December 2001); 'UNICEF Concerned about Impact of Violence on Palestinian and Israeli Children Geneva', UNICEF, 15 November 2001 www.unicef.org/newsline/01pr87.htm.

[79] 'Intifada Toll 2000–2005', *BBC News*, 8 February 2005 http://news.bbc.co.uk/2/hi/middle_east/3694350.stm.

[80] Roy, 'Reconceptualizing the Israeli–Palestinian Conflict', 82.

[81] Pearlman, *Violence, Nonviolence*, 44, 67, 104, 156.

[82] PSR, *Polls Nos 39–42*.

[83] Issacharoff and Harel, 'Palestinians are not Battling with Israel'; Akram Atallah Alaysa, 'Popular Apathy and Cumulative Skepticism over September', *Ma'an News Agency*, 3 September 2011 www.maannews.net/eng/ViewDetails.aspx?ID=417219; Linah Alsaafin, 'How Obsession with "Nonviolence" Harms the Palestinian Cause', *Electronic Intifada*, 10 July 2012 http://electronicintifada.net/content/how-obsession-nonviolence-harms-palestinian-cause/11482.

'weariness',[84] 'malaise',[85] 'indifference',[86] and 'political exhaustion'.[87] 'They don't want to hear of a third intifada,' a Palestinian analyst said of his compatriots. 'The public suffered so much from the second intifada, why would they ask for that again? No man wants to see his children die again, or get injured.'[88] A Palestinian columnist noted that, while external conditions encouraged revolt, the small protests in the Palestinian territories were 'very different from the Arab Spring revolutions . . . because the internal situation is not yet ready for such a revolution. Palestinians are not confident that change is possible.'[89]

Against this backdrop, it was not surprising that Palestinians evidenced only lukewarm support for Abbas's bids in 2011 and in 2012 for UN recognition of Palestine's statehood. Some did come out into the street to cheer the international community's legitimation of the Palestinian quest for statehood. Yet these demonstrations were one-time events in honour of a symbolic victory and did not represent a definitive break from the generally cynical mood. In September 2011 the International Crisis Group summarized Palestinians' sentiments about Abbas's new strategy in a report tellingly titled *Curb your Enthusiasm*:

> Many if not most Palestinians . . . appear to be greeting the entire UN episode with considerable scepticism . . . In general, the Palestinian public seems broadly apathetic about the UN initiative and expresses clear doubts about the impact it will have . . . A Palestinian analyst added: 'People aren't engaged in the idea . . . it's just political blah-blah that goes in one ear and out the other.'[90]

Three years later, on 30 December 2014, when a resolution providing for recognition of Palestine's statehood failed to secure adoption by the UN Security Council, the Palestinian public again avoided holding out too many hopes for this kind of diplomatic initiative.

[84] Alaysa, 'Popular Apathy'; Avi Issacharoff, 'In Ramallah, No One Wants Another Intifada', *Haaretz*, 16 September 2011 www.haaretz.com/print-edition/news/in-ramallah-no-one-wants-another-intifada-1.384717.

[85] Associated Press, 'Low Turnout as Palestinians Vote in First Local Elections in West Bank since 2005', *Haaretz*, 20 October 2012 www.haaretz.com/news/middle-east/low-turnout-as-palestinians-vote-in-first-local-elections-in-west-bank-since-2005-1.471170; Adrian Bloomfield, 'Analysis: Is a Palestinian Revolt against Mahmoud Abbas Brewing?', *Telegraph*, 4 May 2012 www.telegraph.co.uk/news/worldnews/middleeast/palestinianauthority/9244982/Analysis-Is-a-Palestinian-revolt-against-Mahmoud-Abbas-brewing.html.

[86] Bloomfield, 'Analysis: Palestinian Revolt'.

[87] Brown, 'Palestine: The Fire Next Time?'.

[88] Issacharoff and Harel, 'Palestinians are not Battling with Israel'.

[89] Al-Ajami, 'A Palestinian Spring?'.

[90] International Crisis Group, *Curb your Enthusiasm: Israel and Palestine after the UN* (Ramallah/Jerusalem: International Crisis Group, Middle East Report no. 112, 12 September 2011), 14, 16.

JUST A MATTER OF TIME

Palestinian national history has been one of ongoing resistance. This was dramatically symbolized in three mass uprisings, but is no less embodied in Palestinians' everyday steadfastness under occupation or as refugees in exile. Palestinians' history of violent and non-violent protest achieved formidable successes—namely, preserving their culture, identity, and political struggle, and increasingly compelling the world to recognize the legitimacy of their quest for self-determination. Yet, as in cases discussed in other chapters in this book, the Palestinian experience also highlights the special problems that civil resistance faces when it takes place in the context of a conflict in which violence is pervasive and a multiplicity of internal and external political forces compete to advance their interests. Given the difficulties of mounting effecting civil resistance—or, for that matter, political or armed strategies—Palestinians have yet to achieve their goal of an independent Palestinian state. Meanwhile, human-rights abuses, by Palestinian governing authorities as well as by Israel, are ongoing. Palestinians voice continued frustration with lingering domestic problems, such as political corruption, economic hardship, and factional rivalries destructive to the national interest.

There was reason to think that the 2011 Arab uprisings might offer the spark to set aflame that tinder of grievances. Palestinians followed, identified with, and cheered on their Arab brethren who took to the streets. Yet Palestinians' likelihood of launching their own rebellion in 2011 did not depend primarily on diffusion of a revolutionary mood, transnational activist networks, or the demonstration effect of successful tactics in neighbouring countries. To a larger extent, it was a product of their own circumstances. Palestinian civilians and groups engaged in various forms of localized or episodic protest. However, the spatial, political, and emotional conditions reigning in the West Bank and Gaza Strip did not facilitate mobilization of a new, mass-based uprising. Given the devastating toll of the intifada that had begun in the year 2000, it was understandable that many Palestinians longed for a measure of calm and recovery and hesitated to embark on another major upheaval.

Nonetheless, policies undermining Palestinians' rights never ceased. In 2013 Israel continued to expand illegal settlements, imprison Palestinians without charge or trial, restrict Palestinians' freedom of movement, and block people and goods from flowing into and out from Gaza. Pushed by the United States, Israeli–Palestinian negotiations resumed with the goal of a final agreement by April 2014. They collapsed when that deadline passed unmet. That month, Fatah and Hamas announced yet another agreement to create a unity government and hold new elections. The initiative, while resonating with the population's long demand for an end to infighting, was propelled by each faction's interest in escaping its own mounting pressures more than a genuine commitment to forging a common front.

On 12 June 2014 two Palestinian men kidnapped three Israeli teenagers in the West Bank. Though the suspects' identities remained hazy, Israeli Prime Minister Benjamin Netanyahu accused Hamas of responsibility. On these grounds, Israeli forces raided West Bank communities for eighteen days, while the Israeli public passionately followed the search for the abducted boys. Six Palestinians were killed and hundreds arrested, mostly Hamas members, before the boys' corpses were found. Two days later, Israelis abducted a Palestinian teenager in East Jerusalem and beat and burned him to death. As clashes erupted in East Jerusalem, Palestinian rocket fire from Gaza and Israeli airstrikes on Gaza intensified. On 8 July Israel declared the start of what would become a seven-week war on Gaza. Fighting killed more than 2,100 Palestinians and 70 Israelis, displaced up to 500,000 Gazans, and destroyed billions of dollars in homes, factories, and infrastructure in Gaza.

Against this backdrop of political vacuum and tension inflamed by violence, an uptick of acts of protest and violence in the East Jerusalem and West Bank renewed musings about whether an uprising was imminent or had in fact begun. 'The current upsurge in protests and violence has been called the silent intifada, the individual intifada, the children's intifada, the firecracker intifada, the car intifada, the run-over intifada, the Jerusalem intifada and the third intifada,' Nathan Thrall wrote.[91] In his opinion, conditions resembled the period of uncoordinated, leaderless violence that had preceded the 1987 uprising, with the crucial difference that the much-weakened state of Palestinian civil society was significantly less able to organize such sporadic acts into a cohesive strategy. Shibley Telhami remarked that, unlike prior intifadas, the current campaign was a hybrid of peaceful work, such as the BDS movement, and violence that included 'lone wolf' attacks not organized by any political faction.[92] Ramzy Baroud added that the new phase of mobilization against Israel demonstrated the fruitlessness of tired conversations weighing the relative merits of armed or unarmed resistance. In his view, that debate was being replaced with 'an organic approach' in which Palestinians were simply 'opting to use whatever effective form of resistance they can'.[93]

What these developments demonstrated, yet again, was that Palestinians' will and capacity for revolution would persist as long as the goal of self-determination remained unachieved. The history of prior uprisings suggested that the impetus activating that revolutionary potential was most likely to

[91] Nathan Thrall, 'Rage in Jerusalem', *London Review of Books*, 36/23 (4 December 2014), 19–21 http://www.lrb.co.uk/v36/n23/nathan-thrall/rage-in-jerusalem.

[92] 'Is Incitement to Blame for Growing Middle East Violence?—Part 2', *PBS Newshour*, 18 November 2014 http://www.pbs.org/newshour/bb/is-incitement-to-blame-for-growing-middle-east-violence/.

[93] Ramzy Baroud, '5 Reasons why 2014 was a Game Changer in Palestine', *Palestine Chronicle*, 23 December 2014 http://www.palestinechronicle.com/5-reasons-why-2014-was-a-game-changer-in-palestine/#.VLwGKHZfdl8.

come from young people. This cohort was as sizeable as in other Arab countries: as of 2011, an estimated 40 per cent of the 4.17 million Palestinians in the West Bank and Gaza Strip were under the age of 14.[94] Tremors from young cohorts were felt when the Tunisian uprising was barely underway. They gained one powerful expression at the end of 2010, when an anonymous group of students in Gaza posted an online document titled 'Gaza Youth's Manifesto for Change'. In impassioned language, the declaration expressed exasperation with abuses and closed horizons. It suggested the kind of revolutionary energy that could be mobilized to fight anew for change:

> We want to scream and break this wall of silence, injustice and indifference . . . scream with all the power in our souls in order to release this immense frustration that consumes us . . . We are sick of being caught in this political struggle; sick of coal-dark nights with airplanes circling above our homes . . . we are sick and tired of living a shitty life, being kept in jail by Israel, beaten up by Hamas and completely ignored by the rest of the world. There is a revolution growing inside of us, an immense dissatisfaction and frustration that will destroy us unless we find a way of canalising this energy into something that can challenge the status quo and give us some kind of hope.[95]

Similar sentiments existed in the West Bank. Observing November 2012 protests against Israel's bombing in Gaza, Linah Alsaafin judged that declaration of a Third Intifada remained premature. 'The real test of courage', she wrote, 'would be to channel these efforts and actions into a sustainable united front, not brought about from the old men in the outdated national, leftist, and Islamic factions, but from the youth.'[96] Indeed, such had been the case for nearly 100 years. It was thus just a matter of time before another upsurge in Palestinian civil resistance began, though it never actually ceased.

---

[94] 'PCBS: Palestinian Population "Youth Bulge"', Ma'an News Agency, 11 July 2011 www.maannews.net/eng/ViewDetails.aspx?ID=404099.
[95] Reproduced under the title 'Gaza Youth Breaks out with a "Manifesto for Change", Mondoweiss website, Chicago, 2 January 2011 http://mondoweiss.net/2011/01/gaza-youth-breaks-out-with-a-manifesto-for-change.
[96] Alsaafin, 'West Bank Protests: Waiting for a Tipping Point'.

11

Civil Resistance and the Fate of the Arab Spring

Adam Roberts

The chapters in this book have described the extraordinary variety of national and individual experiences that the Arab Spring comprised. They have also recounted how the hopes inspired in the first months of 2011 were followed, in many of the Arab countries of the Middle East and North Africa, by bitter disappointment. They have suggested explanations for why events developed as they did. This concluding chapter draws together threads running through the separate stories, and seeks also, using some additional material, to address some of the general issues these events raise: what they tell us about the character and capacity of civil resistance, about the problems of transitions to democracy, about the roles of outside powers, and about what might be salvaged from the disasters that followed the Arab Spring.

The pace and intensity of events in the first months of the Arab Spring were extraordinary. On 17 December 2010 the 26-year-old vegetable-seller, Mohammed Bouazizi, set fire to himself in the Tunisian town of Sidi Bouzid after police had harassed him as he plied his trade. This incident set off a series of demonstrations, first locally, then across Tunisia, and then in other parts of North Africa and the Middle East. Within two months, the movements that rapidly emerged had resulted in the departure from office of two long-standing autocrats—President Zine Al Abidine Ben Ali of Tunisia on 14 January 2011, and President Hosni Mubarak of Egypt four weeks later, on 11 February. Then in Yemen, following protests that began in February 2011, President Ali Abdullah Saleh resigned from the presidency in November 2011.

Yet even from the start there were setbacks and reverses. Three early cases stand out, in ascending order of the scale of the disaster: Bahrain, Libya, and, above all, Syria. In both Bahrain and Syria the demand for fundamental reform, and for autocratic regimes to step down, was articulated in sustained campaigns involving demonstrations, strikes, and countless other acts of non-compliance. However, both regimes survived, buttressed by significant domestic and external support. In particular, the government of Bahrain defeated the revolution, thanks in part to the arrival of a Saudi-led intervention force on 14 March 2011. This can be seen as the first major setback for the Arab Spring, but other problems were burgeoning. In Libya civil resistance in February 2011 (and some distinctly uncivil resistance) was followed rapidly by an open civil war, direct military involvement by NATO (from 20 March), the killing of Gaddafi, and then the decline of the country into endemic violence. The situation in Syria rapidly became one of civil war in a particularly horrific form, leading to the exodus of millions of refugees into neighbouring Jordan, Turkey, Lebanon, and Iraq, adding destabilizing pressures to the entire region.

The years that followed 2011 saw some important, albeit modest, achievements. The most important, but still fragile, achievement was in the country where it all began. In Tunisia there was a major change towards a functioning democratic system, which in 2014 survived one of the most critical tests of any such system: the peaceful transfer of legislative and presidential power from one party to another. Indeed, this was the first time in the region that Islamists had lost an election and immediately conceded defeat.

Yet in many other countries the demonstrators who had called for the fall of existing regimes faced bitter facts, not the least of which was the continuance of authoritarian rule and repression. In Egypt, which had for a time seemed to bear the hopes of the Arab Spring, there was a reversion to military rule in 2013. In Yemen, the successful overthrow of a hated ruler weakened but did not remove the entrenched power structure, and was followed by unofficial violence, warlordism, and war. In many countries there was growing intolerance of minorities, not least religious minorities, and some regimes and factions exacerbated sectarian animosity as a strategy for survival. Several of the different conflicts in the region came to be seen as parts of a larger transnational struggle between the Sunni and Shi'a branches of Islam. This bitter struggle was not created by the demonstrators of 2011—in its contemporary manifestation it can be traced back to the Iranian revolution of 1979, and it became a defining feature of regional politics after the 2003 invasion of Iraq—but in several countries it has been exacerbated by the Arab Spring's after-effects.

What does this pattern of setbacks mean for the cause of civil resistance as a means of opposing oppression and autocracy? And for the cause of advancing democratic systems of government internationally? Are we at the end of an era of unwisely high hopes in these twin causes, each aiming at the reduction or even elimination of many forms of political violence? Do such hopes have to yield to a more cautious view of the possibilities of political progress? Or are there historical reasons specific to the Arab world precluding civil resistance from being more successful?

From the very beginning of the Arab Spring, civil resistance was the principal public form of action through which fundamental reform was sought. In 2011, in one country after another, huge crowds demanding change—and doing so in a predominantly peaceful manner—became not just a preferred form of political action, but also the symbol of the Arab Spring. The civil nature of the movements helped them to attract huge participation, won much international support, and contributed to the undermining of the legitimacy and power of several regimes. The very achievements of the Arab Spring, and the scale of the subsequent reverses, suggest a need to look rigorously at the phenomenon of civil resistance, its relationship to other forms of power, and its capacity to achieve goals and also to bring about unintended change. There has been little discussion of this matter, and it is hard to identify anything like received wisdom on it.

The previous book produced by the Oxford University Research Project on Civil Resistance and Power Politics focused on two issues that are germane to our consideration of the fate of the Arab Spring:

> The explorations in this book are based on two core propositions. First, that civil resistance cannot be considered in isolation from all the other factors of power, domestic and foreign, civil and military, which help to determine outcomes. And second, that civil resistance, while it has had many successes, can sometimes contribute to adverse, or at least ambiguous, outcomes.[1]

These introductory propositions could easily serve as the concluding propositions to the present work. However, there is more to say about the Arab Spring than that. Six questions will be tackled here, and form the structure of the six sections of this chapter:

1. How unified, or diverse, were the phenomena covered by the term 'the Arab Spring'?

2. How did power politics—including the full range of factors of power, within and beyond the region—affect the outcomes?

3. Why was a new constitutional order, with a settled system of checks and balances, so difficult to achieve in so many of the countries involved?

4. Did civil resistance constitute a serious challenge to those advocating resort to political violence and terrorism?

5. Did the Arab Spring contribute, albeit unintentionally, to a revival of authoritarian ideas in the region and elsewhere, and do advocates of civil resistance need to recognize the strength of appeals to security that have contributed to that revival?

6. What lessons can be learned about the possibilities of political change, and the capacity of civil resistance to achieve it? In particular, is there a problem with the view of civil resistance as essentially about undermining dictators?

---

[1] Adam Roberts, 'Introduction', in Adam Roberts and Timothy Garton Ash (eds), *Civil Resistance and Power Politics: The Experience of Non-Violent Action from Gandhi to the Present* (Oxford: Oxford University Press, 2009), 2.

Underlying all these questions, and particularly the sixth one, is a recurring theme in much debate and writing about civil resistance: what is most decisive in determining outcomes? Is it the choice of methods and the quality of leadership of a struggle? Or is it the specific conditions that the resisters face, such as the resources and degree of determination of the adversary, the broader power-political context, the prevailing customs and belief-systems in a society, and a people's capacity to adopt fundamental changes, not least in the direction of constitutional democracy in some form? In other words, is civil resistance universally applicable, or is it limited by circumstance and place?

Similar questions about methods versus conditions have arisen in many studies of, and debates about, democracy promotion; and the troubles of the Arab Spring have been largely those of seeking to establish new democratic constitutional systems in difficult conditions. This question of methods versus conditions recurs at many points in the analysis that follows. It is essential to any attempt to make sense of the Arab Spring and indeed to learn from its failures.

UNITY AND DIVERSITY

Revolts, Uprisings, Awakening, or Spring?

The very term 'Arab Spring' is often questioned. Other terms have been suggested, each carrying distinct connotations. 'The Arab revolts' and 'the Arab uprisings' have been used frequently. 'The Second Arab Awakening' has particular attractions. The term has been used in conscious evocation of George Antonius's classic 1938 work *The Arab Awakening*—the famous history of the Arab national movement from the mid-nineteenth century to the 1930s.[2] It had been largely about the growth of an overall sense of Arab nationhood. However, it foreshadowed later events in that it also said much about the matter of nationalism and patriotism within the bounds of the existing and new states in the region; and it recognized the drawbacks of relying on violence, drawing a significant distinction between the Arab movement and some acts of violence committed in pursuit of its goals—even arguing at one point that 'violence defeats its own ends; and such immediate gains as it may score are invariably discounted by the harm which is inseparable from it'.[3] The term 'Second Arab Awakening' has been chosen in the titles

---

[2] George Antonius, *The Arab Awakening: The Story of the Arab National Movement* (London: Hamish Hamilton, 1938), 409.

[3] Antonius, *Arab Awakening*, 409.

of books by the historian of Arab nationalism Adeed Dawisha;[4] and by Marwan Muasher, a Jordanian diplomat and former foreign minister, who has suggested that the term Arab Spring 'implied expectations of an immediate transition from autocratic regimes to democratic ones'.[5] Both Dawisha and Muasher saw the first Arab Awakening as having fallen short of its founding aspirations. They saw the events of 2011 as challenging precisely that historic failure of Arab states. As Muasher puts it:

> In the end, colonial autocracies were replaced with domestic ones—often military-backed single parties that took advantage of their revolutionary legitimacy to cement their grip on power. New regimes paid little attention to developing political systems whose checks and balances guaranteed access for all. They saw pluralism as a potential threat.[6]

In short, some of the alternative terms, especially 'Second Arab Awakening', have merit. However, 'Arab Spring', as mentioned in the Preface, is succinct, widely understood, and captures some of the special features of these events. Its hint of their time-limited character tallies with our focus on civil resistance, most of which happened in 2011–13. One criticism is that the term 'Arab Spring' reflects Western media preoccupations, and is deemed to be an echo of a distinctly European event, the Prague Spring of 1968. Yet the term has also been widely used in the region itself, and indeed can trace its origins to the Damascus Spring of 2000–1. It captures both the evanescence of a moment that did not last, and the distinctiveness of these events when compared with older forms of political action in the Middle East and North Africa. True, it has resonances with some European events, but some of these are appropriate. It evokes the 1848 'springtime of nations' in which more than ten European countries experienced revolutions—most of which were reversed within a year or two, by means not wholly unlike what has been witnessed in the Arab world since 2011.

Eight Features of the Arab Spring

There were many common themes detectable in the popular movements that together made up the Arab Spring.[7] Eight such features stand out.

---

[4] Adeed Dawisha, *The Second Arab Awakening* (New York: W. W. Norton, 2013).

[5] Marwan Muasher, *The Second Arab Awakening: And the Battle for Pluralism* (New Haven: Yale University Press, 2014), 2.

[6] Muasher, *Second Arab Awakening*, 1. Similarly, Adeed, *Second Arab Awakening*, 65–8.

[7] The most substantial thematic work exploring the roots, social basis, and mental frameworks of the Arab Spring is Charles Tripp, *The Power and the People: Paths of Resistance in the Middle East* (Cambridge: Cambridge University Press, 2013).

1. *Political and demographic conditions.* The circumstances that gave rise to these movements included growing awareness of, and anger towards, the corrupt and oppressive nature of many Arab governments, which were often supported by outside powers, including Western ones. There was also a more general sense of the humiliation experienced under post-colonial political systems. Youth under the age of 25 formed a high proportion—in many cases over 50 per cent—of the population of the countries considered in this volume: combined with high unemployment rates, including for those who had completed tertiary education, this constituted tinder for revolution.[8]

2. *Precursors.* The use of non-violent methods had many precursors in the region: in their introductory chapter, Chibli Mallat and Edward Mortimer outline 'a long stream of imperfect precedents', and emphasize that 'the Arab Spring derives from long traditions of civil resistance in the Middle East'.[9] The other chapters amply confirm that in the years before 2011 there had been an increase in the number of demonstrations and social movements using non-violent methods in many Arab countries.

3. *Choice of particular non-violent methods.* The various movements sought change by resorting to predominantly non-violent means. The most visible manifestations of the Arab Spring were the many large demonstrations in symbolically important spaces, but there were also strikes, petitions, and use of new media. When there was a risk of demonstrations getting out of hand, 'peaceful, peaceful' was a commonly used invocation. There were many reasons for the decisions to pursue such methods, including disillusion with, and fear of, political violence; the need for forms of action in which large numbers could participate; and awareness of many civil resistance movements in the Arab world and elsewhere. Here, as in other cases, the use of non-violent confrontational tactics in demonstrations was not based on a presumption that the authorities would not use tear gas and bullets in response. Indeed, they did: in most countries touched by the Arab Spring, some demonstrators were shot—in some cases hundreds were killed. With certain important exceptions, the movements generally carried on, and many gained in legitimacy and support because of the perceived illegitimacy of the violence of the incumbent regime. Yet some demonstrators did use violence in certain circumstances, and the movements should not be presented as more homogeneous, and more committed to total avoidance of violence, than they actually were.

4. *Political goals.* The various movements had many common aspirations. They sought to end patterns of authoritarian rule, abuses by police and

---

[8] For statistics on population, GDP, and unemployment, see Table 11.1.
[9] See Chibli Mallat and Edward Mortimer, Chapter 1, this volume.

security services, corruption, dishonest elections, and poor economic per-formance. Demands for change were not couched in ideological terms (whether communist, Islamist, or other) but were mainly pragmatic in nature, centring on hopes for a decent life and the possibility of earning an honest wage. The notably active role of women in the demonstrations was accompanied by demands that the rights of all citizens, including women, be reflected in public life. In short, the movements demanded jobs, dignity, and rule of law. Explicitly or implicitly, they called for an effectively functioning constitutional system within their own states, giving people some control over their rulers. However, notions of constitutionalism, and the degrees of commitment to them, varied greatly, posing a major problem for the capacity of the movements to achieve lasting structural changes.

5. *Leadership.* These popular movements generally did not have formal leadership structures. They were not summoned or led by any one organization or political party. As events developed, some individual leaders, and leadership structures, did emerge. However, new ad hoc leadership arrangements often proved to be an insufficient basis for decision-making in such matters as developing policies, preparing constitutions, and negotiating with other parties. The result was that better-organized bodies could often move in and take a leading role in constructing a new political system. The revolutionary movements, in short, were effective in revolution, but their success did not translate into politics. This left the political scene open for existing social actors (often Islamists) who were able to mobilize through networks of mosques, or who in some cases were already established political actors. This reflected the fact that, through the years of authoritarianism, the only institutions really allowed to function had been the religious ones.

6. *Means of communication.* In the Arab revolutions, the 'new media' played a significant role alongside traditional media, and indeed those fundamental forms of human communication on which meetings in public spaces have always relied. Social networking media such as Face-book and Twitter, together with satellite television channels such as Al Jazeera, and the widespread use of mobile phones, helped both in enabling people to mobilize, and in letting the outside world know what was happening. Civil resistance was used as a means of struggle, partly because, thanks to media both old and new, it could help mobilize international support. The new media, important as they were, are far from being the sole explanation of the uprisings, which continued even when, as in Egypt, Internet and mobile phone services were shut down completely for several days. Without the bravery and skilful strategic thinking of the protesters, new media would have achieved little. A further limitation of the role of the new media was exposed by the

ways in which, both during and after the struggles against existing rulers, older forms of social organization—mosques, the Muslim Brotherhood, political parties and armies—often played a more central part than the new media in shaping political outcomes.

7. *Participation.* The movements were predominantly urban, and in many cases the capital city was the main locus of action. However, the Tunisian uprising began in small towns in the poor, neglected interior; the Yemeni demonstrations took place in all the capitals of governorates, some of which are barely more than small towns, and there was a notably heavy involvement of rural people because of their high presence in towns; and the Syrian Uprising began in Dara'a, in the south-west of the country. Although the movements had some working-class participation, they have been seen as mainly middle class.[10] Young people took a major part, and the role of women in street demonstrations represented a striking change from the formal and traditionally male-dominated politics of the region.

8. *Mutual learning.* The movements learned from each other's experiences. The most common slogan, 'The people want the fall of the regime', moved from one country to the next (perhaps even too easily, as will be discussed later in this chapter). In a rolling sequence, Egyptians were deeply influenced by the events in Tunisia in January 2011, and in turn Bahrainis, Yemenis, Syrians, and others were influenced too by the events in Egypt. This process bore some similarities to the way in which the east European revolutions of 1989 were inspired by events in Poland, then Hungary and East Germany.

Alleged Conspiracies

Some have suggested that there was a more sinister unity in the Arab Spring— that it was run or at least manipulated by foreign states and ideologies. The common language, culture, and history of the Arab world have made the region susceptible to transnational ideological influences of various kinds. For example, both pan-Arabism and pan-Islamism pose difficult challenges to the states of the region, heightening their sense of insecurity. As regards civil resistance, it is beyond dispute that there had long been transnational influences; and the events of 1989 and the subsequent 'colour revolutions' had naturally provoked interest in many parts of the world. Political ideas have always crossed borders, and did so in the Arab Spring. This is a normal part of political give-and-take. Yet, from 2011 onwards, several governments faced

---

[10] Francis Fukuyama, 'The Middle Class Revolution', *Wall Street Journal*, New York, 28 June 2013. His article also referred to events in Turkey, Brazil, and elsewhere.

with waves of demonstrations interpreted civil resistance as enemy interference. For example, at the end of the first month of the Syrian Uprising, in a
long speech to the Syrian parliament, President Bashar al-Assad said:

> our enemies work every day in an organized, systematic and scientific manner in
> order to undermine Syria's stability. We acknowledge that they had been smart in
> choosing very sophisticated tools in what they have done; but at the same time we
> realize that they have been stupid in choosing the country and the people, for
> such conspiracies do not work with our country or our people.... So, they mixed
> Today, there is a new fashion which they call 'revolutions'.... So, they mixed
> up three elements: sedition, reform, and daily needs. Most of the Syrian people
> call for reform, and you are all reformers. Most of the Syrian people have unmet
> needs; and we all discuss, criticize, and have our disagreements because we have
> not met many of the needs of the Syrian people. But sedition has become part of
> the issue and started to lead the other two factors and take cover under them.
> That is why it was easy to mislead many people who demonstrated in the
> beginning with good intentions. We cannot say that all those who demonstrated
> are conspirators. This is not true, and we want to be clear and realistic.[11]

This is one of several cases of rulers adopting an apparently reasonable tone
while appealing to national pride against sedition and conspiracy. The Syrian
press took a similar line. No serious evidence was offered, then or later, about
details of the alleged 'conspiracies', nor was there any specificity about the
reforms that Assad was proposing. However, as Raymond Hinnebusch, Omar
Imady, and Tina Zintl point out in their chapter on Syria in this volume, the
originally baseless narrative of an armed and extremist foreign-backed opposition slowly became a reality.[12]

This emphasis on external seditious interference formed part of a pattern.
In Egypt, from 2011 onwards, and especially after the coup of July 2013, many
newspaper articles alleged that the civil resistance of the pro-democracy
movement was instigated, planned, and funded by external actors.[13] Reflecting
an enduring proclivity for conspiracy theories, and drawing on exotic and
evidence-free areas of the Web, these articles saw any and every sign of foreign
influence as proof of master-and-puppet control by external actors for mal-
evolent purposes that form part of a grand overall plan. In responding to two
such articles in the Egyptian newspaper *Al-Dostoor*, Professor Stephen Zunes
summarized the Egyptian attacks thus:

---

[11] Bashar al-Assad, speech to the Syrian parliament, 30 March 2011 http://www.al-bab.com/
arab/docs/syria/bashar_assad_speech_110330.htm.

[12] Raymond Hinnebusch, Omar Imady and Tina Zintl, Chapter 9, this volume.

[13] e.g. Amro Amer, 'April 6 and the Revolutionary Socialists are Parts of a Scheme to
Overthrow Egypt', *Al-Dostoor*, Cairo, 24 December 2013; and Amer, 'April 6 behind an
American Plan to Empower Muslim Brotherhood', *Al-Dostoor*, 12 January 2014.

As part of this effort to blame the United States for homegrown movements, pro-military writer and political analyst Amro Amer asserts in *Al-Dostoor* that the Egyptian 2011 pro-democracy protests were part of a US government plot 'to dismantle the strongest Arabic armies' which began with the invasion of Iraq, and later shifted to 'nonviolent wars.'

Amer also claims that 'the main instruments to wage those wars are the books and publications of Gene Sharp and Peter Ackerman,' that 'Gene Sharp's book is a book to overthrow Egypt', and 'those political activists in Egypt are following the book of Gene Sharp and trying to create chaos and break the rules'.[14]

Zunes's article offered a point-by-point refutation. There is other evidence of the limited impact of US-based theorists of non-violent action. Gene Sharp himself gave a bemused account of how he saw the Arab Spring and his alleged influence on it.[15] In a highly critical study of *Political Aid and Arab Activism*, Sheila Carapico touched on a theory that had been circulating about the influence of the Belgrade-based Center for Applied Non-Violent Actions and Strategies (CANVAS), which has advocated Gene Sharp's approach:

> The progressive Egyptian intelligentsia found this legend of Western-backed Serbian inspiration for their mass popular mobilization insulting. There was even a facetious hash tag on Twitter, GeneSharpTaughtMe.... I never saw or heard any hint of Euro-American instigation of the Tunisian uprising that started the whole 'Arab Spring' or the Yemeni protest movement ... nor of foreign encouragement of labor strikes, sit-ins, and 'parallel revolutions' roiling Egypt and the region for several years. At most, Sharp and CANVAS would count among an array of inspirations that also included Che Guevara, Nelson Mandela, Palestinian *intifadas*, the American civil rights movement, Mahatma Gandhi, the Paris Commune, Franz Fanon, *The Battle of Algiers*, and indigenous regional, national and local cultural symbols, slogans, and performances.[16]

Notwithstanding the strength of the evidence supporting such observations, the vilification of civil resistance and pro-democracy movements has continued. Such vilification, which conveniently distracts attention from the local causes of dissatisfaction, has perennial appeal to authoritarian rulers in and beyond the Middle East. For example, in his speech about Ukraine in March

---

[14] Stephen Zunes, 'How to Discredit your Democratic Opponents in Egypt', openDemocracy, 17 February 2014 https://www.opendemocracy.net/civilresistance/stephen-zunes/how-to-discredit-your-democratic-opponents-in-egypt. Zunes co-chairs the academic advisory board of the Washington-based International Center on Nonviolent Conflict (co-founded by Peter Ackerman). As noted in the acknowledgements, Peter Ackerman, through ICNC, contributed to the funding of the Oxford University Project on Civil Resistance and Power Politics.

[15] Even Nord Rydningen, 'Gene out of the Bottle: An Interview with Dr Gene Sharp, Author of "From Dictatorship to Democracy"', openDemocracy, 17 February 2012 https://www.opendemocracy.net/opensecurity/even-nord-rydningen/gene-out-of-bottle-interview-with-dr-gene-sharp-author-of-from-dict.

[16] Sheila Carapico, *Political Aid and Arab Activism: Democracy Promotion, Justice, and Representation* (Cambridge: Cambridge University Press, 2014), 195–6.

2014, President Vladimir Putin of Russia criticized several movements in terms remarkably similar to those of President Assad—as will be mentioned in the discussion of Putin's critique of civil resistance, which is in this chapter's section on revivals of authoritarianism.

Diversity in the Arab Spring

The countries involved in the Arab Spring vary enormously in their political cultures, political systems, relations with neighbouring countries, and involvement with external allies. There are especially striking differences in population sizes and levels of development. However, they also share some common features: many have populations in which more than 50 per cent are under the age of 25; all have high rates of unemployment; and, in the countries for which figures are available, the proportion of unemployed who have received tertiary education is remarkably high. The age structures and high levels of unemployment certainly created pressures for revolution. However, these and other pressures were not the same in any two countries. Table 11.1 illustrates some of these features on the eve of the Arab Spring.

Table 11.1. Population, GDP per capita, and unemployment rates of selected states in the Middle East and North Africa, 2010

State/ territory	Population at mid-year 2010	Population aged under 25 as % of total population	GDP per capita in 2010 (except Syria, 2007) (US$)	Unemployed as % of total labour force	Males with tertiary education as % of total unemployed
Bahrain	1,251,513	44	16,722	7.0	21.0
Egypt	78,075,705	52	1,550	9.0	40.0
Jordan	6,046,000	54	2,818	13.0	34.0
Libya	6,040,612	47	9,099	19.0	n.a.
Morocco	31,642,360	47	2,349	9.0	17.0
Syria	21,532,647	55	1,637	8.0	n.a.
Tunisia	10,549,100	42	3,848	13.0	32.0
West Bank & Gaza	3,811,102	64	1,345	24.0	n.a.
Yemen	22,763,008	65	878	18.0	n.a.
Total population	**181,712,047**				

Sources: Columns 1 and 3–5: World Bank data http://data.worldbank.org. Gross Domestic Product per capita is in constant 2005 US dollars. The relevant tables do not have figures for Syrian GDP for 2008 or subsequent years. The World Bank states that the figures for unemployment rates are International Labour Organization estimates. Column 2: The figures for percentage of population aged under 25 in 2010 are from *The Economist*, London, 3 February 2011, citing various sources.

Within and beyond the region, many viewed the Arab Spring as a cascading set of near-identical events, in the face of which regimes would tumble wholesale. This idea of a non-violent 'domino effect' did not do justice to the inevitable complexities of different societies. In each of these countries the Arab Spring assumed different forms and had different effects. The remarkably varied character of the outcomes is largely attributable to different historical, social, and international factors—especially each Arab state's ethnic and religious composition, political traditions, and the ideas about how both government and opposition should operate. The Arab Spring was neither a monolith nor a row of dominoes.

Some observers expected that in the West Bank (mainly under Israeli occupation) and Gaza (under Hamas rule, but besieged by Israel) there might be a revolt comparable to the uprisings in Egypt and Tunisia. There were some demonstrations against the Israeli occupation, but nothing on the same scale. Why? As Wendy Pearlman shows, there was reluctance to embark on what might have ended up as a new intifada, particularly in the light of the weariness resulting from previous struggles. Furthermore, there was a fear of disrupting ongoing economic activities, especially the building boom, which was most notable in Ramallah; and it was not obvious against which of the potential targets—the Israeli occupation, or the Palestinian administrations in the West Bank and Gaza—a campaign should be directed.

Whereas in many cases the demonstrators' demand was the fall of the regime, in two countries, Jordan and Morocco, both pro-Western monarchies, the movements took a distinct form. As Jacob Amis and Driss Maghraoui show in their respective chapters, the movements there called not for revolution, but for constitutional and other reforms. In both cases the reformist stance of the demonstrators framed the way the monarchy reacted, and the monarchy shaped aspects of the demonstrators' proposals and actions; the modest constitutional reforms that resulted remained under the control of the monarchy. In Jordan in 2014—faced with the huge challenges of refugees from the Syrian war, threats from the Islamic State in Iraq and the Levant (ISIS), and the Israeli war on Gaza in July–August—King Abdullah had to maintain a particularly delicate course between the popular demands for reform and his advisers' preoccupation with security (see Figure 11.1).

Wider Echoes

In some other countries not examined in detail in this book, confrontations typical of the Arab Spring did not happen. For example, Saudi Arabia—deeply involved in repressing some of the consequences of the Arab Spring in Bahrain, Egypt, and elsewhere—itself experienced little of the massive and open public opposition that was so widespread elsewhere during the years from 2011. The Saudi government

Figure 11.1. Some protesters were keenly aware of the need to capture the international spotlight. Here demonstrators from the Islamic Action Front in Jordan hold up carefully prepared English-language posters with their reform demands during a demonstration on 2 February 2011 near the prime minister's office in Amman.
© *AP Photo/Nader Daoud*

deployed multiple strategies to ensure that protests were never large scale. Thanks to its oil wealth, it could buy off its citizens with big increases in subsidies. In addition, it suppressed the many Shi'a protests in the Eastern Province vigorously, arrested many non-sectarian activists in Riyadh, Jeddah, and other cities, and encouraged Islamist clerics to issue fatwas banning protests as 'unislamic'. A 'day of rage' planned for March 2011 failed to gain ground.[17] Some of the protests in Saudi Arabia reflected the interests of particular segments of society—the women's campaign for the right to drive cars being a clear example.

Yet, like many revolutionary events throughout history, the Arab Spring was not neatly confined to a particular group of countries. The events in Tunis, Cairo, and elsewhere inspired civic action movements in the broader Middle Eastern, Arab, African, and Muslim worlds. For example, in Algeria, from 28 December 2010, there were protests in many parts of the country, concentrating on unemployment, housing problems, and food prices; and there were several self-immolations in January 2011. Fear of a return to the violence of the 1990s was one factor in inhibiting the population from engaging in attempts to

---

[17] Elham Fakhro, 'The Kingdom Divided', Carnegie Endowment for International Peace, Washington, *Sada*, 8 March 2012 http://carnegieendowment.org/sada/2012/03/08/kingdom-divided/fjca.

replace the regime, and an increase in subsidies was another. In Sudan, from January 2011 onwards, there were extensive protests against the regime of President Omar al-Bashir, in many cases demanding his departure. Several Gulf states were affected: Oman was the scene of protests from January 2011 onwards, with a wide range of demands, and Kuwait saw numerous protests in 2011–12, mainly calling for political and electoral reform, and with some actions also reflecting the interests of a particular group, the *bedoon* (stateless people) campaigning for the right to nationality. Similarly, in Mauritania there were numerous protests in 2011–12, mainly making demands for reform. And, in Turkey, there was a year of protests that started in Taksim Square in Istanbul on 28 May 2013. Many of these events resembled those of the Arab Spring—in the types of demonstration, in the issues addressed, in social composition, and in forms of organization. Some of them, like some Arab Spring events, involved stonethrowing and rioting. In none of these other cases mentioned here was a regime removed in a revolution, but in some there were changes in government policy or personnel. In most of them, the US and European states urged the governments to avoid violent repression and to recognize the rights of citizens.

Many events far from the Middle East and North Africa were influenced by the spectacle of people power in Tunis, Cairo, and other cities. In September 2011, when the Occupy Wall Street movement erupted in the USA, it was widely seen as inspired by the Arab Spring. Exhibiting deep disquiet about the global financial system, it led to similar demonstrations in hundreds of cities around the world. Then, when in December 2011 Russian citizens protested against irregularities in the Russian legislative elections, US Senator John McCain tweeted cheekily to Prime Minister Vladimir Putin: 'Dear Vlad, the #Arab Spring is coming to a neighbourhood near you.'[18] This can only have reinforced Putin's view of civil resistance as linked with US power politics.

POWER POLITICS: THE EFFECTS ON OUTCOMES

The predecessor of the current work, published in 2009, noted the continuous interplay between civil resistance and power politics, both within and between states.[19] This conclusion is amply, and tragically, borne out by the experience of the Arab Spring. If the success of some of the movements in early 2011 briefly encouraged the attractive idea of a democratic 'domino effect'—a

---

[18] John McCain, tweet of 5 December 2011. Matt Cover, 'McCain Tweets Putin: "Dear Vlad, Is It Something I Said?"', *CNS News*, 15 December 2011 http://cnsnews.com/news/article/mccain-tweets-putin-dear-vlad-it-something-i-said.

[19] Roberts, 'Introduction', in Roberts and Garton Ash (eds), *Civil Resistance and Power Politics*, 4–7.

rolling democratic and civil revolution, starting with Tunisia and Egypt, and leading to similar outcomes throughout the Arab world—it was not to be. While civil resistance does represent a significant break from the normal methods of power politics, hard facts of power, which varied hugely in the countries involved, had a bearing on the causation, the course, and the outcome of each episode of the Arab Spring. The revolutions involved not only some crude and cruel acts of repression, but also some more subtle and complex interactions between non-violent demonstrators and various forms of power, including military strength. As so often happens, the leaders of civil resistance movements directed their actions to particular audiences and wielders of power, both at home and internationally.

The rest of this section looks mainly at six countries in which significant domestic movements, either initially or after pursuing more modest demands, sought fundamental change, including a change of regime. In four of these countries—Tunisia, Egypt, Libya, and Yemen—there was a fairly prompt change of regime. In two, Bahrain and Syria, the domestic movements were unsuccessful. The following analysis outlines, first, some of the internal power-political factors that affected outcomes, and then explores at greater length international power-political factors that may have facilitated, shaped, or prevented change.

Power within the State

Civil resistance is often based on a proposition that even dictators depend on various pillars of support, so their power can be undermined from below. Thus the effect of a major campaign of civil resistance aiming at the overthrow of a regime depends considerably on the state of domestic power structures.

This was clear in the first case, Tunisia, where quick results were achieved. The heavy-handed authoritarian regime of President Zine El Abidine Ben Ali with its large security apparatus had neither a strong ideological base nor sufficient financial resources to make significant economic concessions to its people. It tried and failed to stop demonstrations by brute force in the form of police shootings. The demonstrators, as is common in campaigns of civil resistance, consistently sought to discourage the police from using force, and to discredit them when they did so. The Tunisian armed forces largely kept out of the conflict, because they were historically (and especially since independence) small and apolitical: members of the military and internal security forces are not allowed to vote—a rule that was reaffirmed in the electoral law of 2014. Ultimately the Tunisian regime ran out of options because of its own weakness and poor decisions, and the rapid growth of demonstrations. The sudden flight of President Ben Ali on 14 January 2011, an iconic moment of the Arab Spring, was due more to factors within the country than to international pressure.

In Egypt, by far the most populous Arab state, the constellation of power within the state was of critical importance. Indeed, the centrality and complexity of the role of armed forces were most evident there. A key slogan of the Egyptian demonstrators on Cairo's Tahrir Square in 2011 was 'The army and people are one'—an unusual and paradoxical, but far from illogical, chant for a non-violent movement. After the 2011 revolution, cracks in this claimed unity, and inherent problems arising from reliance on the armed forces, became apparent. In his chapter, Cherif Bassiouni suggests that from the start Egypt's military leadership opposed Mubarak's plan to appoint his son Gamal (who was supported by the police) as his successor.[20] By appearing to be pro-reform, they could ride the wave of popular protest and at the same time advance their own agenda. After 2011 relations between the popular movement and the armed forces became even more complex and tangled. In June 2013 many in the movement, by supporting the call for the removal of the elected president, Mohamed Morsi, implicitly supported the *coup d'état* of 3 July that overthrew him (see Figure 11.2).

Figure 11.2. Popular demonstrations return to central Cairo but this time in favour of an army takeover. On the day of the coup, 3 July 2013, demonstrators hold aloft portraits of the army chief Abdel Fattah el-Sisi after he announced he was replacing the elected Islamist president Mohamed Morsi, who had been promptly arrested and jailed; Sisi became president himself in June 2014.

© *Khaled Desouki/AFP/Getty Images*

---

[20] M. Cherif Bassiouni, Chapter 3, this volume.

From very early in its history the Egyptian movement had to confront certain uses of force, not by the army, but by the police and, very dramatically, by pro-regime thugs. It was the latter, many of them riding on horses and camels, who attacked the demonstrators in Tahrir Square on 2 February 2011. In response, some in the crowd retaliated used a degree of force, including throwing stones at their attackers and arresting a number of them. One demonstrator tweeted that afternoon: 'I came to a peaceful protest, this is not one.' And then, eight hours later: 'I did not take part in the violence, which is a real moral dilemma for me right now, for it's the people who did who saved me.'[21] After seeing off the thugs, the demonstrators reverted to their peaceful methods of protest. It was as if they accepted that sometimes it is necessary to use force in a defensive cause, but it should not be the main means of achieving political change.

In both Tunisia and Egypt, there was always a concern that things might get out of hand—that largely peaceful protests could quickly degenerate into riots. Was this also a factor in inducing at least parts of the state establishment to turn against the hated ruler? In both countries, there were certainly enough incidents of stone-throwing, looting, and arson to raise that possibility. For example, in the early days of the Egyptian revolution there was a good deal of rioting and arson, but it was significantly curtailed by the movement's leaders, not least because of concern that such violence played into the regime's hands by giving it a justification for repression. Indeed, in many of the Arab uprisings, governments went to some lengths (for example, sending in thugs, releasing criminals from prisons, and provoking demonstrators) to encourage violence and disorder as part of an attempt to justify their own use of violence in the name of restoring order. The loyalist and officially inspired discourse in many countries became one of order and stability versus the chaos of protests. Whether in particular cases the possibility of violent mayhem on the streets led to a hardening of regime attitudes, or to a willingness to make concessions to the demonstrators, it is not possible to say at this stage.

In Yemen, vividly described by Helen Lackner, there was another rapid process of defections from the regime—a classic case of weakening a ruler's sources of power. Apart from all the other causes, such as declining living standards, a contributory factor in the opposition was President Saleh's scheme to stay in power long enough to be able to hand over to his son. This was similar to the fall-out in Egypt as a result of Mubarak's ambitions to hand over to his son, and it had similar effects both within Yemen and internationally, contributing to the formation of an effective anti-Saleh coalition.

Overwhelmingly, however, it was the peaceful, determined character of the protests and strikes in Tunisia, Egypt, and Yemen that induced recognition,

---

[21] Nadia Idle and Alex Nunns (eds), *Tweets from Tahrir: Egypt's Revolution as it Unfolded, in the Words of the People Who Made It* (New York: OR Books, 2011), 107, 116.

both domestically and internationally, that the old regime could not be saved, and that fundamental changes in the leadership and constitutional structure of the state had to be made. A key part of the process leading to change was the skilful appeal to the wielders of force in their respective societies—and also to their external allies. The international factors involved will be discussed further in the next section of this chapter.

In some other countries—most notably Bahrain and Syria—the regime had a large (albeit minority) social base. In Bahrain the power structure within the state, and its economic and strategic dependence on outside powers, has long militated against attempts to replace the Al-Khalifa ruling family, though the country's history is rife with examples of movements seeking such a change. In the decade before 2011, opposition activists mostly focused on modifying the constitutional system. However, the suppression of protests led to some renewed calls for regime change. A country where the system of government largely represents a demographic minority that is associated with Sunni Islam, but where there is an under-represented mainly Shiʿa majority, is always likely to have a significant section of the population that fears revolutionary change, even if non-violent. The history of Iranian claims to the territory of Bahrain compounds the delicacy of the position of both sectors of the population. Elham Fakhro presents a convincing picture of how local power political factors, as well as the roles of outsiders, created an extraordinarily difficult environment within which opposition actors pursued the cause of change with only limited effect.

The continuing multi-sided civil war in Syria represents the most worrying example of the problems, both domestic and international, that can ensue when a civil resistance movement has confronted a powerful, obstinate, and violent regime. Demonstrations began in Syria in March 2011, initially with modest demands. By April they were demanding that President Bashar al-Assad resign. The demonstrations—vilified by the regime as foreign inspired and as consisting of 'armed terrorist groups'—were brutally attacked by the armed forces. There were large numbers of deaths even in the pre-civil-war phase in 2011, and many of those who were arrested were tortured. The regime survived the non-violent campaign against it, and then went on to survive the first years of the civil war. It owed its survival partly to the fact that, in a society that was ethnically and religiously very diverse, it had a strong power base among the Alawite community, and it also played on the divisions in Syrian society, making it hard for any opposition to secure the support that it needed in all sectors of the population. Both within Syria and abroad, many recognized at the time that it was structurally difficult, or even impossible, for Syria to reform itself.[22] It is even arguable, but not proven, that Assad may

---

[22] e.g. Emile Hokayem, Senior Fellow in Middle East Security, International Institute for Strategic Studies, in a talk at IISS, London, 6 April 2011.

have encouraged the growth of extremist Islamist groups as part of a strategy to force the West to negotiate with him. Whether or not this is so, the events in Syria, like those in Iraq with which they are closely connected, are examples of how security vacuums, however caused, can provide space for extremist groups to gain traction.

In each state in the region, the movements of the Arab Spring had to operate in the same space as Islamist parties. The rise of the latter can be understood as a response to authoritarianism: where there were no avenues for civil society to mobilize, the only institutions capable of mobilizing are religious ones. Further, the widespread sense that in different ways various Arab societies had been dominated by outside forces contributed to the Islamic upsurge. Within many states in the region, Islamic movements of various kinds were large and had a clear leadership structure, posing a challenge to more secular-minded civil resisters. In short, the power-political circumstances within the states of the region, as briefly outlined here, were extremely difficult for the civil resistance movements.

Role of Outside Governments and Organizations

There was another dimension of power politics in the Arab revolutions: the role of outside governments. In all four cases where there was a change of regime, external pressures on the leader to quit played some part—perhaps minor in Tunisia, but definitely considerable in Egypt, Libya, and Yemen. All these were countries in which Western powers, especially the USA, had considerable influence.

A wide range of countries and regional bodies had to address questions about whether they should support incumbent governments or assist a process of change. And, if change it was, they had to consider what forms any support should take: direct support for opposition movements, freezing of regime assets, pressure on governments not to use forceful repression, withdrawal of defence cooperation, military intervention, public statements, refugee assistance, or provision of aid? Among outside powers there were genuine differences of perception and of interest that hampered international cooperation in addressing the internal conflicts of the region. In addition, despite many conspiracy theories attributing extraordinary powers to foreign plotters, the actual capacity of outsiders to affect the politics of particular countries is limited and uncertain: indeed, too much help may be interpreted as evidence of outside colonial domination and may thus result in friction and resentment.

Western countries had a particularly awkward starting point. They had, and have, a range of interests in the Middle East and North Africa, not least in relation to maritime defence, energy, security, arms sales, and support for Israel. The USA and many European countries had a record of close association with dictatorial regimes, which were sometimes preferred, or at least tolerated, on the grounds that they provided stability. The USA and some European states also had a no less troubling record of occasionally intervening against particular regimes, as in the US-led invasion of Iraq from 2003 onwards, in ways that demonstrated a shocking lack of understanding of internal political dynamics and international responses, with baleful effects still unfolding. Two US practices have been viewed in the region as deeply hypocritical. First, while supporting democracy in theory, the USA rejected certain electoral outcomes, such as the Hamas victory in the 2006 Palestinian parliamentary elections; and, second, the USA has been very selective about the states it criticizes and those it does not.

The USA had, and has, close military relations with several states, including a major base in Bahrain, home to the US Fifth Fleet and US Naval Forces Central Command. However, like other Western states, it also had a record of calling for reforms in the region. For example, in 2005, at a time of political ferment in many Middle Eastern countries, US Secretary of State Condoleezza Rice said in a speech in Cairo: 'For 60 years my country, the United States, pursued stability at the expense of democracy in this region here in the Middle East—and we achieved neither. Now, we are taking a different course. We are supporting the democratic aspirations of all people.' She was particularly critical of the way in which the governments of Saudi Arabia and Egypt had imprisoned, or subjected to violence, citizens who acted peacefully in petitioning their government and promoting democracy. She continued:

> There are those who say that democracy leads to chaos, or conflict, or terror. In fact, the opposite is true: freedom and democracy are the only ideas powerful enough to overcome hatred, and division, and violence. For people of diverse races and religions, the inclusive nature of democracy can lift the fear of difference that some believe is a license to kill. But people of goodwill must choose to embrace the challenge of listening, and debating, and cooperating with one another.[23]

As was pointed out at the time in 2005, this classic expression of American optimism about democracy not only risked alienating Cairo and Riyadh, but also 'could open the way for more Islamist governments'.[24] The actual consequences of the US-led invasion of Iraq strengthened doubts in the region about US democracy promotion as being highly selective, mismanaged, and providing a trigger for sectarian conflict. The enduring tension in US policy between supporting autocracy and promoting democracy was perpetuated by the administration of President George W. Bush. Barack Obama sought

---

[23] Condoleezza Rice, speech at the American University in Cairo, 20 June 2005 http://2001-2009.state.gov/secretary/rm/2005/48328.htm.
[24] The BBC's Security Correspondent, Frank Gardner, 20 June 2005 http://news.bbc.co.uk/1/hi/4109902.stm.

to make a new start. Partly on the basis of the Iraq experience, he generally put less emphasis on democracy promotion than some of his predecessors; and, unlike any previous US president, he repeatedly referred to non-violent action as a key instrument of change. President Obama made a wide-ranging speech in Cairo in June 2009 calling for a new beginning in relations between the USA and Muslims around the world. Key parts of the new beginning were to be democratic reform and the pursuit of change through non-violent means. In speaking about the Israel–Palestine issue, Obama claimed that only non-violent struggle can achieve change:

> Palestinians must abandon violence. Resistance through violence and killing is wrong and it does not succeed. For centuries, black people in America suffered the lash of the whip as slaves and the humiliation of segregation. But it was not violence that won full and equal rights. It was a peaceful and determined insistence upon the ideals at the center of America's founding. This same story can be told by people from South Africa to South Asia; from Eastern Europe to Indonesia. It's a story with a simple truth: that violence is a dead end. It is a sign neither of courage nor power to shoot rockets at sleeping children, or to blow up old women on a bus. That's not how moral authority is claimed; that's how it is surrendered.[25]

Impressive as Obama's Cairo speech was, it left two questions hanging. What exactly did his rhetoric, or indeed that of Condoleezza Rice four years earlier, imply for US policy and actions? And how might democracy work in Egypt, where the best organized political force was the Muslim Brotherhood?

Well before the Arab Spring, many observers had concluded that Western policy was in deep trouble in the region. In a book published in 2009, David Gardner, a senior *Financial Times* journalist specializing in the Middle East, argued for a total reappraisal of what realpolitik means in the region. He suggested that the traditional shibboleths—support Israel, build up a network of reliable strongmen, mollify the Saudis, suppress Islamism—simply would not do in the twenty-first century. But he did concede the worrying point that democracy might not bring stability to the region. Holding out hopes of what might transpire under the newly elected President Obama, he proposed a complete change in the role of the Western powers, especially the USA:

> That role has to change. It is not a question of 'regime change', or of actively destabilizing the existing order. Instead of propping up tyrants for short-term (and often illusory) gains, western policy needs to find ways of stimulating and aiding those elements in Arab and Muslim society that might, eventually, replace

---

[25] President Barack Obama, 'Remarks by the President on a New Beginning', Cairo University, 4 June 2009 http://www.whitehouse.gov/the-press-office/remarks-president-cairo-university-6-04-09.

them. Arabs and Muslims, at the very least, have the right to expect that the USA and its allies do not actively support those who deny them their freedoms.[26]

In her memoirs, Hillary Clinton, Obama's Secretary of State, described the situation on the eve of the Arab Spring:

Despite its problems, most of the region's leaders and power brokers seemed largely content to carry on as they always had. And despite the best intentions of successive American administrations, the day-to-day reality of US foreign policy prioritized urgent strategic and security imperatives such as counterterrorism, support for Israel, and blocking Iran's nuclear ambitions over the long-term goal of encouraging internal reforms in our Arab partners. To be sure, we did press leaders to reform, because we believed that would eventually provide greater long-term stability and inclusive prosperity. But we also worked with them on a wide range of security concerns and never seriously considered cutting off our military relationships with them.

This was a dilemma that had confronted generations of American policymakers. It's easy to give speeches and write books about standing up for democratic values, even when it may conflict with our security interests, but when confronted with actual, real-world trade-offs, choices get a lot harder. Inevitably, making policy is a balancing act. Hopefully we get it right more than wrong. But there are always choices we regret, consequences we do not foresee, and alternate paths we wish we had taken.

I talked with enough Arab leaders over the years to know that for many of them, it wasn't a simple matter of being content with how things were; they accepted that change would come but only slowly. I looked for ways to build personal relationships and trust with them, to better grasp the cultural and social views that influenced their actions, and, when possible, push for more rapid change.[27]

On 13 January 2011, about one month after unrest had broken out in Tunisia, Hillary Clinton made a speech to a regional conference in the Qatari capital, Doha, outlining the region's challenges—unemployment, corruption, and a sclerotic political order: 'In too many places, in too many ways, the region's foundations are sinking into the sand.'[28] Yet, in the rapid pace of events leading to President Ben Ali's departure from Tunisia the very next day, outside powers do not appear to have had a decisive role. Thanks to Wikileaks revelations in 2010, the USA was publicly known to be highly critical of Ben Ali. As Michael Willis indicates, that fact no doubt encouraged the Tunisian opposition movement. Meanwhile, European support for change in Tunisia was probably less important; and France, the former colonial power, lost much of its standing in Tunisia because it appeared to be mainly concerned with treating the civil insurrection there as a public order problem. Of the four

---

[26] David Gardner, *Last Chance: The Middle East in the Balance* (London: I. B. Tauris, 2009), p. xviii.

[27] Hillary Rodham Clinton, *Hard Choices* (New York: Simon & Schuster, 2014), 332–3.

[28] Clinton, *Hard Choices*, 337.

revolutions in the Arab Spring that unseated their countries' leaders, the Tunisian one was the nearest to being free of outside interference and external military involvement. The authenticity of the Tunisian revolution was an inspiration to the citizens of other countries, but it would prove a hard act to follow.

From the beginning of 2011, when faced with incontrovertible evidence not just of the unpopularity of many Arab regimes but also of the pent-up popular demand for change, both the USA and European countries took an increasingly critical stance towards certain Arab states. First they called for unspecified reforms, then for an eventual transition to democracy, and then for immediate change. Ultimately, along with a number of countries in the region, they contributed in various ways to the pressure on Ben Ali, Mubarak, and others to go. The civil resistance on the Arab street was having a direct effect in Washington, London, and Paris.

The US position during the events in Egypt that started on 25 January 2011 has been the subject of controversies. These centred on whether the different parts of the US government—the White House, the Pentagon, the State Department, and the CIA—actually had a coherent policy or four competing ones, whether any US policy was likely to be counterproductive because of the unpopularity of the USA in Egypt, and whether the USA was urging democracy on Egypt without having much idea of how it could work out in practice. The USA seemed to be permanently caught between being accused of interference if it pressed too hard for particular solutions, and betrayal if it did not. Hillary Clinton has identified some of the dilemmas faced at the time:

> Contrary to popular belief among many in the Middle East, the United States has never been an all-powerful puppet master able to achieve any outcome we desire. What if we called for Mubarak to step down, but then he refused and managed to stay in power? What if he did step down and was succeeded by a long period of dangerous disorder or by a successor government no more democratic and actively opposed to our interests and security? Either way, our relationship would never be the same and our influence in the region would erode.[29]

According to one well-informed but possibly charitable interpretation, the administration consciously refrained from placing itself at the centre of events. It avoided grandiose rhetoric in favour of specific efforts to achieve an 'orderly, meaningful transition'. Putting the Egyptian people at the centre of events, it saw that siding more aggressively with the protesters could backfire—'by triggering a backlash against an America seen as opportunistically claiming a movement not its own, and by hardening the demands of protesters and thus making a settlement with the military less likely'.[30]

---

[29] Clinton, *Hard Choices*, 340.
[30] Marc Lynch, 'America and Egypt after the Uprisings', *Survival*, 53/2 (April–May 2011), 36.

Yet there was no way that the USA could stand idly by when Egypt was the scene of a great popular movement holding out the promise of a kind of democratic transition that chimed with US visions of how a better world might come into being. During the early days of the Arab Spring, especially in Egypt, US officials were essentially playing 'catch up'.[31] The USA did consistently emphasize that reform was urgently needed; and also that demonstrations should be handled with restraint. There were also statements that the repression had to end, and some indications that, if there was insufficient progress in these matters, US aid to Egypt would be cut. Finally on 2 February President Obama called for the departure of President Mubarak. In the ensuing days there was still some confusion on the key question of whether Mubarak should leave office immediately. Overall, US policies constituted one of the factors leading to the departure of Mubarak on 11 February.

Perhaps emboldened by this outcome, President Barack Obama went on to embrace the Arab Spring movements in a general way: in an interview in May 2011 he spoke of the 'moral force of non-violence' and asserted that 'the United States stands on the side of those who through non-violent means are trying to bring about a better life for themselves and their families'.[32] However, even as he spoke, advocates of systemic change faced visibly shrinking prospects—especially in Syria, Libya, and Bahrain, where the incumbent regimes had all used lethal force against demonstrators. It was far from obvious what actions, apart from the ongoing NATO campaign in Libya, might be implied by standing on the protestors' side. The USA, having run into trouble in its attempts to bring stability and democracy to Afghanistan and Iraq, and facing growing domestic opposition to further ventures abroad, had little will to get engaged in further conflicts.

In some Arab countries the balance of outside forces, far from helping the demonstrators, made conditions tough for them. This was manifestly the case in Bahrain, where courageous citizens demonstrated repeatedly for basic democratic rights. The USA was concerned about maintaining its naval base there. Neighbouring states were worried about the possible ramifications of genuine democracy establishing itself in Bahrain and perhaps elsewhere in the Gulf; and they were particularly concerned about the possibility of the majority Shi'a population gaining a significant degree of control in Bahrain. Saudi forces entered the country on 14 March 2011, under the authority of the Gulf Cooperation Council, and with the stated purpose of protecting essential facilities including oil and gas installations and financial institutions. The obvious effect of this intervention was to reduce the chances of a democratic

---

[31] A phrase used by US officials in interviews with Elham Fakhro, who provided this information in February 2015.

[32] Barack Obama, interviewed in the White House by Andrew Marr, broadcast on the *Andrew Marr Show*, BBC One, London, 22 May 2011.

deal between the government and the demonstrators, and to demoralize supporters of non-violent action. After the Saudi tanks had rolled in, one human-rights activist, who had believed that peaceful revolution could be achieved in Bahrain, said ruefully to a *New York Times* correspondent in Manama: 'We thought it would work. But now the aggression is too much. Now it's not about protest any more, it's about self-defense.'[33]

Libya was the one country in which the Western powers did act militarily in 2011. As George Joffé shows, the reasons for this unique engagement were relatively straightforward. After peaceful demonstrations in February 2011 had been met with violent repression and blood-curdling threats from the regime of Colonel Gaddafi, civil resistance rapidly changed into armed uprising. In this case, outside powers could assume a major role, because Libya's defences were so run down, and also because over the years Gaddafi had succeeded in antagonizing so many foreign governments that he was bereft of support.[34] By the end of February, the Arab League, the African Union, and the Secretary-General of the Organization of the Islamic Conference had all condemned the Libyan government's violations of human rights and international humanitarian law. The United Nations became directly involved almost from the beginning. A UN Security Council Resolution of 26 February 2011 deplored 'the gross and systematic violation of human rights, including the repression of peaceful demonstrators', and provided for an arms embargo, travel ban, and asset freeze.[35] Then, in the following month, as civil war spread in Libya, with Benghazi threatened by government forces, a further Security Council resolution authorized certain member states 'to take all necessary measures ... to protect civilians and civilian populated areas under threat of attack ... in the Libyan Arab Jamahiriya, including Benghazi'.[36]

What was the doctrinal basis of these resolutions and the resulting NATO military action, including the seven-month NATO bombing campaign in Libya? In their preambles, both resolutions referred briefly to the responsibility of the Libyan authorities to protect the population. However, it is doubtful whether the Western policy-makers saw themselves as at last showing how military muscle could be used so as to give teeth and global reach to the doctrine of 'Responsibility to Protect' (R2P), which had been adopted by the UN General Assembly in 2005.[37] There were many other factors involved that cast doubt on any such grandiose interpretations: not only Libya's weakness,

---

[33] Michael Slackman, 'Bullets Stall Youthful Push for Arab Spring', *New York Times*, 17 March 2011 http://www.nytimes.com/2011/03/18/world/middleeast/18youth.html?pagewanted=all&_r=0.

[34] George Joffé, Chapter 5, this volume.

[35] UNSC Res. 1970 of 26 February 2011.

[36] UNSC Res. 1973 of 17 March 2011.

[37] UN General Assembly, '2005 World Summit Outcome', 16 September 2005, UN doc. A/RES/60/1 of 24 October 2005, Articles 138, 139.

but also its proximity and importance to Europe both as a source of energy supplies and as a potential source of refugee flows.

The UN Security Council resolutions and the ensuing actions could be seen as suggesting the emergence of a doctrine that killings of peaceful demonstrators are unlawful, and when such killings lead on to civil war they may provide a legitimate pretext not only for sanctions but also for an international military response. Any such doctrine, which overlaps with R2P, is as deeply problematic as R2P itself. This is partly because its application is bound to be selective, as the absence of any comparable action on Syria soon demonstrated, leading to accusations of double standards; and also because its military implementation may be intensely controversial—as evidenced by the repeated Russian and Chinese criticisms of the NATO action in Libya. All these problems only confirm the extent and complexity of the interconnections between civil resistance and power politics.

In the intense polemics about the action over Libya, there has been a tendency to blame the NATO powers for stretching the elastic of UN Security Council resolutions to breaking point. The NATO campaign did indeed undergo an apparent shift from protecting civilians to regime change. Yet, if a military operation's mission is to protect civilians, which is an inherently difficult task, and it does not have its own boots on the ground, then the main way in which it can act effectively is in conjunction with one of the parties to the conflict. Even then, while it may succeed in removing an existing regime, an externally assisted military operation may achieve little if, as was the case in Libya, a strong social and administrative base for building a new governmental system simply does not exist. Western armed forces have proved, unsurprisingly, to be better at war than at reconstruction. NATO's problem was exactly that of the Arab Spring itself: little is gained by toppling a dictator if there is not a coherent force to put in its place. Many Western leaders expressed the hope that the Libyan revolution would lead rapidly to freedom: UK Prime Minister David Cameron, on a visit to Libya with French President Nicolas Sarkozy in September 2011, said that the victory of the Libyan revolt was the moment 'when the Arab Spring could become the Arab Summer' in which 'we see democracy advance in other countries too'.[38] The military action in Libya led also to optimistic expectations elsewhere that the NATO cavalry would come to the rescue: this problem was to be especially serious in discussions, from 2011 onwards, about how to stop the carnage in Syria.

Yemen was the one case in the Arab Spring in which there was a negotiated transition between a regime and the movements opposing it. President Saleh's agreed departure in 2011–12 was partly due to the strong pressure from the

---

[38] Vanessa Allen and Tim Shipman, 'Cameron Flies in for Libya Tour', *Daily Mail Online*, 16 September 2011 http://www.dailymail.co.uk/news/article-2037693/David-Cameron-Libya-visit-PM-Nicolas-Sarkozy-compete-glory.html.

Gulf Cooperation Council, the UN, the EU, and the USA. His replacement in February 2012 by the Deputy President, Abdo Rabbo Mansour Hadi, was the transition that met with the highest degree of unanimity in the international community, and the fact that it took place within the framework of an internationally agreed plan facilitated its peaceful character. There has been criticism of this transition as shoehorning in an unimpressive president, preventing the pro-democracy movement from coming to power.[39] However, the movement lacked the capacity to run the country. The case of Yemen illustrates the truth of a general proposition: because civil resistance often produces a stalemate between government and opposition, each of which can deny the other the concessions that it wants, there is significant scope for negotiation between the parties and also for third-party mediation. Civil resistance could succeed in displacing Saleh because of some international midwifery. However, the difficulty of the task of building a post-Saleh constitutional and social order, and the rise of armed insurgencies, contributed to the collapse of the government of President Hadi in January–February 2015.

The situation in Syria was completely different. International opinion was divided. Throughout, the Syrian government had support from certain states—notably Russia and Iran, and also from Hezbollah. The UN Security Council was divided over key aspects of the Syrian conflict: in 2011 and 2012 China and Russia together vetoed several draft UN Security Council resolutions on Syria. Moreover, the USA and other Western states lacked a clear policy.

The horrific events in Syria in March–August 2011—including killings of perhaps 2,000 demonstrators—were seen by Western leaders, and many others too, through an 'Arab Spring' lens. On 18 August 2011 President Obama and European leaders, in a prepared statement, said that President Assad of Syria had to go. It was Obama's first explicit call for Assad's resignation—something critics had been urging him to say for months.[40] It was already obvious that Assad had no intention of following the Arab Spring script. The 'Assad Must Go' policy forced Western leaders into a self-created dead end, making negotiations with the Assad regime on almost any matter difficult if not impossible. 'Assad Must Stop' might have been a less-constraining formula.

Similarly, calls for the International Criminal Court (ICC) to take action against President Assad reflected a belief that the Arab Spring model of unseating dictators might apply to Syria. In June 2011 former US Secretary of State Madeleine Albright urged 'the international community to lay

---

[39] Stephen Zunes, 'How the US Contributed to Yemen's Crisis', *Foreign Policy*, Washington, 20 April 2015 http://fpif.org/how-the-u-s-contributed-to-yemens-crisis/.
[40] Scott Wilson and Joby Warrick, 'Assad Must Go, Obama Says', *Washington Post*, 18 August 2011 http://www.washingtonpost.com/politics/assad-must-go-obama-says/2011/08/18/gIQAelheOJ_story.html.

down a marker that mass killings to suppress non-violent political dissent are unacceptable everywhere'.[41] By 2013 many countries (though not the USA, not a party to the ICC) supported the idea of a referral to ICC.[42] In the event, the ICC did not get involved in the Syrian case—not least because any resolution invoking the procedure whereby the UN Security Council can refer a matter to the ICC Prosecutor was certain to be vetoed by Russia and China.

In the second half of 2011 the Syrian opposition underwent a fateful transition to violence. While up to that point most of the anti-regime activity had been based on using largely peaceful resistance, there had already been armed resistance of various kinds, including attacks on government buildings and sabotage of pipelines. At the end of July 2011 the formation of a 'Free Syrian Army' was announced, with its leadership in Turkey. It stated that it would support demonstrators and protect civilians.

That the non-violent Syrian opposition had continued for so long in 2011 was remarkable. Its impact was, and would continue to be, blunted by deep internal divisions. Its political leadership, representing many distinct groupings, had to be organized from abroad: it was in Istanbul that in August 2011 the new Syrian National Council (SNC), a broadly based umbrella group, was formed. The Council, which was to be plagued with dissension and had a lack of credibility on the ground in Syria, initially stated that the Free Syrian Army must 'limit itself to defensive actions', but it was far from clear what 'defensive actions' really meant in the Syrian context. The Council supported the on-going non-violent demonstrations, and warned of the high price of violent opposition to Assad.[43] On 1 March 2012, against the background of the appalling situation in Homs and elsewhere, SNC leader Burhan Ghalioun announced at a news conference in Paris the formation of a new military bureau. He said the uprising had begun as a non-violent movement, but the council had to 'shoulder its responsibilities in light of this new reality'. Mr Ghalioun said the bureau would function like a defence ministry, controlling the supply of arms, and tracking and organizing armed groups. He insisted that the function of the bureau was only to protect peaceful protesters and said the main armed group, the Free Syrian Army, had agreed to the new organization.[44] Implicitly, the SNC was calling for foreign military intervention.

---

[41] Madeleine Albright and Marwan Muasher, 'Assad Deserves a Swift Trip to The Hague', *Financial Times*, 29 June 2011, p. 11.

[42] Letter of 14 January 2013 from the Permanent Mission of Switzerland to the UN, jointly with the governments of fifty-six other countries https://www.admin.ch/gov/en/start/documentation/media-releases.msg-id-47431.html.

[43] Noah Blaser, 'In Fight against Assad, Syrian Opposition Looks for its Own Model of Revolution', *Today's Zaman*, Istanbul, 28 October 2011, citing SNC spokeswoman Bassma Kodmani http://www.todayszaman.com/newsDetail_getNewsById.action?newsId=261271.

[44] 'Syria Crisis: Opposition Sets up Military Bureau', report of 1 March 2012 http://www.bbc.co.uk/news/world-middle-east-17217284.

The repeated failure of the UN Security Council to agree substantive resolutions on Syria from January 2012 onwards, owing primarily to the use or threat of the veto by Russia and China, seriously undermined the strategy of the Syrian National Council. The Security Council did pass some resolutions in 2012, but they lacked bite.[45] For the Syrian opposition, the choice now seemed to lie between an improbable self-liberation and an even more improbable liberation from outside. Already in early February 2012 a Damascus-based diplomat had been quoted as saying: 'The SNC's whole strategy was for the cavalry to come over the hill—whether that meant the Arab League, the UN or NATO.... They don't have an alternative. Their whole *raison d'être* has disappeared.'[46]

The failure of outside powers to act in Syria to stop a brutal and chaotic war has serious implications for the doctrine of Responsibility to Protect. Here was a case that challenged every aspect of the doctrine. The incumbent government persisted in a policy of extreme brutality towards its own citizens, and was resistant to all calls for a change in its approach. Yet the USA was weary of military intervention because of its bitter experiences in Afghanistan and Iraq; and it was conscious that Syria was a harder problem to tackle than Libya had been. It was far from clear how any international intervention could actually bring about a new constitutional order, or indeed whether it could be authorized at all, by the UN Security Council or any other body. For R2P, Syria was a case from Hell. With no protection at home, millions fled as refugees.

Syria also cruelly exposed the weaknesses of Western policy. As in so many crises, the USA and allies were caught in the trap of for ever searching for a force that they could decently support—a 'moderate opposition', the very term sounding like a kiss of death. They also tried to keep firm control of the number and type of weapons that they supplied. Some other groups in Syria, especially ISIS, had less punctilious external backers. Above all, the awkward lesson of Syria is that outside military support for an incumbent regime—notably the Russian and Iranian support for President Assad—can sometimes be effective against both civil resisters and insurgents.

How should the overall role of the Western powers in relation to the Arab Spring be evaluated? It has certainly been the subject of much criticism. With the very arguable exception of action regarding Libya, their role sometimes seemed to be incoherent and indecisive. Yet in several cases the Western powers did usefully urge rulers to avoid the extremes of repressive force, as, for example, in their pressure on the Egyptian government in 2011; they did

---

[45] UN Security Council resolutions on Syria included SC Res. 2042 of 14 April 2012, calling for a cessation of armed violence; and 2043 of 21 April 2012, establishing a UN Supervision Mission in Syria consisting of unarmed military observers, whose mandate ended on 19 August 2012.

[46] Ian Black, 'Everything is Clearer Now: We Must Liberate Ourselves', *Guardian*, London, 6 February 2012, p. 1.

try to help in certain transition processes—for example, in Yemen; and they generally spoke in favour of elections and constitutional politics in the region. Some of this support came from the European Union, which tried to cobble together a coherent response but did not have any convincing success.[47] The EU role was largely geared to following 'the well-beaten path of economic support in exchange for political and economic reforms'; and it lacked coherence, not least because certain states disagreed about particular actions, as Germany did in opposing the UN resolution authorizing the use of force over Libya.[48] In none of these situations could the Western powers determine outcomes—especially when they were carrying so much historical baggage, from the Crusades in the eleventh century to Iraq in the twenty-first, with a great deal in between.

Were there missed opportunities? And, in particular, if Egypt had been handled more skilfully in 2012 and 2013, might there have been a less troubling outcome? It is doubtful whether there was much that outside powers could have done to ensure a secular, liberal, middle way to success: that stream was too small. The real missed opportunity was for the Muslim Brotherhood, having won the elections in 2012, to show wisdom by both making a deal with the Egyptian armed forces (for example, to respect the military's core economic interests) and not alienating the secularists.

After the Egyptian coup of July 2013, hopes that the Western powers could play a positive international role in the region yielded to a more cautious view. The USA and Western states were reduced to standing on the sidelines, their attachment to liberal constitutionalism proving hard to square with the resolve of many in Egypt to prevent any possibility of Muslim Brotherhood rule. In December 2013 Susan Rice, the new US National Security Advisor, struck a note of wan aspirationalism when, resorting to the language of road maps, she responded to the new and thoroughly illiberal Egyptian law prohibiting demonstrations:

> We have spoken out about the deleterious impact the new demonstrations law and its heavy-handed enforcement is having on freedom of assembly in Egypt, and we will continue to urge non-violence and progress on Egypt's roadmap towards an inclusive and stable democracy.[49]

---

[47] European Commission Memo, 'EU's Response to the "Arab Spring": The State-of-Play after Two Years', Brussels, 8 February 2013 http://europa.eu/rapid/press-release_MEMO-13-81_en.htm.

[48] For an informed critical assessment of the EU role, see Chiara Steindler, 'The European Union and the Arab Spring: Business as Usual in Unusual Times?', *E-International Relations*, 6 July 2013 http://www.e-ir.info/2013/07/06/the-european-union-and-the-arab-spring-business-as-usual-in-unusual-times/.

[49] Remarks by Susan E. Rice, 'Human Rights: Advancing American Interests and Values', Human Rights First Annual Summit, Washington, 4 December 2013 http://www.whitehouse.

A notably sober US response to the Arab Spring is evident in the long-delayed February 2015 White House document on *National Security Strategy*:

> The road from demanding rights in the square to building institutions that guarantee them is long and hard. In the last quarter century, parts of Eastern Europe, Latin America, Africa, and East Asia have consolidated transitions to democracy, but not without setbacks. The popular uprisings that began in the Arab world took place in a region with weaker democratic traditions, powerful authoritarian elites, sectarian tensions, and active violent extremist elements, so it is not surprising setbacks have thus far outnumbered triumphs. Yet, change is inevitable in the Middle East and North Africa, as it is in all places where the illusion of stability is artificially maintained by silencing dissent.[50]

Perhaps the biggest worry about Western policy, before, during, and after the Arab Spring, is that it contributed to the increased turbulence of Middle East politics generally, including the rise of animosity between Shi'a and Sunni Muslims. In his account of post-Arab Spring developments in the Gulf, Toby Matthiesen wrote: 'The Arab Spring has led to the sectarian Gulf.... Through their close alliance with the GCC states, the United States and EU member states have played a role in the creation of the sectarian Gulf.'[51]

The case of the Arab Spring confirms the general proposition that there are many inherent difficulties and limitations in outside powers getting involved in revolutions in other countries. There are also difficulties in inaction. A key question, insufficiently discussed, is whether democratic states did enough, both before and during the Arab Spring, to help in some of the long-term practical aspects of democracy building.

DIFFICULTIES OF CHANGING
A CONSTITUTIONAL ORDER

The revolutions in the Arab world have furnished new examples of an old problem: the need to follow up—or indeed accompany—a successful campaign of civil resistance with an effective programme of governmental and societal change involving a wide range of partners, domestic and international.

By no means all of those involved in the campaigns had a clear aim of democratization along liberal lines. In some countries, political Islam had a

gov/the-press-office/2013/12/04/remarks-national-security-advisor-susan-e-rice-human-rights-advancing-am.

[50] *National Security Strategy* (Washington: The White House, February 2015), 20 http://www.whitehouse.gov/the-press-office/2015/02/06/fact-sheet-2015-national-security-strategy.

[51] Toby Matthiesen, *Sectarian Gulf: Bahrain, Saudi Arabia, and the Arab Spring that Wasn't* (Stanford: Stanford University Press, 2013), 126.

distinct approach to constitutional order that was hard to reconcile with proposals regarding, for example, the rights of the legislature to enact laws independently of religious authorities. In many societies, most notably in Egypt, ideas of illiberal democracy survived and even made a comeback. In none of the societies concerned was there a really strong tradition of constitutional democracy such as might offer a natural pole of attraction in debates about the constitutional future.

In at least three countries—Tunisia, Egypt, and Yemen—civil resistance did its job in facilitating the departure of three long-established rulers. However, in these and other countries, the next phase, which necessarily involved setting in place a new constitutional order, proved to be more complex and harder, requiring different skills from the leadership of a resistance struggle against an incumbent ruler.

Before looking at democratization in the Arab and Muslim worlds, drawing particularly on the experience of the Arab Spring in some of the countries of the Middle East and North Africa, it is first necessary to look briefly at the inherent difficulties of the democratization enterprise.

Difficulties of Democratization

Long before the Arab Spring, the literature on civil resistance contained warnings that merely getting rid of one ruler was but the beginning of a long and difficult process. In the early 1990s, in a passage that resonates, even if imperfectly, with the events in Egypt in 2011–13, Gene Sharp wrote:

> Aristotle warned long ago that '...tyranny can also change into tyranny...' There is ample historical evidence from France (the Jacobins and Napoleon), Russia (the Bolsheviks), Iran (the Ayatollah), Burma (SLORC), and elsewhere that the collapse of an oppressive regime will be seen by some persons and groups as merely the opportunity for them to step in as the new masters. Their motives may vary, but the results are often approximately the same. The new dictatorship may even be more cruel and total in its control than the old one.
>
> Even before the collapse of the dictatorship, members of the old regime may attempt to cut short the defiance struggle for democracy by staging a *coup d'état* designed to pre-empt victory by the popular resistance. It may claim to oust the dictatorship, but in fact seek only to impose a new refurbished model of the old one.[52]

---

[52] Gene Sharp, *From Dictatorship to Democracy: A Conceptual Framework for Liberation* (Boston, MA: Albert Einstein Institution, May 2002), 63–4. This was the first US printing of this essay, which had originally been published in Bangkok in 1993 (in Burmese and English) by the Committee for the Restoration of Democracy in Burma, and was subsequently published in numerous other languages. The Aristotle quotation is from *The Politics*, trans. T. A. Sinclair (Harmondsworth: Penguin, 1962), bk V, ch. 12, 233.

It is well established that democratization of previously autocratic and/or colonial political systems is a hazard-strewn process that frequently results in conflict and war. The risks are greatest when there is a high level of distrust between different communities, and the very borders and system of governance of the state are contested. It is because of problems of this type that almost all conflicts in the world since 1945 have involved civil wars in postcolonial territories. The experience of such problems leads to a proposition that is simple to state but often difficult to implement: a commitment to constitutional democracy requires a willingness on the part of political parties, civil resistance movements, and also armed forces to make compromises and even to accept that their favoured candidates may lose an election.

Remarkably, the literature on non-violent action does not generally place much emphasis on the significance of constitutionalism as a means of reducing and controlling violence in society, nor does it contain much exploration of the ways in which civil resistance is often initiated in support of constitutional rights and procedures. Chibli Mallat's new work *Philosophy of Non-violence* seeks to address this omission, particularly as regards what happens after a regime has been deposed. He states early in his discussion: 'Despite the adverse circumstances in which constitution-writing unfolds, this exercise marks the first port of call for a successful revolution.'[53]

A further hazard of democratization is that parliamentary institutions are unlikely to be respected, and to survive, if there is not an effective governmental, administrative, and judicial structure that can give effect to the decisions they take and the legislation that they pass. Francis Fukuyama's book *Political Order and Political Decay* emphasizes the importance of such factors:

> A stable, well-functioning liberal democracy involves the interaction of a number of different institutions: not just elections for a president or legislature but also well-organized political parties, an independent court system, an effective state bureaucracy, and a free and vigilant media. In addition, there are a number of cultural conditions necessary: politicians and voters cannot have a winner-takes-all attitude toward their opponents, they must respect rules more than individuals, and they must share a collective sense of identity and nationhood.[54]

Democratization in the Arab World

The growth of multi-party democracy has been a remarkable feature of global politics since the early 1970s. Between then and 2013 the number of electoral

---

[53] Chibli Mallat, *Philosophy of Nonviolence: Revolution, Constitutionalism, and Justice beyond the Middle East* (New York: Oxford University Press, 2015), 133.

[54] Francis Fukuyama, *Political Order and Political Decay: From the Industrial Revolution to the Globalization of Democracy* (London: Profile Books, 2014), 428.

democracies around the world increased from 35 to 120.[55] Before 2011 the Arab countries of the Middle East and North Africa had been largely excluded from this process. The question arises: what are the identifiable historical and political features that have hampered the development of constitutional democracy in the Arab Middle East? And what does the experience of the Arab Spring show about the possibilities of establishing democratic systems there?

In their chapter Chibli Mallat and Edward Mortimer—citing the poisonous legacy of colonialism and wars, and the Western acceptance of autocratic regimes in oil-producing states—vigorously challenge the myth of Arab exceptionalism. They offer a strong historical explanation for the emergence, and endurance, of various forms of absolutism—all of them shrouded in what they memorably call a 'fog of constitutionalism'.[56] The Arab Spring provided evidence that these forms of government have failed to satisfy large sections of the population, and now need to change.

A central question about the Arab Spring concerns the extent to which the movements in it were, or were not, committed to constitutional democracy. Marwan Muasher, in his book on *The Second Arab Awakening*, answered this question negatively in a note on the aftermath of the events in Cairo in the summer of 2013:

> what has happened so far supports one of this book's major arguments: that the Islamist and secular forces in the Arab world, both before and after the Arab uprisings, have shown no solid commitment to pluralistic and democratic norms. Each side has denied the right of the other to operate and has often ignored the popular will.[57]

This is far too sweeping. For example, Lebanon and Kuwait, while far from being ideal political systems, do have vigorously contested parliamentary elections in which the parties concerned accept election outcomes.

What explains the dramatic difference in the nature of politics across states with large Muslim populations? Several Muslim-majority countries, including Indonesia, Senegal, and Turkey, have managed to develop and retain democratic systems, while others have not. There are tensions between Islam and the state in some of these countries, not least in present-day Turkey, but there remains an awareness that religion and state can coexist without either taking over the other. Furthermore, in some countries with a non-Muslim majority, such as India, large Muslim minorities have a notably positive view of their country's democratic system.[58]

---

[55] Fukuyama, *Political Order and Political Decay*, 33.
[56] Chibli Mallat and Edward Mortimer, Chapter 1, this volume.
[57] Muasher, *Second Arab Awakening*, p. xi.
[58] Alfred Stepan and Juan J. Linz, 'Democratization Theory and the "Arab Spring"', *Journal of Democracy*, 24/5 (April 2013), 17–18.

Plainly, particular forms of militant political Islam, such as al-Qaeda and ISIS, are incompatible with the development of democracy. Even without such extremism, if a society is divided into rival faiths or sects, each of which denies the legitimacy of the other's position, multi-party democracy will be very hazardous. Alfred Stepan and Juan Linz have put the matter thus:

> Conflicts concerning religion, or between religions, did not figure prominently in either the success or failure of third-wave attempts at democratic transition. The Roman Catholic Church of course played an important and positive role in the democratic transitions in Poland, Chile, and Brazil. But conflicts over religion, which were so crucial in Europe in earlier historical periods, were not prominent. For this and other reasons, religion was undertheorized in scholarly writing about the third wave. Yet the hegemony, perceived or actual, of religious forces over much of civil society in the Arab world, especially in the countryside, had no parallel in the third wave. Thus the central role that Islam has played in the Arab Spring presents students of democratization with a novel phenomenon, and prompts them accordingly to come up with new concepts and fresh data to shed light upon it.
>
> Samuel P. Huntington argued controversially that religion, especially Islam, would set major limits to further democratization. That suggested to one of us (Alfred Stepan) the idea of exploring what democracy and religion need, and do not need, from each other in order that each may flourish. Stepan argued that neither *laïcité* of the French sort (generally recognized not merely as secularist but as positively antireligious), nor a type of secularism that decrees a complete separation between religion and the state, was empirically necessary for democracy to emerge.
>
> What was needed for both democracy and religion to flourish? The answer was a significant degree of institutional differentiation between religion and the state. This situation of differentiation Stepan summed up as the 'twin tolerations'. In a country that lives by these two tolerations, religious authorities do not control democratic officials who are acting constitutionally, while democratic officials do not control religion so long as religious actors respect other citizens' rights. Many different patterns of relations among the state, religion, and society are compatible with the twin tolerations. There are, in other words, 'multiple secularisms'.[59]

The development of democracy in Tunisia took place against a background of exactly this kind of twin toleration. Long before 2011, the An-Nahda Party, often called Islamist but very different from Islamist groups in other countries, developed in a strongly democratic direction, in which it consistently demonstrated respect for other political forces. An-Nahda had learned an important lesson from its earlier experiences. When it staged large public demonstrations demanding democratic reforms in 1987, and again after fraudulent elections in 1989, it faced a massive crackdown in which some 30,000 of its members were jailed and thousands more fled into exile abroad. As a result of this

---

[59] Stepan and Linz, 'Democratization Theory and the "Arab Spring"', 16–17.

Figure 11.3. The achievement of transition in Tunisia: a new constitution. The Islamist prime minister, Ali Laarayedh, holds up a copy of the constitution on 27 January 2014 a day after its approval by the constituent assembly. Behind him from the left stand his more secular coalition colleagues, President Moncef Marzouki and assembly speaker Mustapha Ben Jaafar. The new constitution took more than two years to draft but represented a successfully negotiated consensus.

© *Fethi Belaid/AFP/Getty Images*

experience, after the departure of Ben Ali in January 2011, rather than going it alone as in the 1980s, it moved much more cautiously and, as much as it could, in concert with other political parties. In particular, the contribution of Tunisia's An-Nahda Party to constitution-making was to search for consensus: its lack of an overall majority in the constituent assembly forced it into a coalition and encouraged consensus. It recognized that forcing through an Islamist constitution would have threatened the transition to democracy, which is a priority for the party, in part because it is the best guarantee against being repressed and jailed as members had been over decades (see Figure 11.3).[60]

---

[60] For information on the history of An-Nahda I am grateful to Rory McCarthy. Regarding its role in constitution-making I am also indebted to Selim Ben Abdessalem and Said Ferjani for their presentations at a seminar at the Middle East Centre, St Antony's College, Oxford, 5 December 2014. Ben Abdessalem was a secularist member of the Tunisian National Constituent Assembly 2011–14, representing at one point the Nidaa Tounes party. Ferjani is a member of An-Nahda's Political Bureau.

Stepan and Linz rightly emphasize the importance of careful preparation for constitutional change:

> In Tunisia, secular liberals and Islamists began meeting regularly eight years *before* Ben Ali's fall to see whether they could reduce mutual fears and agree upon rules for democratic governance. That is, they began to create a political society.... Such efforts helped to lay the ground for the near-unanimity with which the roughly 155 consensually selected members of the country's key post-Ben Ali reform commission voted for six major rules and principles to govern the selection and proceedings of a constituent assembly.[61]

There were many superficial similarities between the aftermaths of the popular revolutions of 2011 in Tunisia and Egypt. The elections held in these countries in 2011–12 saw wide participation in the electoral process. In both, Islamist parties proved the best organized, and did very well at the polls. However, the processes were very different. In Egypt, the political dialogue from 2011 onwards was mainly between the Supreme Council of the Armed Forces (SCAF), the Muslim Brotherhood, and the secular liberals. All these groupings, while they accepted democratic tenets, also sought 'to protect themselves in certain areas by placing limits on the right of democratic institutions to make public policy'.[62] In this and other matters, there were striking contrasts between the wary and dogmatic Muslim Brotherhood in Egypt, and the worldly wise and flexible An-Nahda Party in Tunisia, which clearly recognized that to cooperate in creating a democratic system requires a degree of mutual trust, which has to be earned. Furthermore, the electoral system in Egypt tended more to a winner-takes-all outcome, whereas that in Tunisia left more scope for coalition and compromise.

The different outcomes in Tunisia and Egypt have been widely noted. Tunisia faces numerous difficulties. There have been deadly terrorist attacks, some other episodes of political violence, and also many complaints that Tunisia is now run by an old guard, not by the youth that took such a major part in the revolution. Yet Tunisia has at least set out on the difficult path to recovery. As Borzou Daragahi, a journalist specializing in the Middle East and North Africa, put it in late 2013: 'It could all still go horribly wrong. But so far, Tunisia has emerged as the one Arab country that has managed the transition from authoritarianism towards pluralism without veering off the rails.'[63]

In Egypt, the way in which a newly created constitutionalism was abandoned in July 2013 indicated that the society remained deeply divided, with very low levels of trust between secularist-inclined demonstrators and the Muslim Brotherhood, and even a low level of respect for constitutionalism

---

[61] Stepan and Linz, 'Democratization Theory and the "Arab Spring"', 24.

[62] Stepan and Linz, 'Democratization Theory and the "Arab Spring"', 21.

[63] Borzou Daragahi, 'Tunisia Deserves outside Help as Respect for Democracy Fades', *Financial Times*, London, 25 September 2013, p. 6.

as such. The Tamarod ('rebellion') movement, founded in April 2013 with many participants from the 2011 Tahrir Square movement, announced on 29 June 2013 that it had collected over twenty-two million signatures calling on President Morsi, the Muslim Brotherhood leader who had been elected to office only one year earlier, to resign. Morsi was given until 2 July to step down: if he did not, civil disobedience would follow. On 30 June, a date that marked a year since Morsi's inauguration, a huge demonstration in Tahrir Square repeated this demand. This was followed by the Egyptian Army's *coup d'état* of 3 July, in which Morsi was deposed. There had also been strong external pro-coup pressure from Saudi Arabia, with Saudi–Qatari rivalry playing out in Egypt. Since the coup there has been harsh suppression of supporters of the Muslim Brotherhood, whose beleaguered supporters have in response resorted to civil resistance as well as to some violent actions.

It is not difficult to understand the reasons why there was widespread dissatisfaction with the government of President Morsi. He was seen as taking Egypt in an authoritarian direction—and it was this, rather than any attempt to Islamize the country, that was the crux of the Morsi problem. In addition, his rule was marked by incompetence and the lack of a serious economic plan for the country. The message of the demonstrations and subsequent coup was essentially reducible to that old slogan with a worrying provenance: 'No freedom for the enemies of freedom.'[64] It was an extraordinarily serious step for a movement hitherto identified with the use of non-violent methods to support the military overthrow of an elected government, however authoritarian. There is likely to be a price: in the country generally, a widespread lack of trust in any future constitutional settlement; and, for the Tamarod supporters, a degree of dependence on the army and the state apparatus.

In addition, these events undeniably pose the question whether democracy should always be the stated and indeed first goal for civil resistance movements in deeply divided and politically underdeveloped societies; and, if so, how it should be pursued. Even if elections can be achieved in a particular situation, more is required if they are to lead to stability and to improvements in peoples' lives. Pessimism about the effects of democracy in the region has been a major theme of those who have questioned whether the Arab revolutions are likely to lead to any positive outcome. The obvious response—that the processes leading to democracy in Britain, France, and many other countries was anything but linear—contains much truth but is hardly a rallying-cry.

The core argument that there were dangers in the Arab Spring was asserted particularly strongly in Israel. In December 2011 the Prime Minister of Israel, Benjamin Netanyahu, referred to the developments in the Arab world as

---

[64] This quotation is attributed to Louis Antoine de Saint-Just (1767–94), a principal organizer of the 'Reign of Terror' in the French Revolution. He, in turn, was guillotined.

'a step backwards, not forwards'.[65] His central theme was that Islamist parties hostile both to democracy and to Israel were likely to triumph in most Arab countries. This analysis reflected the experience of Iran in 1977–9, in which a civil resistance movement against the Shah resulted in the triumph of an Islamic theocracy. Another consideration may have been that Israel's oft-repeated and questionable claim to being the only functioning democracy in the Middle East would be open to fresh challenges if new Arab democracies emerged.

Even if the various dogmatic denials of the possibilities of constitutional democratic progress in the Arab and/or Muslim worlds are rejected, the lesson of the Arab Spring is clear: bringing in a new constitutional order in societies with deep divisions and little experience of constitutional democracy is a complex and multifaceted task. The general proposition that the fall of an authoritarian regime can be quickly followed by a democratic order, without adequate resources, training, and preparation, is illusory. In these circumstances, there might be a temptation to believe that the solution lies in providing more democracy promotion support from outside. However, a cautionary tale needs to be noted: in all the countries concerned, the numerous governmental and non-governmental Western efforts at democracy promotion were steeped in controversy, and their long-term effects are far from self-evident. As Sheila Carapico states, in concluding her study of democracy promotion in the region: 'The ultimate paradox is that political aid projects might support or thwart Arab activism; or they might be irrelevant to organic struggles for social justice and decent governance in a region long denied either.'[66]

A CHALLENGE TO ADVOCATES
OF POLITICAL VIOLENCE

Civil resistance by its nature poses a challenge to practices and belief-systems based on political violence. After the beginning of the popular uprisings in Egypt and other Arab states, al-Qaeda and similar groups had ambiguous reactions to the unarmed people's revolution. The Arab Spring was problematic for them, not only because of the methods of struggle used in it, and the active role of women on demonstrations, but also because of its evident popularity and its early successes. Indeed, the success of the revolts in Tunisia and Egypt also undermined the central jihadist contention that tyrannical

---

[65] Benjamin Netanyahu, speech in the Knesset, Jerusalem, 7 December 2011.
[66] Carapico, *Political Aid and Arab Activism*, 211.

regimes could be overthrown only by violence—either against the regimes themselves or against their international backers ('the far enemy'). Moreover, the underlying programme of the Arab Spring—to reform the existing states of the region—conflicted with the jihadists' rejection of existing state frontiers and Western-style democracy, both of which they saw as threats to their idealized vision of a unified Muslim Umma that would transcend the existing artificial division of Muslim peoples into separate states. In the face of the Arab Spring, jihadists often appeared to be woefully out of touch. When they did issue statements and commentaries giving their views and analyses for the guidance of their followers, their objective was often to show their concern for the state of Muslims; to impress on their audiences that, up to a point, they supported the protests and even had a hand in them; and to steer them in an Islamist direction.

Political violence also poses challenges to civil resistance. These too were evident in the Arab Spring. Violence was sometimes advocated as a means of protecting vulnerable demonstrators, or as a means of advancing the cause when a stalemate had been reached. It was also increasingly presented, with purportedly religious certainty, as the one path to a wholly new Islamic order. In addition, accusations of violence were used in attempts to discredit civil resistance: ruling regimes often insinuated that behind a non-violent movement there lurked a violent and dangerous force. President Assad's regular verbal tirades against the demonstrators in Syria in the early months of the uprising are a classic case, providing a superficially plausible justification for violent repression.[67]

Al-Qaeda's Response to the Arab Spring

Al-Qaeda and its network of affiliated bodies responded promptly to the Arab Spring. For example, al-Qaeda in Islamic Maghreb issued a video in January 2011 that called on demonstrators to extend their movements in Tunisia and Algeria to overthrow the governments there, to institute sharia law, and 'to send us your sons so that they receive military training'—which rather missed the point of the civil nature of the demonstrations.[68]

The most significant jihadist statements on the Arab Spring were made by Ayman al-Zawahiri. Born in Egypt, Zawahiri was Deputy Leader of al-Qaeda, becoming Leader after Osama Bin Laden's assassination in May 2011, and was believed to be in hiding in the Pakistan–Afghanistan borderland. His 'Message

---

[67] For an extract from Assad's speech of 30 March 2011, see the section 'Alleged Conspiracies'.

[68] 'Al-Qaeda Supports the Events in Tunisia and Algeria', Ennahar Online, Algiers, 14 January 2011 http://www.ennaharonline.com/en/news/5541.html.

of Hope and Glad Tidings to Our People in Egypt' was delivered in eight instalments between February and December 2011.[69] In the third message, issued on 27 February, he began to respond to the events of the Arab Spring, showing respect for it, but of course seeking to steer it in a fundamentalist direction:

> The events of Tunisia and Egypt, the results of which have reached Jordan, Yemen and other Muslim lands, must be studied carefully, so that the anger of the noble and uprising of the freeborn do not go to waste, and the fruit born of their efforts are not stolen after they watered its tree with their souls, blood and years of imprisonment.[70]

In this and subsequent messages, Zawahiri avoided any serious discussion of whether the peaceful methods used in the Arab Spring constituted a challenge to al-Qaeda's commitment to acts of violence as a means of achieving change. In the fourth message, issued on 3 March, he emphasized, rightly, that it was easier to get rid of one ruler than to establish a new system. He assumed that he knew exactly what the peoples of the countries in the Arab Spring wanted— sharia law, establishment of the Umma, and so on. In his discussion of the fall of Mubarak, drawing analogies from his own medical training and experience, he said:

> So the removal of this tyrant, rather the uprooting of this whole government, is only a step, or a few steps of the cure. It is like making an incision into the abdomen of a cancer patient; the patient will not be cured unless the cancer is totally removed. The abdomen then must be sutured, and then the patient must be placed under observation and care. As for merely removing the tyrant, it is more like opening the abdomen and then leaving the patient altogether.[71]

This simplistic surgical analogy with the rooting out of cancer is, ironically, one often used by advocates of military counterterrorism, including Tony Blair.[72] This raises the worrying prospect of two cancer surgeons both operating zealously and at the same time on an unfortunate patient. On 12 February 2012 Zawahiri returned to this analogy when he issued a video message saying that the Syrian rebels had the right to use whatever means

---

[69] Ayman al-Zawahiri, 'A Message of Hope and Glad Tidings to Our People in Egypt', an eight-part series of audio/video recordings issued on 18 February 2011 (pt 1), 24 February (pt 2), 27 February (pt 3), 3 March 2011 (pt 4), 14 April (pt 5), 21 May (pt 6), 5 October (pt 7), and 1 December (pt 8). All are available at or from http://jihadology.net, the first six under the heading 'Jihadist Works Related to the 2011 Uprisings in the Arab World'. Note that the first instalment was addressed to 'Our Fellow Muslims in Egypt'; this changed from pt 2 onwards to 'Our People in Egypt'. All the instalments were published after the fall of Mubarak on 11 February, but the first three were evidently composed and recorded before that date.

[70] Ayman al-Zawahiri, 'Message of Hope', pt 3, English translation issued 28 February 2011.

[71] Ayman al-Zawahiri, 'Message of Hope', pt 4, English translation issued 4 March 2011.

[72] Ruth Gledhill, Religion Correspondent, 'Blair Condemns "Cancer" of Terrorism', *The Times*, London, 26 September 2013 http://www.thetimes.co.uk/tto/faith/article3879714.ece.

they saw fit to get rid of a 'cancerous regime'.[73] This was at a time of growing involvement in the Syrian war of two Islamist bodies: the Jabhat al-Nusra, operating mainly in Syria and Lebanon, which announced its formation in January 2012 and is widely perceived to be a branch of al-Qaeda; and ISIS, a successor body to what had previously been known as 'al-Qaeda in Iraq'. The existence of two rival Islamist bodies led to clashes between them, as well as with the Syrian Kurds and with the more secular opposition movement in Syria. In November 2013 Zawahiri attempted from afar to abolish ISIS as such, insisting that it revert to its former area of activity—namely, Iraq—under one of its earlier names, Islamic State of Iraq.[74] This order was not carried out—a sign of al-Qaeda's lack of grip, not only over the Arab Spring movements, but also over its own affiliates. In 2014 ISIS renamed itself Islamic State, controlling a large swathe of territory in Syria and Iraq and providing horrific evidence of the power of violence.

Continuing Role of Violence

The Arab Spring had other effects on the development of movements using political violence. The initial impact of the Arab Spring on such movements was to call into further question the adequacy and relevance of al-Qaeda's vision of the world and its favoured terroristic methods of waging conflict. However, in the troubled world that emerged from the Arab Spring, movements such as al-Qaeda and ISIS—especially the latter, with its emphasis on holding territory and creating a caliphate now—still had millenarian appeal. They had special opportunities because an effect of the Arab Spring was to increase the number of ungoverned spaces in the region—for example, in Sinai, in Yemen, and in the mountains on the Tunisian–Algerian border—within which al-Qaeda and ISIS could and did become more active. Moreover, there were sources of funding available, especially for some Sunni Islamic movements that could be viewed by their backers as the wave of the future.[75]

A report on Jihadist attacks worldwide for one single month—November 2014—showed that they caused 5,042 deaths overall, with well over half of them in five Arab countries: Iraq 1,770, Syria 693, Yemen 410, Libya 39, and

---

[73] Jason Burke, 'Al-Qaida Leader Zawahiri Urges Muslim Support for Syrian Uprising', *Guardian*, London, 12 February 2012 http://www.theguardian.com/world/2012/feb/12/alqaida-zawahiri-support-syrian-uprising.

[74] 'Zawahiri Disbands Main Qaeda Faction in Syria', *Daily Star*, Beirut, 8 November 2013. See also https://now.mmedia.me/lb/en/reportsfeatures/520205-520205-message-from-ayman-al-zawahiri.

[75] On sources of funding from Qatar of movements elsewhere, see Elizabeth Dickinson, 'The Case against Qatar', *Foreign Policy*, Washington, 30 September 2014 www.foreignpolicy.com/2014/09/30/the-case-against-qatar/.

Egypt 5. The authors note that their data suggest 'that the concept of terrorism is no longer sufficient in capturing the actions or strategies of jihadist groups: the eight groups that are responsible for most of the deadly attacks are all involved in large-scale ethnic conflicts and/or civil wars, engaging in a whole range of tactics and methods.... More than ever, jihadists are now holding territory and fighting against conventional forces...'.[76]

This pattern of jihadist violence varies greatly from country to country. It is worst in Iraq, which, mainly because of the security vacuum there since 2003, was less affected by the Arab Spring than most countries in the region. Yet the figures do strongly suggest that, if civil resistance had been a general challenge to Islamist philosophies of violence in those early months of 2011, the effect did not endure.

Even in Tunisia, where political violence remained at a lower level than elsewhere, Islamic millenarianism appears to have held appeal for many: in 2011–14, Islamist groups fighting in Syria are believed to have attracted approximately 2,400 recruits from Tunisia—believed to be the largest number from any country.[77] What are the explanations for this paradox? Salafism grew discreetly in Tunisia in the 2000s, fuelled by satellite television channels from the Gulf and in opposition to the official, self-seeking state Islamic rhetoric, and in the wake of the very harsh state-led repression of the mainstream An-Nahda Islamist movement in the early 1990s. Salafist recruitment in Tunisia has tended to be in areas of large social and economic dislocation, often among unemployed youth in urban areas. It is thus another of the effects of the broad socio-economic crisis that triggered the 2011 uprising. Many key Salafist figures escaped from jail or were released during the 2011 uprising and began to be much more active in the political power vacuum that followed. Finally, lax border controls allowed many young men (and some young women) to leave Tunisia bound for Syria and Iraq via Libya and/or Turkey.

The terrorist attack in the Bardo National Museum in Tunis on 18 March 2015, and the establishment of Islamic State cells in the country, were further evidence of the threats Tunisia faces. There is no shortage of internal and external forces that want to see Tunisia's move towards constitutional democracy fail; and the troubles of the country's economy will mean that there continues to be a potential source of recruits to movements that can pay their fighters.

---

[76] Peter R. Neumann et al., *The New Jihadism: A Global Snapshot* (London: International Centre for the Study of Radicalisation and Political Violence, December 2014), 13–18 http://icsr.info/2014/12/icsr-bbc-publish-global-survey-jihadist-violence.

[77] Eileen Byrne, 'Tunisia Becomes Breeding Ground for Islamic State Fighters', *Guardian*, London, 13 October 2014 http://www.theguardian.com/world/2014/oct/13/tunisia-breeding-ground-islamic-state-fighters; and, with higher figures attributed to Tunisian government sources as of April 2014, Richard Barrett, *Foreign Fighters in Syria* (New York: Soufan Group, June 2014), 13 http://soufangroup.com/category/research.

What has been the overall effect of the Arab Spring on violent movements? In the early months, the civil resistance that began in Tunisia in December 2010 posed a serious challenge to Islamic fundamentalism and to advocacy of political violence. It was almost as if people power had changed the subject of political discourse. Yet by 2014 and 2015 it was only too evident that the effect of getting rid of hated rulers, or of seeing them hang on determinedly, as in Syria, had been to create a series of weak, rival, or non-existent governments. The result was the growth of ungoverned space in which the gun generally ruled. Along with other factors, civil resistance had contributed both to state dysfunction and to Sunni outrage, which in turn fed the growth of ISIS.[78] The tables had been turned. Now it was the lure of the gun that posed a major problem for supporters of civil resistance—and not only in Tunisia and Syria.

REVIVALS OF AUTHORITARIANISM

The Arab Spring was a reaction against certain authoritarian regimes, but it has also been followed by, and perhaps contributed to, revivals of authoritarianism—not only in the Arab world, but also more widely. Three issues arise. The first is whether the Arab Spring itself contributed in any way to a revival of authoritarian ideas and practices within and beyond the region—a revival that also has other causes. The second is more specifically about President Putin's critique of civil resistance generally and of the Arab Spring. The third issue is about the appeal to security that authoritarian rulers regularly make—and more specifically about whether advocates of civil resistance need to recognize the strength of such appeals.

Civil Resistance and the New Authoritarianism

Even if the picture is not uniformly bleak, it is necessary to take account of some obvious and uncongenial truths emerging out of the Arab Spring. Confronted by widespread civil resistance, both in the Middle East and more generally, worried authoritarians have fought back, with help from Iran, Russia, China, and others. They have emphasized the principle of the sovereignty of states. They have prioritized security above both democracy and fundamental human rights. They have tended to vilify, threaten, and attack civil resisters; tar them with the brush of violence; insinuate that they are under foreign control; outlaw even peaceful demonstrations; and devise means

---

[78] Patrick Cockburn, *The Rise of Islamic State: ISIS and the New Sunni Revolution* (London: Verso, 2015), 150.

of controlling the Internet, mobile phones, and social media for the benefit of the state rather than civil insurgency.

One of the key targets of the new authoritarianism has been civil resistance itself, now presented as a foreign import. Certain forms of such resistance have been banned in many countries. The Egyptian law of 24 November 2013 prohibiting demonstrations is a case in point. This did not happen in a vacuum. In matters such as this, the Arab Spring has unfortunately been followed by and perhaps even contributed to this new authoritarianism, both domestically and internationally. There is persuasive evidence that a majority of the Egyptian population, after the upsets and economic troubles of the years since 2011, is prepared to settle for what is essentially authoritarian rule, while also maintaining hope for a more democratic system.[79] Further, the regime is deeply dependent on outside support, especially from Saudi Arabia. That fact has contributed to the authoritarian direction of travel.

Even in the midst of this authoritarian drift, it is not hard to detect a deep and abiding fear on the part of many rulers that they may yet be faced with mass non-violent uprisings. From Beijing to Tehran, the events of the Arab Spring accentuated these fears. In Moscow that concern has been explicit.

The Putin Critique of Civil Resistance

Of the many political attacks on civil resistance, the most significant and explicit have been those of the President of Russia. Vladimir Putin has a long record of concern about civil resistance, dating back to the 1989 revolutions in eastern and central Europe. He subsequently saw the 'orange revolution' in Ukraine in 2004 as unforgivably detaching Russia's frontierland from the mother country. This led to the founding in 2005 of the Nashi (Russian for 'Ours'), a youth movement, the stated mission of which is to protect Russia from liberals, communists, and fascists.

In 2014, in two of his most important statements about Russian foreign and security policy, President Putin went to some lengths to present 'colour revolutions' as part of a sinister external plot. His speech to the Russian State Duma in March, containing an interesting mix of political empathy and baseless slur, began with a polite reference to the demonstrators in Kiev in 2014:

---

[79] On polling evidence about Egyptian political opinion, I am indebted to Dr Gamal Soltan of the Department of Political Science, American University in Cairo, presentation on 'Religiosity, Activism, and Mobilization' at a conference at Pembroke College, Oxford, 13 March 2015, providing evidence of a continuing strong majority in favour of Egypt moving in the direction of constitutional democracy.

I would like to reiterate that I understand those who came out on Maidan with peaceful slogans against corruption, inefficient state management and poverty. The right to peaceful protest, democratic procedures and elections exist for the sole purpose of replacing the authorities that do not satisfy the people. However, those who stood behind the latest events in Ukraine had a different agenda: they were preparing yet another government takeover; they wanted to seize power and would stop short of nothing. They resorted to terror, murder and riots. Nationalists, neo-Nazis, Russophobes and anti-Semites executed this coup. They continue to set the tone in Ukraine to this day....

There was a whole series of controlled 'colour' revolutions. Clearly, the people in those nations, where these events took place, were sick of tyranny and poverty, of their lack of prospects; but these feelings were taken advantage of cynically. Standards were imposed on these nations that did not in any way correspond to their way of life, traditions, or these peoples' cultures. As a result, instead of democracy and freedom, there was chaos, outbreaks in violence and a series of upheavals. The Arab Spring turned into the Arab Winter.[80]

This critique of colour revolutions and the Arab Spring, with its clever use of the passive tense to avoid pointing the finger at any individual country or intelligence agency, is subtler than some of the conspiracy theories that swirl around these events. It is an example of a worrying trend of portraying civil resistance movements as an external imposition on societies, when in reality they more often represent a reaction of societies against the impositions of their rulers.

During a visit to Ukraine in September 2014, Adam Michnik, the distinguished theoretician of the Solidarity movement in Poland in the 1980s, commented on Putin's deep fear of colour revolutions:

When he saw Egypt's ex-president Hosni Mubarak in the dock after the revolution, he thought it could be his fate, too. And when he saw that a similar revolution was taking place next door, in Kiev, and President Yanukovych fled Ukraine, he realized it was the last alarm bell. I have a feeling that at that moment Putin believed he saw Kiev's Maidan on the Red Square in Moscow. His policy, in my view, follows a simple logic of muffling all possible threats both inside Russia and in neighboring post-Soviet countries.[81]

In his Valdai Club speech of 24 October 2014, in the context of discussing the troubles in Ukraine, President Putin returned to the theme of attacking the colour revolutions: 'Apparently, those who constantly throw together new "colour revolutions" consider themselves "brilliant artists" and simply cannot

---

[80] Address by President of the Russian Federation to State Duma deputies, Federation Council members and others, Kremlin, Moscow, 18 March 2014 http://eng.kremlin.ru/news/6889.

[81] Adam Michnik, interview published on the *Day* website in Kiev, 10 September 2014 http://www.day.kiev.ua/en/article/day-after-day/what-going-russia-revenge-black-hundreds-democrats.

stop.' He also made a more general attack on colour revolutions (including by implication the Arab Spring) and on the alleged double standards manifested in the Western press:

> The next obvious threat is the further escalation of ethnic, religious, and social conflicts. Such conflicts are dangerous not only as such, but also because they create zones of anarchy, lawlessness, and chaos around them, places that are comfortable for terrorists and criminals, where piracy, human trafficking, and drug trafficking flourish.
>
> Incidentally, at the time, our colleagues tried to somehow manage these processes, use regional conflicts and design 'colour revolutions' to suit their interests, but the genie escaped the bottle. It looks like the controlled chaos theory fathers themselves do not know what to do with it; there is disarray in their ranks.
>
> We closely follow the discussions by both the ruling elite and the expert community. It is enough to look at the headlines of the Western press over the last year. The same people are called fighters for democracy, and then Islamists; first they write about revolutions and then call them riots and upheavals. The result is obvious: the further expansion of global chaos.[82]

Again, Putin is relying on vague insinuations, unsupported by evidence, to tar civil resistance movements with the brushes of anarchy, lawlessness, drug trafficking and terrorism. All this represents something more than the predictable reaction of a regime inclined to authoritarianism: it is also one key foundation of Russian foreign policy. It provided part of the ideological cover for Russian military interventions in Georgia in 2008 and Ukraine in 2014, and for Russia's support for a range of authoritarian regimes. In turn, these Russian actions have led to intense international concern about Russian encroachments on the sovereignty of other states. The decline in US–Russian relations in the years since the Georgia war of 2008 owes something to the Russian suspicion of colour revolutions.

The Authoritarians' Challenges for Civil Resistance

The occurrence of counter-revolutions in certain countries, and the revival of authoritarian ideas more generally, pose many challenges for advocates and practitioners of civil resistance. One such challenge concerns the accusations of foreign control of civil resistance movements. Lacking in serious evidence as they may be, these accusations do call for responses. However, any such responses face the unavoidable difficulty associated with trying to prove a negative; and, in any case, as will be discussed in the next section, political ideas cross frontiers all the time.

---

[82] Vladimir Putin, speech at Valdai International Discussion Club, XI session, Sochi, 24 October 2014 http://eng.kremlin.ru/transcripts/23137.

Security is a trickier issue to address. It is easy to dismiss terms such as 'stability' and 'security' as conceptually vague and open to abuse in the interests of power. Yet it is hard to deny that there is a natural human preference for stability. Civil resistance, like democracy, is sometimes, damagingly, associated with disorder—especially in those cases where it has caused widespread economic disruption or has been followed by violence or lawlessness. In practice it is by no means necessarily the opposite of stability. It can take the form of notably orderly actions, such as some of the huge and dignified demonstrations of the Arab Spring; and it can serve purposes compatible with order, such as demonstrations opposing acts of terrorism. Concern about order confirms that it is vital that a movement has a leadership and decision-making structure that can, in the right circumstances, persuade a crowd not to march to a particular location, call off demonstrations, terminate particular phases of a campaign, and engage in negotiations with an adversary.[83]

LESSONS FOR CIVIL RESISTANCE

Interpreting the course and fate of the Arab Spring, and its lessons for civil resistance, is a difficult enterprise. What lessons can be learned about the possibilities of political change, and the capacity of civil resistance to achieve it? I first revisit the question of methods versus conditions, then explore the implications of this study for understanding the role of civil resistance in the contemporary world, and finally ask whether there can be any victory after the many defeats of the Arab Spring.

Methods or Conditions?

In the literature on civil resistance, there is a long tradition of concentrating on the choice of method of struggle as a key factor in determining outcomes. The clearest expression of this approach is in Erica Chenoweth and Maria Stephan's influential study of *Why Civil Resistance Works*. On the basis of their Nonviolent and Violent Campaigns and Outcomes data set, they observe:

> The most striking finding is that between 1900 and 2006, nonviolent resistance campaigns were nearly twice as likely to achieve full or partial success as their violent counterparts.... The effects of resistance type on the probability of

---

[83] All these issues are explored in Timothy Garton Ash's discussion of 'the individual and the people' in Roberts and Garton Ash (eds), *Civil Resistance and Power Politics*, 377–82.

campaign success are robust even when we take into account potential confounding factors, such as target regime type, repression, and target regime capabilities.[84]

The analyses in this book suggest that, in the particular case of the Arab Spring, a modification of this approach may be required. The issue is not whether non-violent or violent means of struggle are more likely to achieve success in reconstructing a constitutional order: it is whether, granted the conditions that are faced, either approach has a chance of success when measured in such terms.

Some have interpreted the failures of the Arab Spring as largely due to a failure to adhere to, and persevere with, the use of non-violent methods. In particular, exponents of civil resistance have criticized the resort to armed struggle in Syria in late 2011 and early 2012. In 2013 Maciej Bartkowski and Mahja Kahf argued that the decision to engage the Assad regime on its own violent terms—that is, by a contest of arms—was based on misplaced beliefs in the efficacy of armed protection and on inadequate knowledge of the effects of civil resistance:

> One major reason for abandonment of civil resistance in favor of armed struggle is not understanding what civil resistance can achieve, and with what benefits for a people's liberation. The narrative void about civil resistance during ongoing conflict is often filled by armed insurrectionists with their own ideologized discourse, which tries to discredit the effectiveness of nonviolent resistance and underestimates the costs of violence....
>
> The impact of the nonviolent resistance in Syria—before it was largely overshadowed by an armed uprising in early 2012—was tremendous. It mobilized hundreds of thousands, perhaps millions, of until-then apathetic citizens, produced hundreds of 'leaders' from people who were mostly unknown except locally, united diverse cross-sections of the Syrian population, both rural and urban, as no other internal struggle since the anti-colonial period, and shook and weakened Baathist one-party rule.
>
> Widespread, organized, yet non-hierarchical, nonviolent resistance succeeded in weakening the power of the regime to a degree that armed resistance (notably in Hama in 1982), a few valiant souls from an intellectual elite (such as the signatories of the Damascus Declaration in 2005), and one ethnic group isolated in their armed rebellion (the Kurds in 2004) had all failed to accomplish. All this was achieved while the ranks of civil resisters were being decimated by massacre and detention, and when they had to undergo a mounting humanitarian crisis.[85]

---

[84] Erica Chenoweth and Maria J. Stephan, *Why Civil Resistance Works: The Strategic Logic of Nonviolent Conflict* (New York: Columbia University Press, 2011), 7. See also their earlier article, Stephan and Chenoweth, "Why Civil Resistance Works: The Strategic Logic of Nonviolent Conflict," *International Security*, 33/1 (Summer 2008), 42.

[85] Maciej Bartkowski and Mahja Kahf, 'The Syrian Resistance: A Tale of Two Struggles', open-Democracy, 23 September 2013 www.opendemocracy.net/civilresistance/maciej-bartkowski-mohja-kahf/syrian-resistance-tale-of-two-struggles.

Bartkowski and Kahf are right to be critical of the decision to embark on armed struggle. Armed resistance in Syria since 2011 has indeed failed to provide protection, it has led to a civil war within a civil war, it has blunted the possibilities and impact of non-violent action, and it has contributed to the refugee exodus from Syria. However, a difficult question does need to be faced. Granted the consistent and large-scale brutality of Assad's response to the civil resistance in 2011, and the evident absence of necessary preconditions for democratic change in Syria, how long could open non-violent opposition have been expected to continue? And how long could the resort to armed struggle by certain groups be prevented?

Of all the adverse conditions faced by demonstrators in the Arab Spring, the greatest were two: repression by the regime, and the absence of the preconditions for peaceful transition to a stable and pluralist constitutional order. The two are interlinked: autocrats typically claim that their repression is justified in order to prevent anarchy, disorder and vulnerability to external threats. Repression is sometimes effective, but it is by no means sure to work against civil resisters. It frequently leads to international opposition, as it did when Gaddafi's forces attacked Libyan citizens in February 2011. It can also arouse internal opposition—as in Tunisia, where the first killing of a demonstrator, on 27 December 2010, hastened the spread of protests; and in Yemen, where the killings in Sanaʻa on 18 March 2011 became the occasion for bringing together a larger coalition against President Saleh.

The absence of preconditions for peaceful political transition is a key part of the explanation of the troubles of the Arab Spring. In 2011 many compared the revolutions of the Arab Spring with those of 1989 in central and eastern Europe. There was the same rapid spread of highly telegenic events from one country to another, the same sense of an old order under threat. A key difference was that the countries of central and eastern Europe had at least distant memories of more or less functional constitutional democracy, and also had western Europe close at hand to serve as model and helper. In the Arab world, the transition was exceptionally hard to tackle, and many citizens could not believe in it. Francis Fukuyama, whose emphasis on the preconditions for democracy was cited earlier in this chapter, also wrote with specific reference to the Arab Spring:

> Bringing down dictators like Ben Ali or Mubarak eliminates only one source of authoritarian power. Putting the other institutions in place is not a process that happens overnight. The American architects of the 2003 Iraq invasion expected that democracy would appear spontaneously in the wake of the removal of Saddam Hussein. They discovered to their dismay that they had to preside over a chaotic and violent society from which institutions were largely absent.[86]

---

[86] Fukuyama, *Political Order and Political Decay*, 429.

The partial exception to this rule is Tunisia. Despite many problems, which continue to this day, it has made a steadier transition to constitutional democracy than any other country involved in the Arab Spring. A prime reason for this success is the clear recognition by the An-Nahda Party that constitutionalism necessarily means willingness both to support a constitution that does not favour one party over others, and to accept unhesitatingly the result of elections—a strikingly different approach from that of some of the principal political actors in Egypt. The Tunisian case shows that it is possible for a far-sighted movement to shape the conditions it faces, and thus to prepare the way for the long haul.

It is sometimes assumed that non-violent movements tend particularly to lead to democratic outcomes. Yet clearly they do not always do so. What the case of Tunisia suggests is that, if they are to have this outcome, there needs to be serious preparatory work, on the part of would-be political leaders, to build up a necessary minimum of confidence in the likely shape of a democratic system and in the willingness of politicians to abide by its rules. In other words, conditions, whether favourable or adverse, should not be conceived of as objective facts about which little or nothing can be done: it is up to political forces and civil resistance movements not merely to pursue particular methods of struggle, but also to shape conditions.

Civil Resistance and the Arab Spring: Twelve Propositions

Granted the disasters encountered in the Arab Spring, and in the light of the proposition that conditions are crucial to the outcome of civil resistance movements, what conclusions follow, both in the region and more generally?

1. If conditions are as important in determining outcomes as this analysis suggests, more attention needs to be paid to them both in academic analysis and in the practice of civil resistance. To have a prospect of success, movements need to adjust their political aims, their methods of struggle and their preparations for negotiation, in order to take the particular circumstances of their society into account. They often do so, but sometimes fail in aspects of this difficult task.

2. A lesson of the Arab Spring is not that civil resistance is too weak. On the contrary, it is powerful, maybe sometimes too powerful. It offers the possibility of achieving basic change even in societies that have been under apparently stable authoritarian control. However, on its own it can only open the door to, and perhaps prepare the way for, the unavoidably complex and hazard-strewn process of making a new constitutional system.

3. Civil resistance is by no means bound to succeed. The repression of the demonstrations in Iran in 2009, protesting against a fraudulent election

result, had already confirmed this point, which has since been manifested in many of the Arab uprisings that started in 2011. However, even when costly and initially unsuccessful, civil resistance may undermine the claim to legitimacy of an authoritarian system. In short, both success and failure need to be judged in a long-term as well as a short-term perspective. To depose a regime is hardly a success if the long-term effect is social chaos or war. Civil resistance is not a panacea, and presenting it as such unnecessarily limits discussion of what it can and what it cannot achieve.

4. Civil resistance can play some part in larger tragedies. If it displaces a regime without providing for an effective succession, it can lead to power vacuums and ungoverned spaces, with disastrous results. It can even form part of the story of how wars begin—the case of Syria being a particularly worrying example. Civil resistance has a complex relationship with other forms of power, and cannot be fully understood in isolation from them. Yet it remains a very distinct form of struggle, and combining it with the use of force is often deeply problematical.

5. Constitutional democracy, despite all its numerous and well-known faults, is the principal means by which political conflicts are played out with minimal violence in most advanced societies. Practitioners of civil resistance are often, and understandably, impatient with the compromises and horse-trading involved in party politics. Yet there are links between the practice of civil resistance and the achievement of democratic outcomes. One such link is that civil resistance has often been used in campaigns, many of which have been successful, to reverse the fraudulent stealing of elections. The larger issue, of how civil resistance can be one means of moving towards the overall goal of constitutional democracy, has been comparatively neglected and needs attention.

6. In the Arab Spring, it was not always analytically enlightening or prescriptively helpful to refer to each and every leader being opposed as a 'dictator'. In some cases, even in the absence of formal democratic constraints, such leaders are continuously engaged in reacting to a range of regional, confessional, or other pressures within the state, as well as from outside. The implicit assumption of characterizing rulers as dictators is that, if the ruler who is the source of oppression is removed, all will be well—which has plainly not been the case in many countries affected by the Arab Spring.

7. The movements' initial success in overthrowing rulers in Tunisia and Egypt was a great achievement. It was also misleading—for three solid reasons. First, because of the power of the 'deep state' to continue within the administration and security services despite the decapitation of the regime; second, because, in those countries where a regime was overthrown, building a constitutional political order proved to be a longer

and harder task; and, third, because in some other countries the existing regimes had a greater degree of legitimacy or capacity for survival—so could not be overthrown as easily as those in Tunis and Cairo in those early months of 2011. Because of these three considerations, the question arises: was it wise—especially in deeply divided societies—to call for the removal of the regime? In some cases, including Syria, such calls undoubtedly aroused dark fears and caused severe problems. In other cases, including Jordan and Morocco, Arab Spring movements concentrated on more modest calls for reform, and in the particular circumstances they faced were probably right to do so. In the case of Tunisia, the movement began with modest demands, calling for the fall of the regime only after the first two weeks of protests. Similarly, many civil resistance movements in other parts of the world, including those in central and eastern Europe in the 1980s, started with more modest demands regarding workers' rights, human rights, and freedom of movement, and only later, as circumstances made such a transition inevitable, aimed at more ambitious goals. Yet it has to be admitted that in Egypt and Tunisia, in the first decade of the present century, there had been significant opposition movements demanding limited reforms— and they had not been notably successful. There is no general rule about whether civil resistance should have revolutionary or reformist demands: all depends on the circumstances, and on the extent of preparation for implementation of whatever demands are being pressed.

8. The decentralized and ad hoc quality of the leadership of the movements in the Arab Spring did not help in the performance of three key tasks: preparation for post-revolutionary governance of the country, making necessary compromises with other political forces, and producing a convincing plan for economic development. There were failures on all three fronts. In many Middle Eastern and North African countries it might not be realistic to respond to such failures by urging young activists to form or join a political party: such parties as currently exist are commonly seen as ineffectual bit-players in a political pantomime. Yet, as the story of An-Nahda in Tunisia shows, it can be political parties' careful preparation for transition that makes ultimate success thinkable. As indicated earlier in this chapter, An-Nahda had learned an important lesson from its experiences in the 1980s.

9. Citizens can become weary of prolonged or repeated civil resistance campaigns, especially if they are seen as damaging the economy of a country. Leadership of a movement requires skill in ending campaigns, or pursuing them in imaginative ways that do not antagonize the public.

10. There is sometimes a tendency in civil resistance movements to regard the crowd as itself a fount of legitimacy. In Egypt in June 2013 the Tahrir

demonstrators conveyed a message implying that an elected government should step down, or be forcibly replaced, on their say-so. Such a view of the legitimacy of crowds becomes a problem if it assumes superiority over constitutional arrangements, demonstrates over-confidence about the capacity of crowds to remove regimes, or becomes a justification for a *coup d'état*. Moreover, as evidenced in Cairo, Damascus, and Manama, ruling regimes can often assemble large crowds as a means of demonstrating that they too have crowd-based legitimacy.

11. Civil resistance, if it is to be effective, often needs both strong local roots and external support. Its application in any given country, and the outcome there, depends first and foremost on the interests, beliefs, and political culture of its citizens. It may also benefit from outside support, not least if that helps to level the playing field against a powerful government apparatus. Such external support can sometimes be counterproductive. However, in the Arab Spring all of the four regimes that were overturned had been under significant pressure from other states, including the USA, to quit or at least make major reforms.

12. The evidence for the propositions put forward by President Assad of Syria and President Putin of Russia, that civil resistance is the product of an international conspiracy, appears to be flimsy. This is not to deny all international influence. Civil resistance is often assisted by the power of example (including in other countries); by the spread of ideas through books, pamphlets, and media; and by the fact that a few key people have had training in its basics. Transnational influences have for centuries been facts of life, including in the fields of medicine, business, and politics. Although often controversial, some external help may be necessary to help to level the playing field between government and opposition.

Victory of a Defeat

The Arab Spring is over, but the story of change in the Arab world is not. As Laurence Whitehead has written, 'once spring has been experienced it will be expected again'.[87] In the countries that it touched, the Arab Spring captured imaginations and raised hopes of a different and more decent society. It exposed the brittleness of entrenched regimes, and helped people to lose, albeit temporarily, their fear. The method of struggle used, civil resistance, is seen to have had a capacity not just to upset some powerful rulers, but also to exemplify the strengths of civil society and the qualities of the new kind of

---

[87] Laurence Whitehead, 'On the "Arab Spring": Democratization and Related Political Seasons', in Larbi Sadiki (ed.), *Routledge Handbook of the Arab Spring* (London: Routledge, 2015), 26.

Figure 11.4. From Sidi Bouzid, the town in Tunisia where the Arab Spring began, to the rest of the world. A portrait of Mohammed Bouazizi in his home town photographed on 17 December 2013, the third anniversary of the start of the Arab Spring, showing how his actions began an uprising that inspired the 'revolutionary movement in the world'. The pictures above him show events in many different countries. But even at this moment young Tunisians were still protesting social exclusion, high prices, and unemployment.

© *Fethi Belaid/AFP/Getty Images*

revolution that was sought. It is not just a technique, but exemplifies a spirit. There have been some significant, albeit fragile, results, especially in the country where it all began—Tunisia (see Figure 11.4).

Yet the disasters that followed early triumphs in Tunis and Cairo were inherent in the Arab Spring itself. It is not good enough to say that civil resistance did its job of helping to unseat dictators, and that the failure came only afterwards and from others. That is like saying: 'The operation was successful but the patient died.' The fact is that many people in the pro-democracy movements, as well as many outside them, failed to recognize how complicated and dangerous the process of building a new constitutional order would prove to be, how necessary it was to prepare for it, how different the conditions were in each country, how deep social and religious divisions within societies could be, and how tenaciously some rulers would hang onto power. When civil resisters call for the fall of the regime, but fail to address these issues, they became part of the problem.

Defeats can sometimes lead on to victories. It is tempting here to cite an eastern European parallel. In 1968 the exiled Hungarian historian Miklós Molnár wrote a book, with the brilliant title *Victory of a Defeat*, about the fate of the 1956 Hungarian revolution.[88] In Hungary, 1956 was never forgotten, just as in Czechoslovakia 1968 stayed in memories. In both, apparent defeat was followed by success in 1989, when circumstances had changed and a series of revolutions ended communist rule in countries of eastern and central Europe. Generations have grown up in a world that has strong memories of 1989; and generations of journalists have remembered that moment when the media and history marched hand in hand.

Within the region, other parallels, closer to home, probably had more appeal. For example, many citizens had heard, from their parents' generation, stories of Gamal Abdel Nasser and the end of colonialism—and how those were days of hope and glory. Such stories strengthened a desire to take ownership of the future.

However striking the parallels, change in the Arab world is not likely to follow such remembered histories. The Soviet empire was able to change, because its centre, the Soviet Union itself, changed. The Arab countries of the Middle East and North Africa are not one single empire, but a collection of states each with its own political system and its own external allies. One size will not fit all. The events in the Middle East and North Africa in 2011 were initially seen by many through a 1989 lens, perpetuating the belief that the same kind of revolution could happen in many very different countries. This latter-day domino theory has now been discredited. Revolutions certainly travel, but they do not necessarily travel well.

Will there be a place for civil resistance in the future politics of the region? There are rival visions aplenty: a new authoritarianism that views civil resistance as part of disruptive foreign plots; and the millenarian visions of some Islamist movements whose very hallmark is violence. They will not hesitate to say that the Arab Spring and civil resistance should lie in a common grave.

Yet, despite the disasters, civil resistance has shown a capacity to mobilize publics and to achieve change. It has had a significant psychological effect on large parts of the ordinary populations in the Arab world. There was, at least for a time, a shift from the deep fatalism and depressing cynicism about the potential for change that had characterized popular attitudes, especially among the young, for decades before. Much of this cynicism has returned on account of the dashed hopes of 2011, and by 2015 a form of civil resistance in several countries was the tragic one of becoming refugees. If there is to be a place for civil resistance in the politics of the Middle East and North Africa, it will need to assume new forms, and to have more constructive purposes than simply the fall of the regime. It will need to work with the grain of each society. This analysis has emphasized that, in the debate about what determines success or failure in civil resistance, the specific conditions of the society where it happens are all important.

---

[88] Miklós Molnár, *Victoire d'une Défaite* (Paris: Fayard, 1968). See also the discussion of it in Timothy Garton Ash, 'Introductory Essay', in Csaba Békés, Malcolm Byrne, and János M. Rainer (eds), *The 1956 Hungarian Revolution: A History in Documents* (Budapest: Central European University Press, 2002), p. xxiii.

Index

Note: Figures/photographs are indicated by an italic *f* following the page number; footnotes by an italic *n* with appropriate number.